The Last of Lands

A nation of trees, drab green and desolate grey
In the field uniform of modern wars
Darkens her hills, those endless, outstretched paws
of Sphinx demolished or stone lion worn away.
They call her a young country, but they lie:
She is the last of lands, the emptiest,
A woman beyond her change of life, a breast
Still tender but within the womb is dry;

FROM 'AUSTRALIA' BY A. D. HOPE

THE LAST
CONSERVATION

OF LANDS

IN AUSTRALIA

Edited by

L. J. Webb
D. Whitelock
J. Le Gay Brereton

FREDERICK WARNE & CO. LTD

First published 1969 by
JACARANDA PRESS PTY LTD
46 Douglas Street, Milton, Q.
142 Victoria Road, Marrickville, N.S.W.
162 Albert Road, South Melbourne, Vic.

United Kingdom edition
first published 1970 by
FREDERICK WARNE & CO. LTD
1-4 Bedford Court, London WC2E 9JB

Type Setting by Queensland Type Service,
Brisbane, Australia, in Times New Roman, Series 327
Printed in Hong Kong
ISBN 0 7232 1300 3

To Jock Marshall, whose love of the Australian living landscape, and whose untiring fighting spirit in his work for its conservation were too early ended, we dedicate this book. His memory remains to animate all patriots and lovers of this land.

All royalties from this book will be donated to the Australian Conservation Foundation.

The editors wish to thank those who kindly supplied photographs for use in this book.

Contents

Foreword ix

Introduction xi

PART I

The Ecology of Conservation: *M. F. Day* 3
The Australian environment — The web of life — Man's role — Man's uniqueness — Development — Competition for land — Habitat preservation — — Population pressure — Decisions regarding land use — Summary

Conservation in Relation to the Land and Its Use: *R. G. Downes* 11
Conservation — The community and land use — Conservation philosophy — Basic information to determine land use — The need to manage land for chosen use — Land use and management for preservation — The conservation task

An Economic Framework for the Conservation Decision: *J. A. Sinden and W. F. Musgrave* 18
Natural resources, economics and ecology — The meaning of conservation — The decision framework applied to conservation — National park problems in the decision framework — Application of the framework — The role of uncertainty — Conservation and income distribution

Recreational Demands and Conservation: *R. D. Piesse* 26
Numbers of visitors — International tourism and Australia's visitor attractions — Conflict between ideals and recreation use — Differing recreationer requirements — Problems of recreation use of parks and similar reserves — Increasing dominance of future recreation demands — Applying recreation-projection techniques — Some policy implications

Management Problems of National Parks: *J. D. Ovington* 36
Man's concern with rural and urban environments — Demands on national parks — Need for research, and the problems of change — Scientific functions of national parks — Essential planning

The Role of Public Opinion in Conservation: *Judith Wright* 43
Man and nature — The population explosion — Old and new attitudes — — Aesthetics, morals and self-interest — The potential for science — Education and the unified view

International Perspectives in Nature Conservation: *W. C. Robison* 52
Conservation policies and kinds of reserves — Threats to wildlife — International co-operation — Summary

PART II

Australian Ecosystems and their Origins: *J. Le Gay Brereton, B. N. Richards, J. B. Williams* 61
Limiting factors — Dependent or regulating factors — Origin of Australian ecosystems — The mechanisms of change — Conclusion

The Australian Flora: *J. G. Tracey, L. J. Webb, W. T. Williams* 74
Special life-forms — Primitive plants and living fossils — Plants of direct economic importance

Australian Plants and Chemical Research: *L. J. Webb* 82
Aboriginal foods and drugs — Chemical research begins — New alkaloids — Other poisons — Chemical curiosities — Glossary of chemical terms

The Vertebrates: *J. H. Calaby* 91
Freshwater fishes — Amphibia — Reptiles — Birds — Mammals — Conclusions — References

The Invertebrates: *E. N. Marks* 102
Introduction — Living fossils and missing links — Some especially interesting or vulnerable species — Conclusion

Marine National Parks and Reserves: *D. F. McMichael* 115
Recent threats — Some basic data on conservation problems in the sea — The need for conservation areas in the marine environment — Some principles for their establishment and management — Development of the marine national parks movement — Some aspects of management — References

PART III

Three Parks, Three Rangers: *D. Whitelock* 125
New England national park — Gibraltar Range national park — Dorrigo national park — Conclusions

National Parks and Other Reserves of Queensland: *J. K. Jarrott* 133
Geographic features and environment — Evolution of the reserve systems — Distribution of the parks — Problems in Queensland

New South Wales: *A. A. Strom* 142
The environments — Evolution of the parks and reserves systems — Status of parks and reserves — Table of national and state parks — Legislation and administration — Problems

National Parks and Nature Conservation Reserves in Victoria: *J. Ros Garnet* 151
Environment and ecological factors — Evolution and status of national parks — Administration and legislation — Problems — The future

Scenic Reserve and Fauna Sanctuary Systems of Tasmania: *J. G. Mosley* 160
The environment — Evolution of the reserve systems — Scenic and historic reserves — Fauna sanctuaries — Administrative organization — Management problems — Remedies

National Parks and Reserves in South Australia: *C. W. Bonython* 170
Geographical features and environment — Evolution of the national parks and reserves system — A select list of national parks and reserves — Other reserves — Administrative organization — Problems and remedies

Nature Conservation in Western Australia: *V. Serventy* 179
The environment — Present national parks — National parks needed — Legislation and control — Fauna and flora protection laws — Public education — The future

Reserves in the Northern Territory: *L. Rose* 187
The environment — Reserves — Legislation for reserves board — Procedure in acquiring reserves — Reserves already committed — Conclusion

Australian National Parks and Equivalent Reserves 194

Notes on Contributors 195

Further Reading 199

Foreword

It seems almost incredible that Australia should have gone from the problems of settling a wilderness to the problems of the conservation of nature in little over 100 years. Even to-day there are many Australians who find it hard to believe that the problem of conservation exists at all. Unfortunately these people are not likely to read this book.

This book about the broad conservation issues in Australia is particularly well timed; the situation is not hopeless yet, but nothing useful can be done until the problems have been properly analysed and considered. Each contributor writes from a wide knowledge and experience of his subject and taken together they paint an objective picture of a subject which can rouse fierce passions.

It's never too early to care about the conservation of our natural inheritance but the time may come all too quickly when it is too late. I hope this never happens in Australia.

Philip

DUKE OF EDINBURGH

Foreword

It seems almost incredible that Australia should have gone from the methods of ... [illegible] ... to the [illegible] ... [illegible]

[illegible]

[illegible]

[illegible]

Introduction

The message of this book is clear: not another acre to be alienated, not another native habitat to be gutted, until we take stock. Modern man has already proved that he can create a physical, chemical or biological desert in anything from a day to a decade. What we don't rescue now, we shall never possess.

The virgin land bonanza is nearly over; the harvest of Australia's renewable resources is becoming a job for science and land husbandry. Significantly, those who want quick economic returns are switching their attention to minerals, a non-renewable resource, whose exploitation implies no further responsibility to its origin than a hole in the ground — in any case, you won't see it until the dust settles.

In a celebrated outburst, the poet Andrew Marvell protested:

> Had we but world enough, and time,
> This coyness, Lady, were no crime.

In the context of nature conservation, if we had more world and time, then the indifference, the short-sighted greed (usually euphemized as 'development') and, not to put too fine a point on it, the stupidity that has characterized many aspects of European settlement in Australia might, just conceivably, be no crime.

But, as this book shows, there is no longer world enough to be coy about decisions for nature conservation, not even in the 'last of lands', sequestered *Terra Australis*, which managed to elude acquisitive Europeans until the late eighteenth century. Sheer size and the sun-blasted bleakness of much of its area hindered for many years the despoliation of nature in Australia. Yet, if the pioneers came late, they soon had the technology of the Industrial Revolution to draw on. It took Europeans a thousand years to establish their present-day pattern of cleared and forested land: we in Australia have tried to do it in something more than a century, and we must now face the fact that we have had but limited success. The limit was imposed by the characteristics, the inherent features, and — admit it or not — by the shrinking size of what is durable and manageable in the continent itself. It's a big country, and that has been the trouble. The myth of infinite natural resources, what Francis Ratcliffe calls the 'Big Country Mystique', that faith in a shining El Dorado around the corner of the next billabong, died hard.

And the frenzy of exploitation that began soon after the anchors of the First Fleet dropped in Port Jackson is still not spent. If in the early nineteenth century hunters almost exterminated the fur seals, sea lions, whales and penguins round the Australian coasts, then we in the 1960s have risked the extinction of the Red Kangaroo by a poorly managed kangaroo industry and lack of co-ordination between the states. If the pioneers razed the 'Big Scrub' in northern New South Wales and stripped the red cedar from the ranges, then we in the 1960s have permitted the flattening of practically all the brigalow vegetation and the slow ooze of holiday 'development' along some of the finest shorelines in the world — a state of affairs which delights only real estate agents.

The moral of *The Great Extermination* by Jock Marshall is clear if unpalatable: the environmental sciences in Australia such as agriculture may no longer simply design and abet the increased exploitation of natural resources, but must accept a major responsibility to repair and prevent the ecological disasters which unbalanced development provokes.

Responsible people are beginning to ask would it be worthwhile to destroy all the beauty, character and unknown potential of our living landscapes and replace them with uniform crops, when the total increased food production would have only a trivial impact on world food demands?

We can, of course, take consolation from the growth of national parks and reserves documented state by state in this book, but we might also reflect that carloads of weekend Nimrods with guns looking for something (besides riddled road signs) to shoot at, roadside gibbets of wedge-tail eagles, cemeteries of ringbarked eucalypts, and weed-choked paddocks are more noticeable features of the Australian bush than national parks.

Already we have paid a heavy price for the development of our resources, for development in the old narrow way of the Australian 'short cut' and 'scrub-bashing', in obedience to that grand old maxim: 'If it moves, shoot it; if it stands still, cut it down.' Practically all the original eucalypt woodland in New South Wales and Victoria — about 100 million acres and half the area of central Europe — has been destroyed or drastically modified by the advance of the wheat and pastoral industries. Most of the 23 million acres of brigalow country — the last area of relatively fertile and well-watered virgin land in Australia — has been cleared, at least temporarily. Of the tropical and subtropical rainforests, which originally covered about four million acres in the north-east, fragments survive mainly on steep slopes and infertile soils unsuitable even for forestry, the last of the peck order and generally excluded from the definition of development. Fast disappearing and sentenced to the axe and the bull-dozer are about five million acres of coastal wallum in Queensland and thirty million acres of heath and eucalypt vegetation in south-western Australia. And these are but a few examples.

Less obvious forms of destruction of the natural environments have occurred more slowly: changes in the botanical composition of native pastures ranging from the alps to the arid zone which followed grazing; the decline and near extinction of many species of small marsupials after their habitats were modified; the concentrations of pollutants and the destruction of non-target species by pesticides; the spread of the Crown of Thorns Starfish and the threat to the whole ecosystem of the Great Barrier Reef; the deepening scars of wind and water erosion inland and along parts of the coast; the infiltration by weeds and other pests.

All these changes have meant that within a century or so we have destroyed many unique ecological systems and probably more individual species of plants and animals than we dare admit even to ourselves.

Not that we need mourn the simple qualitative fact of loss, for if a land is to be populated, loss there must be. If our forbears had taken the extreme attitude that no alien plants or organisms were to be introduced to disturb our superb environment, there would be no wheat, no sheep and no cattle in Australia; we should all be hungry or, more probably, not here at all. The mistake was simply that of considering only one side of the equation. We extolled the value of what had been gained, and disregarded entirely the value of that which had been lost.

And the characteristics of the Australian environment itself have clamped a limit on our success. Of all the continents, Australia is probably the most dependent on nature, on the stability and productivity of low fertility soils and native pastures over vast areas of the arid and semi-arid zones where one-third of our sheep and cattle graze; on rainfall, which in some regions is the most variable in the world; on unusual weather such as severe frosts in subtropical areas; on intermittent but certain cyclones, bushfires, and floods; and on the explosive liability of certain habitats, once disturbed, to be monopolized by alien plant and animal pests such as cacti and rabbits.

Now we cannot escape the responsibility of making a choice, if our natural resources are to satisfy our physical, aesthetic and psychological needs in the future. Are we to be like the philosopher Buridan's logical ass, which starved to death between two equally large and succulent bundles of hay because it could see no reason for going to one rather than the other? Throughout the Middle Ages this unhappy beast epitomized for mankind the uncomfortable fact that the continuance of all human life depends at every moment on the resolution of choices; and that to make no choice may be more disastrous than making the wrong one. For most of us, however, the problem is not that of being unable to find reasons, but of finding too many; reasons for going in both directions are valid and persuasive but manifestly conflicting. This is particularly true if the choice is one that concerns not merely a single individual, but a community, a city, a nation, or the whole of mankind.

Before we can play any part in making decisions concerning the greater choices, we need to know two things: the nature of the choice, and the reason why it needs to be resolved. So it is with the latest of the choices which now faces all mankind, what we have come to know as conservation, and what ranks with nuclear war and multi-racial strife as the central challenge of our time.

Although the concept of conservation — care of the human habitat — is simple, it can perhaps most easily be understood by considering what it is not. It is not just the preservation of objects or things, whether these be rocks, sands, or living organisms such as corals, koalas or tree ferns; it is the maintenance of processes. In our context, this means those processes which are naturally occurring in the sense that they have not been consciously initiated or controlled by man. Processes involve change, and the systems with which ecology and thus conservation are concerned are themselves enternally changing. The nature of the choice, as it concerns any particular natural system, is whether we are to permit it to continue to change in those directions which arise from its own structure (and which ecology must ascertain), or whether we are to impose one of those irreversible changes, of which the extreme is complete destruction, that man devises and accepts so readily.

As for the need for choice, it must be realized that the concept (and the problem) of conservation is not new. Our early ancestors conserved, for their own survival, those natural systems which provided them with food, and the word 'conservation' was in use in English, in precisely its present sense, as long ago as 1490. An Act passed in the fourth year of the reign of Henry VII was largely concerned with the illegal netting of fish, and appointed the Mayor of London as 'conservator having the conservacie of the Watir and Ryver of Thamys'.

In western Europe at least, only a stylized version of nature was considered of any aesthetic merit. Marie Antoinette's bijou version of a shepherd's cottage at Versailles had not the remotest connexion with the real thing. Gentlemen of a liberal education, like Edward Gibbon, preferred to draw the blinds on their coach windows while travelling through Switzerland, lest their sensibilities be affronted by the sight of the Alps. Earlier still, monastic orders like the Cistercians built their abbeys in the wilderness as a deliberate penance. It took a Wordsworth to make the ruggedness of the Lake District aesthetically acceptable.

Only in the last century has conservation come to be regarded as a world-wide problem. Before that time the living world consisted of rather few men and a lot of what was collectively called 'nature'. Nature was seen as an enemy to be subjugated to the greater good of mankind, and if a little of it was destroyed as a result, there was plenty left. In our time we have come to realize that, as a result of the fantastic rise in population during the last century, there are today a lot of men, and rather little of nature.

By delaying our choice we have inadvertently initiated a steady progress towards a world clothed, outside its cities, only by those few animal and plant species already domesticated by man. The fact that few people want this does not make the decision easier in any particular case. Too often in the past the problem has been seen in black and white as a conflict between good and evil, between the good, who wish to preserve nature in all its beauty, and the bad who wish to destroy it for personal gain; or between the farsighted and practical, who wish to harness the opulent productivity of the natural world for the greater good of man, and the muddle-headed idealists, who would prefer starvation to enlightened exploitation. Too often the problem has been resolved by appeal to prejudice or strength, too often the decision has been made by the simple process of avoiding making a decision.

Nature conservation means different things to different people. To the scientist it can mean the salvage from the wreck of the natural environment of specimens for clinical study and the deduction of facts which may or may not be of material value to humanity. To the hunter and angler it can mean an assured supply of prey. To the tourist promoter it can mean attractive scenery and fauna sanctuaries. To the aesthete it can mean the safeguarding of patches of nature for contemplation and hence inspiration. Some biologists have even suggested that, since man almost certainly evolved in the forests of the tropics and subtropics, his need for nature may be genetically built into his psychological make-up, and some psychiatrists believe that man's alienation from his natural environment may be a contributory cause to the rising incidence of mental sickness in big cities. Most men seem impelled sometimes to escape to wider vistas, to the surf, the bush or the desert, where walls no longer confine, where the light is no longer controlled by a switch, where the gum trees do not talk back and friar birds and kookaburras only do so as a joke. And to the ecologically minded agronomist and agricultural economist, nature conservation is an essential part of a pattern of balanced use which ensures the health of the land. There are other interpretations, but the point is that nature conservation is not only a many-sided affair but also that it appeals to and derives support from a wide cross-section of human interests and needs.

In deciding the nature of our choice, there is another difficulty besides the sheer complexity of the Australian environment and its often 'trigger-happy' response to disturbance. This difficulty is of our own making. We have a tradition of alienation from this kind of land; expatriates to a man, we generally assumed that we lived in a second-class environment at whose demolition the world would shed no tears. John White, Chief Surgeon of the First Fleet, made a typical eighteenth century judgment on the physical appearance of New South Wales: 'a country and place so forbidding and hateful as only to merit execration and curses'. Anthony Trollope commented in 1876 that 'it is taken for granted that Australia is ugly', and Marcus Clarke in 1894 considered Australia to be 'a fantastic land of monstrosities'. The gibber plains and sandy gorges, leathery-leaved eucalypts filled with screeching birds, and the eerie, monotonous bush were usually considered repulsive by colonists fresh from the hedged landscape of the pretty English shires. Small wonder that Australia was treated for many years by its white settlers as a barbarous environment which needed rough treatment before it would yield its riches! For many years our artists went to Europe to finish their training, and our scientists to the United States. It was not that careful appraisal had shown that, in the discipline at issue, some other country had more to offer; it was simply that the idea that there might conceivably be fields in which we were pre-eminent had not entered the national consciousness.

But at last all this is changing, and Australia is awakening to a consciousness of her own nationhood, even though unlike Europe we have no ancient architecture, no Appian Way, no folk costumes; only natural monuments like termite-mounds and Ayers Rock, the tracks of the overlanders, and the vivid garments of the wattles on the plains.

Conservation has become articulate and the nature of the choice has become clear. The publication of books — such as *The Great Extermination* edited by Jock Marshall — has exposed the problems to a wider public. And at long last we have the Australian Conservation Foundation with a national charter and the noble aim 'to make every effort to ensure that the land and waters of the Commonwealth and its Territories are used with wisdom and foresight and that competing demands upon them are resolved in the best long-term interests of the nation'.

With greater assurance yearly, there is a quite remarkable surge of public concern and a striking interest on the part of state governments in nature conservation. National parks and reserves are growing in number, especially in New South Wales, where the government's new attitude towards a realistic and expanded provision for nature conservation is epitomized by the National Parks and Wildlife Act, 1967. Newspapers and magazines, which are supposed to mirror the public mood, can often be relied upon to raise an outcry about plans to declare open seasons on rare species such as the Hairy-nosed Wombat or the Cape Barren Goose. There is a strong groundswell of interest in a move to have the whole of the Great Barrier Reefs dedicated as a marine national park, there are petitions to rescue some remnants of the coastal sand dunes from mining, and several almost extinct habitat-types on the tropical humid lowlands of north Queensland will be preserved following local compaigns. Wildlife preservation societies, bushfire prevention leagues etc. continue to erupt in towns throughout the countryside. There is concern even outside the towns, in some of the homesteads, and graziers themselves recently made the first practical move to reserve the only surviving fragment of typical brigalow country in southern Queensland.

The new generation of tourist promoters realizes that nature conservation is very much in their interests, that the much-coveted foreign tourist will not bring himself and his money into Australia to see merely Antipodean versions of American holiday-land extravaganzas. They know that the tourist wants to see kangaroos thumping over paddocks, koalas in gum trees, Aboriginal rock paintings, well-preserved relics of the gold-rush, unspoiled bush and uncluttered coastlines. It is of significance, surely, that among the most popular attractions of the Gold Coast (Queensland's notorious Miami imitation) are the various fauna sanctuaries and the adjacent Lamington national park. Australia's national parks, however remote, attract hundreds of thousands of visitors — campers, hikers, naturalists, photographers — each year. Fauna and flora reserves such as those at Lone Pine near Brisbane, Healesville near Melbourne and Cleland near Adelaide are bustling with people every weekend.

Thus, in the end, conservation is the sum of its parts, and the problems of choice must deal with those local areas which have to be conserved. This is the level at which conservation battles are ultimately fought, and the level at which any one of us may at some time become involved. It is the most difficult level of all, for it involves not only generalities, not only ecological principles, but also people; people with hopes and ambitions and fears, people to whom a decision in the national interest may or may not represent aesthetic or economic disaster. At this level it will no longer suffice to release accusations or emotional diatribes, to appeal only to sentiment or the power of the purse; we owe it to our country, whether it is ours by birthright or adoption, to ensure that all future discussions on conservation of particular areas are argued on the nation's behalf, with all the rigour and the knowledge that is currently available to us. And it is the duty of all of us to be forearmed with this knowledge.

That is the purpose of this book which arose out of a Summer School on national parks and nature conservation held at the University of New England, Armidale, in 1964. As a result of this School, and of the similar meetings in succeeding years, many Australians were able, for the first time, to gain some insight into the importance and complexity of the conservation problem, and to acquire some at least of the scientific knowledge which would sustain them if later they were involved in decision-making in this field. But not every one of us has the time, or even the inclination, to attend annual schools or scientific meetings, however interested we may be in the problem. So some of us have become increasingly aware of the need for some source of information to provide in an accessible and palatable form, that background of knowledge of which any one of us may suddenly find the need. It would have been better, it is always better, if this book could have been written by one man; but the subject is now too large for this to be possible, and the presentation of what is essentially a symposium does at least ensure that the divergent views have some opportunity of gaining a hearing.

We have aimed to cover three aspects: to outline the principles of conservation in greater detail than is possible in an introduction such as this, and to indicate the problems of management and of economics that these entail; to draw attention to those features of our natural environment whose over-familiarity may have deadened in us that sense of awe and wonder which is felt by outsiders; and to give some indication of what has already been done by the different states in this field.

It is our wish to provide, to the best of our several abilities and in the space available, a framework of knowledge on which decisions which we believe to be vital in the national interest must ultimately rest. We believe that this book will be useful, and we hope it will be interesting; but above all we hope that it will assist those who may not postpone their choice and who have to take a stand in this field; and we hope it will help them to make decisions which will not later give them cause for regret, nor their children and grandchildren cause for reproach. In this simple hope we lay this book before you.

Part I

The Ecology of Conservation

M. F. Day

Australia was the last of the settled continents to be inhabited by man. Its animals and plants evolved in the absence of man and of his domesticated animals, and they are ill adapted to the activities of exotic animals such as sheep, rabbits and cattle.

In the course of a single generation, we have seen great changes in the native animals and plants of the Australian continent. Are these changes producing conditions that are a cause for concern? If so, is any remedial action desirable, or possible? A ready answer to these questions is, yes: but the questions are complex and we need to understand them better. What was Australia really like before the advent of Europeans? In what way has it changed? How were the changes brought about? These questions will inevitably lead us to consider 'the web of life' — and thence to the theme of this book.

The Australian Environment

It is more difficult to get an adequate picture of Australia before 1788 than might at first appear. The journals of early explorers are frequently inadequate and even the early drawings and paintings generally reveal a misleading picture of the landscape. The trees often look more like European than Australian trees. But a few early authors are more helpful. One of the pioneer landholders in western Victoria was John G. Robertson, at once a perceptive observer and a careful writer:

> When I arrived through the thick forest land from Portland to the edge of the Wannon country I cannot express the joy I felt at seeing such a splendid country before me . . . the grasses were about four inches high, of that lovely dark green, the sheep had no trouble to fill their bellies, all was eatable . . . I looked amongst the 37 grasses that formed the pasture of my run. There was no silk grass, which had been destroying our Van Diemen's Land pastures . . . But soon the picture was to change . . . The sheep at first made little impression on the face of the country for three or four years. The first great change was a severe frost, 11th November, 1844; before this catastrophe all the landscape looked like a park with shade for sheep and cattle.
>
> Many of our herbaceous plants began to disappear from the pasture land; the silk grass began to show itself in the edge of the bush track and in patches here and there on the hill. The patches have grown larger every year . . . When I first came here I knew of but two landslips, both of which I went to see; now there are hundreds found within the last three years. . . .
>
> Over Wannon country is now as difficult a ride as if it were fenced. Ruts, seven, eight and ten feet deep, and as wide, are found for miles . . . I find from the rapid strides the silk grass has made over my run, I will not be able to keep the number of sheep the run did three years ago, and as a cattle station it will be still worse. . . .

Robertson's vivid description of the reduction in carrying capacity of the Wannon country is characteristic of much arid and semi-arid sheep country in Australia. In the whole of the Western District of New South Wales there are now less than one third the number of sheep carried at the peak of sheep productivity in the 1890s. Without doubt the introduction of sheep has produced tremendous and irreversible changes in the Australian environment. But the effects of the rabbit have also been immense. Its spread and subsequent reduction by myxoma virus has been described by Fenner and Ratcliffe; it is a story of vast significance, and indeed an epic in biology.

Man, sheep, rabbits, fences and artesian bores have brought so many changes that today we can hardly visualize the country as Robertson saw it about a hundred years ago, and this picture is true over the greater part of the continent. An early lithograph, see photograph, depicts 'Lake Patterson' near Newcastle, 1824.

This ancient continent has been more weathered, its soils more leached, and its flora and fauna more isolated than any area of comparable size anywhere in the world. It is for this reason largely that so many of the trace element deficiencies in soils were first recognized in Australia. Introduced plants and livestock were ill adapted to living with deficiencies of these minor elements like cobalt, copper and zinc. Even so-called macro-elements like phosphorus and sulphur were in some places deficient and symptoms of deficiency diseases were soon recognized. Today we see the primary productivity of vast areas increased many fold by dressings of phosphorus or nitrogen, or in some cases by small amounts of copper, zinc, manganese, cobalt or boron, or combinations of these. In a remarkably short time the changes in the land have been vast and many of them are irreversible.

The Web of Life

The study of ecology makes it clear that living organisms are bound together in a complex 'web of life'. Perhaps the most important aspect of this web is the 'food chain', wherein organisms are related as 'eaten' or 'eater'. A significant feature of food chains is that there is a loss of energy at each of the stages in the progression from plant to carnivore. At each succeeding level there are fewer individuals (a 'pyramid of numbers'), and greater dependence upon the lower levels.

The food chain is important also in its effect on the accumulation of some persistent materials. For example, a pesticide was sprayed on the waters of Clear Lake, California, to control gnats. It was applied and was effective at the great dilution of 0.02 parts per million (ppm) of water. The plankton accumulated the substance and was found to have 5.3 ppm. Small fish feeding on plankton had 10.0 ppm in their tissues, and predatory fish and birds had about 1600 ppm. This was a toxic concentration and a substantial change was thus brought about in the environment by an apparently minute dose of pesticide.

A second important feature of the web of life is that in stable systems the basic nutrients are eventually recycled, often through very complicated and devious pathways. Thus, there are in nature 'cycles' of carbon, nitrogen, minerals, and so on. Interruption of any of these cycles must eventually result in reduced productivity. Organisms that decompose dead tissues play an important part in these 'cycles'. Thus, in the absence of fungi or termites, dead wood would accumulate in massive amounts.

The absence from Australia of insects capable of feeding upon or dispersing dung of sheep and cattle has resulted in the failure to return much material to the soil and thus to be re-introduced into the nutritive cycle. Attempts are now being made to introduce some beetles adapted to dispersal of cow dung, mainly in the hope of controlling the buffalo fly which is a serious pest of cattle in northern parts of the continent. But a significant additional function of dung beetles is to aid in the recycling of nutrients.

A third important principle is that all the biological systems we see today are in process of change. In any examination of any such system we see, as it were, a single frame of a continuing, moving film of change. Such changes may be induced in many ways. There are seasonal changes; there are changes brought about by introduced plants and animals and changes in plant cover occurring as the result of repeated fires. Slow changes in climate may be reflected in the change of distribution of plants and animals, or the increase in numbers of a particular animal may cause loss of plant cover, with subsequent erosion and the eventual change in plant species.

On another scale, species of animals and plants eventually become extinct, to be replaced by others with new characteristics for exploiting the resources of the environment. Slow changes in any biological system are thus inevitable. It requires great insight and knowledge to know whether changes which we observe are man-induced, or not. The British biologist Tansley, seeking a name for these biological 'systems' suggested that it was useful to consider that living organisms and their environments together form 'an ecosystem'. The study of these ecosystems is the work of 'ecologists' and an understanding of the principles of ecology is absolutely basic to the study of conservation.

A fourth principle of ecology is that a change induced in an ecosystem may sometimes set in motion a compensatory reaction tending to bring the system back to a condition approaching its previous state. This concept is sometimes referred to as the 'balance of nature'.

It is a common observation that the numbers of many species of animals fluctuate, but that over a period of time these fluctuations average out, so that one species is thought of as being 'abundant', another as 'rare'.

A simplified example will illustrate the concept of 'balance'. Increase in numbers of a herbivore, following a 'good' season, is not infrequently followed by an increase in numbers of its predators; these eventually reduce the numbers of the herbivore until the predators have insufficient food and their numbers are in turn reduced. In most ecosystems the predators have alternative hosts and the situation may then be greatly complicated, so that the 'balance' may even be obscured.

If a system is pressed too far, then the balancing checks may be overtaxed. This may result in a period of disorganization until a new system is established. A great deal of understanding and energy may then be needed to re-establish the previous condition. We have too little information about the complexity of most ecosystems to be sure that we could re-establish these earlier conditions. Such man-induced changes may have repercussions far wider than at first imagined.

Early man was like other animals in his complete dependence on his environment, and his efforts to change it were not particularly effective, even after he began the cultivation of crops. But, with time, his ability to bring about modifications in the environment has increased, until today the effects are felt in every remote corner of the earth. Much has been written on this but the report in 1965 by the United States President's Science Advisory Committee entitled 'Restoring the Quality of Our Environment' is one of the most revealing. This report makes it clear that man's new-found ability to modify his environment is matched by inadequate knowledge of the effects of the changes he is bringing about. We cannot predict the effects and some of these may cause irreparable damage. President Johnson in his foreword to the Report states: 'Pollution now is one of the most pervasive problems of our Society'. He recommends that 'highest priority of all' be given to increasing the number and quality of people able to contribute to the control and management of these problems.

Man's Role

Of course, change in landscape is inevitable. The whole evolutionary sequence is a constant demonstration of the extraordinary changes that make up the past. But, except for a few periods of catastrophical upheavals, the rate of change has been infinitesimally slow. The majority of animal and plant species have long been extinct, but the rate of extinction and of evolution of new species was until recently as slow as changes in climate.

The intrusion of modern man into slow-changing ecosystems has produced new effects unlike any previously known agent of change. Man is highly adaptable, and he is a tool-using animal; his tools are becoming remarkably efficient.

By his manipulations, man has frequently interrupted the recycling of nutriments, but he often attempts to make good these interruptions by further manipulations of the environment. He fertilizes his crop with nitrogen, phosphorus, or the 'minor elements'. He produces ever-increasing yields by these inputs, by pathogen control, by genetic improvements and other means.

But his greatest effects have been upon the environments themselves. There is no time now for the slow evolutionary adaptation of the past. Forests are cleared, fertilizers applied, new plants and animals are introduced, competing pests are destroyed by potent chemicals and the environment becomes irrevocably changed. Pine trees are planted where eucalypts grew before. This may give a short-term advantage by the provision of soft woods, but the qualities of the environment may deteriorate unexpectedly. Even greater changes are brought about by the spread of cities and all the accompaniments of civilization.

Ancient civilizations also destroyed their environment — and today the hills of Syria and Lebanon support only a fraction of the population they maintained in Roman times. But the rate of change today is so much greater that the problems induced have become very urgent. Today, misuse of land is continuing in many parts of the world and new biological deserts are in process of formation. Much has been learned about land use, and many errors of the past would not be allowed to occur today. But there is still a long way to go before we understand our environment sufficiently to know for certain that gross and costly errors are not still occurring over very large areas of land. There is an urgent need for research in Australia's arid land where changes over a vast area are still taking place.

Man's Uniqueness

In this 'space-age' the uniqueness of man cannot be stressed too frequently. No other planets appear to be habitable; no other solar systems are approachable. Of this earth 71 per cent is covered by water; of the land two fifths are frigid or desert, and only one tenth is arable. This fraction supports roughly three billion people, and to this an additional sixty-five million are added each year. It is this current exponential rate of increase of human population that is the source of so many current human problems and the basis for the need for conservation.

Conservation involves the best use of resources. The resources of man may be roughly divided into 'renewable' or 'non-renewable'. The first category includes plants, animals and water in place. The second includes such things as minerals, fossil fuel and landscape. It has become clear that, although a resource may be replaceable, it may be so altered in quality as to be unusable. Thus, pollution by pesticides or by radioactive contamination could render water, soil or air useless for the maintenance of life. Atmospheric pollution by smoke and exhaust fumes is now a feature of most large cities of the world, and pollution of waters of rivers and streams is now characteristic of most civilizations. The insidious nature of these changes makes their control difficult and costly. They generally slowly worsen, until government intervention becomes the necessary solution.

How do these considerations apply to the question of wildlife conservation in Australia?

Development

Australians hope to maintain or increase their standards of living. This implies increase in development of resources, and almost every plan for development envisages some change in the environment. The population is increasing by immigration, in addition to natural increase, and will continue to do so while present policies continue. All this demands an ever-increasing rate of development. Any plans for economic development and all projections of national productivity call for increases in food production. Schemes to ensure this development visualize clearing of virgin country (e.g. brigalow or the mallee); increasing stocking rates and the establishment of alien legumes; the improvement of crop yields, and other measures of this kind. Increasing national income involves increases in fibre production, in wool production, in mineral output, in highway construction, in irrigation, and in hundreds of other facets of primary and secondary industries. Land, and — even more — water, is limited for all these developments, and it is because of these increasing pressures on all forms of land use that a degree of planning, hitherto impracticable, is fast becoming a necessity. Some competing forms of land use can co-exist, some are mutually exclusive. Because there now is not enough land, it is important that every project for development be examined to make sure that its implementation will provide the greatest benefit for the greatest number of people for the longest period of time, and will not entail long-term hazards.

Competition for Land

All will concede the need for a variety of kinds of land use, and so particular difficulties arise when a decision is taken to use land for nature conservation to the exclusion of other purposes. It is a natural reaction to think that a reserve for wildlife or for a national park should be on somebody else's land. Opposition to this form of land use stems from private owners who may claim the loss of grazing land, the loss of timber rights, or that the land is 'locked up' and is non-productive. Or it may be said it is a breeding ground for vermin or weeds; that fires are uncontrolled and spread into nearby 'productive' land. Or opposition may stem from local government bodies who fear loss of taxes, or from industrial companies who may lose the opportunity to exploit mineral deposits, or from public authorities who require the tops of mountains for TV stations or repeater stations, or from power authorities who require dam sites and sites for power lines. The military authorities require training grounds, and it is a rare statesman who will write like President Roosevelt in a time of national emergency (1941), because of a threat to the breeding ground of the trumpeter swan:

> . . . Please tell Major General Adams or whoever is in charge of this business, that Henry Lake, Utah, must immediately be struck from the Army planning list for any purposes. The verdict is for the Trumpeter Swan and against the Army. The Army must find a different nesting place.

What is not readily appreciated is that land for a national park or a wildlife reserve may, in fact, be a productive form of land use in the face of other requirements. But experience has shown that this is so (see, for example, 'First World Conference on National Parks', United States Government Printing Office, 1962).

Habitat Preservation

It becomes pointless to attempt to preserve a species in a zoological garden. Only very rarely has a threatened species been re-established after having become extinct in its original environment. (Amongst interesting exceptions are the Hawaiian goose and the American bison.) All animals are dependent upon plants or upon other animals and the inter-relationships of the components of an ecosystem make it more sensible to protect a habitat than a species.

A good deal has been said of the need to preserve individual species of animals or plants. This may sometimes be desirable but to do so *requires* the preservation of the *habitat* of the species.

Some plants and animals are wide ranging, others are highly restricted. Some are migratory yet require areas along the migratory routes. Few generalizations are possible and all species threatened with extinction require special consideration. Examples of these problems are given in *The Launching of a New Ark*, edited by Peter Scott for the World Wildlife Fund. The above considerations also provide an explanation for the necessity for areas to be of reasonable size. No more precise statement is possible, for a large, wide ranging migratory marsupial obviously requires a larger area than a small, highly-localized plant. But, in order for the area to be a self-perpetuating unit it must be of sufficient size to provide all the requisites for the ecosystem. Unless the ecosystem is to be a self-perpetuating unit, it is generally a waste of money, effort and resources to establish it as a reserve.

It is common experience that more devastating outbreaks of disease may overtake a plant grown as a crop than the same species growing sparsely in a mixed community. Such a community has resilience to invasion, and it has a much greater stability than a monoculture. There is thus a virtue in diversity, and yet man continually wishes to grow plants in monoculture, largely because of ease of harvesting. He must therefore be prepared to introduce energy into the system in the form of cultivation, weedicides, fertilizers and so on, whereas these are unnecessary in the ecosystem in its native condition. A small insult to such a diversified ecosystem such as, for example, wildfire or defoliation by insect attack, may be tolerated, and a succession of compensatory changes is begun which generally eventually re-establishes the original situation. Even a major fire may not permanently alter a system, but repeated firing not infrequently allows the establishment of fire-resistant species which can become dominant.

Such considerations stress again the need for reserves to be relatively large areas. A small one will generally not be self-perpetuating and may be too easily damaged. In ecosystems showing great diversity of species, a tropical rainforest for example, a smaller area may be less viable than a simpler ecosystem containing relatively few species.

It should now be clearer why ecologists insist on the idea that the only effective way of conserving a species of animal or plant is to preserve its habitat, as much of it as possible, and in as natural a condition as possible.

It should also be apparent why the biologist sees a need for some degree of 'management' of the necessarily smaller area that can be incorporated into reserve systems. The mere fact that the area is restricted in terms of geographical range of some of its component species means that there is interference with part of the web. It requires great ecological knowledge to understand what this interference may do to the ecosystem, and even more penetrating understanding to know what compensating measures need to be taken. These are the measures we think of when we talk of 'management' of the ecosystem. We do not imply that the area should be managed for man, or even that an attempt be made to maintain the *status quo*, because, as already has been stressed, the essential feature of a biological ecosystem is change. To appreciate whether changes in, for example, the number of a particular mammal are man-induced, or are 'normal' fluctuations, requires ecological skills which are available for few environments, and yet are needed for many.

But if we are to generalize, it may be said that the simpler the ecosystem, the greater is the need for management practices. Of course, in an area that has been badly damaged, reclamation projects can be carried out. Some highly valued wildlife reserves in the U.S.A. are on areas that have been reclaimed.

Population Pressure

The dilemma of man is that, as his numbers increase, so does the pressure upon available resources. At the same time his needs increase, and so it seems inevitable that populations will tend to 'overshoot' their resources.

Almost within living memory there was somewhere else to go to take up land. But 'squatters' can never again find a place on this earth. There are good ecological reasons for the shifting cultivation practised by the New Guinea natives, and indeed by people in all tropical countries. As land becomes limited this form of agriculture, which allows natural regeneration of essential organic matter, is being replaced by more permanent cultivation. This will require fertilizers which are easily leached in the high rainfall tropics. Any errors in methods of cultivation will result in impoverishment then far more difficult to set right. In a place where land is limited, the way it is treated will determine the future of the population it supports. In parts of Australia it is already too late to divert the course of events, but over much of the land there is yet time to plan adequately for future expansion.

This is not true of some parts of the earth, and within a generation we will begin to see the limiting factors to further expansion. The limit may be water in one area, it will be food in another, and space in yet a third. Control of population expansion is the only eventual solution, but the need for control will arise at different times, in different areas. But it is *now* that people need to understand what is yet to come because only with such knowledge can adequate planning be conceived.

Decisions Regarding Land Use

From the viewpoint of the future, therefore, before decisions are taken on the most appropriate form of land use for any piece of land, all conflicting uses should be considered and a decision reached on the basis of the greatest good for the largest number as far ahead as we can see. To arrive at such a decision requires a view of future needs and these needs will certainly change with time. So we cannot expect future generations to view all of today's decisions with equanimity. But it takes no imagination to anticipate their reaction to the decay of the visual environment as illustrated in *Australian Outrage*.

In Australia, we at least have the advantage of being able to view in some perspective the problems facing people in more populated parts of the world which have been settled for longer periods. We can say with assurance that land needed for many purposes will become an even more precious resource, but that in the face of pressure we must include space for national parks and wilderness areas. We can say that experience has shown that there are never enough of these; that they bring unsuspected wealth to people of the area; that they soon become in danger of over-use; and that once damaged they can either never be reclaimed or, if reclaimable, can be reclaimed only at great cost. Alienating influences are so strong, and are often so thoroughly organized, that substantial efforts are needed to retain those inadequate remnants that remain.

Stewart Udall, United States Secretary of Interior, in his inspiring book *The Quiet Crisis* has called for a renewed effort to understand man's role in this environment. There is need for a new 'land ethic' that will help man to understand his own role in the 'web of life'.

As the National Parks Association of New South Wales repeats: 'The Wilderness we now have, is all that we or any man will ever have . . .'

Summary

By way of summarizing the arguments presented above, the following are the principles of conservation which apply to our problem in Australia; most have a wider relevance also:

(1) Man is the dominant ecological force on earth. He is alone in the solar system and there is no foreseeable possibility of his inhabiting other planets. His environment is therefore circumscribed.

(2) The cardinal criterion for man's activities must be that future generations should have as full opportunities as we have today. Part of all available resources must be left unimpaired, not damaged and not depleted. This is what we call conservation.

(3) Resources are of many kinds and their conservation varies depending upon the resource.

(4) Many animals, when they become too numerous for the resources provided by their environment, damage it. This does not matter when the area is small, because the environment generally has considerable recuperative ability.

(5) But the entirely new factor is that man now covers the entire earth and very soon NO habitable part will be left untouched.

(6) All animals, including primitive man, have mechanisms preventing their numbers from becoming too excessive.

(7) Modern medicine and agriculture have reduced most of these curbs so that man is in the midst of a population increase that is exponential.

(8) This rate of growth has already had the effect of making many resources more difficult of access and it is in the nature of man to carry his exploitation of resources to the point where they can no longer recover.

(9) Because so many living things are so interdependent, damage to the resources of one may have repercussions far beyond those at present anticipated.

(10) Our lack of foresight is due to a lack of ecological knowledge, but, even when the knowledge is available, a short-term gain is at present more likely to prevail than a long-term view providing hypothetical benefits for hypothetical future generations.

(11) Although the need for more detailed ecological knowledge is very great, so many resources are now known to be damaged or reduced that the urgent need for their conservation is the most pressing need of mankind.

(12) The need for a new attitude towards resources is thus a requirement of all men of all nations.

Conservation in Relation to the Land and Its Use

R. G. Downes

Man's attitude to land and how it should be used has changed according to the degree to which he has been capable of modifying it to suit his purpose.

Primitive man lived within his environment like other animals and had no significant influence on it. He was entirely dependent on the available natural productivity and fared according to its seasonal changes. Because primitive man lived within the environment in this way, conservation was achieved at low levels of productivity and comfort and with some degree of hazard for many individuals; but he threatened neither the continued productivity of the environment nor his own existence as a species.

Modern industrial civilization is at the other extreme. Today, man has such a degree of technological skill that he can modify his environment significantly and quickly. He is now the ecologically dominant species on earth and the future biological condition and continued productivity of the planet are virtually in his hands. This means that he can threaten not only his own future as a species, but that of the existing flora and fauna. During his rise to this place of ecological significance, man has caused considerable destruction. Whole civilizations have failed to survive because they have tried to produce from the environment more than was possible on a sustained basis.

Our present civilization is making an effort to avoid some of the obvious mistakes of the past, for example by the mitigation of soil erosion, but it has still failed to recognize some of the less dramatic but more insidious forms of environmental destruction and pollution. Man must now look critically and responsibly at his effect on the environment in which he lives, and clarify his objectives so that appropriate action can be taken. The population explosion, the possibility of nuclear warfare, and the widespread pollution and destruction of environments constitute a serious threat to life on earth.

Conservation

Conservation is concerned with man's attitude toward his environment and its resources, involving the study of how man can satisfy his physical and aesthetic needs from the resources of his environment without spoiling its capability to go on satisfying those needs. The development of conservation knowledge is a constructive process requiring integration of scientific knowledge from many disciplines to provide suitable systems of use and management for the various kinds of environment.

Because conservation is achieved by the proper use and management of dynamic biological systems, there are no absolute means for determining what is right or wrong action. Any decisions are based on relative values which must be assessed for each set of circumstances. The only firm basis for achieving conservation is the acceptance of the ecological principle that change within an environment causes other changes. If man is to use and continue using the environment for the benefits which he desires, he must ensure that any change to achieve his ends is made in a way which maintains stability or creates new stability.

Throughout the course of evolution, many

species have become extinct because they could not adapt themselves to the changing conditions of an environment. Man's survival will require all the scientific knowledge and ingenuity which he can command. In addition to solutions for technical problems, there must be an enlightened public opinion, so that the conflicting interests and demands for different kinds of uses for our natural resources can be resolved after the scientific, economic and social requirements have each been given appropriate consideration.

A philosophy of conservation leading to a united, rational approach by all those interested in the conservation of natural resources will not emerge until persons interested in any particular resource perceive and understand the multiple needs of the community in the use of natural resources; that the demands to fulfil these needs can be conflicting; and, that an acceptable basis for resolving these conflicts in the public interest can be devised.

The Community and Land Use

Man needs land for production — the production of food, fibre, timber and water — and he needs land for industrial and urban purposes and for the associated transport systems, roads, railways and airports. Man also needs some land for recreation and scenic enjoyment so that city dwellers in particular can escape at times from their unnatural confining environment to associate with nature. Areas in their natural condition are needed for ecological reference and scientific study, and for the preservation of the other species which inhabit the earth.

Some people look on the need to preserve plant and animal communities as an impractical emotional desire, but this is not true. Environments are being changed in many ways, and so there is a basic scientific need to preserve the widest possible range of genetic material represented in the multitude of existing plant and animal species. Although economically unimportant now, some of these species could become important to man. The present pool of flora and fauna is the source from which species will be obtained to occupy the man-created conditions of the future.

Of the various forms of land use which man requires, some are flexible because a change to another use can be achieved easily. Some are inflexible because once the use is imposed it must be continued for a long time. Some uses are compatible, and in these circumstances 'multiple use' is a desirable objective. Some uses are incompatible, and someone must decide how land shall be used.

Ideally, the use should be determined in accordance with the nature of the land itself: its characteristics, weaknesses and capabilities. Irrespective of how the land is to be used, conservation principles must be applied; the imposed system of use and management must ensure that the land shall continue to be useful for the chosen purpose.

Conservation Philosophy

Whatever their particular interest, all conservationists are basically concerned with the study of environments and their use. The character of an environment not affected by man is due to the particular combination of the individual features of which it is composed, namely climate, topography, soils, hydrology, flora and fauna. Each environment must be studied to determine the interaction of the critical features by which the equilibrium of the system is maintained, and what is likely to happen if particular changes are made. Only in this way can disastrous, and sometimes irreparable, mistakes be foreseen and avoided.

Each environmental unit is an ecological system which has evolved to achieve its current stability. Undisturbed, it represents the optimum combination and relative abundance of the available plant and animal species which can continue to live and compete with each other in the prevailing soil, topographic, hydrological and climatic conditions.

These undisturbed ecosystems seem to have a dynamic stability. There are seasonal changes of species composition and populations but these tend to oscillate about a normal or average condition. If any particular species threatens to get out of hand, factors operate which tend to check it. In man's lifetime there is little permanent change unless, by chance, there is a major catastrophic climatic or geological event. In these circumstances, the system begins on a path of development toward a new dynamic stability.

Throughout the world the character of many ecosystems has been changed to a greater or lesser extent. In some, man has been successful in raising productivity; in others, man's effects have been equivalent to some of the major natural catastrophic events and they have created instability followed by a chain of reactions ultimately leading to another stable condition at a lower level of productivity.

Whether man has been successful in his attempts to change the environment to achieve higher productivity has depended to a large extent on the nature of the original stability of the ecosystem. Different systems have varying degrees of stability. The more stable appear to be those in which there is the greatest variety. Presence of many species and many ecological niches makes a system resilient to imposed changes. The more vulnerable are those in which the stability is dependent upon some special set of circumstances such as a specialized vegetation. A system of this kind has a vegetative weakness. If any imposed change destroys or weakens the vegetation, the system becomes unbalanced and changes take place which can lead to permanent change. Other systems have topographic, soil or hydrologic weaknesses.

This kind of knowledge about an ecosystem enables us to determine what is possible in the way of land use or at least to determine what kinds of use or development are likely to lead either to undesirable and irreparable changes, or to advantageous changes which provide productivity and continued stability. With such information it is possible to turn more confidently toward resolving the conflicting demands for the use of land in a modern society.

Conservation of land being used for agriculture, forestry or grazing requires that man's management of introduced species of plants and animals must provide an over-all and lasting equilibrium within limits set by the climate, topography, soils and other organisms. Stability of undisturbed systems seems to be less vulnerable when there is a wide array of plant and animal species, and so it is not surprising to find that multiple use and broad rotation systems are more likely to give stability than single purpose, single crop, or single species of animal production.

Conservation requires that the most useful land — that capable of many uses — should be kept under flexible forms of land use so that its capability of a variety of future uses is maintained. Then the form of use and production can be altered to suit changing needs. Ideally, the building of towns, roads and airports on first class agricultural land should be avoided. Frequently decisions to use land in this way are not based on proper criteria but on economic insistence. Industrial and urban users can afford to pay much more for land than those wanting to use it for primary production, preservation or recreation.

A conservation attitude can be applied to the use of land for industrial and urban uses. The building of cities and towns on flood plains should be avoided, not only because it is an inflexible use of good land, but also because it becomes increasingly difficult to maintain its usefulness for its chosen purpose. Sewage disposal and drainage is difficult and flooding can be a major problem.

Land chosen for roads, airports and railways must be used in accordance with conservation principles. These structures must be stable and maintain their usefulness with a minimum of maintenance. For example, it is useless to choose sites for roads where it becomes virtually impossible to stabilize them because of landslips or erosion, or where the cost of maintaining the stability is exorbitantly high. A consideration of conservation principles in selection and design will avoid such difficulties.

There are many different concepts of conservation with respect to national parks, wildlife reserves and primitive areas. In fact many ardent amateur naturalists tend to regard themselves as being the only real conservationists because they hold rigidly to a narrow view of preservation. Unfortunately their concept of conservation is often based on emotional ideas about individual plants and animals and not the species, or on the species and not the plant and animal community. As conservationists they should be concerned with the whole environment — the topographic, soil, biotic complex — and not just part of it. People who are concerned about the preservation of land just for the sake of preserving areas of land in a wild state without some specific objective, are as far removed from true conservation as are those who look on land as only something to be altered and developed.

For systems of land use and management to have continuing usefulness, they must provide the environment with ecological stability so that, depending on its particular purpose, there will be no loss of soil or deterioration of its fertility, no deterioration of a structure built on it, no loss of value as an area of scenic beauty, or for recreation or for the preservation of plant and animal communities.

Basic Information to Determine Land Use

Because conservation is fundamentally an ecological problem of adjusting the system of land use to suit the environment, it is essential to obtain all possible data concerning the various features of each environment. Complete studies of areas reveal that environmental units can be recognized, each of which by virtue of the integration of its particular soils, climate, vegetation and topography provides the basis for determination of suitable forms of land use. The recognition and study of these units is essential for devising appropriate systems of management to avert the problems and hazards which a unit may present in productive use, and in maintaining stability of the plant and animal communities when the use is preservation.

These units can be recognized at different levels of generalization according to whether the determination of land use needs to be at the broad scale (that is, whether the unit is suitable for agriculture, forestry, recreation or preservation uses); or at the narrow scale (for individual farm planning where the problem is the assessment of the suitability of areas for specific crops or pastures, silvicultural methods, or for the maintenance of specific plant and animal communities).

Soil and ecological surveys for land use have now been rationalized on a reasonable basis which enables the recognition and mapping of units at different levels of intensity, and at the same time provides a means of correlating the units and their relative significance at these different levels. The Soil Conservation Authority has recognized four units — the component, the land unit, the land system, and the land zone.

The component is the unit recognized in the most detailed investigation and is consequently the basic unit for considering detailed land use. A component is uniform with respect to its potential, problems and hazards, and is an area of land in which the climate, parent material, soil, vegetation and topography are uniform within the limits significant for a particular form of land use. In practice, when studying land for potential development, this is interpreted as being the most likely form of land use. Agronomic investigations need to be based on components because they cannot be truly related to a wider range of conditions.

The land unit is an area in which there are a limited number of components occurring in a consistent sequence forming a characteristic pattern or landscape. It is the unit most commonly used for mapping.

The land system consists of a combination of land units, land form frequently constituting the major basis for grouping.

The land zone is a unit used for portraying the variation of a large area of country for initial consideration of land problems. It is an area in which similar land systems are included, the chief land forms of the system being common.

To indicate the relative levels of generalization, the scales of the final maps are: components, 40 chains = 1 inch; land units, 2 miles = 1 inch; land systems, 8 miles = 1 inch; geographic zones, 32 miles = 1 inch.

Surveys in which land units are mapped provide a compromise by which sufficient knowledge of the country is obtained for the determination of land use with a reasonable speed of survey. Information is obtained about all the components which occur within the land units and about their relative proportions and locations in relation to each other.

By means of diagrams and an accompanying table, the way is shown in which the land components, of which a land unit is comprised, occur in the field in relation to each other. Also provided is the information concerning the nature of each of the environmental features such as climate, topography, soils, vegetation, potential and hazards when used for productive purposes. Such a survey provides the preliminary information for a detailed component survey if this is required later—e.g. for farm subdivision and planning.

In conjunction with soil-ecological surveys at all levels, every effort is made to understand the origin and development of the land forms, the soils, and the vegetation types; in fact a knowledge of the dynamics of the environment is an important aspect of the investigations if the problems and hazards of management under likely forms of land use are to be foreseen.

Because these surveys cover all features of the environment, they provide factual data for resolving problems of conflicting land uses. They can furnish information by which the value of an area for a national park can be judged as readily as its value for agriculture, forestry or urban and industrial use.

The Need to Manage Land for Chosen Use

Man must learn how to manage land for its chosen use. Management means the manipulation or alteration of conditions to achieve desired objectives, but there must be some degree of confidence that the objectives are correct for the particular circumstances. Some examples of the conservation approach to land use and management problems in water catchments, agricultural land and wildlife reserves will serve to illustrate this.

For instance, in some catchments the maintenance of at least a certain rate of water yield throughout the year is the important characteristic which must be safeguarded; while in others a reduction of sediment load, even if it means a reduced water yield, may be the most desirable objective. In pursuing these objectives, manipulation must be based on an understanding of basic principles of ecology and of their effect on the hydrology. This requires a knowledge of how catchments work and how the various operating factors affect the fate of water which falls on the catchment as rain or snow.

The prime objective of catchment management in a dry country like Australia must be water production, and in some small vital water supply catchments it may be necessary to restrict all other forms of land use. However, in large catchments, multiple use is most desirable and should be attainable without detriment to water production.

Agriculture abounds in ecological problems — weed control, pasture establishment and management being excellent examples. But in addition to such facets of agriculture in which the ecological implications are obvious, it is important to understand that the agricultural use of land is an ecological problem. Farm planning is the co-ordination of technological knowledge to provide a system of land husbandry in which each part of the farm is put to its best and proper use. Ideally, good farming is a situation in which man manages his plants, animals and soils to produce a dynamically balanced productive ecosystem.

It is useless to consider individual technological advances in isolation because any change imposed on the environment results in other changes which can be either beneficial or detrimental from either the physical or the economic aspect. Farm planning consists of an assessment of the land and water resources of the farm and their potentiality. For this purpose the farm needs to be classified into its land components or the somewhat comparable units known to conservationists as land classes. The components can be readily characterized in terms of land classes. From this basic information the alternative safe and profitable farming systems may be determined and when the choice is made detailed planning can begin.

As an example of such an approach, the factors influencing the final paddock size on a sheep grazing property can be elaborated. Initially the soil, slope, climate and aspect will determine the type of pasture and potential productivity. The type of pasture will determine the type of grazing management with respect to the grazing pressure to be applied in accordance with the season of the year, and the frequency with which it shall be left for a hay crop. To obtain the proper grazing on the right occasions requires careful flock management procedure, and, according to flock management methods and breeding programme, so does the paddock size need to be designed. In addition to these criteria the water supply facilities need to be arranged so that the combined pasture and flock management programme can be carried out as planned. So farm planning for conservation and proper use of an environment is a process of integration of knowledge of the behaviour of plants and animals in relation to each other and their environment — truly a problem of applied ecology.

The whole basis of soil conservation, erosion control and reclamation is ecological. For soil conservation there is a need to assess the nature and dynamics of environments so that systems of land use can be devised to give the desired production on a permanent basis. Erosion control is basically an understanding of the reasons for the upset equilibrium and of the mechanics of erosion processes, so that methods can be devised for re-establishing a balance. Reclamation is a matter of assessing the nature of the modified environment so that suitable primary and secondary colonizers can be found to occupy the available niches and so begin a succession to a new equilibrium.

In a wildlife reserve the objective is the maintenance of the animal community. Strict preservation in the sense of merely prohibiting the destruction of the fauna is never likely to succeed unless associated with it is an attempt to conserve and manage the environment in which the animals exist.

Damage of environments has probably had a more adverse effect on the maintenance of wildlife than any depredations of casual hunters. This means that the environment, the whole system, must be managed even to the extent of deliberately reducing the animal population from time to time so that the animals themselves will not irreparably damage their environment and threaten their own existence. For some animal species, proper wildlife management may even require manipulation of the environment to make it more satisfactory for their survival. This approach is likely to be needed more and more in the future because of possible adverse effects of uses imposed on land round wildlife reserves.

Land Use and Management for Preservation

Land required for preservation purposes could well amount to a significant proportion of the total available land. For this reason, proposals to use land for preservation purposes will need justification if they are to compete successfully with the rising demand for land for other purposes. Those interested

Welcome facilities at Ayers Rock National Park, Northern Territory. PHOTO COURTESY AUST. TOURIST COMMISSION

ffects of the disastrous 1939 fire in *Eucalyptus* *gnans* forest, Victoria. The regeneration is about years old. PHOTO COURTESY VICTORIAN ORESTRY COMMISSION

atherine Gorge National Park, Northern erritory, is an unusual type of oasis which ppeals to tourists. PHOTO COURTESY UST. TOURIST COMMISSION

art of the Stirling Ranges National Park, south-western Australia, a typical wilderness rea without mechanized access. Regions of great geological nterest occur in some of our ational parks. PHOTO COURTESY . WALDENDORP

Skiers at Mount Buller, Victoria. This village and resort are in a reserve administered by the Forests Commission, but are not favoured by hikers who prefer wilderness areas. PHOTO COURTESY AUST. TOURIST COMMISSION

This sign, disfigured by trigger-happy Nimrods, is unfortunately only too typical of forestry reserves in Queensland. PHOTO COURTESY J. G. TRACEY

Pulling Brigalow scrub (*Acacia harpophylla* etc.) with chain and cable, west Moura, Queensland. Most of the Brigalow-dominated vegetation in Queensland has now been cleared for pastoral development and cereal growi PHOTO COURTESY S. L. EVERIST

Dove Lake and Cradle Mountain, centr Tasmania. Australia's only overland wilderness area trail of any extent (53 miles) within a park commences nea this point. PHOTO COURTESY AUST. TOURIST COMMISSION

in the preservation of land for national parks, primitive areas, wildlife reserves, scenic and recreation areas must have clear objectives concerning both the proposed land use and the future management of the land. Irrespective of whether land is to be a national park, a primitive area, a wildlife reserve, a scenic or a recreational area, it must be suitable and adequate for the purpose, and it must be managed so that it will continue to fulfil its function. Land should not be just set aside in the vain hope that preservation alone will ensure that it will remain useful.

Ideally there is a need for the preservation of a viable example of each type of ecosystem. This is desirable for scientific reasons both as a means of preserving the widest possible range of plant and animal species and as a basic reference by which the effects of imposed systems of land use and management can be judged. These areas would need to be primitive areas and, as such, would not serve the great need of the community for open space walking, hunting and other outdoor recreation. Other areas of land should be allocated for these purposes, some of which will be preserved because of outstanding scenic value or some special geological or topographical feature.

Most people would agree that these are all justifiable reasons for the preservation of land. However the management of the areas should be related to an objective. There is no valid reason to believe that all land set aside for preservation purposes should be treated as primitive areas.

It is even unreasonable to expect that the whole of a national park should be managed as a primitive area although the purists would expect this. In practice it is impossible because national parks are set aside for the benefit of the people and for this reason many parts of the park must be subject to a certain degree of human interference. Management of parks must recognize this and provide for the effect of man's intrusion into some parts of the various ecosystems. A properly constructed road or track is much more stable and will finally cause less destruction to the environment than some poorly constructed means of access attempted in the hope that it looks more natural, or does not cause too much initial destruction. On the other hand parts of parks set aside as primitive areas should be managed as such and have very restricted public access.

The Conservation Task

Although there are many arguments between people about the use and management of land, the only real point of conflict between people who want land for productive purposes, and those who want it preserved, is the initial decision. Once a decision has been reached both groups are confronted with the ecological problem of maintaining an environment so that it will continue to serve its chosen purpose. This is the basis of conservation and all conservationists should be concerned with how land is being managed whether it be an urban or industrial environment, agricultural or forest land, water supply catchment, national park or wildlife reserve.

Conservationists must recognize that the public needs land for many purposes and until they can agree on how decisions should be made, the public and politicians alike will be confused, frustrated and annoyed with the endless arguments about land use which are common at present. In this atmosphere productive use will always have the advantage because man tends to think of the present rather than the future.

Conservationists have a real task to perform, to agree on the basic philosophy of conservation and to see that the public understand it. In this way there can be some hope that before it is too late a more rational and scientific approach will prevail in determining how we shall live within our environment so that it will continue to serve the needs not only of the present but of subsequent generations.

An Economic Framework for the Conservation Decision

J. A. Sinden
W. F. Musgrave

Natural Resources, Economics and Ecology

Conservation concerns the use of natural resources; more specifically it concerns their rate of use, that is output per unit of some input. Although the term 'natural resources' is difficult to define, it has come to mean those attributes of nature which are of value to man. Natural resources include coal deposits and national parks, land and scenery, commercial fisheries and kangaroos.

Resources are valuable because they can be used to satisfy the wants of man and because they are scarce. Society's wants are diverse. They may be satisfied by the food values of animals which can be grazed on land which has been cleared of native forest, or by the aesthetic values of that same forest in its undisturbed state. If a resource is of value, then men will make decisions about the rate of use of that resource. Sometimes these decisions excite public discussion. If the resource is a natural one this discussion will usually involve use of the word 'conservation'.

Both ecologists and economists consider that man is a source of disturbance and that because of his actions old ecological states become irrelevant and new states emerge. The economist believes that his discipline can contribute significantly to the assessment of the social desirability of different states. Put another way, economics can contribute to the evaluation of alternative uses of resources. Definition and analysis of these alternatives in relation to individual and social man is the crux of the economist's concern and is highly relevant to the conservation decision.

The Meaning of Conservation

At any one time we are in a particular state of resource use which will produce a stream of benefits to society through time. Alternative states of resource use will produce other streams of social benefits. Similarly, each state will have a cost stream. Choices among states of resource use involve the valuation of costs and benefits which occur in each time period. These costs and benefits are reduced to a common point in time, usually the present, by discounting at the appropriate rate of interest. These discounted values are called present values and measure the value today of a cost or benefit which occurs in future time periods. The optimal state of resource use is that which maximizes the present value of social benefits net of costs. This sort of decision is being made frequently. Sometimes the problem involves questions of land use such as: shall we continue to use prime wheat land for state forest or to use good sand mining areas for wildlife reserves? At other times it involves questions of intensity of resource use within a particular land use such as: what is the optimal stocking rate of sheep or the optimal number of park visitors per day?

Conservation involves questions of alternative forms and rates of resource use and so the optimal state of conservation is that which maximizes net social benefits. Presumably then, those who deplore a lack of conservation of certain natural resources believe that the current use rate is sub-optimal in this sense. A 'conservation problem' exists because the use rates are considered to be too high or perhaps too low and an alteration in the use rate would improve social welfare.

Literally, 'conservation' can mean both the state of resource use and the act of conserving. In this chapter the act of conservation is taken as the process of movement towards the optimal state. This is an accepted meaning in resource economics and it provides a basis for the subsequent formulation of a decision framework. In its second meaning, i.e. as a state of resource use, 'conservation' signifies the maintenance of the present state, for example, the maintenance of specific areas which are of scientific interest in their present state. This *status quo* interpretation is used in this chapter in only a limited way. 'Conservation' is taken as the act of movement towards an optimum: the optimum may of course be the *status quo*.

The conservation of natural resources, now defined as movement towards some optimum, involves two types of decision. First, to what use should a particular resource, say land, be put? The previous example of wheat and forests as alternatives is relevant here. Another, and more specific example, is provided by the need confronting the New England National Park Trust to decide if, and at what rates, Bellingen sawmillers should selectively log portions of the park.

The second type of decision concerns the optimum level of use of a resource after it has been committed to a particular alternative. For example, having dedicated an area as a national park, the decision still remains as to the intensity of use which should be permitted. As an example, in portions of the Royal National Park current over-use is impairing future use capability. The slopes of the Hacking River receive excessive human pressure and this leads to erosion. This human pressure can be specified as a rate of use in terms of visitors per acre per unit of time. It would seem that a reduction in the rate of current use would decrease the erosion and so increase future use capacity. In economic terms such an action is regarded as a redistribution of rates of use of the river area to the future.

In a dynamic world the optimal state of conservation is almost certainly unstable. At any point in time some changes in tastes or technology may make a change in the state of resource use desirable. For example, in terms of the Royal National Park again, technological improvements in erosion control or fire control may permit more peak visitors than the present 25,000 per week. In this case the technically optimal state would incorporate a higher use-capacity.

So far our examples have tended to involve resource 'improvement' — more visitors or more sheep per acre. However, it should be emphasized that new optimal states may represent resource depletion rather than improvement; that is, the new optimal state may require an eventual decline in the rate of use. While such a change may be dubbed exploitation, it should be recognized that it is possible, and that sometimes it is desirable.

The Decision Framework Applied to Conservation

In this section the fundamental concepts of social benefits and costs are developed further. They are vital components of the choice between land use activities as well as the choice of the optimal state for a given activity. They recognize both the private and social dimensions of well-being. The need for such recognition is emphasized by the accusations of commercial exploitation and the pleas for protection of resources. These issues typify most conservation debates.

A Conceptual Framework

The general relationship between the price of a good and the quantity which is purchased is portrayed by the demand curve. At high prices, say OH in Figure 1, only small quantities are purchased, that is OS. In general the quantity of purchases will rise as the price of the good falls. Accordingly the demand curve can be expected to slope downwards to the right.

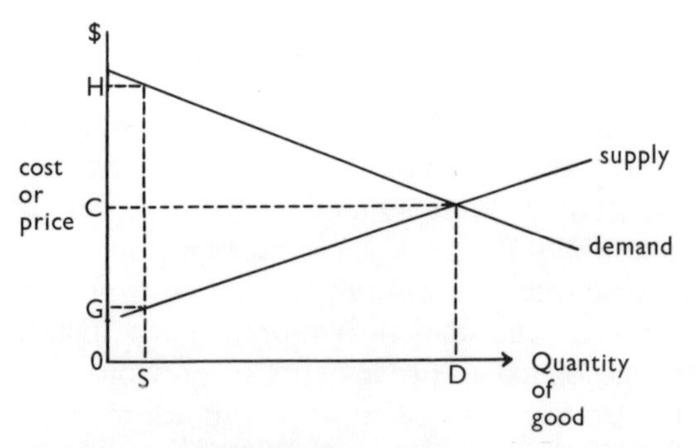

FIGURE 1: *Supply and Demand Curves for a Hypothetical Good*

A supply schedule depicts the relationship between market prices and the quantity of a good which producers are willing to produce and sell. At high prices producers will devote more of their resources of land, labour and capital to the production of the good. For example, a farmer can afford to purchase more fertilizer and labour and to use poor land at higher prices. All of these factors tend to increase output at high prices. Thus supply curves tend to slope upwards to the right.

Supply curves are also known as marginal cost curves because each point on them relates the cost of one marginal or extra unit of output to total output. For example, a price of OG in Figure 1 is shown to call forth a supply of OS units. As the price rises to OC the farmer in the above example supplies more inputs of fertiliser to his land to raise his output to OD. The cost of the ODth unit is OC: the cost of production of that unit (the marginal cost), which includes a profit allowance for the farmer, just equals the price which it will receive. A complete marginal cost or supply schedule shows this relationship between the cost of the marginal unit of output and the total output. It therefore shows how the amount that producers will sell varies with market price.

Equilibrium of supply and demand is reached at an output of OD. At OD the consumer is willing to pay price OC for quantity OD: at this price producers can profitably produce and market OD units. All units greater than OD cost more to produce than the competitive market is prepared to pay. Similarly at outputs less than OD it is still profitable for producers to raise output. Thus the equilibrium price at which production and consumption are equated is OC: the equilibrium output is OD.

The Framework in Terms of Park Use

Gross benefits from the use of any resource are measured by the total willingness to pay for such use by all those who benefit. The corollary that the degree of financial support is a measure of the true degree of benefit is subsequently considered in the context of wombat preservation. Individual willingness to pay was described above in terms of a single demand curve. Total willingness of society to pay is portrayed by a total demand curve which is built up by the aggregation of the demand curves of all individuals.

This concept of benefit can be applied to national park use but in this case it is more meaningful to talk about total cost to the user rather than a single price. Users' willingness to pay is then portrayed as the quantity of annual visits in relation to the total costs which he himself incurs directly, i.e. fees, travel and preparation (the demand curve of Fig. 2). In the general framework the quantity demanded increased as price was reduced. Now the quantity of visits is assumed to increase as the total costs are reduced.

Gross costs of supplying a particular conservation facility are the money value of goods foregone by individuals throughout the economy to establish, maintain and use it. There are two types of cost: the costs which are borne by the public at large for park establishment and maintenance, and the private costs of travel and preparation which are borne directly by the users. The sum of private and public costs is called the 'social costs' of resource use. Some items within these cost classes may, of course, be difficult to calculate. Some of the benefits may also be difficult to calculate.

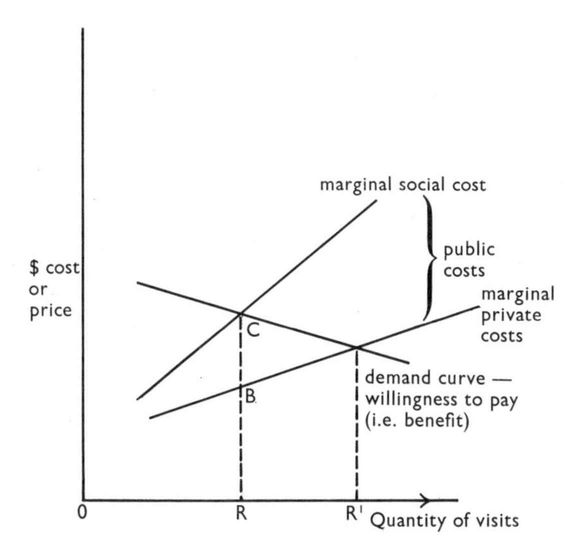

FIGURE 2: *Supply and Demand Curves for National Park Use*

The distinction between social costs (public and private) and private costs is shown in Fig. 2. In this figure users do not bear all the costs involved. As well as costs of establishment and maintenance, public costs would include the costs of resource protection or of restoration of exploited areas. These latter costs may give much more steeply rising marginal social cost curves if the costs of protection rise rapidly with increasing use. These represent the costs of protection in the face of increasing recreational use.

Total social marginal costs of the ORth unit can be interpreted as follows. RB represents the private cost of travel; BC represents the marginal public cost for the unit, i.e. the direct costs of park maintenance and any other costs which do not fall on the private user in the given time period. Hence RC is the total marginal social cost.

Maximum net social benefits occur when the quantity of visits per time period is OR. For a quantity greater than OR each visit has a social cost greater than the benefit or willingness of all individuals to pay: this is indicated by the demand curve. To maximize the present value of net social benefits through time it is necessary to compare time streams of benefits and costs and to select that pattern of use rates which gives the highest net benefits.

The social equilibrium rate of use is OR visits. This contrasts with the private optimum OR^1. The difference in desirable quantities of use (RR^1) gives rise to one of the most serious problems of park management.

This framework can be used in choosing between alternative forms of land use. However, in so doing, the concept of 'opportunity cost' must also be used. Opportunity cost is the income lost because land is used for a park rather than, say, timber or agricultural production. If the opportunity costs, or foregone agricultural income is high enough, comparison of net benefits from the optimal intensity of park use with these opportunity costs may show it would be best to have no park at all.

National Park Problems in the Decision Framework

The problem of over-use can be considered as a case of sub-optimal resource management. In Figure 2 the optimum level of use in a social context is OR where net social benefits are maximized. But, if it is first assumed that no fees are charged, then the actual level of use is determined solely by the relationship between private costs (as marginal private costs) and willingness to pay (the demand curve). The private optimum rate of use is therefore OR^1 visits per year. If there are any public costs at all, then OR^1 will always be greater than OR which is the socially desirable quantity of visits: RR^1 is the extent of over-use.

The framework not only clarifies the problem of over-use but enables the problem to be identified in a clear and rigorous manner. It also suggests the remedy of raising of the effective level of costs of private use. Thus fees could be charged for park use. In the United States for example, the price of a 'car sticker' for entrance to Yellowstone National Park has risen from $3 to $15 in recent years. Whether this is actually to control quantity of use or to provide revenues is not at issue. Fees can be charged and varied, and they can be set at appropriately high levels. Another remedy is to ration use. Even in this situation although the price system is not employed, the economist's framework is still relevant. The optimal rationing policy would be to restrict use to OR visits in Figure 2.

The problem of resource protection or preservation is considered subsequently in the context of uncertainty.

Application of the Framework

The criterion of maximization of the present value of net social benefits is a general criterion and its implications are relevant to the activities of all decision makers — individuals, groups or governments. In fact, there would be no need to distinguish private and social optima if all decision makers considered identical benefits and cost data, used the same discount rate, and used the same criterion. However, in reality, different data and criteria are often used by different decision makers. For example, the 100 acres or so of the Wilson's River Reserve of the New South Wales Forestry Commission has commercial timber with a total value of some $10,000: it also has considerable but less tangible value as a recreational reserve. The government, in dedicating the reserve to the latter use must have compared the alternatives and made a choice which, we assume, was the social welfare maximizing choice. It is very doubtful if a private owner of the area would have made the same choice because some of the benefits of such reserves are difficult to capture in a market price and because of differences in attitudes to benefits received in the future. The private owner's choice would then have been a private optimum but it would not have been a social optimum.

The divergence between private and social optima is one of the two main causes of conservation problems. Another is uncertainty, which is discussed later. Both of these reasons may justify increased public action for the conservation of natural resources.

Two of the main difficulties in applying the above conceptual framework to real world conservation and related problems are what economists call 'externalities' and 'intangibles'. The meaning of the word intangible is rather obvious. Externalities are a little more complex. External costs and benefits are those losses and gains, if any, which do not enter into the decision process associated with an act.

Externalities are frequent. A case involving wildlife, human health, and agriculture is the use of pesticides to raise farm output. The use of pesticides may simultaneously benefit farmers and damage biological units external to the farm. We can call this outside damage an externality or external cost because farmers would not consider them in deciding how much pesticide to use. Such an external effect could justify public intervention, in a variety of forms. Taxes on pesticides, subsidies or assistance to restore the damage or various regulations to restrain the farmers themselves may be appropriate. The purpose of public policy in such instances would be to 'internalize' the externality so that pesticide use would approach the level the farmers would have chosen had they recognized the 'cost' of the external effects in making their decisions.

Policies to 'internalize' externalities sometimes need the creation of some overall decision-making agency. This can be hard when the relevant external effects are very diffuse, as is certainly true of some pesticide effects.

Intangibles are an important aspect of the conservation and wildlife question. Many conservation benefits involve subjective, even aesthetic, qualities which are not readily capable of evaluation. The fundamental problem with these benefits is that there is no market in which a price can form. But the determination of socially optimal policies requires some assessment of them. Several methods have been used. The first and most commonly used is the 'opportunity cost' approach which sets the intangible benefit equal to the net revenue which could be obtained if the resources involved were diverted to their most profitable alternative use. In this way the intangible effect is, *de facto*, removed. For example, the unique rainforest outlier at Iluka in New South Wales lies on sands which are valuable to rutile miners. If this natural area is maintained by society then it is argued that the monetary value of the intangible benefits of preservation of the forest are at least equal to the potential income from mining.

The second method is an attempt to generate a quantitative measure of the benefits received: the intangible is again rendered tangible. This approach has been developed most intensively for the study of recreation benefits. An attempt is made to simulate the demand curve by the determination of a population's willingness to pay for visits: this involves survey-techniques of specified population groups. While fraught with difficulty, this technique and the opportunity cost approach do provide an acceptable way of attacking an otherwise insurmountable, but increasingly important problem.

Of course, every now and then an opportunity arises for an *ad hoc* evaluation of an otherwise intangible phenomenon. Such an opportunity was provided by the attempt to save the Hairy-nosed Wombat in South Australia. The Natural History Society of South Australia managed to raise $18,000 to purchase land which was the habitat of the animal. Thus we know that the value of the preservation of the Hairy-nosed Wombat is at least $18,000 to those who were the object of the campaign.

Any attempt to value a benefit which does not pass through a market or which cannot be measured precisely can never be wholly satisfactory. But abuses of these two methods of evaluation are probably less than abuses which may follow from alternative vague, arbitrary and often emotional assessments of the so-called 'public interest'.

The need for government intervention in the case of externalities and intangibles means that decisions about resource use will be made in that other market place, the political system. Economic analysis along the above lines is not regarded as being capable of displacing the political process but it is regarded as being able to help the process work better.

The Role of Uncertainty

A characteristic of most decisions is that they are made in the light of some lack of knowledge. Decisions which encompass long time spans are subject to obvious uncertainties as to future prices, costs and technology. In effect, every decision is subject to some difficulties in the definition of production relationships and market prospects.

In using natural resources man plays three roles: that of a user or destroyer of resources, that of a creator or discoverer of resources, and that of a pool of skills and labour. Individual men fill each of these roles to varying degrees. While some may be classed as resource users, others may be classed as resource creators or discoverers. Both classes of men make substantial impacts on social welfare. Fuel sources for power generation epitomize this dichotomy: on the one hand man is consuming known stocks of fossil fuel, while on the other hand he is creating new kinds of fuel, for example nuclear fuel, or discovering new reserves of fossil fuel, or improving his technology for utilizing existing fuels.

The creation, and probably to some extent the discovery also, of resources is essentially the product of man's creativity and an appropriate cultural and scientific environment. As long as there is technological advance man will probably continue to use natural resources more efficiently. There is no denying that man's creative capacity is fundamental as an engine of economic growth. But because of uncertainty we can never predict just where this engine will take us, nor what fuel it may require.

Uncertainty, together with man's creative capacity, is a fundamental justification of a system of wildlife reserves. The scientific value of such reserves depends entirely on man's capacity to use these 'pools of genes' to produce new plant varieties, to develop scientific knowledge, and thereby generally to promote the welfare of society as a whole. Uncertainty about the future may be adequate economic justification for investment in these reserves because it is felt that the welfare of future generations may be increased more by these investments than by, say, investment in bridges or roads. For public investment to be devoted to this issue on the scale that many conservationists advocate, society's expectations of the net benefits of this scientific hedge or insurance must be as great as the net benefits from alternative investment opportunities.

One effect of uncertainty about the future is that conflicts arise as to man's ability to fill the role of creator or discoverer of resources. If the oft-evinced expectations of sustained and high growth rates are any guide, it would seem that the majority of members of modern Western societies believe that the role will be effectively fulfilled. In its most advanced form these expectations amount to a belief that if man is preserved in a suitable cultural environment he can then invent, discover, substitute and economize to satisfy all of his wants.

In contrast to such optimistic expectations of man's technological abilities, many conservationists are concerned that there is a limit to what man can create or discover. This is symbolized in Liebig's (1855) law of minimum which effectively states that the rate of a process is limited by the pace of the slowest factor. The concern that Australia's economic growth may be limited by the total available energy in the aggregate ecosystem demonstrates a faith in Liebig's law. The apparent difference between this viewpoint and that of the optimists in the above paragraph leads to conflicts of opinion within society which are difficult to resolve because of our uncertainty about the future.

To date it certainly would seem that the expectations of the optimists have been justified. For example, study of this conflict in the United States indicates that, while there are indeed some cases of resource insufficiencies such as timber, and some undesirable ecological disturbances such as the dustbowl, domestic natural resources have proved adequate for sustained growth and, in fact, have been playing a progressively smaller role in economic growth. In general, due to advances in technology and to the possibilities of resource substitution it has been possible to sustain adequate growth rates without serious threat to the natural resource base or without dangerous disequilibria of major ecosystems.

Due to uncertainty of the future, a society could wish to transform our previous general criterion of net social benefit maximization to the maximization of the present value of net social benefits subject to a constraint. The constraint is a residual level of productivity which requires that the users leave the resource in a certain productive condition at the end of the planning period. Just what this condition should be is essentially a question of expectation, with which value judgments will inevitably be intertwined. At one extreme it may be judged that the resource should not be depleted in any way whatsoever, as with wildlife reserves: at another extreme an optimistic judgment may result in a policy to deplete a renewable resource below some 'safe minimum standard'.

This concept of a constraint on the basic objective is a useful way to accommodate uncertainty into the decision framework: its application in park management illustrates the concept. A major objective of national park policy is the maintenance of the current state of resource protection or preservation:

in terms of day-to-day management this contrasts with a productive or use function. However, it can be incorporated into our decision framework in the form of a restraint as to a residual level of productivity. For example, the guiding principle of a park trust could be to maximize visitor satisfaction subject to the restraint that some critical number of specific wildlife groups will be unchanged. Our decision criterion then becomes the maximization of the present value of net social benefits subject to the maintenance of such desirable levels of species preservation.

Conservation and Income Distribution

Total welfare is not determined by aggregate wealth alone, i.e. by the maximization of a net benefit function. Most societies are also concerned with the distribution of this wealth among their members. Conscious policies to effect this distribution are invariably the province of the public sector, i.e. the government, whereas aggregate wealth is generated by both the public and private sectors.

Conservation programmes are frequently used to redistribute income to low-income groups such as farmers, as well as to achieve conventional conservation goals. The analysis of programmes now becomes rather more difficult because of this non-efficiency goal, i.e. a goal which does not aim to maximize net benefits or economic efficiency.

A frequent objective of park systems is to make recreational facilities available to low income groups, i.e. a redistribution objective. If this is the sole objective, then our decision framework can be adapted to this situation. If it is an objective which can be specified as a constraint on the action, then the framework can be applied in the usual manner. This is an economic method of systematizing what are often regarded as non-economic problems. Similarly constraints as to desirable residual levels of productivity can also be accommodated.

Recreational Demands and Conservation

R. D. Piesse

One must wonder when the landscape will be altered to such a degree that it will be no longer worth our while to own vehicles to enjoy our leisure.—ALLAN M. FOX.

At one time in the brief history of conservation it seemed that it would be enough to preserve the great beauty spots — the Yosemites and Yellowstones, Lamingtons and Lake St Clairs — while controlling forest resources, eradicating noxious weeds and vermin, and preventing soil erosion. Who, before the early fifties, could have foreseen the multiplying effect of three escalating factors: exploding city populations, increased leisure, and the tremendous mobility afforded so many by ownership of cars? Four-week paid vacations are being applied already in the New South Wales Public Service, a stage most other Australians may expect to achieve before the end of the century. By that time, it has been predicted, Sydney and Melbourne will each be sprawling conurbations of about five million people. According to Speechley,

> . . . the Australian population will have jumped from about 12 million today to 22 million; we may have a four- or even a three-day working week; income per head in real terms will have trebled; our three million cars will have become 10 million and they will be used 1¾ times as often as today.

Some eighty-two per cent of Australians now live an urban life, with its growing pollution, noise, traffic congestion and other forms of strain, its impersonality and divorcement from daily contact with the soil. No wonder a yearning exists in hundreds of thousands of people to 'seek nature' through some form of outdoor recreation. This recreation is taken to imply participation outdoors in casual leisure-time activities of a non-organized sport type. The U.S. National Recreation Survey divides outdoor recreation into five classes: physically active recreation of youth; winter sports; water sports; 'backwoods' recreation (camping, hunting, hiking, mountain climbing); and passive outdoor pursuits such as driving or riding in a motor car for pleasure.

The word 'conservation' has been known in the United States for sixty years or so, and the term 'national park' there, and in Australia, has always connoted public recreational use. But it is now realized that 'although the tourist industry played a notable part in the early history of national parks in Australia, modern tourism is a doubtful ally for conservation'.

Nevertheless, one clear fact should be recognized at the outset. If Australian governments are to provide more adequately for the growing outdoor recreation needs demanded of them, it will be primarily the spendings of tourists and 'recreationers' to which they will most readily respond, as have governments elsewhere.

No official statistics or even reliable estimates are compiled on the volume and value of domestic tourism. Some states have made rough estimates; for example Tasmania, 150,000 visitors in 1965 believed to have spent $15 million; Northern Territory, 41,000 visitors in 1966 spending about $13.3 million. Intra-state tourism's dimensions are 'unguesstimated'. However, one very rough estimate puts the total economic value of all domestic recreational and tourist spendings in 1967 at around $800 million.

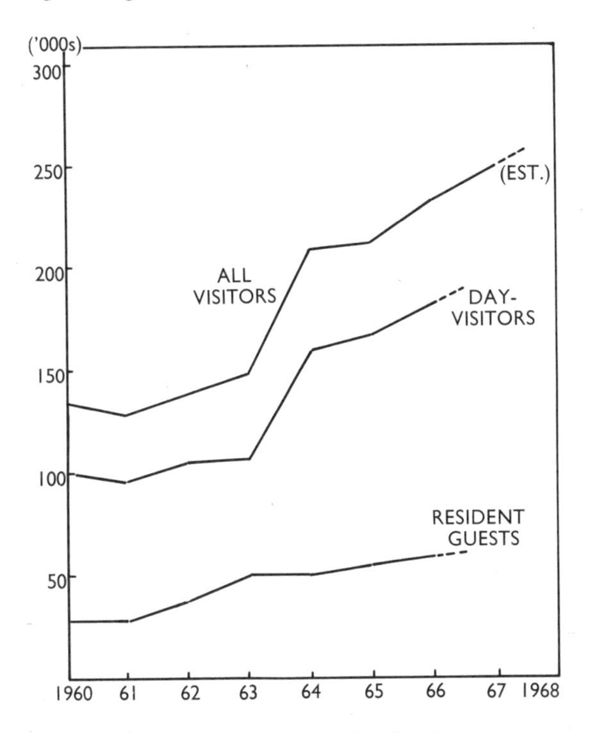

FIGURE 1: *Visitors to resort islands, Great Barrier Reef region, 1960-67.* (SOURCE: QLD. GOVT. TOURIST BUREAU)

The number of visitors to some national parks is known reasonably accurately. Ayers Rock attracted over 19,000 visitors in 1967, and registered a 337 per cent increase over the previous seven years; the Barrier Reef islands received approximately 250,000 visitors — 50,000 of them resident guests — in 1967, a ten per cent increase over 1966 (see Figs. 1 and 2). In north Queensland, at Mackay, a 1965 survey indicated that nearly 31,000 people passed through that city on the way to cruise or vacation on islands in the Whitsunday Group.

Estimates in New South Wales for 1966-7 of visits to certain national and state parks show a big range from The Royal National Park (1,500,000 cars), Ku-ring-gai Chase

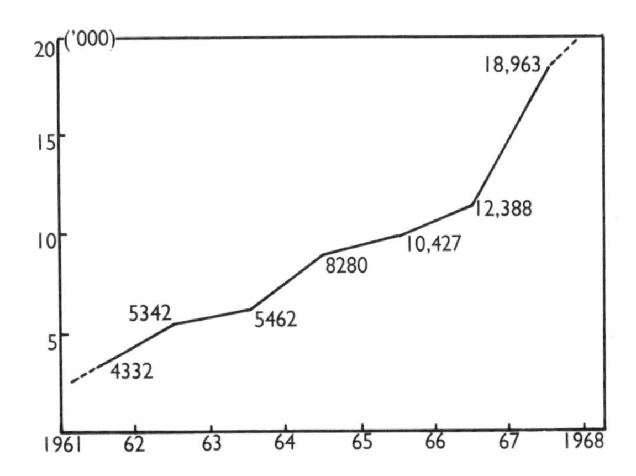

FIGURE 2: *Visitors to Ayers Rock-Mt Olga National Park, 1960-61 to 1966-67.*

National Park (335,000 cars) and Kosciusko National Park (350,000 people), to New England National Park (13,500 people).

Visitors to Victoria's national parks are estimated to have almost doubled from approximately 176,000 in 1958-9 to over 350,000 in 1966-7 (see Fig. 3, page 28). Examples of the increasing pressure on two parks, Wilson's Promontory National Park and Fraser National Park, abutting Eildon Reservoir, are also illustrated (see Fig. 4, page 29). The first, a primarily non-day-visitor park popular with campers, caravanners and walkers, experiences saturation-levels in two summer months when over half the present annual total of 78,590 visitors is received. Numbers of visitors have increased over two and a half times inside eight years. At Fraser, visitors, mainly motor-boatsmen and water skiers, increased about three times between 1962-3 and 1966-7.

At Mount Field National Park, in the upper Derwent Valley, Tasmania, where snowfields help to even out the seasonal attractions for visitors, the 1959-60 recreationer traffic of about 35,000 grew to 54,500 in 1966-7, a fifty-six per cent increase.

These examples provide some indication of the recent growth in demand for outdoor recreation activity.

International Tourism and Australia's Visitor Attractions

It is not yet widely appreciated that the largest and fastest-growing item in international trade is the spendings generated by travel. Some 130 million people travelled from country to country in 1967 spending about $US14 billion in the process. This represented about six and a half per cent of total world export earnings. It is expected that 1970 will see about 190 million international visitors. While international tourism had a growth rate of eight per cent in 1967, Australia received 222,000 visitors (an almost nineteen per cent increase over 1966) who spent some $A76 million; it expects 605,000 visitors spending over $A200 million by 1975.

It is significant that major attractions for most overseas visitors depend largely for their appeal on protection of the natural environment; for example, the outback (including Ayers Rock), the Great Barrier Reef, Australia's unique flora and fauna, and those landscapes involved in outdoor recreational activity. Lord Casey, when Governor-General, stressed that without sound conservation, the country will lose some of its unique flavour and attraction to other peoples.

Conflict Between Ideals and Recreation Use

In the Yosemite Valley, authorities have warned that forty thousand people and 12,000 cars cannot be brought into eight square miles in a single day without drastic consequences to the environment.

All over the world, park administrators and conservationists are asking how far can national parks and reserves have a distinctive recreation function while satisfying other needs, notably those of science, education, and the preservation of species.

Legislation concerning national parks in Queensland, New South Wales, Victoria and South Australia follows overseas practice in emphasizing use and enjoyment of the people without impairment of the natural heritage, as the object of management. However, South Australia's National Parks Act, 1966, adds the significant words 'as far as practicable', thus reflecting the reality of the management problems such a 'use-without-impairment' objective creates. The traditional approach has been to ignore the competition between uses and to treat the total reserve as serving all allowable purposes. This 'unitary system' of park management, as Mosley points out, 'does not provide the distinctive conditions required for each use . . . and the legislation is almost always vague as to the priorities to be observed in management'.

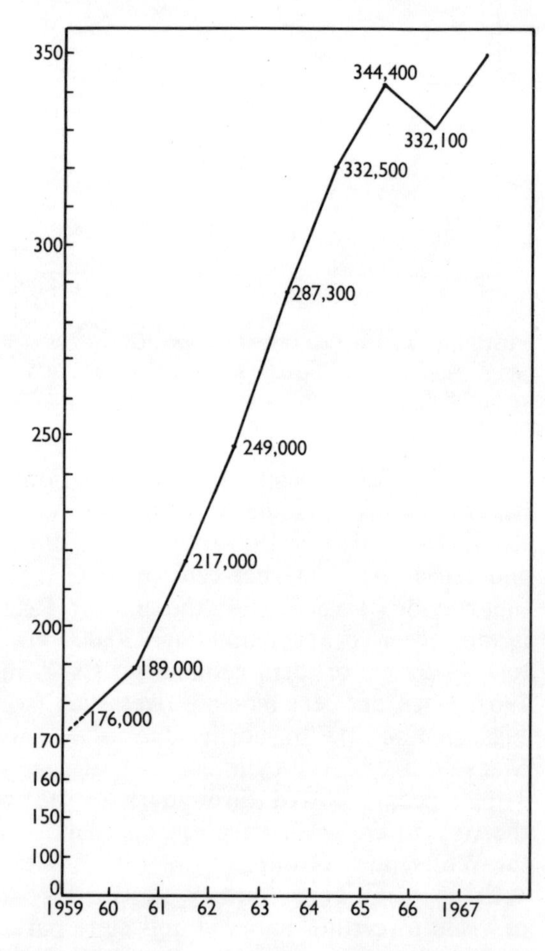

FIGURE 3: *Victoria. Visitors to all national parks, years ended 30 June, 1958-59 to 1966-67.*

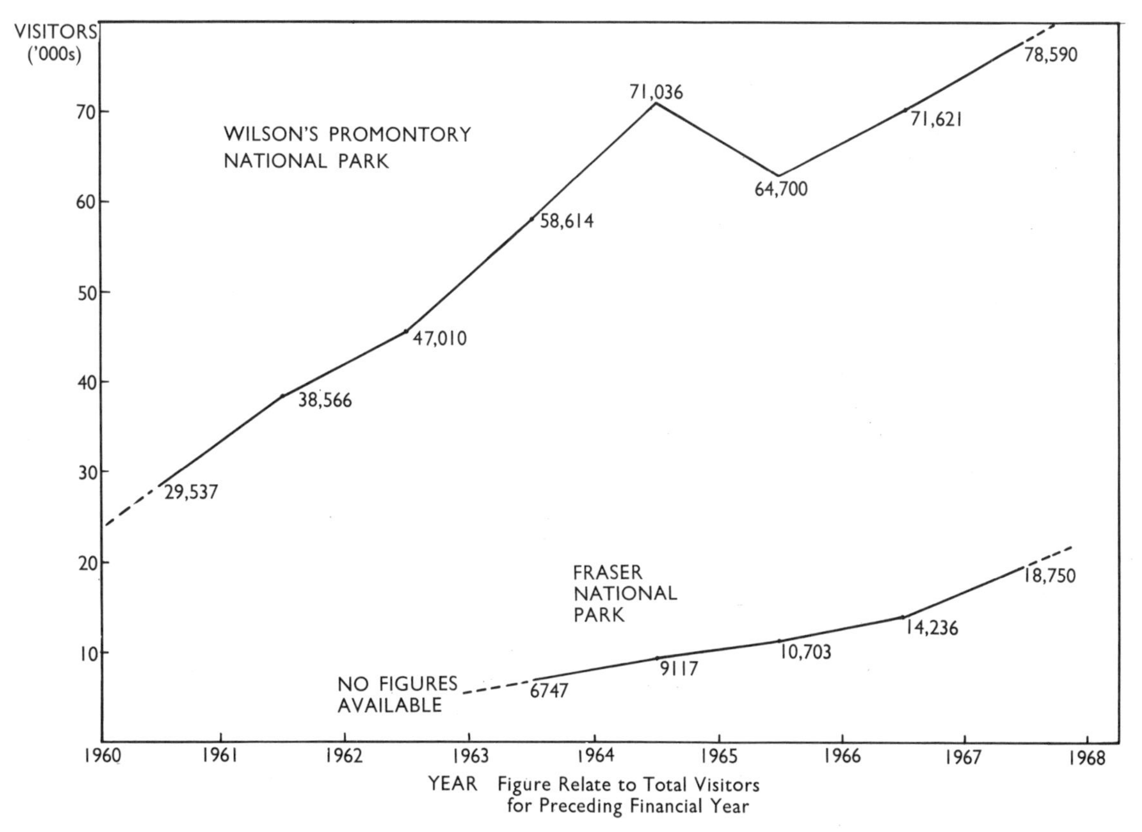

FIGURE 4: *Wilson's Promontory National Park and Fraser National Park.* (SOURCE: NATIONAL PARKS AUTHORITY, VICTORIA)

The conflict is complicated further by the importance of the recreation and tourist industry to the national parks systems. In Canada and South Africa, for example, the parks provide the major tourist attractions and management is traditionally oriented towards serving the majority group of vacationing motorists. Canada's National Parks Service has embarked on a crash programme to develop camping facilities in the western provinces, in expectation that visitor traffic to the national parks between 1966 and 1973 will double to twenty-four million persons annually.

South Africa's experience indicates that a very strong national parks organization, provided it enjoys the unequivocal support of government, may not only maintain nature conservation in its parks, but can do so in the best interests also of hundreds of thousands of tourists.

The attitude of South African tourist authorities is clear-cut on such fundamental issues, and the Tourist Corporation has stated:

> National Parks, Game and Nature Reserves, constitute our greatest single tourist attraction, giving the visitor . . . unequalled opportunities of seeing unspoiled nature and . . . proof of . . . what has been done to preserve nature.
>
> During the last fifteen years the old conflict, so long alleged, between the well-being of the animals in the reserves and that of their human visitors, has been solved in an admirable manner. Furthermore, accommodation in the Parks has improved greatly — no mean achievement when

one realises, for instance, that the Kruger Park's 71,279 visitors in 1951 had risen to 136,705 by 1961. [And to over 270,000 in 1967 — of whom 70,000 were in private cars.—Author's Note.]

The general African approach, according to M. Jones, is that 'nature conservation is a case of people-planning and of treating tourism as part of the fauna of a park. The conservationist holds the key to conserving the capital of the tourist industry — the land and the wildlife that the tourist comes to see.'

It is clear that the conflict between conservation and recreation uses is only avoidable by clarifying use, provided that the reservation is large enough to enable zoning to be effective. This requires initially an adequate survey of resources leading to master-planning or zoning of user-purposes.

Certainly, this is the ideal to aim for in future. However, Dr A. B. Costin of CSIRO has pointed out that

> the problem of accommodation . . . recreational development and nature conservation (in the sub-alpine and alpine zones of the Kosciusko area) would be easy to solve *if a fresh start could be made by setting aside primitive areas* to be managed primarily *as single purpose nature reserves*, and encouraging . . . recreational developments in most of the rest.

It is unfortunate that because recreational use originally was the main justification for establishing many of our parks and reserves, developments within them which facilitated visitor use (such as roads and chalets) were at first encouraged. As a result, Costin goes on to observe,

> . . . many parks and reserves in Australia, including those in the high mountain areas, have become multiple-use resources, and nature conservation in the strict sense has suffered. Similar action (viz. zoning for use) is required in . . . Tasmania, where the alpine and sub-alpine ecosystems are different in several important aspects from those at Kosciusko.

How true all this is, and why the Kosciusko lesson still needs to be learnt in Tasmania, is evident in the case of the water storage development planned in the Lake Pedder area of that state. In the absence so far of any multiple-use plan, radical changes in the present 'backwoods' recreation use of the Lake Pedder National Park (which forms part of what is perhaps Australia's finest wilderness area) unfortunately would appear to be inevitable. The Hobart *Mercury* felt government had a duty to 'make the best' of the large new lake as a 'tourist asset'. It hoped that the government did not intend to be content with the access road put in by the Hydro-Electricity Commission because the area would 'need to be opened up with other roads and tracks if this great lake is to be more than a sheet of water which tourists will be told has a setting of spectacular rugged grandeur'.

So much for the sacred cow of progress, 1968-style.

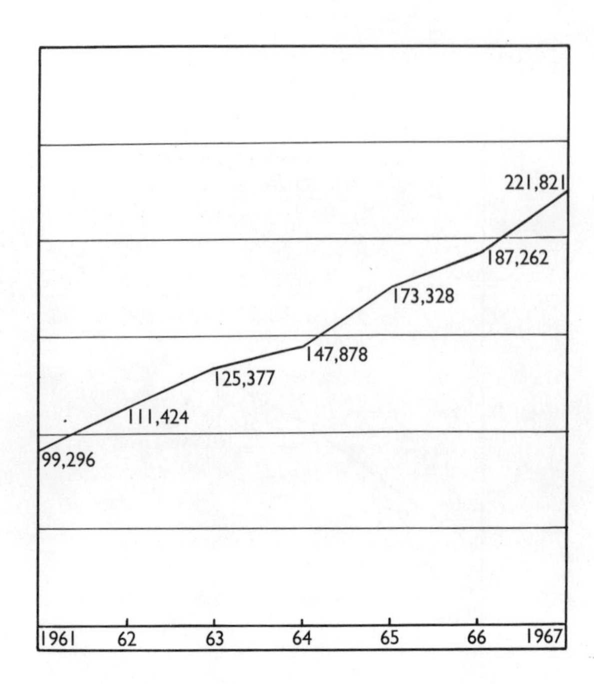

FIGURE 5: *Visitors to Australia (short-term arrivals excluding cruise, 'through', etc.)* 1961 *to* 1967.

Differing Recreationer Requirements

The requirements of various park-user groups, which have been analysed by conservationists such as Mosley, differ considerably as regards dominant recreation purpose and the facilities each desires to use.

At the 'low density recreation' end of the spectrum are walkers, ski tourers and nature lovers seeking adventurous, unconfined forms of recreation and solitude in areas of natural beauty large enough to provide lengthy trips on foot or on ski away from sophisticated facilities. This calls, as will be seen later, for a primitive park or area set aside for the purpose, among other things, of wilderness recreation. Few have been so zoned, except in New South Wales (although plans for zoning of park-use are now well advanced in several Victorian national parks).

What may be regarded in fact as wilderness recreation areas, that is areas trackless or with long-distance tracks or marked routes but without mechanized access, are diminishing in extent. This is due to the gradual infiltration of hydro-electricity and forestry authorities by means of aqueducts and roads in various types of parks and similar reserves.

Australia's only overland wilderness trail within a park of any extent (fifty-three miles) is to be found in the Cradle Mountain-Lake St Clair National Park, and it is traversed by over 800 walkers of all ages every year; we have no equivalent to the John Muir Trail along the Sierras in California. However, the creation of a similar trail straddling the Dividing Range in north-east Victoria and southern New South Wales would, in itself, be a most worthwhile investment in youth training, national health and education in conservation values.

In 'intermediate density recreation' the dominant purpose is active enjoyment of park attractions including winter and summer sports and natural history, using man-made facilities (tracks, ski tours, etc.). This purpose involves classification of general outdoor recreation areas or zones within a park for limited recreation development. Thus it provides land in semi-primitive conditions for short walks by day-trippers and residents at resorts, and contributes to general scenic amenity.

But the dominant purpose involved in the visits of most motorized visitors, Mosley reminds us, will be for passive enjoyment. This requires areas or zones the primary purpose of which is to furnish roads, lookouts, picnic areas and the like within a general recreation area.

'Higher density recreation' requires classification of a reserve or zone to provide visitor reception facilities, accommodation for winter sports, etc. The Tidal River 'village' at Wilson's Promontory, the 'home-beach' leasehold resort areas on the Barrier Reef islands and ski villages within the Kosciusko National Park are all examples of this type of zone, created for, if not actually described as, higher density recreation use.

Turning to general outdoor recreation needs outside national parks and similar reserves — the situation is dominated by mechanized recreationers touring through scenic areas, or demanding convenient day-use facilities at beaches or in the countryside. For instance, hundreds of thousands of Australian city families merely wish to picnic in green and clean recreation areas or enjoy a 'safe' unsoiled beach. Alternatively, and as community affluence increases, they desire a holiday house close to water. Consider a typical case. We will call it Weekenderville, although it has now become popularized and renamed Gold Sand City.

A remote, beautiful beach area, populated by a sprinkling of old residents, mostly fishermen, is suddenly and prematurely opened up by real estate developers. Subdivisions misfire, or thrive. The persuasive influence of the local parliamentary or shire representative helps obtain a sealed road from the nearest highway. Some buyers buy for speculation, but after a period of stagnation, fibro-plaster cottages and shacks mushroom. Picnickers break down the sea-verge flora. Tourist facilities are built: petrol stations, boat launching ramps and tasteless brick or concrete toilet blocks. The new esplanade demands a sea-wall, which alters the environment severely so that wave-erosion almost ruins the fine beach. Because the foreshore trees have disappeared a 'beautification' project is required . . . . The pattern can be found repeating itself over and over again. But was the outcome inevitable? The Chairman of Victoria's Town and Country Planning Board believes

> there can be little doubt that over the next 10 or 20 years the touch of man will spread much more widely over our thousand miles of coastline . . . What we must do, somehow, is to ensure that the touch does not contaminate.
>
> Up to now the depredation has been pretty awful. The speculator has been busy wherever people are likely to go . . . Along the coastline of N.S.W. almost every single beach and headland has been exploited. Many thousands of acres of land have been laid waste by useless subdivision — scenery marred by scattered cottages, usually out of harmony with the landscape . . . In Victoria much the same thing has been happening, but on a much smaller scale.

Fortunately, the protection of the coastline of New South Wales came under a new State Planning Authority in 1964. Development along the whole of the Victorian coast also has been brought under planning control, but at this stage in Victoria the controls are very broad, merely providing that development, including land subdivision within the area affected, must have planning consent. The administrators know this is a holding measure, that further steps must be taken to introduce positive guiding measures, such as land use zoning to assist landscape preservation. If the coastal areas cannot withstand the impact of people, they will surely not remain attractive. Subdivisions for holiday homes have disfigured the landscape of parts of Phillip Island but a rezoning scheme to consolidate titles in many 'failed' subdivisions and to reclassify same as rural purpose land is now before the government.

In Queensland there is the chance that the next stage of subdivision development along the Sunshine Coast, north of Brisbane, may involve creating artificial islands and waterways along tidal estuaries and in swamp lands with consequent serious modification of the existing natural environment. In this regard, the pattern seems to be influenced by Gold Coast development projects; and to a large extent it has been affirmed by the building of a near-shore coast road from Caloundra through to Noosa Heads. It is hard to suppose this will not lead eventually to the same sort of result to be seen between Coolangatta and Southport, which more and more Australians are now starting to deplore.

Problems of Recreation Use of Parks and Similar Reserves

These can be considered conveniently under four groups.

Problems Resulting from Pressure of Numbers

The problems referred to at Wilson's Promontory and Ayers Rock are not only due to seasonality, but relate directly to the concentration of almost the total visitor traffic in or around one general recreation area in which the dominant user requirement is higher density recreation.

Due to insufficient staff for both supervision and interpretation purposes, visitors at Ayers Rock have at times disfigured or 'touched up' the Aboriginal rock paintings found there, and even daubed their initials in large letters on the Rock itself. These graffiti plus empty beer bottles on the 'Dead Heart' spell out another aspect of Australian culture. Due initially to lack of an overall development plan (the building of some chalets pre-dated the gazettal of the park under the Reserves Board), movements of cars and buses on the old two-wheel tracks have gradually become a problem threatening the environment. A 'circle-road' has also

This toilet block is an example of the tasteless and badly-placed functional architecture which mars Australian shore-lines in developed areas.
PHOTO COURTESY JOHN FAIRFAX & SONS, SYDNEY

Research worker recording frog calls, with a parabolic reflector gathering sounds directionally for the microphone.
PHOTO COURTESY DR M. C. BLEAKLY

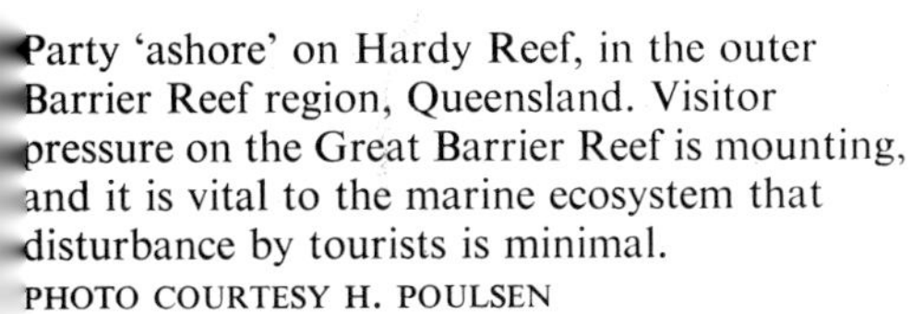

Party 'ashore' on Hardy Reef, in the outer Barrier Reef region, Queensland. Visitor pressure on the Great Barrier Reef is mounting, and it is vital to the marine ecosystem that disturbance by tourists is minimal.
PHOTO COURTESY H. POULSEN

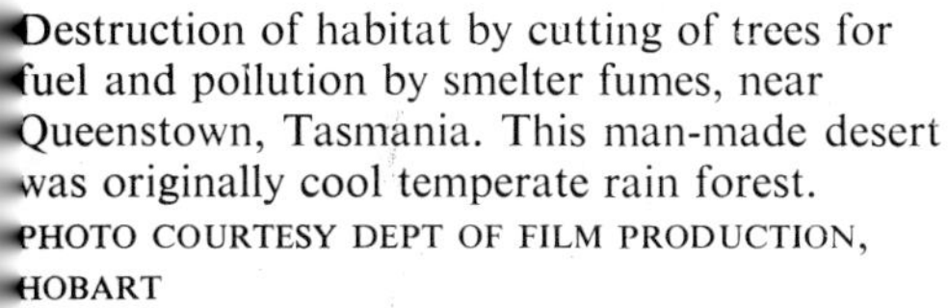

Destruction of habitat by cutting of trees for fuel and pollution by smelter fumes, near Queenstown, Tasmania. This man-made desert was originally cool temperate rain forest.
PHOTO COURTESY DEPT OF FILM PRODUCTION, HOBART

Lake Patterson near Newcastle, N.S.W., reproduced from *Views in Australia* by J. Lycett, published in 1824. This lithograp by a careful observer depicts the great numbers of wildfowl. PHOTO COURTESY NAN KIVELL COLLECTION, NATIONAL LIBRAR OF AUST.

Lake Talbot, N.S.W. More and more Australians own motor cars and speedboats, and seek recreation areas like this. PHOTO COURTESY PHOTOGRAPHIC ILLUSTRATORS, SYDNEY

Location maps, both helpful and in harmony, are featured in Queensland national parks. PHOTO COURTESY QLD FORESTRY DEPT

been built around the Rock. The shortage of water, which precludes any further development of tourist facilities near the Rock, has forced the park authorities to look around for a new village site out in the desert. This time it will be launched only after proper siting and planning (and it is hoped, zoning of the whole park).

Problems Caused by Incompatible Forms of Recreation

These arise locally between the requirements of anglers and water skiers at lakes and rivers; water skiers and swimmers at inlets and bay beaches; and walkers and skiers (the hikers abhorring the villages, tows and other facilities built in mountain areas to serve the needs of the latter). Similarly, passive outdoor recreationers, such as motorists touring Tasmania, would wish to travel by road through the Cradle Mountain-Lake St Clair National Park; there has been pressure from time to time on the Tasmanian government to build such a road, but any road would destroy the essential values of such a magnificent primitive area leaving both walkers and motorists dissatisfied.

It was even suggested a few years ago that a motor road should be built between the two guesthouses — O'Reilly's and Binna Burra — at Lamington National Park, south Queensland. Such large-scale disturbance of a delicately balanced and unique environment — in which several rainforest types such as *Nothofagus* forest exist at their critical limit — would destroy a biological asset which is already much too small.

Different Intensities of Recreation Use

The recognition, in 1961, of the need for alpine wilderness area zoning which excludes recreational (and hydro-electricity) development but without restricting walking and ski touring activities, was an historic breakthrough for nature conservation and the principle of land use zoning. The last section of the road to the summit of Mount Kosciusko was subsequently closed and other steps have been taken to control ecologically harmful intensities of recreation use at higher altitudes.

In California, a source of continuing anxiety to the Parks Service is the trampling of the soils in certain famous redwood groves featuring giant trees visited by hundreds of thousands of tourists each year. A similar situation has caused considerable deterioration along track-verges in Sherbrooke Forest, a forest park situated only a few miles away from Melbourne's outer suburbs.

Geographical Location of Outdoor Recreational Opportunities

This problem is not so much one of acres of land available for recreation, but of effective acres of land available to the public and which are usable for specific types of recreation. Access problems mean that many areas theoretically available for outdoor recreational use are open to very few people. Difficulties of access may be due either to remoteness (such as at the Kinchega National Park west of the Darling River or the Glen of Palms in the Finke Gorge, Central Australia) or to encirclement by land in private ownership.

But effective demand for outdoor recreational opportunities exists closer to Australia's major cities, as anyone will agree who has experienced the summer-time traffic to Sydney's Royal National Park or Adelaide's National Park, Belair.

Increasing Dominance of Future Recreation Demands

Until recently Australia was dependent on agricultural production to balance imports. Observers have pointed out that, following the recent major discoveries of minerals and the increasing contribution minerals are making to export earnings (expected by 1970 to rank with wool as the main export earner, comprising about thirty per cent of the total value of all primary products), Australia no longer 'has all its eggs in the agricultural basket'.

As industrialization proceeds there will be an increasing percentage of employment within the service industries to cater for the spending power generated by ever-rising standards of living. Thus the demand for recreation will become an even more dominant force than it is today. As Costin has stated,

> under these changing conditions Australia can afford to take a new look at how its environments might be used. At this stage, it is also important for Australia to examine what are the likely trends in demand for products of the land in the broadest sense, as an indication of the kinds of land use for which we should be planning.

While no overall assessment of resource requirements has yet been attempted here, a study for the U.S.A. by Resources for the Future Inc., discovered that considering metals, energy, farm products, timber, water and outdoor recreation, the rate of demand for recreation is almost double the rate for any product. The U.S. Outdoor Recreation Resources Review Commission (1962) anticipates that the main recreation forms will simply be driving and walking for pleasure, for which purpose landscape preservation is vital. The Resources for the Future Inc. study concludes that, with the pressures to be expected in the U.S.A. on land for agricultural and other production, it is essential to retain flexibility in land use, combined with multiple purpose use of crop, pasture and forest land for recreation in addition to much greater recreational use of parks and reserves themselves. Australia, of course, is somewhat differently placed due to its smaller population and its concentration in the south. Costin indicates that

> although the situation will not develop over Australia as a whole, nevertheless it is already developing regionally around our cities, and the same kind of thinking, planning and action recommended by the Resources for the Future Group seems inescapable.

To give an economic justification as a prerequisite to such action, studies are necessary on the comparative impact of recreation activity and other industries on incomes and employment. Even in the United States, very few analysts have taken a hard look at the development potentials of the recreation/tourist industry as compared with other types of economic activity. One of the few studies in this area is a 1966 report on the impact of a proposed redwood national park on the economy of a county in northern California. Briefly, the findings were that in the short run (by 1973) more employment and income would be generated if there were no park. But in the long run (by 1983), both income and employment would be greater if a park were established.

We need now, in Australia, studies of this type regarding the feasibility of establishing a Kruger-type wildlife park (of native animals) in an existing or even potential pastoral region as against the economics of raising stock such as buffaloes or more sheep for wool.

Applying Recreation-Projection Techniques

To meet the long range outdoor recreation needs of urban Australians will require us to apply sophisticated recreation projection techniques, such as the application of systems analysis to supply and demand for outdoor recreation activities.

But we will first need to prepare a continuing inventory and evaluation of the outdoor recreation needs and resources of Australia. The Commonwealth Government will have to set up proper statistical measures of recreation use and general tourism on an Australia-wide basis related to origin and destination; to highway traffic flows; socio-economic factors and the like. Many studies concentrating on individual areas are needed, as is the application of computer techniques.

Some Policy Implications

The horizons of government thinking must be drastically enlarged, and policies tethered to the peg of tourist income must be scrapped in favour of a positive concern with the protection of nature as well as with recreational needs. New legislation and new instruments are required, and somewhere men sound and strong enough must be found to break down the old barriers between departments and ensure co-ordination.

Recreation is a prime physical, psychological and social need for Australians: government and communities alike, through research, will have to put an economic value on the conservation of natural attractions — as is now being attempted in the United States. Universities can also help build both knowledge and techniques to solve the problems created by recreational demands on nature. Education programmes and texts are needed to show how vital it is to learn to use leisure properly in the coming age of automation, and how truly vital it is to preserve and restore the quality of the human environment, whether for recreation or for plain survival.

Finally, those interests vested in the tourist and recreation industry may no longer evade their responsibility to replace the short range and ready-profit attitude by a long range fostering of the 'geese that lay their golden eggs'.

Management Problems of National Parks

J. D. Ovington

With improved technology and growing numbers, man's capacity to modify his environment has increased so rapidly that many people feel there is an urgent need to set aside rural areas against further development. Paradoxically, this need has gained momentum as man has become more of a city dweller benefiting from expanding industry and intensive, mechanized agriculture.

Man's Concern with Rural and Urban Environments

Concern with man's rural environment originates partly from a guilt-sentimental complex in which man sees himself as the main despoiler of natural resources in the past, particularly of primeval areas and wildlife. The halting of further exploitation and the preservation of representative examples of attractive landscapes are regarded as inescapable duties to posterity. Concern arises also from a superiority complex whereby man regards himself as a dignified animal possessing the ability to regulate his numbers by common consent at some prescribed level. This population level would enable those permitted to be born to enjoy facilities and privileges regarded as essentials of modern life but which are greatly in excess of the requirements for survival alone.

Both viewpoints can be disputed. It may be argued for instance that change is not necessarily bad since many attractive landscapes are essentially man-made and on balance man's efforts have resulted in improvement rather than deterioration of the rural environment. It may also be pointed out that there is little evidence as yet of a significant slowing down of the rapid multiplication of the human population and that the acceptable requisites of contemporary civilized life vary so much according to population density and affluence that no permanent criteria exist for determining a population level and distribution acceptable to all mankind.

Nevertheless, it cannot be denied that there is a genuine and growing demand to reserve in perpetuity selected rural areas, and the establishment of national parks, nature reserves, etc., throughout the world is an expression of this. The first national park ever to be established was Yellowstone Park in the United States in 1872 as a pleasuring ground for the benefit and enjoyment of the people. By 1960 the United States had 180 parks within its national park system and these extended over twenty-four million acres of land and were visited by more than sixty million people per annum. Because of the complex origin of the concept of national parks and national differences in history and affluence, the creation of national parks has been justified in different ways.

Before the management of any national park can be placed on a sound basis it is essential to have a clear statement of the reasons for its establishment and the aims of management, always recognizing that these aims may have to be modified in a world where man's habits and ways constantly change.

Bourlière (1964) in discussing the history of urbanization emphasizes the recreational role of national parks for city dwellers. He suggests that the benefits of better nutrition and improved control of infectious diseases enjoyed by contemporary man are being counter-balanced by new diseases of civilization. He points out that adult urban citizens tend to suffer, amongst other things, from high blood pressure, higher contents of cholesterol and B-lipoproteins in the blood, and to be more prone to psychosomatic disorders and nervous breakdown. Bourlière considers that the antidotes to these manifestations of man's adaptation to living in overcrowded cities are better balances between work and rest, intellectual activity and physical exercise, pavement grey and forest green rather than dietetics, psychotherapy or tranquilizers. Thus national parks are regarded by Bourlière as an economic investment whereby areas of marginal agricultural value are used, not for subsidized agricultural production, but to provide recreational space wherein to combat the physical degeneration and mental morbidity resulting from urban living.

Stanley (1964) in attempting to define national parks accepts them to be spacious land areas, essentially of a primitive or wilderness character, which contain scenery and natural wonders so outstanding in quality that their preservation intact for the benefit, enjoyment and inspiration of the people is a national concern. It is noteworthy that Stanley, like Bourlière, emphasizes the recreational role (both physical and mental) of national parks but also links this with uniqueness, spaciousness, primitiveness and nationalism. He does not attempt to specify these qualities with any precision nor to show to what extent they are essential if the recreational role is to be fulfilled. In a somewhat similar vein an anonymous article on national parks with particular reference to Australia emphasizes their contribution to the nation's cultural background through the appreciation of natural beauty. National parks are regarded as inviolable sanctuaries for the permanent preservation of scenery, wilderness, and native flora and fauna in their natural condition. The protein-starved nationals of East Africa probably do not think of their magnificent national parks in quite this light.

H. J. Coolidge (1963), in a thought-provoking review paper emphasizing the international significance of national parks, dreams of the day when the entire world will be covered by a network of parks and reserves where principal biotic environments will be permanently preserved for research, education and the enjoyment of future re-generations. Whilst Coolidge also accepts the recreational role of national parks he sees them not only as a means of conserving ecosystems and rare species, but also of publicizing conservation and of providing reference study areas for scientific research. Coolidge recognizes the advantages to be gained for conservation in general by making full use of national parks through talks, films, campfire programmes, signs, markers, exhibits, nature trails with booklets keyed to numbered stakes or stations, trailside exhibits and site museums.

Using Japan as an example of a country where little or no primeval land area remains, Coolidge points out that national parks often include important historical relics and are valuable places for the study of history, archaeology, and the arts and crafts. In the United Kingdom, which lacks vast expanses of virgin land teeming with big game and where almost every acre of land has its place in a complex design of agricultural, industrial or residential use, national parks are seen as a means of preserving beautiful landscapes for public open-air enjoyment and it is accepted that the established land use must continue largely unaltered if the landscape is to be maintained (National Parks Committee 1947). Species protection and scientific research are more the responsibility of the Nature Conservancy with its series of nature reserves in Britain.

Demands on National Parks

Whilst the demands placed upon national

parks are many and varied according to location, they can be summarized as:

(1) to provide special outdoor recreational facilities by virtue of a beautiful and unusual landscape often, but not always, with a wilderness character,
(2) to provide opportunities to see native animals and plants in characteristic outdoor surroundings,
(3) to conserve outstanding natural features, rare species and ecosystems,
(4) to preserve examples of the history and archaeology of man as part of the national heritage,
(5) to encourage interest in conservation and rural activities,
(6) to serve as storehouses of biological evolution both at the species and community level and
(7) to act as reference points for scientific investigations.

Individual national parks may fulfil several of the functions either through multipurpose use over the area as a whole or by the allocation of different activities to different zones of the park. Some of these uses are complementary, other are opposed. The management of a national park must attempt to obtain a working compromise between the different kinds of use in relation to the needs of the area it serves and developments in the foreseeable future.

The demand for recreational use of national parks increases every year and has increasingly come to dominate park management. Recreational use covers a wide range of activities — walking, horse riding, sight seeing, contemplation, swimming, relaxation, boating, picnicking, barbecuing, fishing and hunting to name only a few of the more obvious. Each of these activities has specific requirements and the meeting of these requirements in cases where thousands of visitors are concerned poses difficult management problems. This is particularly true where recreational use is linked with the wilderness concept since the presence of large groups of visitors can be an intrusion countering any impression of unspoiled nature, misleading though this may be. In this era of radioactive fallout and widespread use of toxic chemicals, it is doubtful if any truly primeval areas remain with no human interference.

Various management techniques have been developed to orientate recreational use in desired directions and to lessen the impact of recreational activities on national parks. Many visitors to national parks only wish to stay for a short period to enable them to see wildlife, panoramic views of majestic scenery and spectacular features such as mountain peaks, waterfalls, geological formations, natural bridges and caves. In these cases some organization to best show features of interest is of advantage to both visitors and park authorities. For example, natural vantage points can be developed to give the best views with the minimum of intrusion and to concentrate visitors so as to leave large areas undisturbed. Telescope and photographic facilities at the lookouts are often helpful and, according to circumstances, vantage points may be linked by pathways, rough tracks or roads. If the best use of the vantage points is to be obtained the park manager may have to condone limited interference on a local scale such as the removal of trees blocking a view or the erection of screening to prevent visitors unduly disturbing wildlife. In many national parks vehicular access is prohibited but in large national parks where motor access is permitted, careful siting of roads and stopping places can add much to the attractiveness of a short visit and satisfy many people.

Other visitors to national parks expect to use them as playgrounds and as camping places. Where such activities have to be accommodated the park manager has to decide how best to concentrate them and to what extent they are permissible if the nature of the park is not to be altered. In some instances these activities can be diverted outside the park boundaries. This is particularly desirable when they involve the provision of petrol stations and motels, supermarkets and the like. However, there is always a danger that highly commercialized approaches to national parks may lessen the impact and attractiveness of the parks.

Need for Research, and the Problems of Change

The integration of recreational considerations into the framework of national park management is hindered by lack of information on human behaviour in national parks and the problem of co-ordinating relevant research from different disciplines to obtain comprehensive assessments of complex and changing situations. Before computers can be used effectively to evaluate the consequences of alternative management procedures, as a guide to future management, much more information is required.

The managers of national parks need particularly a better appreciation of the characteristics of both non-visitors and visitors to national parks. Specially designed questionnaires filled in by representative groups of visitors are being used now to discover the background of people coming to national parks, why they visit national parks, the frequency of their visits, their behaviour pattern whilst in national parks, the response of the public to what they have experienced during their visit as well as their complaints and suggestions for improvement.

There is also unlimited scope for observational and experimental research. Burch (1964) has pointed out that individual behaviour varies according to the surroundings and to the nature of the group of which the visitor is a member. Changing some element in a national park may trigger off a whole set of unexpected reactions, e.g. the provision of a viewing point can create demands for improvements in transport facilities and ultimately through public pressure lead to the opening up of an area intended to be left undeveloped. The extent to which the park manager can influence recreational behaviour by the nature and distribution of the amenities he provides is largely unexplored. Another problem arising particularly from recreational use is the question of wardening activities and the need not to alienate public sympathy by too many restrictive regulations. Careful wording of notices can invite cooperation rather than cause resentment. It is necessary to examine management systems carefully lest they create hazards for visitors. Old trees, left for scenic effect or for conservation reasons, become so rotten and insecure through the ravages of time that they are liable to fall on some unsuspecting tourist.

In the more frequented national parks there is growing evidence that the effects of visitor pressure can be minimized through skilful management whereby the areas subjected to heaviest use and more liable to change are rested periodically by being put out of bounds for sightseers. Ultimately, with increasing visitor pressure, a management decision has to be made between giving priority to preserving the area unchanged for succeeding generations or permitting it to be exploited by the present generation. Perhaps the only long term solution to this dilemma is more and more national parks.

Ecological change arising from intensive visitor use takes various forms — tourist feeding and disturbing of wild animals may change animal numbers and habits; plants and plant communities susceptible to trampling may be reduced in number; tree seedlings may be destroyed so that a forest cannot regenerate; and alien plants may be introduced inadvertently. Where visitors congregate, soil compaction may limit plant growth and in critical areas such as the alpine country of Kosciusko State Park in Australia the destruction of vegetation increases the danger of soil erosion. There is some evidence to indicate that sites having soils of high fertility have the greatest resistance to visitor use (Ripley 1962) but, in general, national parks are located on marginal areas where ecological change occurs readily and may be difficult to reverse. Ecological change is not solely the result of tourist activities within national parks. Often change is induced from outside, thus the high density of elephants in some African parks results from persecution of the animals in the surrounding countryside so that the elephants seek sanctuary within a park with devastating effects on the ecology of the area. Few communities are in a static state and change is a natural phenomenon, as when a lake is filled in by organic growth and deposition.

How far park managers should go to reverse unwanted ecological changes artificially by using all means at their disposal is a subject of debate but sometimes these ecological changes are so subtle and insidious that the damage is done before the dangers are appreciated. In the case of African national parks with excessive numbers of elephants, should systematic cropping of the elephants be practised to keep the population at a level where the survival of other living things is not threatened and the danger of soil erosion is lessened? Some native oakwoods in Britain are being invaded naturally by the alien sycamore tree; should the sycamores be harvested or should nature be left to take its course even if it means the replacement of native oakwoods by exotic sycamore wood? To crop the elephants and to harvest the sycamore trees is tempting particularly as these operations could be done with financial profit and the funds provided put to good use.

Once such techniques are used it becomes more difficult to resist further kinds of interference — for instance the use of insecticides to try to control insects defoliating the vegetation and causing unsightly conditions. A different aspect of this problem is the preservation or multiplication of disappearing species by special treatments (often called farming by critics) or the artificial reintroduction of species known to have been present in a national park at one time.

If the conservation concept of a national park is to be fully applied in parks where change is occurring for one reason or another then the national park manager is compelled to change the natural sequence of development or to try to maintain some transitional successional stage.

Some ecological changes occur rapidly and on a grand scale. High winds may blow down extensive areas of forest overnight and natural or man-ignited fires may destroy plants and animals over a wide area. Both of these events can be regarded as natural phenomena but when they occur, the recreational and preservation role of a national park may be greatly diminished.

In the case of windblow there is some evidence that in the long term it may be an essential component of natural forest ecosystems since the ploughing effect, in which soil held by the roots is brought to the surface as the tree falls, may counter soil degradation through leaching and encourage soil weathering to improve soil nutrient status. Drainage of waterlogged areas can reduce the risk of windblow but also modifies the ecological situation.

Elaborate fire control measures can be installed to lessen the fire risk and to extinguish fires once started. However, many ecosystems valuable for national park purposes are there because of fire and the stopping of burning in some savannah and prairie areas for instance would mean that these would be replaced by forest. Several light burns are less dangerous to wildlife than one giant conflagration and regular prescribed burning prevents the build up of combustible material within ecosystems and so lessens the danger of an uncontrolled hot fire. Consequently, in some national parks, prescribed burning is an acceptable management procedure but to be well done requires skilled operators. Despite the extensive use of fire as a management tool and the many arguments for and against it, knowledge of the effects of fire is scanty and there is need for more research.

Whilst more ecological research will provide answers to some of the problems of management in national parks, it would be unwise to expect quick returns from ecological research. Too few trained ecologists are available and much ecological research is long term so that park managers faced with immediate problems are compelled to draw upon the knowledge of other land users such as graziers and foresters. Where ecological research involves destructive sampling, valid objections may be raised against its being done in national parks and the problems of linking fundamental research with practical management are formidable. On the other hand it is often possible to carry out management procedures in such a way that they involve some degree of experimentation and provide facilities for ecologists to examine critically the effects of ecosystem manipulation.

Scientific Functions of National Parks

In relation to the function of national parks as conservation areas, storehouses of biological information and biological reference points, there is a great need to obtain comprehensive records of the living organisms present, their distribution and numbers. Without this kind of information it is impossible to judge the status of different species, the relative effects of different management techniques upon them and whether the global national park system contains adequate representation of world ecosystems. However, ecological research must be more detailed than species recording alone and currently research is actively going on at a number of centres into the functioning of ecosystems and the interrelationships between living organisms and between them and their environments. Whilst the research task is immense, the establishment of international organizations such as the International Union for the Conservation of Nature and Natural Resources is stimulating international cooperative research so that communication between scientists is helped and maximum dividends are obtained from research. In 1962 for instance, this International Union organized the First World Conference on National Parks which resulted in a valuable exchange of ideas so that local management experience could be applied with confidence on a wider scale.

Essential Planning

Long term planning is essential if the management of national parks is to be placed on a rational basis. Foresters with somewhat similar planning problems prepare forest plans, and similar documents can form the basis of management planning for national parks. Well documented management plans help to assure continuity of approach since new or replacement staff can easily assimilate background information and rapidly gain an insight into the purposes and results of any past management treatments.

Generally these plans are composed of three sections:

(1) a descriptive section bringing together all known information of locality factors such as topography, climate, soils, vegetation, fauna and history
(2) a section devoted to the purposes of management and justifying decisions about the allocation of different uses and
(3) a final section in which the future management proposals and the requirements of staff and equipment are given in detail.

Since park management in the early stages is tentative, the plans are revised every five years to include additional information and to introduce any new ideas in the light of experience gained. Unfortunately, descriptive data of the organic and environmental factors present in national parks are usually very limited but, by drawing up a management plan to some standard prescription, a better perspective is gained and inadequacies in knowledge are emphasized. The boundaries and size of national parks are often settled by political compromise rather than biological requirements and a management plan carefully prepared can draw attention to problems arising from this.

The preparation of management plans is a skilled task calling for the integration and assessment by qualified personnel of diverse facts and ideas. More education in conservation is needed if such personnel are to become available and there is a strong case for attempting to encourage interest in conservation by the provision of educational facilities on national parks. Educational activities may take up valuable time but when well organized can yield rich dividends and reduce vandalism.

As people have come to recognize the values of the national park concept, private organizations interested in various types of resources such as forestry, wildlife, soil and wilderness have joined with national park authorities in carrying out educational and research operations and in providing recreational areas. Such activities may help to meet some of the growing pressures on publicly owned national parks. The park manager is fortunate in usually having a sympathetic and interested audience and, whilst the management problems he has to face are considerable, their solution can give untold satisfaction in the pleasure provided for others.

The Role of Public Opinion in Conservation

Judith Wright

To the scientific conservationist, who has had experience in dealing with public attitudes to his programmes, it may easily seem that public opinion is one of the chief blocks on the way to proper planning of resource use and sensible attitudes to carrying out those plans. Conservationists of any kind — whether they are interested in soils, in water, in forests, or in wildlife, and whether they are in professional positions or in humbler jobs, such as helping to conduct private conservational societies, soon realize that their chief problem lies in the inertia, or too frequently the active opposition, of public opinion to the concepts they support. People are seldom awake to the need for conservation at any level until the process of waste has gone so far that it may already be too late to reverse; and propaganda and education are slow processes, while conservationists are busy people impressed with a sense of the urgency of their job. It is easy to feel that that job is action, not preaching.

Yet only public opinion — educated public opinion — will be the decisive factor in the fight. The struggle to reverse the trends of waste and exploitation of resources is a human battle. It represents the biggest problem of our time, a problem which is largely obscured from the public by issues which appear larger, more immediate and more sensational, because it is so large and all-pervading that it has not been thoroughly formulated until very recent years. Even now, it is usually expressed in piecemeal ways, with emphasis on one or other of its aspects which is most immediately apparent in some special field.

It is even a bigger problem than any single worker can really visualize, because it is an emergent problem with application in every field where the exploitation of this planet's resources is going on; and even with application in the human field as well. It is as much a matter of human attitudes and the general climate of human feeling, as it is a matter of economics, politics and the natural sciences.

I will return to this point later, but for the moment I want to drive it home with a quotation from R. C. Haw's recent book, *The Conservation of Natural Resources:*

> Society and its elaboration are resources, on which we are dependent; and society is something which needs to be tended and cultivated, if we are to get a good crop of responsible beings. Conservation is even more a human and sociological problem than a technological one. Technology is available to deal with the wastage of natural resources, but the greatest problems arise when dealing with the people who cause the erosion and wastage. Hence the urgent need for education in conservation matters.
>
> The destruction of natural resources which is so evident today, has a sad counterpart in the increasing manifestations of vandalism and delinquency. Such afflicted youth, lacking roots and with branches of knowledge dropping and diseased, are ignorant of the conservation ideal, which cultivates strong roots and healthy branches of co-ordinated knowledge. Could these tragic actions occur so easily if all were taught the broad aspects of conservation and shown their status as individuals, yet units of society with responsibilities and opportunities?
>
> Is it the aim of education to compartmentalise, categorise, specialise — breaking man into so many unrelated parts without showing him the

whole? Some unifying study is urgently needed to co-ordinate knowledge and enable students to see the whole picture of man's environment.

Man and Nature

This quotation, which could be matched by quotations from other writers, indicates the emergence of a wider vision of the problems presented by man's relationship to nature. Precisely because it is so new, and so wide, and represents the recognition of so large a problem, it is going to be most difficult to get it into perspective. It represents, in fact, the beginning of what must be, if man is to survive at all, a wholly new attitude in his notion of his relationship to his natural and his social world. It represents a new chance for all of us, if we are brave enough, and far-seeing enough, to take it.

This may seem a very large claim to make for the concept of conservation. I want to support it by taking a very summary glance at man's history in relationship with the earth on which, and by which, and as a part of which, he lives.

Primitive peoples, it is clear, must have lived, as a few surviving small tribes and peoples do today, in comparative harmony with a restricted environment. Their resources were limited to what they could reach in their own immediate tribal or racial territory, and their survival depended on their wise use of their immediate resources. A people without technology cannot alter their environment to suit themselves; if they waste the resources immediately given them, there is no alternative but death. Therefore, as consciousness emerged, their energies were directed, not simply to hunting down all representatives of the species of plants and animals on which they lived, in order to satisfy their immediate appetites, but to conserving their resources, and to methods, which may now seem very primitive and even foolish, of ensuring that these resources did now dwindle past recovery.

The Australian Aborigines, for instance, directed a large part of their religious rites and their economic practices to what we would now call 'conservation'. As hunters and gatherers of food, subject to natural disasters such as drought, flood and fire, they developed a relationship to their environment which was intended to ensure that the environment continued to nourish and support them. They had no species, or few, which could be cultivated, farmed and domesticated; but their whole way of living was directed towards the preservation of the food-species and other useful portions of the environment, not only by the magical rites which now seem to us such useless and primitive methods of propitiating nature, but by totemic prohibitions which in fact worked as conservation methods, and by making sure that sufficient seed of useful plants, and sufficient numbers of breeding-aged animals, were always left for survival and increase, even where this meant that they themselves went short in bad seasons, or went without certain articles of food.

The notion of exploitation, of 'using up' what was there completely before moving on to exploit another territory, made no part of their attitude. They regarded themselves, not as a supreme species with absolute rights over nature, but as themselves a part of that nature, with responsibilities towards all that surrounded them. If they had not done so, of course, not only the species on which they lived would have vanished, but they themselves would not have survived. This is why they had extremely strict laws against over-use of any species, and why, in effect, they kept certain areas of land as reservoirs within which certain species could not be taken, so that there would always be replenishment of species. Such primitive peoples, in fact, were the first to practise wise conservation.

Man took his first step out of this primitive Garden of Eden, in which he had formed part of a self-balancing harmony, when he developed the idea of interfering with his environment to ensure that species he found useful for food or shelter should have advantages over those species he did not find so useful. Instead of simply leaving enough seed on the grass or fruit on the tree to keep the species going, or regulating his hunting to suit the supply of food-animals, he began to dig and plant and weed the soil, and to keep herds of edible or otherwise useful animals. He soon found, however, that soils once broken and exposed needed management if they were not to lose their fertility. Either he must somehow look after these soils, or must practise a purely exploitative farming which moved on when soils became impoverished to new soils, leaving the old to regenerate gradually under cover of such weeds as would grow there. When his herds ate out the grasses of a particular region, he moved on and took them with him. He discovered that soils varied in their fertility and their capacity to support crops, and wars began to be fought for the more fertile areas. Nomad tribes in areas that were unsuitable for farming or protracted grazing descended on the luckier possessors of good soils and grasslands. The history of man as an exploitative and covetous animal had begun.

The Population Explosion

More than this, of course, a population explosion had begun. Formerly, man had adapted himself to what his environment provided: his rate of increase had remained within bounds set by the available food. Now that large crops of grain could be produced, and management of herds allowed increase of edible species, man's own rate of increase kept up with this advance. Where disease in crops or herds, or floods and droughts, made sudden inroads into the food available for such an increased population, man found himself with the alternatives of war on other peoples to gain their harvests and animals, or death by starvation, unless he could discover means of controlling such diseases and disasters. He began to invent new agricultural techniques and veterinary methods, and to discover ways of preventing disease in crops by rotational farming, or fertilizing the soil, or using extracts of other poisonous plants to control the pests of cultivation. As population increased, so technology had to increase, if a people were to be successful; and as available land became occupied, ways had to be found to ensure that it remained fertile enough to produce food.

So as time went on, what had been scattered tribes became nations, which by process of increased technical mastery had vitally altered their environment to serve their needs, and had pushed outward to occupy territories whose boundaries were defined either by the sea, or other natural limits, or by the amount of suitable food-producing land which they were able to hold. Human increase within nations depended on the available resources and techniques, and on the amount of warlike pressure from outside national boundaries.

Once the limits of expansion within these resources had been reached, if technology remained static, population also tended to become static, unless some new factor entered. Europe in the Middle Ages was apparently reaching such a static condition, when two new factors entered: firstly, the beginning of the great outward explorations, and secondly the almost coincident beginning of the new attitude towards the world that became the modern scientific movement.

That movement, with its attendant intellectual upsurge and the new tools, machines and methods it made available, meant that the new countries thrown open by explorations were easily overcome and developed to serve the needs of the discovering countries. Wealth from the new world poured back into Europe, where in turn it provided a further impulse in the developing of scientific thought and method. The new techniques in turn were used to exploit and settle the new countries. The tremendous expansion that began in the fifteenth century has culminated today in the compound interest of increasing population encouraged by freedom from disease and victories over natural hazards, and this again is increasing the need for new technological advances to provide for the needs of that increasing population.

No new countries, however, remain to be discovered; the only frontier still pushing outward is that of human mind and technology. We are the masters of our environment. But in the process of reaching its frontiers, we had lost the sense of our belonging to that environment, and begun to believe that the environment belonged to us.

This was very obvious in the development of the new countries. The Europeans who flocked into North America found what seemed an inexhaustible supply of wealth in land, forests, minerals, furs and everything else they needed. Their response was in terms of waste. The great herds of buffalo and fur-bearing animals gave place to herds of people; the forests were burned, cut and wasted in the expansion of agriculture and grazing; minerals and oil, and other natural wealth, were seized on in a frenzy of acquisition. The whole attitude was exploitive. There seemed no end to the available wealth, and techniques of conservation were ignored or forgotten in favour of techniques of exploitation.

When the frontiers were at last reached, it seems to have been almost a physical shock. The inexhaustible wealth of the country had become an article of faith. Now men's minds had to become adjusted to the notion that it was no longer true, and that what remained after the great expansions was what they now had to live on.

To a lesser degree, the same process went on in all the new countries, and the same attitude towards the wealth of the world possessed men's minds. Over the centuries of European expansion and discovery, the whole world was thrown open. The European technical revolution had moved in everywhere, until only in a few smaller and more difficult areas was there any longer wealth waiting to be discovered and exploited. Now we are faced with the results of those centuries of exploitation and expansion — a world whose natural wealth has been largely converted to our use, and a human population increasing yearly to astronomical proportions.

Old and New Attitudes

It was in the United States that the apparently wholly new idea of the conservation of resources first began to make its way. Technological studies on the conservation of soils, forests and water were instituted, government instrumentalities were set up, and research programmes got under way. As the twentieth century began, new studies in the natural sciences were undertaken; but the upsurge of advance in physics and chemistry overshadowed most of them. Nevertheless, other countries than the United States gradually became aware of the need for conservational measures to save their natural resources, and soil and water and forest conservation were gradually taken over by government departments as well as by private enthusiasts.

This movement is one of our own time, and it is in its way a new thing, representing the beginning of a new attitude. Yet it is really the rediscovery of an old attitude from a new angle. We are beginning to realize that the primitive peoples we have overwhelmed in our exploitive adventure lived in a balance we have disturbed or destroyed, and from our own now so much more complex technological level, we have to attempt to re-establish some such kind of balance in order to survive. We cannot continue to exploit forever, because the end of exploitable resources is in sight; and our numbers are becoming so great that we must find means of stabilizing them, or outgrow the possible means of supporting ourselves.

One of the greatest obstacles in the way of the new move towards the conservation of resources is precisely the human attitudes already established in the centuries of exploitation. They may be, in the end, the instruments of the downfall of the human race, as they have been the instruments of its expansion. We have become the enemies of the nature by which we have lived, and in becoming so we have greatly depleted and wasted its supplies. The forests of the world, and the soils which were made fertile by them and their inhabitants, have been denuded and largely given over to human use and occupation. We are nearing the end of known supplies of phosphate rock to fertilize our fields, and are turning our attention to finding substitutes. Erosion has resulted in the spread of deserts in once rich areas; careless mining methods have polluted streams, and rivers are full of wastes and silted with mud that was once topsoil. Water supply is looming as another great problem for our increasing populations.

We are beginning to turn our attention to the sea, as a supplier of necessary fertilizers, of food and of water. If we find ways of using the ocean as we have already used the lands of the world, another period of expansion may be before us. But a period of expansion is followed by a period of stocktaking — and once we have used the food and fertility provided by the ocean, we have come to the end of the resources of this planet. Moreover, there is evidence that we are already polluting the oceans with wastes and pesticides to such an extent that we may be affecting their productivity.

This very brief survey may be concluded with another quotation from R. C. Haw:

> Civilised men may waste and destroy, through greed or ignorance, but society does not allow them to starve or sicken to death. Nature's punishment is evaded (for the time being) by permitting survival on the basis of nature's capital stored elsewhere. Sometime, however, if we continue to deceive ourselves, the world's capital resources will fall below subsistence level.

The operative phrase here is 'if we continue to deceive ourselves'. It is, in fact, up to man himself not to continue to deceive himself. It is the attitude developed over our period of expansion that is our greatest danger as a species. Can we change this attitude to nature in time to save ourselves from extinction, and our natural environment from disaster?

This is the problem I spoke of as the greatest problem of our time. It is all the greater because it is recognized by so few, and in so piecemeal a manner that it is often seen only as a number of separate small problems — the conservation of soil, of forests, or of wildlife, or even of separate species — whereas in fact all these problems are inter-related. It is a question of man's total attitude, a choice between conservation and exploitation, that lies behind all such problems.

I would suggest, therefore, that the whole concept of conservation, which is only now emerging, is possibly the most important and far-reaching concept of our time. Its acceptance on a significant scale requires of us a complete revision of what has hitherto been the attitude of man to nature. We can no longer go on altering, destroying and thoughtlessly wasting our natural resources on the scale to which we have grown accustomed, or use the old excuse that'there is plenty more where that came from'. We must begin to try to understand the whole relationship of man to his environment and the complex interactions of every form of life, from bacteria and fungi in the soils, through plants and animals to man himself. This study can be based only on a policy of massive reservation and conservation of such natural habitats as are left us, for botanical, zoological, biological and ecological study as well as for aesthetic reasons.

The conservationist, on this view, becomes one of the most important people of our time. His responsibility is not only to the natural environment, but to human society as well. He cannot afford to ignore public opinion and its education, for it is on society and its attitudes that his work must depend. If man is not to go on deceiving himself into a belief that all is well, that the present exploitation of resources can go on indefinitely, that the chemists and physicists will be able to solve all problems of man's survival and prosperity, then the conservationist must try to make his voice heard, in politics, in economics, and above all in education. He cannot afford to do otherwise, whether in smaller or larger conservational problems, if our present 'economy of waste' is to be transformed into an 'economy of conservation' before our planet is exploited beyond recovery.

The fact that the concept of conservation is so new in our minds, and that it has so many different aspects, makes it difficult to emphasize its urgency sufficiently to impress a public which has hitherto lived by ideas of quite a different kind. It takes time to put over a new idea. Also, this concept is emerging at a time when human power over the environment is enormous and is daily growing greater, and when the cry is for more and more 'development', and planning and restriction are unpopular, because they are not clearly seen to be necessary. We are fascinated by our own power, and by the modern chemical and physical means of changing the environment. Crop-spraying, aerial agriculture, wholesale forest-clearing methods, are spectacular and modern; their results are obvious. The occasional unexpected side-effects of the application of various new methods have not yet become obvious enough to trouble anyone.

Yet we know far too little of such effects, which sometimes arise even out of our well-meant but ill-informed conservation measures themselves. Chemical warfare against a sudden increase of disease in crops can result in modifying the environment, in the long run, in favour of the pests or diseases themselves, by destroying natural predators; but in addition, ill-directed attempts to preserve certain species can result in their multiplying beyond the capacity of their environment. Instances are the enormous increase in the number of elephants in the Tsavo National Park in Kenya, and the damage done to their own habitat by hippopotami in the Queen Elizabeth National Park, until a great reduction in their numbers had to be undertaken. Seal nurseries in the northern parts of the British Isles, when protected, quickly became overcrowded because of the lack of natural predators, and the seals themselves began dying of disease.

These instances, and numerous others, show that even the trained conservationist does not yet know enough about the problems of conserving species and environment to be sure of the results of conservatory action. An enormous amount of work requires to be done before we can begin to say that we understand how to manage even the conservation of single species. Mistakes may not be so serious where the 'exploding' species is harmless to man and his needs, but this may not always be so. In South Africa, for instance, there is the well-known case of the tremendous increase in the number of baboons, which came about when their natural predators, the leopards, were destroyed. The baboons then became a menace, not only to crops, but even to farm animals. Queleas or Weaver-Birds have increased in Africa to the extent that they are now more destructive to grain-crops than locusts are. And when this kind of explosion in numbers occurs in a protected species, it is the conservationist who will get the blame, and the concept of conservation which is damaged.

Then, of course, the reigning view that our natural environment is given us to make a profit out of, ensures that the notion of conservation is far too easily seen as soft and sentimental. The picture of tenderminded people weeping over the fate of little furry rabbits and mice in cruel traps is often used to obscure the real issues — and would that it were not, all too often, rather a justifiable picture. The real facts are not easy to present against this background; it is hard to put over the image of the conservationist as the only really practical person of our time. But somehow or other this has to be done, and done quickly.

he coral reef at Lord Howe Island has an interesting admixture of tropical and
:mperate marine fauna. It has been suggested for reservation as a marine park.
HOTO COURTESY ELIZABETH C. POPE

Tylophora crebriflora, a rather rare vine in the rainforests of tropical Queensland, has a characteristic mustard-coloured sap, and yields an alkaloid effective against leukaemia. PHOTO COURTESY W. T. JONES

The grotesque Baobab (*Adansonia gregorii*) of north-western Australia, has a 'bottle-tree' form adapted to water storage in tropical semi-arid areas. The termite mounds are characteristic of the terrain. PHOTO COURTESY V. SERVENTY

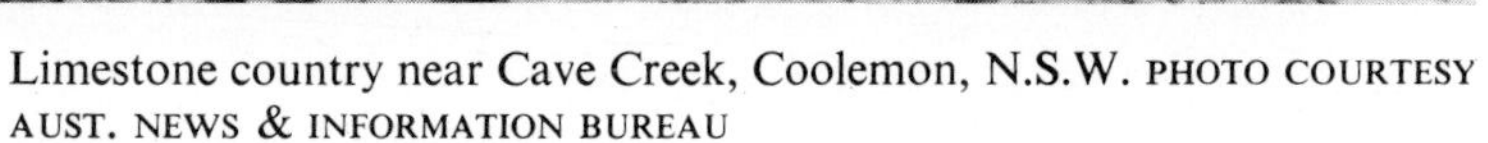

Limestone country near Cave Creek, Coolemon, N.S.W. PHOTO COURTESY AUST. NEWS & INFORMATION BUREAU

Coastal wallum country, south Queensland, with paper-bark tea-trees (*Melaleuca*), Banksias, and many native heath species belonging to the families Epacridaceae, Proteaceae, Leguminosae etc. PHOTO COURTESY S. AND K. BREEDEN

Dinosaur footprint near Broome, W.A Such preservation is a function of geological reserves. In accessible areas, protection of 'fossil reserves' may well a problem unless strict control is exercised by fencing and appointment voluntary wardens as for certain archaeological sites. PHOTO COURTESY V. SERVENTY

Austrobaileya scandens, a vine with a restricted distribution in the tropical rainforest of north Queensland, is one the most primitive types of flowering plant. It was not described until 1929, a is the only member of its family. PHOTO COURTESY W. T. JONES

Aesthetics, Morals and Self-Interest

Moreover, we cannot afford to neglect the very real moral and emotional aspects of the concept of conservation. Properly thought through and presented, these are quite as important as the other aspect of enlightened self-interest, in convincing public opinion of the importance of conservation. After all, man is not a wholly self-interested animal: even when we are most materialistic, we are apt to be in internal rebellion against our own arguments. And most of us like to think of ourselves as rather wider in our outlook than the tyrannosaurus, and as being capable of appreciating the right of other species to live their lives, and even of enjoying their enjoyment of them.

Moreover, as we look around us at the environment we are creating for ourselves, and the results of crowded urban life on the young of our own species, we are beginning to have certain doubts. Like R. C. Haw, in my earlier quotations, we observe a certain rootlessness and ugliness in our own attitudes. We do not yet see what to do about it, but we are becoming uneasy about ourselves. Waste, pollution, exploitation, greed, we begin to understand, are having their effect on human nature as on nature itself. We know, however vaguely, that we need a new kind of attitude towards the world, both the natural and the social world. It is just here that the concept of conservation, in its widest sense, could provide us with what we need.

In fact, many of the battles waged so far for the reservation of natural areas have been waged and won — or, occasionally, lost — in the name of aesthetic and moral values, rather than in the name of enlightened self-interest. The great game-reserves of Africa were made as much on these grounds as on those of providing reservoirs in which big-game could breed undisturbed for tourists or for big-game hunters outside the reserves themselves. The first national parks in the world, and many since, were made for aesthetic reasons.

Nevertheless, it has to be recognized that where reserves are made purely for aesthetic or 'scenic' values, they are too often made grudgingly, and quite without consideration for the survival of species or the preservation of all that needs protection. Often the area granted is otherwise unsuitable for economic human use, and often also unsuitable for species-survival and for study of soils and natural environments. And, where some economic use is later discovered to be possible, these areas are all liable to have their reservation revoked at any time; and public opinion is seldom aroused against such action.

The Potential for Science

The realization of the possible importance of studies of species in their natural environment has emerged too slowly. It is clear that we do not yet know nearly enough about the history of the earth and of the development of its species, and the relationship of soils, plants and animals. In the great upsurge of physical and chemical research, studies of this kind have been comparatively neglected. It is also more than possible that the psychological, physical and social history of man himself has been and is profoundly influenced by environment in ways that we do not yet suspect. Such arguments ought to be among the strongest we have for insisting on the preservation of a complete range of natural environments while there is still time to save them.

Apart from the arguments for large reserves for scientific study, and others for recreational and aesthetic purposes, we urgently need reserves near towns and cities for the education of children from urban schools. This would be a most important factor in the education of public opinion. Even if we of the present generation succeed in reserving enough land for the survival of species, it will be in the hands of succeeding generations to look after them. We cannot possibly expect generations reared in artificial urban conditions to care much about the conservation of rural habitats, unless we undertake this kind of education. No school lessons in biology, zoology, botany and the rest can ever take the place of actual contact with natural environments. Reserves of this kind — 'nature-trails', guided excursions through bushland, even well-planted and well-managed botanical gardens — may make all the difference between intelligent response to teaching in the basic sciences of life, and an apathetic lack of interest.

But all such reserves, whether educational, aesthetic or simply for tourist purposes, are going to depend for their survival on education in their proper use, and on their being actually used for the purposes for which they are intended. Pressures for alienation even of the small number of national parks and reserves we have are already increasing; as development goes on they will be more and more endangered. We are brought back from every angle to the most urgent need of all — the need for education in conservation principles, and education wide and well-based enough to give a balanced view of the processes of nature and of our own place and responsibility in the natural world.

Not long ago a newsreel film was released on Australia's policy of export action. Lavishly photographed in colour, it was an official production obviously intended to convince the audience of the wealth of Australia and our wisdom in using it. It was frankly and wholly a film dealing with the exploitation of resources, and worse, of the shipment overseas of everything resulting from this exploitation. Great gashes appeared in hillsides as mineral was extracted and piled into waiting ships; eucalypts of hundreds of years' growth toppled and were lopped of every branch before they were dragged to the paper-mills where overseas businessmen approvingly examined the quality of the paper they made; beach dunes were denuded and flattened to be run through extracting machinery for rutile which was immediately loaded into holds for overseas. In none of these exploitive processes had man had any hand in the actual production of the exported goods; we were not even shown a plantation of exotic pine trees to give us hope that something was being done to replace them. Yet the burden of the commentary was wholly approving.

Education and the Unified View

While this kind of exploitation reigns, and the attitude of mind behind it is a complacent approval, it is going to be very difficult to convince anybody that conservation can have any other aim or moral meaning than simply putting something aside so that we can exploit it another day. We will have to expect, as time goes on and pressures increase, that even our present parks and reserves will inevitably be exploited, as some are being already. The only answer is to take action now — by education, by protests against the acceptance of purely exploitive attitudes, by presenting the facts in their starkest form, by refusing to allow people to deceive themselves. If we do not yet know the facts — the reserves of wealth that we actually have to draw on, how long it will take to come to an end of them, the actual damage we have done, are doing and will do to this country — then somehow we must find them out. We must, above all, educate and teach. Perhaps we ought even to evangelize — for time is getting short, and extractive techniques and techniques for wholesale land-clearing, pesticide campaigns and the like are becoming more and more efficient in operation. There is little sign, either, that conservationists and scientific workers are gaining ground in their efforts to influence governments towards planning and surveying areas to be cleared, developed or mined, before the jobs are undertaken, so that proper land use methods can be applied and valuable or vulnerable species and biosystems protected.

I said at the beginning of this chapter that public apathy and outright opposition were among the most discouraging obstacles the conservationist has to face. But it is equally true that there has been, over the past few years, increasing interest among far-sighted laymen, as well as scientists, in the idea of conservation, and an increasing distaste for the cruder kinds of exploitation and the wreckage and ugliness they leave behind them. This is what conservationists should work on and develop: and here scientists and workers ought not to scorn the work of the lay enthusiast and his viewpoint, however non-technical and even misguided they may seem. Most lay conservationists are intelligent enough to be able to modify views they have not clearly thought out, and many are only too anxious for guidance in principle and action.

This is a movement which ought to transcend jealousies and bridge the gap between the 'two cultures', between science and the humanities. It is just as important to the writer and painter, the social worker, the philosopher, even the factory-worker and the clerk, that the human race should learn again to live in responsible harmony with its surroundings, as it can possibly be to the scientist, engineer, or farmer. We who are becoming interested in the problem from a lay point of view are trying to educate ourselves; we want help and guidance from those in the scientific side of the battle, so that we in turn may help, whether in passing on that guidance to others or in necessary action.

For we are beginning to realize the truth behind my earlier quotation, that 'conservation is even more a human and sociological problem than a technological one.' If modern society is to be saved from the consequences of the attitudes built up over the exploitive centuries, the conservation movement is certainly going to be one of the most important factors in its salvation.

International Perspectives in Nature Conservation

William C. Robison

'Where can I go now, and visit nature undisturbed?' This question was asked by John James Audubon, the great ornithologist and wildlife illustrator of the early nineteenth century, on witnessing the wholesale destruction of North America's mink and marten for the fur trade. Yet while the continent was changing before his eyes, in Audubon's time there were still many places on the earth where nature remained relatively undisturbed. Only about two human lifetimes ago, the interior of Africa was largely uncharted by Europeans; the North American plains supported vast herds of buffalo and a sparse indigenous population; the interior of Australia had not been crossed; and only a small part of the coast of Antarctica had been seen by men. So it is understandable that there was almost no concern for nature preservation in the world despite the fact that large areas of once-fertile land in China and the Middle East had already deteriorated to unproductive wastelands.

Today, however, the problem of nature conservation is not only far more urgent but also more generally recognized than it was in the nineteenth century, and it is the purpose of this chapter to present a brief survey of the means by which the challenge is being met throughout the world. I am not suggesting that the reduction of the area of wild lands in the world has been altogether undesirable, even though nature lovers may regret the closing of the period of wilderness abundance. As Robert Wernick recently remarked in stating the case against wilderness preservation, ' "Wilderness" is precisely what man has been fighting against since he began his painful, awkward climb to civilization. It is the dark, the formless, the terrible, the old chaos which our fathers pushed back, which surrounds us yet, which will engulf us all in the end.' But there are sound economic and scientific reasons, as well as aesthetic and personal ones, for preserving substantial areas where human interference is at a minimum, for taking whatever steps are necessary to prevent avoidable extinction of animal and plant species, and for preserving adequate representatives of the various types of biological communities that once covered the earth.

Without attempting to enumerate these reasons in detail — for they are already familiar to most of the readers of this book — it is worth noting that not all of the reasons are applicable in all situations, and consequently we find a great variety of policies and reservations that are all concerned in some way with nature preservation. Perhaps the best approach to a world synopsis is to consider first the various types of policies that have been directed toward nature conservation, and the forms which they have taken.

Conservation Policies and Kinds of Reserves

The most obvious, and in some cases the most short-sighted, conservation policy has been one of exclusive concern with a particular species of bird or mammal without consideration of the habitat that it requires for its existence. Too often such concern has been manifested simply in restrictions on shooting after a species has already dwindled to the point where it could not recover, as happened to the Passenger Pigeon which once numbered in the millions in North America. Some misguided efforts in this direction — now happily disappearing — have taken the form of preserving the 'good' species (applying human standards of conduct to determine which species are 'good') by eliminating the 'bad' species or predators. Sometimes such a policy has backfired, and with the natural controls removed, a species was subject to overpopulation and then starvation such as the catastrophe which overtook the Kaibab deer herd of Arizona in the 1930s. Sometimes, however, attempts to rescue or restore a species have been successful when its natural habitat has remained relatively undisturbed. A recent example is the successful re-introduction of the ibex to the Swiss Alps, from which it disappeared some years ago.

The scientific approach, while maintaining an interest in individual species, is concerned primarily with biological communities, for no plant or animal exists independently of the other biota in its environment. The ideal scientific nature reserve is one that is not used for public recreation (nor even by too many scientists), for its essential quality is the maintenance of a 'natural' condition. Such areas were defined as 'strict nature reserves' by the 1933 London Convention for the Preservation of African Fauna and Flora, and as 'strict wilderness areas' by the 1940 Pan-American Convention on Nature Protection and Wild Life Preservation in the Western Hemisphere. Such preserves are closely related to the national park movement in certain countries where many are located within national parks, but their standards are obviously more strict than those of national parks in general can be. Their size tends to be considerably smaller than that of national parks, since many nature reserves exist for the preservation of a single community or ecosystem. The reserves maintained by Britain's Nature Conservancy, established in 1949, and by the Society of American Foresters in its 128 'natural areas', fall into this category. The system of 'state protected areas' (*zapovednik*) in the Soviet Union, which now comprise more than 8,000,000 acres, originated primarily to preserve representative biological communities. The need for international recognition of natural areas, and standards for their establishment, were included in the Scope and Objectives of the International Biological Programme. Under the heading, 'Conservation of Terrestrial Communities', a group of scientists (the Special Committee for the International Biological Programme) representing a number of different countries have drawn up plans for a world survey of natural areas and for standardizing methods of field description and research.

The third major approach to nature preservation is one of combining the two just mentioned — species preservation and maintenance of natural communities — with public recreation and preservation of all scenic values in an area, that is, the national parks approach. Since national parks are the principal theme of this book, it is tempting to treat them as though they were the final answer to the problem of nature conservation. But this simplification would overlook both the unavoidably wide differences between the structure of the national park systems in various countries and the problems of wildlife conservation that still exist despite the establishment of national parks.

Statistically, the situation is encouraging, especially when compared to that of a few decades ago. A survey titled 'National Parks of the World' by C. F. Brockman, was published in 1961 in *American Forests*. This listed fifty countries and territories (most of which are now independent) that had set aside national parks, nature reserves, or other types of reservations for the preservation of wildlife, natural scenery, and vegetation. A further list of twenty-six national parks exceeding one million acres in size, topped by Canada's eleven million acre Wood Buffalo National Park, includes representatives of five continents. The figure of aggregate acreage of these parks and reserves is impressive — but not very meaningful. For these areas include such a diversity of types of land and degrees of protection for their natural life that their effectiveness cannot be measured in terms of acres. Furthermore, to include only areas having the status of national parks or reserves would mean disregarding other areas where the natural conditions receive equal or sometimes better protection. Such conditions are often found in local or regional parks, in portions of national and state forests that have been set aside as wilderness areas, and sometimes in private holdings.

Although some national parks were set aside primarily to protect outstanding scenic areas rather than as nature preserves, they all have the preservation of natural plant and animal life as at least one of their objectives. This has been a gradual development, beginning in the nineteenth century with such acts as reservation of the Yellowstone Park in the United States, the Hluhluwe Game Reserve in Natal, and Royal National Park in New South Wales, all in the 1870s, and reservation in 1882 of the large area on New Zealand's South Island that has become Fiordland National Park. The first European national parks were established in Sweden in 1909; since then a number of countries have followed this example, but limited national areas and intensive land use have required special adaptations in some countries. The largest national park system in Europe is that of Great Britain, which began in 1949 with passage of the National Parks and Access to the Countryside Act. This Act provides an effective method for ensuring the preservation of scenery and wildlife on private as well as public lands, and public enjoyment of them. The outstanding park system in Asia is that of Japan, including nineteen parks in nearly four and a half million acres. Other Asian countries that can boast of national parks or nature reserves are Burma, India, Indonesia, Malaysia, and the Philippine Republic. In Latin America, national parks have been established in Argentina, Brazil, Chile, Ecuador, Mexico, Peru, and Venezuela. Numerous African countries have natural reserves or parks, which offer a hope for preservation of some of the magnificent wildlife of that continent; their problems are many, however, as discussed in the next section.

Threats to Wildlife

The continued existence of many species of wild animals is threatened from a variety of sources which range from uncontrolled killing to extension of agriculture. Killing for sport, using high speed automobiles and modern rifles, is said to have caused the extinction within the past ten years, of the South Arabian oryx. The polar bear seems to be similarly threatened, although there is inadequate knowledge of its numbers and habits. Uncontrolled killing for commerce or food is especially serious in Africa, where souvenirs are made of elephants' feet and zebra tails and there is a brisk market in powdered rhinoceros horn. Killing for the protection of livestock, which is responsible for the elimination of the Bald Eagle from parts of North America, and to reduce competition with livestock as in the case of the Red Kangaroo, presents a special problem in conservation in which legitimate economic interests must be taken into account.

Even if the animals themselves are protected, however, if their natural habitat disappears they will disappear also. In many parts of the world this is happening at an unprecedented pace. The rate at which the natural landscape of Africa is changing is illustrated by a photographic survey that was recently made. Between 1918 and 1924 the botanist H. L. Shantz made a number of trips through Africa to study its vegetation and soils, during the course of which a large number of photographs of the natural plant cover were taken. In 1956 Dr Shantz returned to Africa to document the changes in vegetation at as many of the sites of his earlier photographs as possible. Of 1,309 photographs that were selected for study and reduplication, seventy-nine per cent had to be eliminated because of urban development or agricultural extensions over the original sites; in the end duplications were possible for only 241 of the original photographs.

Similar extensions of 'civilization' are taking place in other parts of the world that formerly were protected by their remoteness and isolation. In Alaska, there has been a heated controversy over the proposed Rampart Dam project that would flood eight million acres or more of land along the Yukon River and its tributaries. A recent report by a committee of experts appointed by the Natural Resources Council of America has declared that 'nowhere in the history of water development in North America have the fish and wildlife losses anticipated to result from a single project been so overwhelming.' Yet the belief is widely held by residents of Alaska that the project is essential to the region's economic development.

One answer to the problems of uncontrolled killing and reduction of habitat is obviously to be found in the establishment of suitable reserves and parks where natural biological conditions can be maintained. But once a park or reserve is established, a new set of problems is likely to be encountered. In countries such as Australia and the United States, which share the attributes of an expanding economy and a high standard of living, these problems are generally associated with over-development, conflicting recreational uses, and attempts to superimpose hydro-electric projects on the natural landscape. In recent years preservationists have found themselves in conflict with 'realists' who were intent on building dams in such widely separated parks as the Swiss National Park, Dinosaur National Monument of Utah, and the Mount Kosciusko summit area.

The problems requiring the greatest judgment and skill on the part of park administrators, however, are usually those deriving from one of the principal purposes for which parks are established — public recreation. To be used for recreation a park must have roads, camp grounds, hotels, service stations, and other improvements, and the pressures are strong to allow uses and developments that are not consistent with the primary functions of a national park. Even in their more remote areas, trails must be maintained and fires must be suppressed, perhaps altering one of the basic ecological factors in the environment. But most of these problems are not insurmountable, and with good management most parks can be maintained largely in a wilderness condition at the same time that certain parts of them accommodate large numbers of visitors.

The recently independent, emerging countries of the world are faced with a different type of problem in attempting to maintain their parks and wildlife preserves, one which in some respects is much more difficult than ours. Although some of these countries inherited from their colonial administrations an admirable system of parks and reserves (no less than eight of the parks on the over-one-million-acres list are in recently independent countries of Africa) and well-trained staffs to patrol and protect them, the political emphasis in such countries is on increased expenditures for education and welfare services. Even the educated elements of the population in these countries see little reason for spending money to maintain wildlife reserves. According to Sir Julian Huxley, 'some of them regard National Parks and Controlled Shooting Areas as relics of white "colonialism", or merely as places for white men to indulge their peculiar habit of enjoying the sight or the pursuit of wild animals; and accordingly to be abolished or at any rate not encouraged'. Nor is it easy to answer their argument that 'You white men have killed all your wolves and bears: why do you want us Africans to preserve our lions and elephants?' At the same time, Huxley found a growing awareness of the prestige value of wildlife: 'In the modern world, as Africa is beginning to realize, a country without a National Park can hardly be regarded as civilized.' It is to this type of attitude — which Huxley believes could be fostered through 'the African zeal for education' — that the world might look for the preservation of Africa's heritage during these difficult times.

International Co-operation

There is also an increasing awareness among the nations of the world that nature conservation is an international responsibility. The interdependence of the world today as well as the habits of many wild species makes some degree of co-operation between countries a necessity if many species and communities are to be preserved.

The first co-operation of this kind to be effective was motivated by purely economic considerations — in the field of marine life. After several unsuccessful attempts to reach agreements for the conservation of fur seals and sea-otters, in 1911 a convention was agreed to and ratified by the United States, Great Britain, Russia, and Japan. This agreement was successful in checking the destructive practice of pelagic sealing and in stopping the decline of the North Pacific seal herds. The population of sea-otters has similarly risen to an estimated 40,000, from its low point of less than 1,000 fifty years ago.

Conservation of fish resources has been achieved by various international agreements which have operated with some success, beginning with the so-called Baltic Convention of 1929. The Canadian-American halibut conservation program has achieved considerable success in its objectives, and Japan and the U.S.S.R. are now signatories to several fisheries agreements in the Pacific.

Whaling has presented a special problem because of its international character, the wide distribution of the resource, and a lack of sufficient knowledge of many species for formulation of sound conservation policies. The first International Convention for the Regulation of Whaling was proposed by the League of Nations and became effective in 1935 after being ratified by seventeen countries. There is now an International Whaling Commission which establishes limits for the catch of various species, the decisions of which are participated in and agreed to by all of the important whaling nations. Thus far, however, rivalry between certain nations has prevented the adoption of an international inspection system, and there is concern for the future of some species such as the Blue Whale and the Blunt-nose Sperm Whale. The most recent agreement by the world's whaling nations provides for the demarcation of whale sanctuaries, and sperm whales are now to be protected within forty degrees north and south of the Equator.

One of the first examples of international co-operation with respect to non-economic wildlife was the Migratory Bird Treaty, concluded between Canada and the United States in 1916. But this was a bilateral undertaking; multilateral action came much later. The most outstanding example of such co-operation has been in the Antarctic. The Antarctic Treaty, signed in 1959 by representatives of Argentina, Australia, Belgium, Chile, France, Japan, New Zealand, Norway, South Africa, the U.S.S.R., the United Kingdom, and the United States, and subsequently acceded to by Czechoslovakia, Denmark and Poland, provided in Article IX for a meeting of the Contracting Parties to formulate and recommend measures, among other things, for 'preservation and conservation of living resources in Antarctica'.

The First Consultative Meeting was held at Canberra in July 1961 and has been followed by two other meetings. The Third, held in Brussels in 1964, adopted a statement of 'Agreed Measures for the Conservation of Antarctic Fauna and Flora' and recommended its approval by all of the governments that were signatories to the Treaty. Although formal approval by all of the Antarctic Treaty nations has not yet been completed, the measures have been informally adopted throughout the Antarctic continent. They prohibit the killing or capturing of any native mammal or bird in the treaty area except under permits which are to be issued only for scientific or essential purposes and limited to the number that can normally be replaced by natural reproduction in the following breeding season. Other provisions restrict 'harmful interference' with native fauna by such activities as allowing dogs to run free, flying aircraft within 200 metres of bird and seal colonies, and use of explosives or firearms near such colonies. The agreement also provides for the establishment of 'specially protected areas' where unique natural ecological systems are preserved; it prohibits the bringing into the treaty area of non-indigenous plants and animals, except under permit; and it provides for the exchange of information between nations as to the status of native animals and birds in the area.

The successful co-operation of many countries in the Antarctic provides a model that might well be emulated in other parts of the world. Perhaps it is not too much to hope that this might eventually come about. In the Arctic regions, a first step toward international co-operation in the interest of conservation was taken in 1965 when scientists from the Soviet Union, Canada, Norway, Denmark, and the United States met at the University of Alaska to discuss the status of the polar bear. In recent years this animal has increasingly been the objective of trophy hunters using long-range rifles and airplanes and concern is felt over its dwindling numbers. But an essential step toward its preservation is the acquisition of reliable information regarding its habits and distribution. This is the present aim of the scientists of the circumpolar countries who wish to determine what measures are needed to ensure the polar bear's survival.

Other notable international meetings have been held in recent years. In October 1965, representatives of the various nations comprising the Organization of American States met at Mar del Plata, Argentina, to consider the question of conservation of the western hemisphere's renewable natural resources, and specifically the progress that has been made toward establishment of national parks and other nature reserves. The group noted that many recommendations that had been adopted by previous conferences had not been carried out, but expressed hope that certain measures would be taken by the member governments even with the limited financial support available. A still more widely attended meeting was the First World Conference on National Parks, held at Seattle in 1962. Attended by more than 400 persons representing sixty-three independent nations, this conference brought together for the first time a truly world-wide gathering of individuals who were directly concerned with the establishment and administration of national parks in their respective countries.

A recent development to meet the varied threats to the world's remaining wild animals is the World Wildlife Fund, established in 1961 with international headquarters at Zurich. The Fund operates through local organizations, helping to train biologists and ecologists in countries where these skills are in short supply, and providing money to meet local emergencies where anti-poaching patrols must be strengthened or land is needed for conservation purposes. Typical activities of the Fund have been the purchase of a large area of wetland near Seville, Spain, to forestall its sale to a shooting group, and of land near the Ngordoto Crater in Tanzania as a wildlife preserve. In 1967 the Fund held its first international congress at Amsterdam.

A further measure that might prove of great value in wildlife preservation would be an international agreement to control the trade in wildlife and its products, and the United Nations has been urged to convene a conference toward this end. If the spirit that has made a success of the Antarctic Treaty and other international agreements for the conservation of wildlife should again prevail, there is reason to believe that much good could come from such a meeting.

Summary

National parks and other types of reserved areas are an essential ingredient of a worldwide programme for preservation of the species and natural communities of plants and animals now on the earth. But if they are to serve this end effectively — as more than mere areas on a map — they must be protected by legal safeguards, adequate patrols, intelligent management, and an interested and informed body of public opinion. Adequate scientific knowledge of the organisms concerned, and personnel trained in their management, are also needed. International co-operation is a necessity in dealing with many species, especially those that spend all or part of their life cycle in international waters, and interchange of information, ideas, and experience between the nations can further the maintenance of world standards for national parks and natural areas. With continued efforts in these fields, we and our descendants may yet be able to give a positive answer to Audubon's question and point to areas throughout the world where one may 'visit nature undisturbed'.

Part II

Australian Ecosystems and Their Origins

J. Le Gay Brereton
B. N. Richards
J. B. Williams

Plants and animals, together with their physical environment, constitute an ecological system or 'ecosystem'. If we examine Australian land ecosystems by travelling westwards from, say, a beach of northern New South Wales, our journey will be marked by changes in vegetation. As we move up the beach we come to spinifex grass, then low shrubs. Behind the dunes we find a higher, denser shrub formation. Next we come to eucalyptus woodland and then forest. Nearer the steep scarp of the Great Dividing Range we may find subtropical rainforest, and close to the top of the scarp in some high wet places there is temperate rainforest. On the tablelands we again find woodland, but farther west this opens out and we move through savannah woodland.

Trekking westward for a hundred miles across the tablelands, we reach slopes and scarpland leading down to the western plains. On the gentle fall, open woodland continues but relics of the rainforest are still found in this region, albeit impoverished in species. On the western plains the savannah woodland opens out still further, and the trees become stunted and give way to shrubs. Areas of dense grassland appear, but later in the sandy and stony deserts, low plants become widely scattered. The changes in vegetation which we have observed during our journey form a pattern i.e. there is an orderly arrangement of different species into plant communities. Each community, viewed on this broad scale, has a characteristic appearance and structure, and is called a vegetation 'formation'. The distribution of formations throughout the world is primarily controlled by climate, and one of the obvious changes during our journey from the dense closed forests of the coast to the deserts of the inland is decrease in rainfall. There are, however, many exceptions to climatic control e.g. the influence of different soils, and historical causes.

Different formations tend to harbour different kinds of animals, and the distribution of animals follows a pattern similar to that of vegetation. Closer investigation will show that, within a single formation, animals are not distributed at random but occur in definite patterns. Thus among birds in a forest, some dwell in the tree canopy, others in the shrub layer, while still others are ground-dwellers. If we make a really diligent and systematic search we should find that most of the animals are invertebrates which live in the leaf-litter and soil.

It would be very easy at this point to think that all has now been said about the living part of an ecosystem. This would be a mistake, for some of the most important components of ecosystems are the least conspicuous, that is, the protozoa, algae, bacteria, and fungi. They are so small that a microscope is necessary to make them visible. Collectively they are known as micro-organisms. Although they are extremely numerous (millions of individuals occur in a pinch of soil) they are frequently overlooked; perhaps it is a case of 'out of sight, out of mind'. Their importance is such, however, that an eminent microbiologist felt constrained to remark that plants and animals were interlopers in a microbiological world!

Ecosystems can be named by the vegetation. From a survey of the pattern it is comparatively easy to place vegetation in one of a number of formations: rainforest, sclerophyll forest, woodland, savannah woodland, shrubland, grassland, alpine complex, desert complex. This description based largely on appearance tells us little about how the system works or functions. There is another way of describing ecosystem structure, and this is in terms of the activities or 'industries' in which the component organisms engage. In most ecosystems we can recognize three such industries: a producer industry, a consumer industry and a decomposer industry. The producer industry in terrestrial ecosystems is composed of green plants, which capture and store the energy of sunlight and so provide a source of energy for all forms of terrestrial life. The consumer industry involves animals that feed on plants or on other animals. The decomposer industry is based on animals and

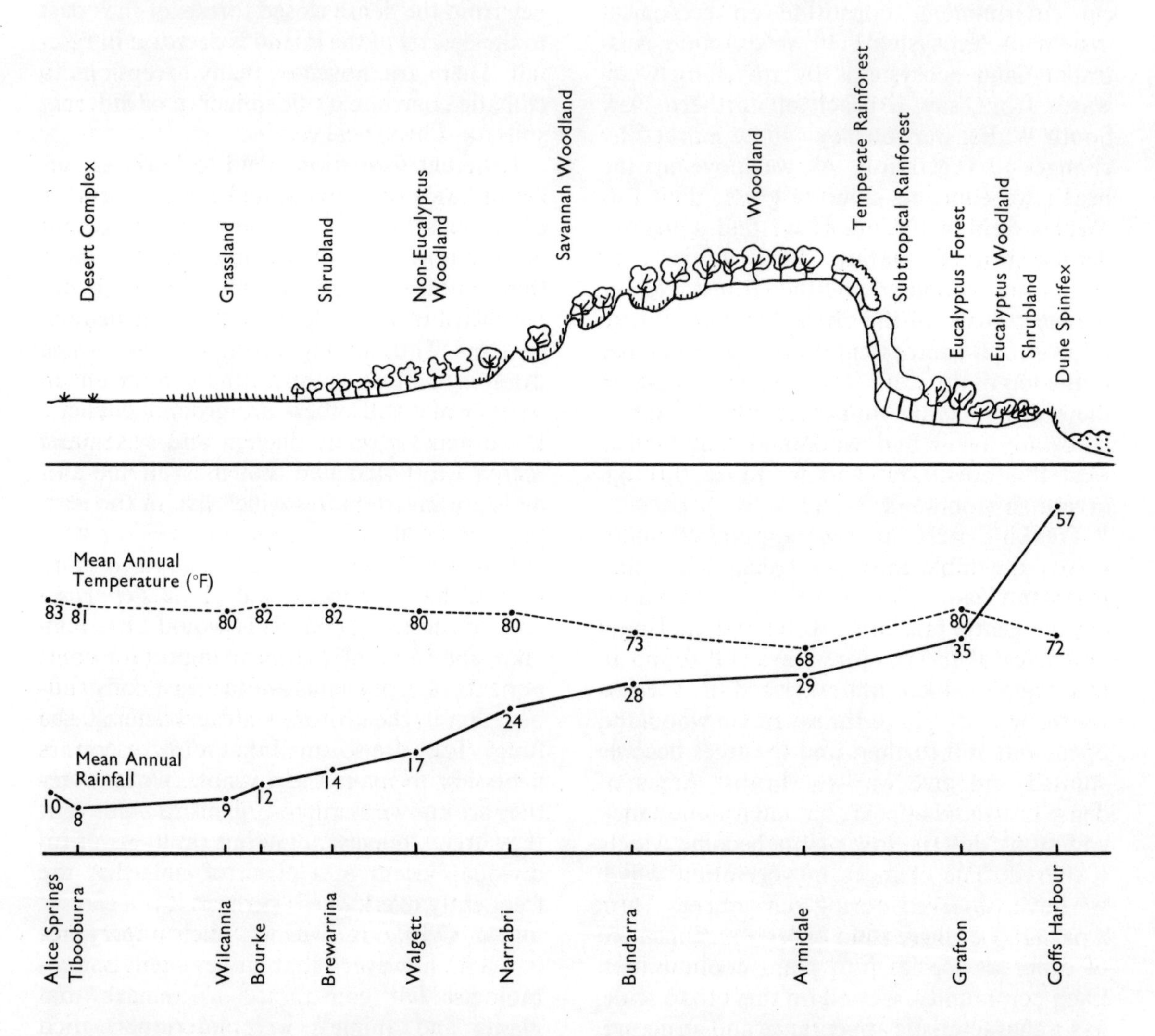

FIGURE 1: *The structure and distribution of terrestrial ecosystems is largely determined by independent factors (see text). The most important of these is climate. Here the distribution of major Australian ecosystems is shown against topography and two components of climate (rainfall and temperature). The correlation is quite good, but far from perfect. Other independent factors as well as dependent factors need to be known for an understanding of ecosystem structure and distribution.*

micro-organisms that feed on dead organic matter.

Limiting Factors

The factors limiting ecosystems are of two kinds: independent and dependent. No understanding of the structure, function and evolution of ecosystems is possible without a discussion of these factors. We shall commence with independent factors. These are factors which have a marked effect on ecosystems, but which are not themselves affected *by* ecosystems. They are soil parent material or rock which is the basis of the soil and nutrients; regional climate, which so greatly influences water availability; topography or relief; the organisms which are available for colonization; and time. The use of just two components of climate (temperature and moisture) goes far towards explaining the distribution of ecosystems, and in doing so, indicates to us that these factors are of great importance (Fig. 1). However, closer examination also shows that these limiting factors are insufficient. Thus high rainfall alone does not explain the occurrence of rainforest. Soil parent material of low nutritional status and the deleterious effects of sea-spray may be the main causes of its failure to occur on the foredunes.

Out on the western plains we come to systems characteristic of more arid conditions: shrubland and grassland. But here we sometimes find woodland and shrubland where we would expect grassland in other parts of the world. This indicates the importance of the availability of species and of evolutionary history in a region.

Time also plays its part in determining the structure of ecosystems. For example, if we examine the steep and crumbling slopes at the bottom of the upstream gorges of the New England Tablelands, we observe bare rocks, older ones covered by lichen, and small herbs in skeletal soil. Higher up where time has allowed more development, shrubs are growing, and as we go higher up the sides to the older gentler slopes, we find trees and grass. Looking at time in another way, we know that the further we go downstream, the older will be the river, and the denser, higher and more stable the vegetation.

With these categories of independent factors in mind we can make sense of the vegetation map of Australia. Many exceptions occur which can only be explained by other factors (see Fig. 2).

Dependent or Regulating Factors

It would be convenient if we could wholly understand ecosystems in terms of independent factors. But this is not so. One only has to protect plants from consumers, or rotting material from decomposers, to see how influential these organisms are. Changes in producers or in dead material bring about changes in the numbers of organisms which feed on these things. It is in this way that some factors must be considered dependent or regulating factors. A sudden increase in herbivores leads to a sudden decrease in pasture; the consequence is a marked decrease in herbivores by starvation, and a subsequent increase in pasture. In general, the effect of the change in one factor leads to a change in another factor, which in turn affects the first. The interacting response of dependent factors contrasts with the lack of response of independent factors. One does not obtain an immediate and systematic change in parent material, regional climate, topography, available organisms, or time, by changing the vegetation of an area, because these factors are independent. But changes in species numbers, biomass (weight of organisms per unit area), microclimate, or soil, lead to reciprocal changes and hence these are some of the dependent factors of ecosystems.

The degree to which compensatory responses of dependent variables stabilize ecosystems is a contentious and difficult question. We have as yet insufficient evidence on which to judge this concept known as balance. It is such a plausible idea that there is a tendency to accept it uncritically.

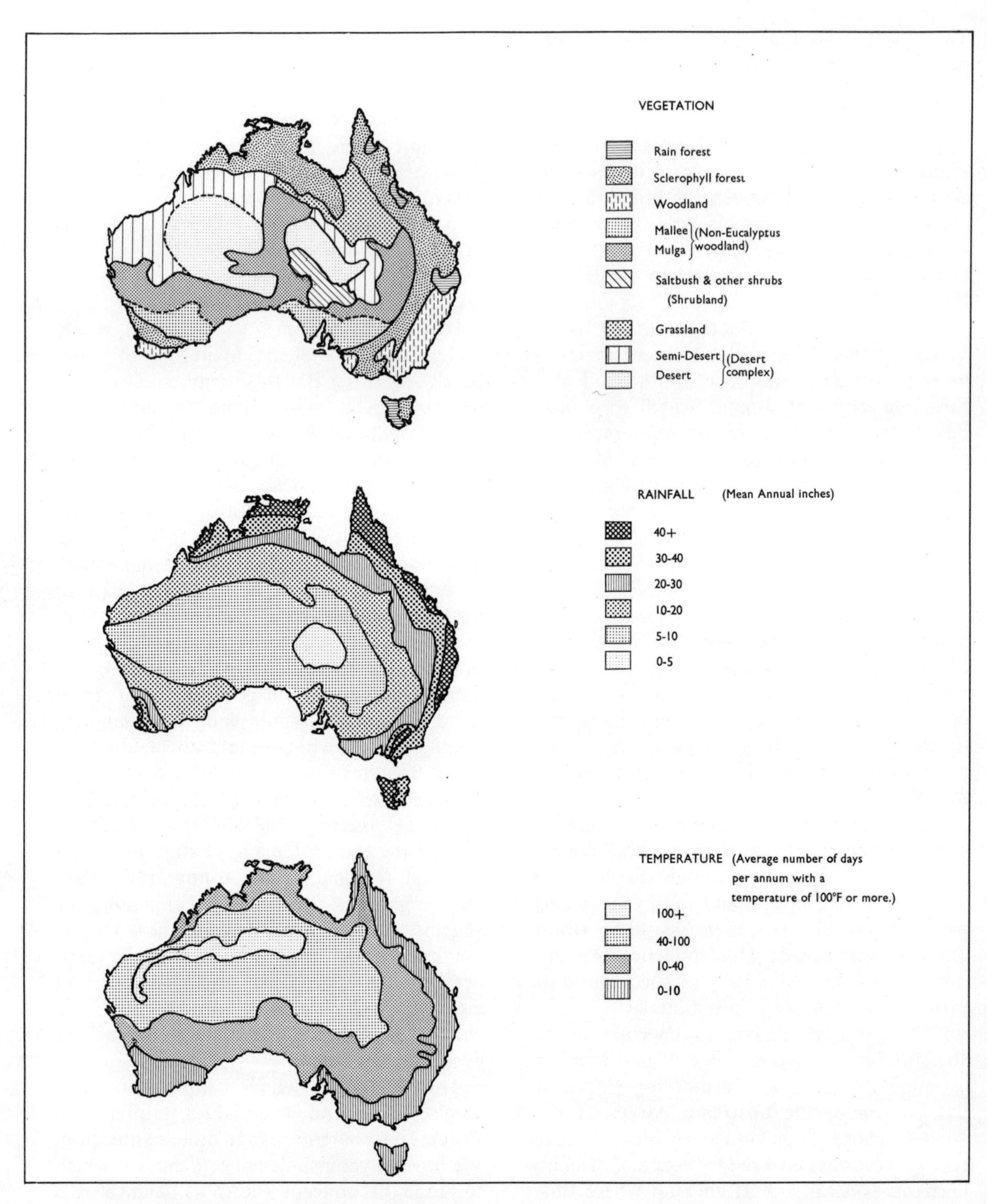

FIGURE 2: *The degree to which the distribution of Australian terrestrial ecosystems is determined by rainfall and temperature is indicated. It is also clear that other factors are involved (see text).*

rested Terns (*Sterna bergii*) in a typical pose, near Teewah coloured sands, outh Queensland. PHOTO COURTESY S. AND K. BREEDEN

uboisia myoporoides, now widely known as 'Duboisia', is a common small tree secondary growth of coastal rainforests in eastern Australia. The powerful rugs hyoscine and atropine are produced commercially from the leaves. HOTO COURTESY W. T. JONES

lank-buttresses and luxuriant trunk epiphytes are characteristic of the wet opical rainforests. The plank-buttresses are flat, vertical extensions of the roots. HOTO COURTESY S. AND K. BREEDEN

The Spiny Ant Plant (*Myrmecodia antoinii*) has a network of tunnels which harbour ants. It is common on trees in the woodlands of Cape York Peninsula. PHOTO COURTESY W. T. JONES

'Blackboys' or 'Grass-trees' (*Xanthorrhoea* sp.), Western Australia. These remarkable plants are restricted to the Australian continent. PHOTO COURTESY V. SERVENTY

Acronychia baueri, sometimes called 'scrub ash' is a smaller tree of the subtropical rain-forests of Queensland and northern N.S.W. The bark contains brilliant yellow alkaloids, one of which has anti-tumour activity. PHOTO COURTESY W. T. JONES

Laportea moroides, the notorious 'Gympie-Gympie' or 'Giant Nettle' has stinging hairs which cause intense and persistent pain when brushed against, usually along tracks in the tropical rainforest. The exact chemical nature of the stinging principle is still unknown. PHOTO COURTESY S. AND K. BREEDEN

The Pitcher Plant (*Nepenthes mirabilis*) is an elaborate insectivorou plant restricted to swampy and infertile soils of the tropics. PHOTO COURTESY W. T. JONES

An ecosystem is in some ways like an organism; it requires energy for maintenance and growth. Almost all ecosystems depend for their energy almost entirely on conversion of sunlight to carbohydrate by the process known as photosynthesis. This is augmented in most ecosystems by energy in the shape of living or dead organisms entering from nearby systems, but this component is usually tiny compared to that supplied by photosynthesis. Nevertheless, there are a few ecosystems which depend totally on organic material supplied from other systems. For example, the dung in bat caves supports a simple decomposer industry and is an ecosystem totally lacking a producer and a consumer industry.

Every ecosystem has certain inputs and outputs of energy and materials; what is gain to one ecosystem is loss to another. This is a factor which must be taken into account when determining the size of a reserve needed for perpetuating any given ecosystem.

The rate of capture of energy over a year by the producer industry will determine the size of the consumer and decomposer industries. Energy flows from the producer pool to the first consumer pool (herbivores). From here it flows to a pool of carnivores which eat herbivores and so a second consumer pool is established. Carnivores are generally preyed on by larger carnivores, so creating a third consumer pool. A similar chain of energy pools is found in the decomposer industry. It is this arrangement of pools which represents the structure of the ecosystem, and three types of ecosystem are shown in Fig. 3.

Notice that the producer biomass of the marine system is small, yet the energy flow is of the same order as the terrestrial system. This comes about because the consumer pressure is very high on the marine plankton, but small amounts of phytoplankton are capable of a high rate of photosynthesis; that is, a small biomass of these microscopic plants can capture the sun's energy at a high rate. Hence a large producer biomass is not an essential prerequisite to a high rate of energy capture, and one must be careful about judging the function of an ecosystem from a consideration of its structure.

A further important point emerging from a comparison of structure and function in grassland and woodland ecosystems is the size of the decomposer industries. This is especially striking in the case of the grassland system, where a huge amount of the producer industry falls into the decomposer industry. Presumably the decomposer industry increases when the consumer industry fails to exploit fully the potential of the producers. Looked at in this way, the decomposer industry is an alternative energy pathway acting as an escape valve for the consumer industry. It is not then simply a rapid transit route for nutrients from the organic to the inorganic phase, but a subsidiary system which allows the consumer industry to have a stable input despite its existence in a very unstable environment. Fluctuations in moisture and temperature affect the producer output enormously. If the input to the consumer industry is set low enough, fluctuations in producer output need not disturb the consumer output. All surplus to consumer input is variable input to the decomposer industry. Being largely micro-organismic the latter can respond almost instantaneously to input variation, and can survive over-exploitation and input scarcity by entering dormant or resting stages. This hypothesis lies between the balance and non-balance theories.

In natural grassland it seems that the input for the consumer industry has been set very low. In grassland managed for meat output, it should be possible to regulate the consumers (grazing animals) so that a greater amount of energy goes into the consumer pathway. Of course there is risk here, for moisture and temperature may become unfavourable for pasture growth, and the large number of consumers will overload the producers. Whereas the natural system tends to take a

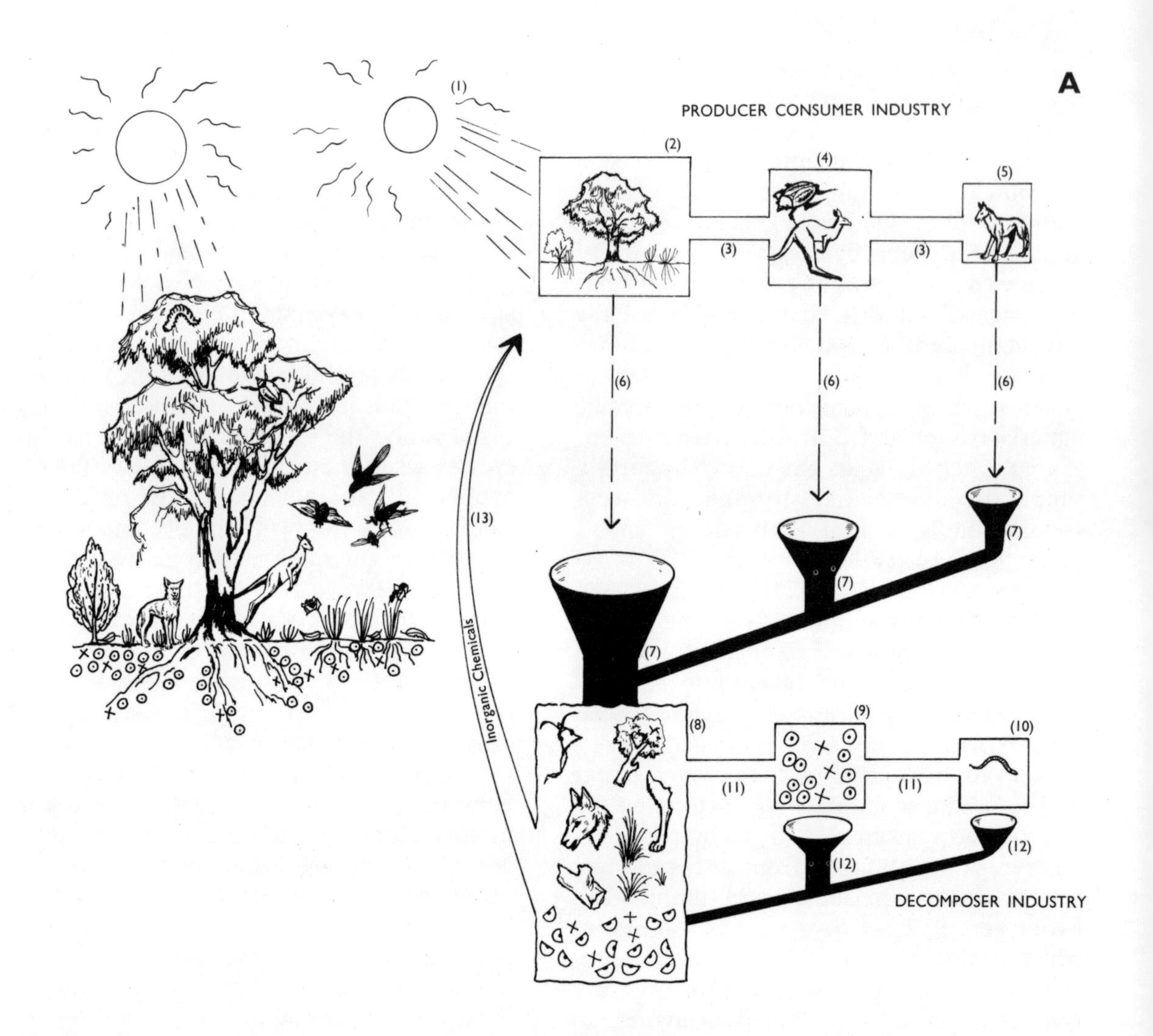

FIGURE 3: *A. The structure and function of a woodland ecosystem is illustrated here. On the left an intact woodland ecosystem is represented symbolically by the tree, shrub, and grass and other organisms. Grazer organisms are shown eating vegetation (caterpillar, chrysomelid beetle, bee, kangaroo), while carnivore 'grazers' (robber fly, bird, dingo) feed on other animals. Dead organisms continually fall to the floor of the woodland where they provide food for the vast decomposer industry, composed largely of micro-organisms (bacteria, fungi, protozoa), as well as worms, insect larvae, mites, larger scavenger organisms.*

On the right the ecosystem is shown symbolically divided into its main structural and functional features. A system of funnels and pipes symbolizes the collection of dead organisms into the pool of 'free organic matter' which supports the decomposer industry.

(1) The sun is the main source of energy.

(2) Producers only capture 1 to 2 per cent of this energy.

(3) Herbivores graze on the growing plants controlling to some degree the biomass of the producer pool and being themselves to some degree controlled by the size of the pool. This determines the rate

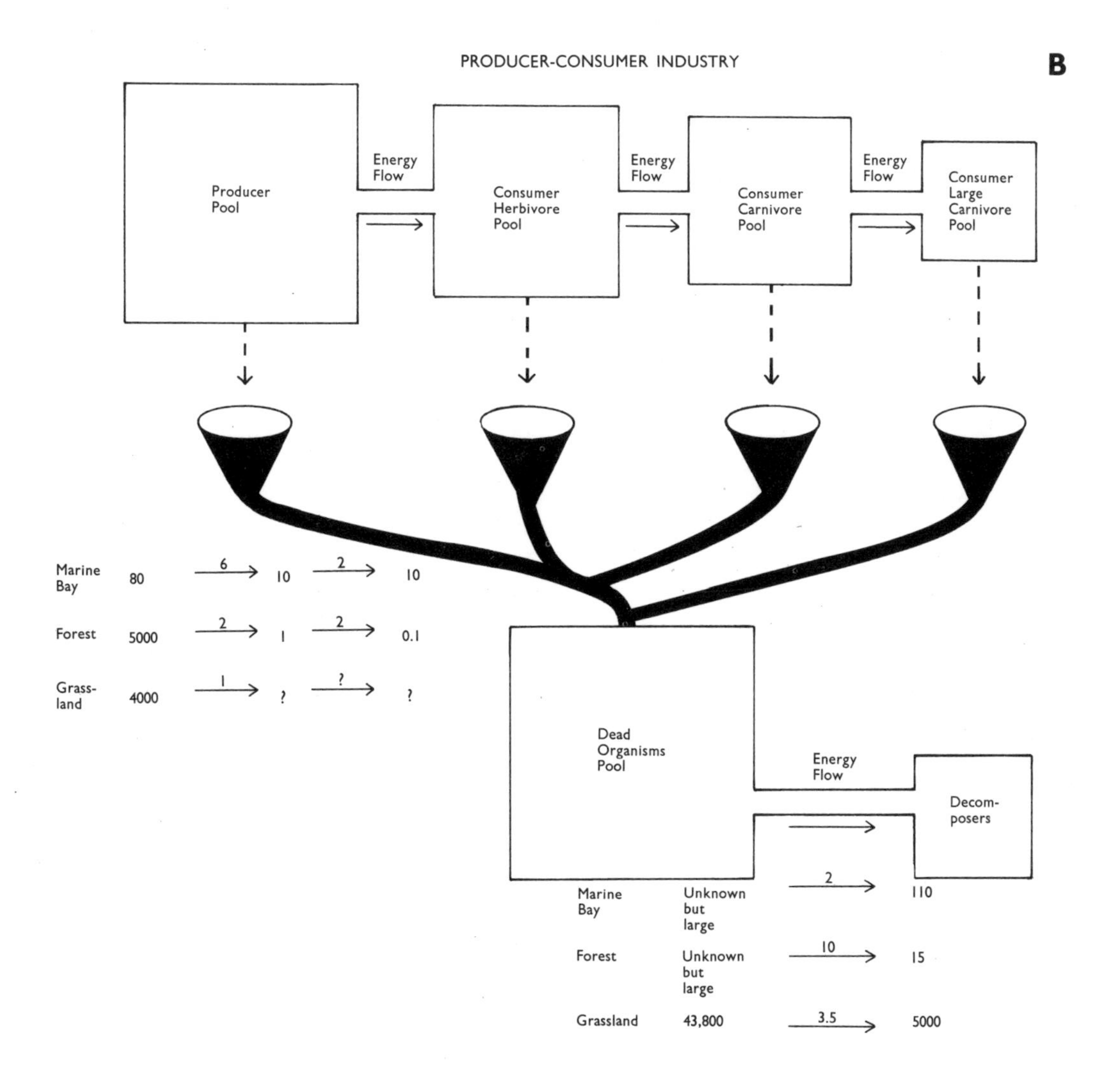

of flow of energy and nutrients to the pool of herbivores (4). Carnivores (5) graze on the herbivores producing a similar reciprocal relationship to that between (4) and (2). Dead organisms and parts of organisms fall (6) to the floor of the woodland (7), and form the litter layer there. This is the pool of dead organisms (8) which supports the primary decomposers (9) and the organisms that prey on decomposers (10), and which determine energetic and nutrient flow rate (11) in this system. These organisms also die (12) and are collected into the dead organism pool (8). The decomposer industry converts the dead organisms to inorganic chemicals which are then again available to the producers for their growth (13).

B. Comparative aspects of structure and function are illustrated here. A marine bay, a forest, and a grassland ecosystem are compared. Note the order of difference in the producer pools. A forest producer pool is over sixty times greater than a marine bay producer pool. However, the initial consumer flow rate of the marine bay is three times that of the forest. Note also the great size of the dead organism pool in grassland. If a grassland could be managed to function more like a marine bay there would be a far greater 'turn off' of animal protein (see text). The figures represent energetic units: pools in kcal/metre^2; flow rate in kcal/metre^2/day. Respiration rate has been omitted from both A and B figures.

long time to respond to this effect, man can reduce the demand of consumers for energy very rapidly (e.g. by movement of stock) and the risk of ecosystem breakdown is thus minimized. In some natural systems adapted to irregular fluctuations, behavioural and physiological patterns occur which have this effect. The Red Kangaroo changes its habitat, breeding behaviour and physiology under drought conditions. To what degree this improves the survival value of the pasture or brings about compensatory responses in the producers is unknown, but there can be no doubt of the advantages for the kangaroos. Sheep and cattle are not so well adapted to Australian ecosystems and must be regulated by man.

Organisms require not only a source of energy, but must also find in their environment all the chemical elements they need to build and maintain their cells and tissues. We can study the structure and function of ecosystems in relation to nutrient requirements just as we did for energy. Thus the producer, consumer and decomposer industries can be considered as pools of nutrients and these, together with the nutrient pools in the soil and air, represent the structure of an ecosystem. The rates of movement of nutrients between pools is an aspect of ecosystem function and this is governed by regulatory processes just as is energy flow. One important difference between energy and nutrients, however, is that whereas energy is gradually dissipated and lost to the system forever, individual nutrient elements may be used again and again.

To return to the question of regulation: this, whether it be by man or by evolved mechanisms, involves population changes, which of course affect biomass and thus structure. An example comes from the introduction of two organisms well-known to Australia: prickly pear and the moth *Cactoblastis*.

The introduction of prickly pear led to great changes in the producer industry of the ecosystems it entered. This no longer favoured the output man wished to have. The introduction of a new consumer, the moth *Cactoblastis*, led to a vast increase in the numbers of this moth and a vast decrease in the numbers of prickly pear. The total producer biomass may also have been reduced. When *Cactoblastis* numbers fell, there was only a minor increase in prickly pear; we assume that the compensatory increase in the moth was rapid and prickly pear never became abundant again. The interaction of the dependent factors resulted in permanently low numbers of both the plant and the moth. This has added two organisms to the ecosystems, and restores their structure to one favourable for meat and wool output.

The understanding of producer-consumer regulation, whether it be of natural or agricultural systems, requires detailed studies of the behavioural and physiological adaptations of the organisms involved. These studies must be undertaken in the perspective of the system as a whole.

Another important point arising out of the foregoing example and concerning regulation is the significance of species composition. Earlier it was pointed out that one independent factor is the availability of organisms for the construction of ecosystems. African dogs, gazelles and veld do not occur in Australia; dingoes, kangaroos and mulga woodland do not occur in Africa. Function and, to some degree, structure are determined by the availability of organisms. All ecosystems are periodically challenged by new species, as illustrated by the example of prickly pear. Some of these challenges are successful and these events are likely to shift the 'equilibria' and affect the sizes of the various energy pools. They also may cause extinction of some species and reduce the fitness of other organisms, and in this way stimulate adaptive change.

Adaptive change in one organism of course occasions genetic change in other organisms. Compensatory genetic changes will tend to occur. This was well demonstrated with the myxomatosis-rabbit system. The virus became less virulent thereby improving its chance of passing to a healthy rabbit, and the rabbit became more resistant. Each organism was adapting to the other and the probability of survival of the system improved. This is an example of co-evolution. Thus organisms tend to adapt one to the other, and thereby to regulate their systems. If this were universally true we could say that the theory of balance as a mechanism of regulation of ecosystems was also universally true. The evidence at present seems to suggest that balance does occur to some degree in the consumer industry; it may be almost non-existent in the producer industry. Species composition affects regulation and therefore influences the structure and function of ecosystems and this can occur whether there is balance or not.

Origin of Australian Ecosystems

The origin of ecosystems involves the interplay of independent and dependent factors. To obtain some idea of how present-day Australian ecosystems evolved we need to know something of the geological, climatic and biological history of the continent during the Cainozoic. This era of about sixty million years is divided into two periods, the Tertiary and the Quaternary. The Quaternary of about one million years is itself divided into two important epochs: the great ice age (Pleistocene) and the Recent or Holocene of only about 10,000 years. Thus the Quaternary takes up only about two per cent of the time-span of the Cainozoic.

At the beginning of the Tertiary, many of the huge lakes and seas of the earlier era had vanished, and the land surface was spread out flat and featureless. Most of the plants and animals were very different from those seen today. During this period rapid evolutionary changes were taking place. Flowering plants, insects, birds and mammals were becoming more numerous in species and more effective in ecosystems; many forms were becoming extinct, while others were adapting rapidly. Changes in ecosystems must have been very great. As we approach the end of the Tertiary we find that the organisms bear a considerable resemblance to those of today. However, the rivers, the warm humid climate, and the extensive rainforests of this time would have made most of the landscape very different from the present. Volcanic activity occurred about the end of the Tertiary on the east side of the Australian continent. This laid down basaltic parent material favourable for the development of soils which support ecosystems of high biomass, rapid energy flux, and fast cycling of nutrients, as in tropical rainforests. Later the Great Dividing Range was formed. This huge topographic change was followed by the Pleistocene, a sequence of four intensely cold intervals which are also known as the ice ages. These events commenced about one million years ago at the time when ape-men in Africa were becoming men. Only 10,000 years ago did the last ice age terminate. Since that time there has been at least one intensely arid period alleviated by long spells of more humid conditions.

These vast changes in independent factors led to equally great changes in ecosystems: the geographical distribution of rainforest, forest, woodland, shrubland, alpine and desert complexes changed enormously. Temporally continuous ecosystems went through great rearrangements in species composition, so that dependent factors altered and their regulatory processes changed. Some species readapted to the new conditions while some became extinct. Many species were divided into a number of isolates which in time became genetically unique so that these new groups could not interbreed; thus they became new species. Reduction in sea-level favoured migration and thereby allowed new forms to challenge existing ecosystems.

Fully as effective as these great changes in independent factors must have been the spread, sub-speciation, and biological and cultural adaptation of man. Ape-man gave way to man between 1.5 and 0.5 million years ago. From isolation in Africa this animal spread to Europe and Asia and by 300,000 years ago he had fully colonized these continents. However, his arrival in the Americas and Australia appears to have been much later, sometime before 25,000 years ago. It is difficult to evaluate the magnitude of the impact of these migrations and successful colonizations. It is unlikely that man ever arrived without some hangers-on, and these attendant organisms would also have some influence on the ecosystems to which they were introduced. But it is man who is likely to create the greatest amount of disturbance. In fact, one important theory to account for man's very fast evolution involves the concept of massive disturbance of ecosystems. In this theory it is postulated that tool-using and other technological advances by man led to such marked changes in the ecosystems he occupied that man's adaptation changed, and these new adaptations led to further ecosystem changes, thus hastening evolutionary modification. Such a theory implies that almost all terrestrial ecosystems have been in a state of dis-equilibrium and rapid evolutionary change throughout the Recent period.

If these speculations are correct, and they are fully as tenable as any others, we should be wary of assertions about the balance of nature, a concept frequently appealed to by conservationists.

It should be realized that evolutionary change can be rapid. Ape-man became man in about 500,000 years. In a space of about fifty years or less, changes in coat colour in some rabbit populations were evident in parts of Tasmania. But despite the rapidity of some evolutionary change, some forms have shown very little, if any, modification over periods of up to 500 million years. In this way some contemporary ecosystems may be considered as relics of flourishing ecosystems of earlier times.

The Mechanisms of Change in Organisms and Ecosystems

We have so far discussed in broad terms the way in which major changes in independent factors have changed organisms and ecosystems and have thus affected dependent factors and regulation. We must now turn to a closer examination of the mechanism of change in organisms under the topics of extinction, migration, speciation and adaptation, always keeping in mind the implications of these changes for the ecosystem as a whole.

It seems likely that the two most important causes of extinction are climatic change and habitat change by successful migrants. Of the latter the most potent is man. The giant marsupials which became extinct in the late Pleistocene or Recent in Australia may have been unable to adapt to a climate rapidly changing towards aridity. This is the more likely because, being large animals, they were probably few in number, low in genetic variability and slow-breeding: therefore they would be unlikely to adapt at a sufficient rate. On the other hand, man may have been responsible. He appears to have brought big changes of habitat to Australia when he arrived more than 25,000 years ago. He introduced the dingo, a relative of the domestic dog, to the mainland but not to Tasmania, and this seems to be associated with the extinction of the marsupial wolf on the mainland and with its persistence in Tasmania.

Whatever the effect of early man in Australia, far greater changes in habitat have occurred with colonization by white man. By overgrazing the producers of the semi-arid ecosystems, he changed their structure by drastically reducing producer biomass and causing large changes in species composition. This led to reduced productivity the reasons for which were not clearly appreciated by management at the time. In a natural system this may have led to compensatory effects reducing the size of the consumer industry. In the artificial, man-dominated ecosystems, however, stocking rates continued to be high thus forestalling any real possibility of compensatory change. In most cases the trend was not recognized until it was aggravated by drought when, because economic factors restricted or prohibited the movement of stock, regulation was almost totally removed from man's control. The outcome has been the total loss or extinction of some species of animals and plants. The degree of extinction of micro-organisms is almost completely unknown. This example is however only one quite minor example of the enormous changes brought about by white man since 1788.

A short discussion on the implications of extinction is relevant here. To what degree extinction is bad we cannot say, but two things are certain. We cannot anticipate at this moment what Australia's or the world's needs are for organisms. Many forms which are not economically important today may be necessary tomorrow. Furthermore we may require more diversity in agricultural and forest ecosystems if they are to be managed for optimal productivity in the long term. The other certainty is that we cannot preserve every species. There are far more species extinct than there are species living today. Any effort to prevent all extinction is futile, and it may well inhibit further speciation. The obvious strategy to adopt is to make sure that we preserve examples of contemporary evolving ecosystems. To be viable these will need to be large areas. Not only will they provide man with a reasonable chance of retaining sufficient organism diversity for the future, but they will provide us with complete natural ecosystems as research material. Perhaps even more importantly they will preserve places of wild grandeur and great cultural importance.

The Australian continent has an array of distinctive indigenous species of plants and animals, yet many species have close relatives on another continent. For example, it is often found that Australia has one or a few forms of a group that is numerous in species and related genera in the Orient. This suggests that these Australian species have come from the Orient, rather than the converse. If we consider the family of frogs Ranidae, we find that Africa and the Orient have twenty-nine genera, while New Guinea has nine genera and Australia one genus. Moreover this genus exists only in the northern part of Cape York Peninsula. New Guinea has ten genera of twenty-three species of Brush-tongue Parrots while Australia has four genera of six species; on the other hand, New Guinea has only three species of *Eucalyptus* while Australia has over 500 species. We infer from these facts that Australian Brush-tongue Parrots come from New Guinea, while New Guinea eucalypts come from Australia. But this inference is not the only possible one: New Guinea and Australia may have once had equal numbers of species of Brush-tongue Parrots and eucalypts. Differential climatic changes might have encouraged speciation of 'Brush-tongues' in New Guinea and eucalypts in Australia, and a converse form of extinction may have reduced 'Brush-tongues' in Australia and eucalypts in New Guinea. Decisions between rival hypotheses are sometimes possible from the fossil record, and sometimes the process of migration and colonization can be more closely followed.

Current ideas of how new species are produced may be illustrated by following through four cycles in Australian Cainozoic history. One warning needs to be given: the course of events to be described is inferential and is based on all too few facts — as is much of evolutionary biology which seeks on limited evidence to understand events over long time intervals. Facts are slowly gleaned from the biology of contemporary organisms and from the temporal, spatial and evolutionary evidence of fossil organisms. Such findings are impossible if contemporary and fossil ecosystems are destroyed.

A beginning can be made by turning to Tertiary Australia very largely covered by nearly continuous rainforest. During the ice ages, the southern highlands were covered by ice and snow. The southern lowlands probably had extensive grassland, and to the north there would have been, most likely, successive bands of shrubland, woodland, forest, and rainforest. Most opinion seems to incline to the view that moisture was adequate throughout the land except where temperatures were continuously at freezing level or below. Under this regime there would be little opportunity for isolation, and speciation for the most part would be reduced.

By contrast the interglacial periods would encourage speciation. At these times it is thought that rainfall was low and evaporation was high. These conditions would put a stress on all those organisms and ecosystems adapted to the cold, wet conditions of the glacial period. Such organisms and ecosystems would have three courses open to them: extinction, adaptation to the new conditions, or migration up mountains in order to stay in cold, wet conditions. Here they would be isolated on discontinuous ranges. Hence the interglacials would be expected to encourage speciation of forms adapted to cold, wet conditions. With three interglacials and the great period of aridity of about 5,000 years ago, species present at the commencement of the first interglacial could multiply rapidly in species four times. If there were no subsequent extinction, we should expect many closely related species of organisms on each cold, wet isolated region in present-day Australia. It is true there are a few organisms which are adapted in this way and are so isolated; examples are some eucalypts, some frogs of the genus *Kyrannus*, some parrots (*Platycercus*), some insects (Peloridiidae — see Marks, this volume), Dobson flies (Archichauliodes: Corydalidae). However, it cannot be counted a rich and impressive fauna and flora. This may be the result of the sparsity and low elevation of Australian alpine complexes, or it may be that the arid periods were so severe that no refuges remained for the cold/wet-adapted forms.

When it comes to the effects of the ice ages on the ecosystems and organisms adapted to semi-arid environments, we are on surer ground. A number of studies support the view that certain peripheral parts of Australia provide isolated refuges for warm/wet-adapted forms in times of aridity. Sub-species and incipient new species occur there even today (Fig. 4).

How would this speciation system work? In extremely arid times, areas on the periphery of the continent (which were topographically favourable to increased rainfall) would support only forms adapted to semi-arid conditions, and those adapted to cold and wet or warm and wet places would either become extinct or themselves adapt to semi-arid conditions. When the continent became less arid, the semi-arid adapted forms of the isolated refuges would be able to increase their range and ultimately remeet. Competition, sharing, and mutual adaptation would occur depending on circumstances and chance. Restoration of rainforest ecosystems would depend on colonization of suitable areas from contracted patches remaining in Australia, or from New Guinea, or an adaptation to warm, wet conditions or cold, wet conditions by the semi-arid-adapted forms. This seems to be the phase in which we find ourselves today. When it is realized that there are perhaps 600 species of *Acacia*, very many in the semi-arid and arid zones and more birds and mammals in semi-arid ecosystems than in rainforest ones, the effectiveness of these peripheral isolates or refuges seems to be sustained. Extinction seems to be comparatively rare for semi-arid adapted forms but high for those adapted to cold and wet, or warm and wet environments.

Conclusion

This then is one theory to account for the diversity of ecosystems and organisms in the semi-arid area of Australia. With a few patches of rainforest, forest, woodland, shrubland, grassland, alpine and desert complex not greatly changed by primary and secondary industry nor overgrown with tourists, it is still possible to continue research to investigate this idea. However, if man continues in his seemingly unquenchable thirst for development of remote areas, all the grand wild places will disappear and the surface of the earth will be densely covered by a few common organisms, a great number of them men. Then there will not be the slightest possibility of enjoying and understanding natural ecosystems, nor of comparing natural and automatically regulated ones with those partly or wholly controlled by man.

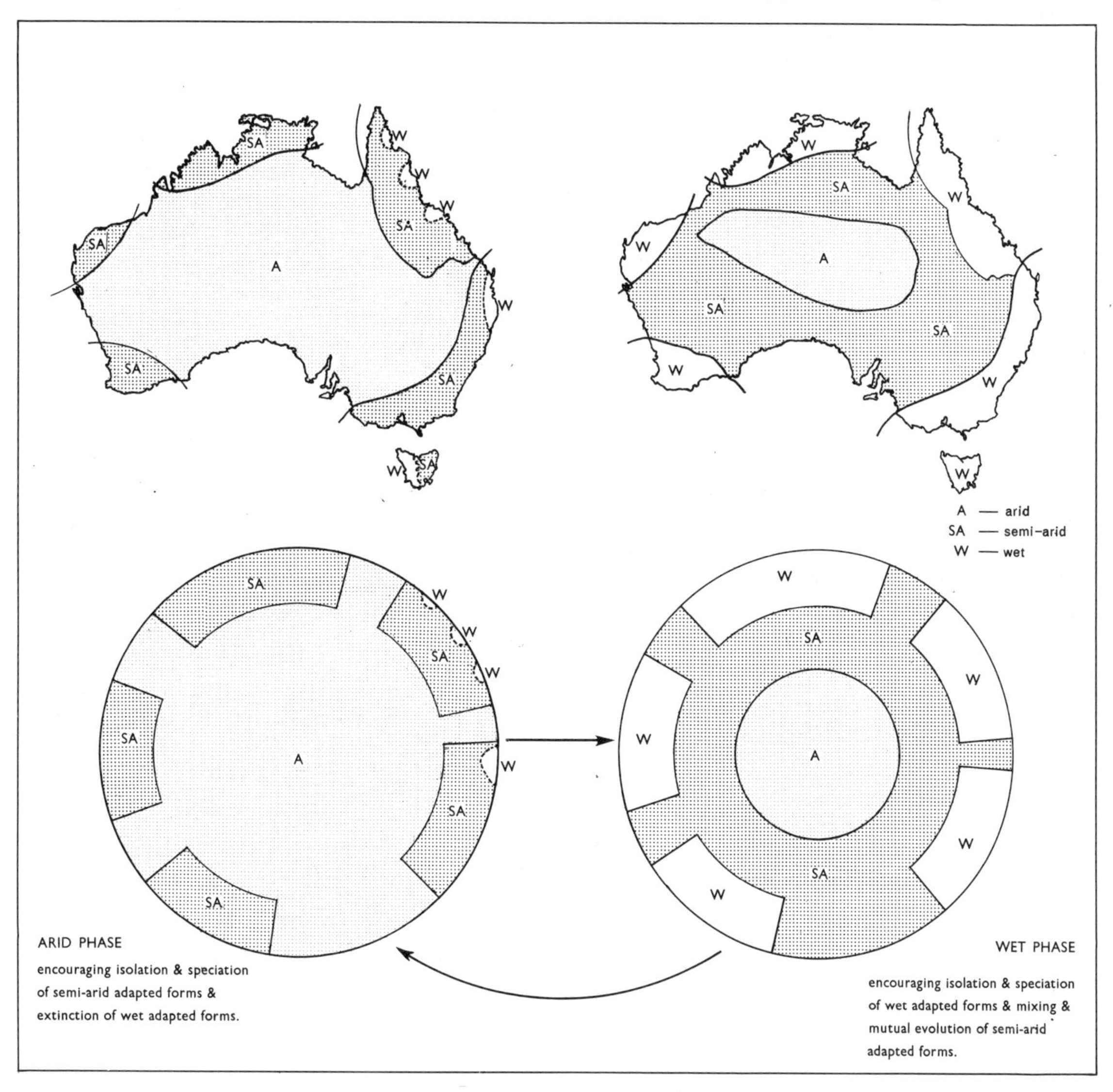

FIGURE 4: *A mechanism of speciation which would account for the richness of species in the semi-arid area. In arid phases a great deal of extinction of rainforest forms would occur but a few would survive in tiny pockets as shown. Very small isolates do not favour speciation. The few survivors in these small isolates plus slow recolonization from New Guinea would account for the low level of diversity of the Australian rainforest. On the other hand, the large semi-arid isolates would favour speciation of semi-arid forms and would account for the richness of the semi-arid ecosystems.*

The Australian Flora

J. G. Tracey
L. J. Webb
W. T. Williams

It has recently been estimated that the Australian flora contains more than fifteen thousand different species of vascular plants alone. No complete list of these exists anywhere; indeed, every botanist is aware that there are, particularly in the forests of the north-east, many species which have never been described and which as yet bear no names. The extinction of any species of living organism is a tragedy to biologists, but the loss of a species from Australia may represent a tragedy which transcends the bounds of the continent. It is true that there is no 'Wallace's line' to separate the plants of Australia from their neighbours as sharply as the animals are separated; but it is also true that the age-long isolation of the continent has allowed evolution to proceed along specialized paths, so that an abnormally high proportion of our plant species are endemic. This alone would justify the most rigorous conservation of our flora, but it is by no means the only feature of interest or importance. The study of the plant-cover of a continent can be approached in two ways: by the physiognomy of the vegetation as a whole, or by the characteristics of the individual species of which it is composed. Nobody, be he professional botanist or enthusiastic naturalist, can fully appreciate the remarkable features of Australian vegetation until he has had the opportunity of seeing it through the eyes of a botanist from the north temperate regions. It must be remembered that even now the great majority of the world's botanists have been trained in the north temperate countries, and everywhere in the world botanical courses still show traces of that temperate environment in which the study of plants grew into the science of botany as we know it today. Such a visitor views the scene with amazement: there are mild temperate regions with no summer-green deciduous forests; cold regions not dominated by conifers; arid zones without succulents. Instead, everywhere, there are evergreen forests superbly adapted to a land of erratic and often inadequate rainfall and to soils of low fertility.

The impact of individual plants is no less great. It has always been true that plants, like prophets, are not without honour save in their own country; and every horticulturally-minded nation has tended to cultivate exotics rather than native plants. Compared with the flora of Brazil, the Australian flora is relatively deficient in showy flowering trees and shrubs — though it is certain that very few of those we do possess have been horticulturally exploited to the extent they deserve — so that it is perhaps not surprising that when a town decides to subscribe to the charming custom of adopting a floral emblem, it usually adopts an alien. So Glen Innes has the rose, Goulburn the lilac, Grafton *Jacaranda*, and Brisbane *Poinsettia*. Gums and wattles are evidently too commonplace, too easy, to merit attention; only Tasmania has had the courage to adopt, as its state floral emblem, the majestic Blue Gum (*Eucalyptus globulus*) rather than a more spectacular flower. To appreciate gums and wattles at their true worth, an Australian must needs spend some time in the south of England and see the years of unremitting effort that gardeners expend in trying to establish eucalyptus or acacia — *any* eucalyptus or *any* acacia —

almost invariably without success. He should note, too, the popularity of wattle flowers, imported to Britain from the south of France, and appearing briefly and expensively in florists' shops. But the greatest impact on our visitors is reserved for those relics of bygone geological ages which, because of our isolation and — until recently — freedom from large-scale human interference, have survived to an unusual extent in this country. Australians are still surprised by the excitement of a visitor when he first sees, on a casually-arranged trip to the south-eastern coast, a tree fern growing — actually growing — negligently by the roadside, or a eucalypt forest with an understorey of *Macrozamia*, which the visitor has probably studied in his youth from a few jealously-guarded fragments preserved in methylated spirit.

This casualness of discovery gives us the key to what is, to the visitor, the single most important feature of the Australian flora: its accessibility. There are places in the world where the Pitcher Plants are more luxuriant, the mangroves more extensive, the palms more numerous, or where the trees have larger plank-buttresses; but there is nowhere else in the world where so wide a variety of life-forms can be seen without privation, without months of preparation, without passports and without fear of attack by man or disease. There is a useful parallel in geology. Every geologist trained in Australia envies his English counterpart, who in a day's drive can visit virtually every major geological formation from the Pre-Cambrian to the Quarternary; in Australia it is all too easy to see nothing but the Ordovician or Silurian. Similarly, every English student of botany must envy his Australian counterpart, who can so easily see living specimens of plants which are little more than legends to the European. This envy is less commonly expressed, because English students learn little or nothing of Australian vegetation; we may hope that this deficiency will one day be rectified, but must do all in our power to ensure, when that day comes, that the Australian vegetation is still there to be studied in its magnificent variety.

The purpose of this chapter, then, is to provide signposts: signposts to those aspects of our flora of outstanding botanical interest, whose accessibility could make a visit to Australia the ambition of every overseas botanist, but whose familiarity within our own country is such that we may be tempted to regard them as unimportant or even expendable. We shall therefore concentrate on the two aspects we have already needed to refer to briefly — the specialized life-forms and the relict 'living fossils'; but we shall also give brief consideration to those species which, by being of direct economic value to man, have in a sense evaded the conservation problem entirely.

Special Life-Forms

Plants have growth-forms or life-forms which, in any one locality, we take for granted, but which characterize definite conditions of the physical environment where they occur naturally. For example, large membranous leaves with drip-tips (long drawn-out points) are typical of the wet tropics, and small toothed leaves of the cool temperate region. In dry inland areas, the leaves of many unrelated families converge to the narrow, sometimes curved shape typical of eucalypts. Palms characterize the tropics, and ferns the temperate zones; the succulents, whose striking life-form characterizes so many of the world's warm deserts are absent from Australia. The greatest variety of life-forms is, however, undoubtedly to be found in the tropical rainforest, whose structure — to quote an early explorer — is like 'forest piled on forest'. Robust lianes ('monkey ropes'), epiphytes forming aerial gardens in the tree crowns, splendid palms and saw-toothed pandans, aroids like elephant's ears, plank-buttresses, strangling figs and a bewildering variety of leaf shapes and lichen-crusts on bark all contribute to an impression of powerful and exuberant nature. Early travellers waxed rhetorical over their first contact with the tropical rainforest and the modern visitor is no less impressed by its awesome magnificence.

Tropical and subtropical rainforests in Australia are restricted to the fertile well-drained soils along the wet north-eastern coast. Although they have mostly been cleared for dairying and agriculture, there are some good samples preserved in mountainous regions in national parks. Unlike eucalypt forests, rainforests have many tree species — in some places over a hundred different species to an acre. The lower part of the trunk of some tree species in the most luxuriant types have flat flanges or plank-like extensions which may extend ten feet or more above the ground. These so-called plank-buttresses are characteristic of certain species, e.g., Crow's-foot Elm or Booyong (*Argyrodendron*), Yellow Carabeen (*Sloanea*), Quandong (*Elaeocarpus*), Rose Marara (*Pseudoweinmannia*), Spurwood (*Dysoxylum*), and some of the Figs (*Ficus*) and Water Gums (*Eugenia*).

Species with plank-buttresses do not have deep tap-roots, and it was originally thought that the buttresses provided support, especially during high winds. It is now generally recognized that plank-buttresses are hereditary features, and like the breathing-roots ('pegs' and 'knees') of mangroves, improve the aeration of the tree roots. Plank-buttresses characterize warmer and wetter climates, and sometimes soils with impeded drainage, and are absent from temperate rainforests or montane forests in the tropics, as well as from the 'vine scrubs' of the dry interior.

Epiphytes are plants growing attached to other plants — on the trunks and branches of trees, and even on the surface of leaves. They belong to a variety of families, but in the Australian tropical rainforests are usually ferns, orchids, aroids and pandans, as well as mosses, lichens and liverworts. They are adapted to a life with scanty soil, excessive drainage, but often high humidity and good illumination. The larger species assume a variety of shapes, such as brackets, nests and tanks, e.g., Bird's Nest Fern (*Asplenium nidus*), Staghorn and Elkhorn (*Platycerium* spp.), and accumulate large quantities of humus. Different epiphyte associations are related to differences in the physical and chemical nature of the bark, and occupy limited positions vertically within the forest. Epiphytes have special problems of seed dispersal and establishment, and must rely on wind-borne spores or seeds, or mechanisms to ensure dispersal by birds, e.g., sticky fruits. Families such as the legumes which tend to have heavy fruits do not contain epiphytic species.

Strangling Figs begin their life as epiphytes and by the downward growth of their roots eventually enclose the host tree in a 'living coffin', as Lane-Poole called it. The bizarre shape of the interwoven trunk, often with a chimney formed where the original tree has rotted away, always attracts camera enthusiasts e.g. the 'Curtain Fig' near Lake Barrine on the Atherton Tableland, north Queensland. According to P. W. Richards, the stranglers are one of the most remarkable ecological groups in the tropical rainforest, and their life-form has no counterpart in temperate forests.

There are, however, many characteristic growth-forms outside the rainforests. Bottle Trees (*Brachychiton* spp.) favour heavy, often calcareous clays, generally in association with vine scrubs. Their swollen trunks, an adaptation for water storage, assume a weird variety of shapes, ranging from squat chianti to tapering hock bottles. Another type, and more grotesque, is the Baobab (*Adansonia gregorii*) of north-western Australia. In Africa, a related species is called 'vegetable elephant', and was thought by some natives to be the only tree which grows upside down. The Bottle Tree life-form is characteristic of extreme seasonal drought conditions in the tropics. As for the opposite extreme — the saline muds of tropical and subtropical estuaries — we have already needed to mention the mangroves. All have developed special structures for aerating their mud-encased root-systems, often by means of 'breathing-roots' which grow vertically upwards into the air. These, too, are remarkably accessible; the best known, *Avicennia*, is within easy reach of the towns of our eastern seaboard. Further afield it is possible to see *Carapa*, the bizarre anatomy of whose breathing-roots has fascinated botanists for half a century. Nor should we forget *Rhizophora*, whose seeds germinate immediately while still on the tree, later to fall, not as seeds, but as seedlings up to a foot long, ready to establish themselves in the mud in their turn.

Less conspicuous, but representing another curious adaptation, are the insectivorous plants; a temperate zone visitor will already be familiar with the small Sundews (*Drosera* spp.), though he will be excited by the Australian *Byblis*. All such plants are found on strongly acid soils with low nitrogen content, and belong to several families. In Australia the most elaborate is the Pitcher Plant *Nepenthes*, restricted to swampy areas of Cape York Peninsula north of Cooktown. The pitchers, about the size of a small tea-cup at the end of strap-shaped leaves, are provided with glands which secrete a fluid capable of digesting animal protein; around the rim of the pitcher is, first, a nectar-secreting zone which attracts insects; but after this is a zone covered with downward-pointing scales of wax, and any small insect which ventures on to this treacherous zone slides helplessly into the pitcher, first to be drowned in the water which collects there, and then to be slowly digested. In this way the plant obtains, or at least supplements the supply of nitrogen that it needs. Another famous Pitcher Plant is *Cephalotus follicularis*, confined to the margins of swamps in the Albany area of Western Australia. It develops a strong system of underground stems from which arise rosettes of leaves — the inner leaves flat and fleshy, the outer ones forming pitchers each surmounted by a small leaf which looks like a lid, though it is not, in fact, moveable.

Other plants are less inhospitable where insects are concerned. Two members of the Rubiaceae are known as 'ant plants'; these are *Myrmecodia* and *Hydnophytum*, whose tuber-like stems develop a network of tunnels which become the home of colonies of small brown ants. These extraordinary plants are sun epiphytes in the rainforest of the Malayan dry tropics, and in Cape York Peninsula are a feature of the tea-tree forests and the margins of mangrove woodlands. *Hydnophytum* has a spineless swollen stem with smooth brittle branches; *Myrmecodia* has a squat tuber covered with spines. The honeycomb-like cavities are formed even in the absence of ants. The aqueous tissue in the tubers suggests that they function as water-storage organs, another adaptation to drought in the monsoon region where little or no rain falls for eight months of the year. It is also possible that the plants absorb nutrients from the ants' faeces: the ants in return live in an air-conditioned and weatherproof aerial house, but it seems fanciful to suggest that the ants have a protective function e.g. against insects harmful to the plant.

Dischidia, which belongs to the Wax Flower family, is another curious epiphyte of north Queensland. *D. nummularia*, often called 'button orchid', has leaves resembling round, flat buttons linked like a string of beads, and *D. rafflesiana* has leaves which form fleshy bladders which are like pitchers with an incurved margin. Adventitious roots from the stem grow into the pitchers, which harbour ants and fill with water during the rainy season. Debris is also collected by the nesting ants. Truly an admirable example of soil and water conservation!

Flowers, too, have features of interest over and above those incidental qualities of beauty of colour or form for which they are usually prized. The most striking example is the adaptation of flowers to ensure pollination by insects, birds, bats, etc. The shape, smell, colour and nectar of flowers attract insects, and vary with the evolutionary status of the plant. The sequence of pollinating agents from Cretaceous times, according to E. J. H. Corner, was birds, insects, wind and water. Clumsy and rather simple-minded beetles pollinate primitive large flowers such as those of magnolia and custard-apple and small open flowers like roses and poppies. The specialization of insect pollinators then led to small, numerous nectar cups, or to few large showy flowers. The former culminated in the daisies and umbellifers. And, as Corner puts it, the large symmetrical flowers of lilies led to the precise flowers of orchids. Thus the structure of flowers reflects the different behaviour of insects — bees which clutch and crawl, butterflies and moths which pause and flutter. The interrelation of length of corolla tube and insect tongue is one example. On the other hand, bird-pollinated flowers such as Coral Tree (*Erythrina*) and other tropical leguminous trees, *Bombax* of the monsoon forests, and wild bananas, are tough, elastic, scentless, with much watery nectar and with the delicate ovary often protected in the inferior position. The favourite colours of flowers for birds is said to be, in descending order, red, pink, orange, blue, yellow, white, green and maroon. Bat-pollinated flowers, such as the Baobab, are also large, tough and watery, with lurid yellow and brown colours.

No discussion of the flowers of Australian plants would be complete without some note concerning the remarkable species of *Xanthorrhoea*, the so-called 'black boys' or 'grass trees', which are entirely restricted to Australia. This group has been difficult to classify; it is related to the Liliaceae, but has been given a family of its own. The inflorescence, like a blackfellow's spear, has millions of flowers, and according to A. J. Eames is rivalled in this respect only by the palm *Corypha*, a species of which also occurs in far north Queensland.

Finally, the common casuarinas or she-oaks should be mentioned. These trees, which superficially resemble pine trees, actually have reduced scale-like leaves and green branchlets with photosynthesize. The *Casuarina* genus has caused great argument among botanists — some consider it to be highly specialized, others consider it to be so primitive that it should be excluded from the flowering plants. Although the genus consists of about thirty species of trees and shrubs mainly of drier habitats in Australia, it has been little studied, and little is known, for example, about the anatomy of the flower. A. J. Eames considers *Casuarina* to be a highly specialized flowering plant, whose simplicity is that of reduction, not of primitiveness. It is the old story; we are often most ignorant about our most common plants. She-oak, Bull Oak, Belah and other casuarinas are examples of trees we take for granted as part of the Australian bush, but which are of profound scientific interest.

There is no space to describe the many other curious life-forms of Australian plants — the 'vegetable sheep' of the Tasmanian Alps, the saltbushes of the interior, the Horsehair Fungus (*Marasmius equinus*), sand-spiders and roly-polies, the world's largest moss (*Dawsonia*), the rare parasitic flowering plant *Balanophora fungosa* which attacks the roots of certain rainforest trees in north Queensland and looks like a puff-ball fungus, and many arresting palms and tree ferns — the list would be virtually endless.

Primitive Plants and Living Fossils

The front cover of the classical textbook, *Morphology of the Angiosperms* by A. J. Eames, features the primitive flower of *Eupomatia bennettiana*, an understorey shrub of the wet subtropical rainforests of eastern Australia. According to Eames, although the Cretaceous flora of Australia is not different in its basic families from floras of other continents, the long isolation of Australia led to the evolution and survival of a great variety of unique types. Nearly ninety per cent of species and thirty per cent of genera of the plants are endemic, i.e. found only in Australia. The major Australian families (e.g. Leguminosae, Myrtaceae, Proteaceae, Goodeniaceae, Rutaceae, Dilleniaceae, Labiatae) possess the most primitive representatives of these groups in the world. The rainforests of north-eastern Australia are famous among botanical authorities because they harbour primitive families of flowering plants such as Annonaceae, Winteraceae, Himantandraeae, Eupomatiaceae and Austrobaileyaceae. Thus *Austrobaileya scandens*, the only member of the family, is a woody vine confined to a few localities in north Queensland. Where it occurs it is common enough, but it was not described until 1929, and the first collection of fruits to be lodged in an herbarium was made only in 1962 (which is another illustration of our ignorance of the local flora). *Austrobaileya* occupies an isolated and ancient position among the angiosperms, and some features of its wood anatomy belong to the gymnosperms. It is being actively studied today in the U.S.A. and U.S.S.R.

Older than all these are the gymnosperms, the group of flowering plants which includes the conifers. Here again, the interest to the northern visitor is that he exchanges his familiar set of 'modern' conifers — the species of *Pinus*, *Larix*, *Cedrus* and the like which are common, and commonly grown, in the northern hemisphere — for a more primitive set comprising, among others, our own *Araucaria*, *Agathis*, *Podocarpus* and *Callitris*. The goal of the botanist interested in this group, though, is Tasmania, the only habitat in the world for the genera *Arthrotaxis* and *Microcachrys*, and the home of several other conifers of very restricted distribution.

Oldest of the surviving gymnosperms, however, are the cycads.

There are nine genera and about seventy-five species of cycads throughout the world and four of the genera occur in Australia: *Cycas*, *Macrozamia*, *Lepidozamia* and *Bowenia*. They are primitive gymnosperms, survivors of a group of plants which dominated the flora of the earth about 200 million years ago, and are an evolutionary link between the flowering plants and the ferns. *Cycas media*, distinguished from *Macrozamia* by the possession of midrib and no lateral nerves in the pinnae, is the most widespread, growing in coastal regions from New South Wales through Queensland to the Kimberley region of Western Australia. Species of *Macrozamia* are found in the subtropical rainforests and the dry vine thickets; *M. macdonnellii* survives as a relict in the Macdonnell Ranges of central Australia *Lepidozamia hopei* reaches a height of sixty feet in the lowland rainforests of north Queensland and is the world's tallest cycad. *Bowenia* species are small plants only a few feet high, with bipinnate leaves which arise from large underground tubers. *B. serrata*, the Byfield fern, is the best known and was used from early times for interior decoration, especially in butchers' shops. Today its plastic replica, which faithfully reproduces the serrated edges of the symmetrical shiny leaflets is a common sight. This species is found in sandy soils at Byfield near Rockhampton, and as a small outlier in a dry rainforest on granite on the Atherton Tableland. *B. spectabilis*, with glossy entire leaflets, is a common understorey species in north Queensland rainforests.

But before there were cycads on the earth there were ferns; and the profusion of ferns in the Australian forests — tree ferns, filmy-ferns, and the spectacular epiphytes — shows that they have, on the whole, adapted themselves to recent conditions more successfully. Two, however, deserve special mention: *Marattia fraxinea* and *Angiopteris evecta*. These ferns have a short 'trunk' but with individual fronds up to twelve feet long and five to six feet wide, with glossy green pinnae;

they are a conspicuous feature of the streams in the tropical rainforests of north Queensland, and *Angiopteris* survives in sheltered gullies as far south as Fraser Island.

Older still are the lycopods or club-mosses, which survive today as small plants usually branched, and with numerous tiny moss-like leaves spirally arranged on the stem; the spore-bearing leaves are arranged in club-like cones. About 330 million years ago they attained their greatest size and abundance when they dominated the forests of the Coal Measures. In Australia we have representatives of the living genera *Lycopodium* and *Selaginella*. *L. phlegmaria* and *L. clarae*, 'tassel ferns', are beautiful pendulous epiphytes in the wet tropical lowland rainforests of north Queensland, but are now rarely seen outside the few specimens which manage to survive in collectors' bush-houses. Most primitive of existing lycopods is *Phylloglossum drummondii*, now confined to Western Australia, Victoria, Tasmania and New Zealand. The nature of its curious tuberous stock still excites much discussion.

Oldest of all, older we believe even than the lycopods, are the two genera of the Psilotales — *Psilotum* and *Tmesipteris*: both occur in Australia, and both deserve our every effort to ensure that these plants, with an ancestry extending back over hundreds of millions of years, survive the onset of man and his civilization.

Plants of Direct Economic Importance

Not all our native plants are neglected or forgotten; some have been pressed into the direct service of man. *Eucalyptus*, with over 600 species, tops the list of native plants of economic importance. In their book *The Eucalypts*, Penfold and Willis describe the genus as Australia's great gift to the peoples of the world. Eucalypts are extensively cultivated in the warmer regions of the globe and have become of value to countless millions of the human race. They are now grown in more than fifty countries and produce some of the heaviest, hardest and most durable woods known.

Well-known species basic to the paper and timber industry are Mountain Ash (*E. regnans*) and Alpine Ash (*E. gigantea*) in Victoria and Tasmania, Blackbutt (*E. pilularis*) in New South Wales and Queensland, Karri (*E. diversicolor*) in Western Australia. All these are giants which reach over 200 feet in height, and there are many more smaller which wear a variety of barks such as box, iron, stringy, gum, and peppermint. Tasmania's own floral emblem, *Eucalyptus globulus*, is itself an important raw material for the Tasmanian paper industry, but is in no danger of extinction; it is widely cultivated throughout the world, and does so well in California that the locals think it came from there, and know it as 'Californian Blue Gum'.

The Australian rainforest, though small in area, yields some of the world's prized cabinetwoods and ply timber, including Maple (*Flindersia brayleyana*), Silkwood (*F. pimenteliana*), Red Cedar (*Cedrela toona* var. *australis*), oaks (many Proteaceae), Hoop Pine (*Araucaria cunninghamii*), and, practically restricted to New South Wales, Coachwood (*Ceratopetalum apetalum*).

Acacia, with more than 500 species, ranks next to the eucalypts as the dominant feature of the vegetation of Australia. Some are used for timber, e.g., Tasmanian Blackwood (*A. melanoxylon*), a famous plywood, but the great majority are smaller trees which are most at home in the drier regions. Probably the greatest financial benefits result from the use of *Acacia* species, notably Mulga (*A. aneura*), as fodder for sheep in times of drought.

Also of positive value to the pastoral industry are well-known native grasses such as the Mitchell Grasses (*Astrebla* spp.), Blue Grasses (*Dichanthium* spp.), and Spear Grass (*Heteropogon contortus*). Recent research has shown that many native herbs and shrubs, which tend to be overlooked, are a much more important element in the diet of sheep than was formerly believed. Thus more than

ıe Grey-headed Fruit Bat is one of ɛ largest bats and is well known as pest of cultivated fruit.
ıOTO COURTESY E. SLATER

Corroboree Frog (*Pseudophryne corroboree*) is a mountain species of southern N.S.W., and distinguished from all other Australian frogs by its striking pattern.
PHOTO COURTESY E. SLATER

The Numbat (*Myrmecobius fasciatus*) is probably the most beautiful of the marsupials. It lives on termites and is still fairly common in parts of the south-west Australian woodlands. PHOTO COURTESY V. SERVENTY

iger Cat (*Dasyurops maculatus*) is a ırnivorous marsupial with remark- ɔle tree-climbing ability; most ımerous in wooded districts of the ıstern coast and Tasmania.
ıOTO COURTESY E. SLATER

anding the Noisy Scrub-bird *(Atrichornis clamosus*). Until a small ɔlony was found in south-western ustralia in 1961, there had been no efinite sighting of this species since 889. PHOTO COURTESY V. SERVENTY

Cape Barren Goose (*Cereopsis novae-hollandiae*) is found in diminished numbers in coastal southern Australia and offshore islands. It is the sole representative of a unique genus of waterfowl.
PHOTO COURTESY P. SLATER

Brush or Scrub Turkey (*Alectura lathami*) is one of the mound-building birds of the tropical-subtropical rainforests of north-eastern Australia. PHOTO COURTESY E. SLATER

The Narrow-footed Pouched Mouse (*Sminthopsis crassicaudata*) is commonly found in savannah woodland, grassland and saltbush steppe in inland N.S.W., S.A., Victoria and south-west W.A.
PHOTO COURTESY E. SLATER

Short-necked Swamp Tortoise (*Pseudemydura umbrina*) of sou western Australia is most rare. First collected about 1839, it w not re-discovered until 1953, wi 25 miles of Perth. It has a very narrow geographical range and specialized habitat requirements
PHOTO COURTESY V. SERVENTY

Wedge-tailed Eagle (*Aquila audax*). Although accused and slaughtered as a lamb-killer in some districts, its food in most areas is rabbits, young dingoes, marsupials and carrion.
PHOTO COURTESY E. SLATER

Red Kangaroo (*Megaleia rufa*). Shooting and drought have seriousl threatened its survival. PHOTO COURTESY E. SLATER

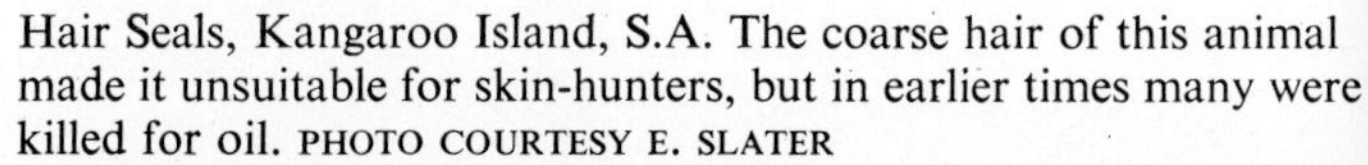

Hair Seals, Kangaroo Island, S.A. The coarse hair of this animal made it unsuitable for skin-hunters, but in earlier times many were killed for oil. PHOTO COURTESY E. SLATER

Sugar Glider (*Petaurus breviceps*) is fond of sugary blossoms and is able to glide fifty yards or more.
PHOTO COURTESY E. SLATER

thirty different native species on the Riverine Plain in New South Wales may be available to grazing sheep at any given time.

But plants can be economically important in a less co-operative sense. In any country which has long been geographically isolated there are apt to be ecological niches which are unfilled, or not exploited to their fullest extent. The fact that there are no native succulents in Australia does not mean that succulents cannot grow here; this was made all too clear when the introduced prickly pear, *Opuntia*, commandeered vast tracts of land, and was only brought under control by the introduction of one of its own native pests, the moth *Cactoblastis*. It now seems very likely that the story will be repeated by the even less desirable cactus *Harrisia*, for which no counterpart of *Cactoblastis* is yet available. The problem can be particularly important if there is interference with the native vegetation. When the white man first came to Australia, he cleared rainforests; in their place, if the land was then neglected, would arise a eucalypt forest or another rainforest; there was no pioneer shrubby species capable of invading and persisting to the exclusion of the forest. All this has changed since the introduction of *Lantana camara*; now, in the warmer regions, if a rainforest is cleared and the land neglected it too easily becomes replaced by a thicket of *Lantana*. Again, a form of biological control is being actively sought; but we should do well to remember that, just as the *Opuntia* problem has been replaced by a *Harrisia* problem, so the clearance of *Lantana* might well open up the same niche to yet another undesirable alien.

However, the economic value of the plants we have been discussing is actual, either positive or negative; but there are others whose economic value is as yet only potential, and whose survival is therefore less secure. Far and away the most important of these are the plants which produce physiologically active substances — 'drugs' in the ordinary sense of the term. These are so important, and the work done on them is now so extensive, that they deserve — and have received — a chapter to themselves. We cannot, however, avoid in this chapter considering their relevance to the overall conservation problem. We are all aware of the lives saved by the discovery of quinine; but suppose *Cinchona*, the plant from which it was derived, had been an uncommon plant of our northern rainforests? It might well have been exterminated, from Australia and the world, before its vitally important properties had been discovered. And so we return to the beginning of this article, to those plants — especially to be found in the rainforests — not yet described, named, or studied. More than conservation is needed here; we need exploration, to ensure that we know what it is that we have to conserve. In this chapter we have been concerned to draw attention to those features of our known flora which are botanically interesting and important; but we must never forget that, even now, much of our flora is still unknown.

Australian Plants and Chemical Research

L. J. Webb

Touch the tree with your hand; it is only wood,
A pillar of rain and earth; and what will you find
But rain and earth in its flower or curious blood?

DOUGLAS STEWART.

What will you find, indeed? The living cell is the best architect of all, and out of a pinch of earth, a shower of rain, a shaft of sunlight and just air, plants can build complicated and vivid forms of life. The curious blood of plants conceals a mild and serenely efficient alchemy beside which the most sophisticated apparatus and theories seem incongruous.

With the aid of minerals which they absorb from the soil, plants convert water and carbon dioxide from the air into carbohydrate materials and at the same time release oxygen. The energy required for the conversion is provided by sunlight and hence the process is known as photosynthesis. It enables plants to manufacture their own food reserves and structural materials and is in a very real sense the primary biological act. Animals are incapable of photosynthesis and ultimately all of them depend on plants for their food.

There are Australian plants to nourish, shelter or poison animals; plants which are fragrant or foetid; plants which sting, blister or blind; plants to heal or stupify; plants elegant or grotesque; useful for timber, shade and decoration, fibre and honey — there seems no end to their versatility. Plants are perhaps more interesting when they are related to human activities and needs in the broadest sense: as Edgar Anderson observed, 'botany equals plants plus man'. Yet only now it is becoming generally appreciated that plants have and have had values other than those of satisfying obvious material needs. Studies by chemists, anatomists, geneticists, ecologists, geographers, historians, anthropologists and others continue to reveal unsuspected complexities in the relationships between plants and man.

The structural theory of organic chemistry has been described as one of mankind's greatest intellectual achievements, and its development is due in very large measure to the influence of natural product chemistry. Modern production of polymers and plastics, drugs, vitamins, hormones, oral contraceptives, etc. would have been considerably delayed — if possible at all — without the knowledge derived directly from the chemistry of natural products. And there is another reason, apart from the economic ones, why the latter is important. It leads to knowledge and understanding (and so foreshadows control) of our environment: this, of course, is one of the features that distinguishes man from beast.

Aboriginal Foods and Drugs

As Judith Wright points out elsewhere in this book, Aboriginal man in Australia had a deep and subtle understanding of his natural environment, and modern research on Australian medicinal and poisonous plants has been partly guided by the empirical traditions of the Aborigines. From 'eat, die, and learn', the Aborigines had developed an intimate knowledge of physiologically active plants. Their food harvesting revealed ingenuity and patience, and they were able to extract a meal from such unlikely sources as the inside of *Pandanus* fruits or the bulbs of Nardoo (*Marsilea drummondii*). There is, indeed, some evidence of elementary food production by the

Aborigines: fragments of yams (*Dioscorea* spp.) were sometimes replaced in the soil, and there are a few reports that seeds (e.g. *Portulaca*, Bunya Pine, quandong and some grasses) were planted in limited areas, especially in the ashes after fire.

Palatable fruits used by the Aborigines include Wongi (*Manilkara balata*) of Torres Strait, Millaa Millaa (*Elaeagnus latifolius*) of the Atherton Tableland, Bunya Bunya (*Araucaria bidwillii*) of south-eastern Queensland, figs (*Ficus* spp.), White Raisin (*Securinega virosa*), Nonda (*Parinari nonda*), Lady Apple (*Eugenia suborbicularis*), Peanut Tree (*Sterculia quadrifida*), and Macadamia Nut (*M. tetraphylla*, *M. ternifolia*) — all from the tropical and subtropical rainforests. In drier areas, grass grains, including Mitchell Grass (*Astrebla pectinata*), *Sorghum* spp. and Wild Rice (*Oryza fatua*) were harvested, but tubers and yams, characteristic of a flora adapted to arid conditions (geophytes), were the staple food, e.g. *Amorphophallus variabilis*, *Dioscorea* spp., *Tacca* spp., *Ipomoea* spp., *Stemona australiana* and *Microstemma tuberosa*.

Other foods were eaten by the Aborigines only after careful preparation to remove poisonous principles. Thus Black Bean (*Castanospermum australe*) and Matchbox Bean (*Entada scandens*) were ground and washed in running water to yield a saponin-free flour. Some foods were roasted before washing, e.g. the yam *Dioscorea sativa* var. *rotunda*, to remove steroids. The caustic part of the Australian cashew nut (*Semecarpus australiensis*) was removed by Aboriginal women who are reported to have protected their hands and arms with clay, then the seed was pounded, cooked and washed. Fruits of Zamia Palms (*Cycas*, *Macrozamia*) were scorched, cracked, mashed and soaked (q.v.).

The most famous Aboriginal drug plants, and the earliest investigated, belong to the genus *Duboisia* of Solanaceae, a family well known in pharmaceutical chemistry for its powerful alkaloids from Belladonna, Stramonium, Deadly Nightshade and Tobacco. There are three Australian species of *Duboisia*, and *D. hopwoodii* of the inland was used as a source of 'pituri'. This was a preparation of dried leaves and wood ashes, chewed for its narcotic effect. It contains nicotine and related alkaloids. It was first examined nearly a century ago by Dr Joseph Bancroft, who lived in Brisbane, and who, with his son T. L. Bancroft, pioneered the pharmacological study of our native plants. *D. myoporoides*, found in coastal rainforest areas of Queensland and northern New South Wales, and sometimes called 'Corkwood', was also used by the Aborigines to prepare a narcotic drink, and to stupefy fish and eels in freshwater pools. This and the related *D. leichhardtii*, which has a restricted distribution in south-eastern Queensland, have been shown to contain large amounts of the alkaloids hyoscine and hyoscyamine. These plants have been developed commercially since World War II as major sources of these drugs for the world market.

It is interesting that at least three different genera of plants (*Duboisia* and *Nicotiana* in family Solanaceae, and *Isotoma* in Lobeliaceae) were used as chewing tobacco by the Aborigines. The first two contain nicotine, and the latter contains lobeline with a physiological action like that of nicotine. This convergence of use as a native tobacco of quite different-looking plants illustrates the success of Aboriginal empirical medicine.

And there are many other Aboriginal 'bush medicines' which recent research has shown to contain biologically active compounds. For example, Bitter Bark (*Alstonia constricta*) was used to prepare a kind of tonic, and is now known to contain the alkaloid reserpine which has a tranquillizing effect and lowers blood pressure. The use of the latex of species of *Euphorbia* and *Excaecaria* (Euphorbiaceae), *Ficus* (Moraceae), *Sarcostemma* (Asclepiadaceae) and *Ervatamia* (Apocynaceae) on sores and wounds may have a rational basis, because these plants contain proteolytic enzymes (like papain) and possibly antibiotics.

Spilanthes, a native daisy, was used to treat toothache; a related species in South Africa — also used for toothache — has been shown to contain spilanthol, a local anaesthetic.

The crushed leaves of Headache Vine (*Clematis glycinoides*) were inhaled to relieve headaches, and have a sharp odour like smelling salts (ammonia). Numerous plants were used to treat diarrhoea or 'running belly', and include the kino ('gum') from certain eucalypts, and decoctions of *Sida*, *Grewia*, *Musa*, *Cymbidium* and other plants containing mucilages and tannins. Cures for coughs and colds included preparations from the leaves of tea-trees (*Melaleuca*) and *Eucalyptus*, well known for their medicinal oils.

Other plants were used for a variety of complaints and disorders ranging from constipation to fever, snake-bite and stings from marine animals, soreness of the chest and general 'body pains'. Even love potions were not neglected, and the scent from the bruised oily roots of *Pittosporum venulosum* was reputed to have aphrodisiac effects. There are also a few records of 'oral contraceptive' plants, e.g. *Morinda reticulata*. This contains large amounts of selenium, and is poisonous to livestock, but it is not known whether selenium has oestrogenic effects.

The Aborigines also used various plants as fish-poisons. Chemical research has shown some of these to contain active compounds, e.g. rotenone in *Derris* and *Tephrosia*, saponin in *Planchonia*, *Barringtonia* and *Ternstroemia*, and alkaloids in *Stephania*. So far as we know, plants were rarely used for homicidal purposes, but recent records include *Castanospermum australe*, *Codonocarpus cotinifolius*, and *Strychnos lucida*, all of which are known to yield toxic compounds.

Chemical Research Begins

Starting with the empirical knowledge of the Aborigines, there is a long history of plant chemistry in Australia. In the first year of European settlement, the essential oil of *Eucalyptus piperita* was distilled and used as a substitute for oil of peppermint. Bosisto and von Mueller later established the Australian essential oil industry, and towards the end of last century H. G. Smith commenced his pioneer work on the chemistry of the eucalypts and conifers. About that time Rennie investigated the pigments of Sundew (*Drosera*), and the Bancrofts had begun their pharmacological studies on *Duboisia*. By the early part of this century, the large numbers of species poisonous to stock had attracted the attention of botanist, veterinarian and chemist. But the modern era of plant chemistry in Australia dates from World War II, when strategic drugs were in short supply, and a systematic survey of the chemical potentialities of the flora was begun by CSIRO and the universities.

The achievements of what came to be known as the Australian Phytochemical Survey are summarized in the Proceedings of seven national conferences held between 1947 and 1965, and are reported in many hundreds of chemical papers in journals in Australia and abroad. Australian research on plant products over the last twenty years has received international acclaim. Entirely new classes of compounds have been discovered and many known ones identified, new theories to explain the biosynthesis of various plant chemicals have been advanced, and several new alkaloids have been shown to have therapeutic promise in the treatment of human diseases, including leukaemia and hypertension. Over 4,000 species of higher plants in Australia were screened for the presence of alkaloids (such as strychnine, cocaine and nicotine) and for other substances with certain physiological effects on man and animals.

A summary of the chemical findings is given in Table I. The numbers of each type of compound identified are very approximate estimates, and are conservative. The organic chemists who kindly provided the estimates are acknowledged in the Table. In addition, helpful advice from Professor E. Ritchie in the collation of the chemical results in

TABLE 1: Approximate numbers of selected chemical compounds identified in Australian plants during the past twenty years

compound	estimated by	new	already known
alkaloids	J. A. Lamberton	200	250-300
terpenes and sesquiterpenes	H. H. G. McKern	20	210
diterpenes	P. R. Jefferies	63	20
triterpenes and steroids	J. J. H. Simes	36	70
glycosides (cardiac)	T. R. Watson	6	16
flavonoids and other pigments	R. G. Cooke	51	30
lignans, triketones, coumarins	E. Ritchie	40	20
glycosides (non-cardiac)	N. V. Riggs	5	6

Table 1, and in the preparation of the chemical glossary is gratefully acknowledged.

To describe the chemical significance and potential economic importance of this vast array of plant compounds would require a book by itself, so only a few examples can be mentioned.

New Alkaloids

The family Rutaceae (which includes citrus, boronia and Queensland maple) is one of the most versatile in alkaloid production, and one of the most thoroughly studied of all plant families. Seven structural types of alkaloids have been identified in nine genera of Australian Rutaceae; only one other type occurs in this family elsewhere. All the Australian alkaloidal species referred to occur in tropical and subtropical rainforests, and J. R. Price's suggestion that the alkaloid versatility might reflect rapid evolution is therefore of great biological interest. *Acronychia baueri*, sometimes called 'scrub ash', is a small tree with vivid yellow inner bark, glossy leaves and waxy petioles, confined to the drier rainforests of Queensland and northern New South Wales. It was first shown by chemical tests in 1945 to contain alkaloids. These are remarkably stable, because strongly positive tests were also obtained on fragments of a sample collected by Alan Cunningham in 1824! F. N. Lahey published his first paper on the structures of five alkaloids in this plant in 1949: it was shown to be a rich source of a new class of acridones. But it was not until 1966 that Eli Lilly, a large pharmaceutical firm in the United States, disclosed that one of the alkaloids, acronycine, gave 'a new lead in cancer research' and was active against a wide range of test tumours. The time lag of twenty-one years from the first alkaloid test to discovery of therapeutic promise illustrates how long this type of research takes, and how important it is to take a long-range view by preserving native species until they are thoroughly investigated.

Cryptocarya pleurosperma, popularly known as 'Poison Walnut', and a member of the Laurel family, is a medium-sized tree of the wet rainforests in north Queensland. Shaw and de la Lande showed that it contains a vesicant alkaloid, cryptopleurine, with an action on the skin like mustard gas, and toxicity rivalling that of strychnine. Its molecular structure is rather complicated, and a diagram of it was used to decorate the brochure for the Symposium of the International Union for Pure and Applied Chemistry which held its first meeting in Australia in 1960. Botanists and foresters who collected the first samples of bark of this tree were unaware of its toxic properties, and several of them who came in contact with the sap spent some time in hospital. One forester became sensitized to the plant and had to be transferred from the area in which it grew. Later, gloves and protective clothing were used by collectors. Despite precautions, laboratory workers such as N. V. Riggs were also affected by dermatitis and general *malaise*. The National Cancer Institute, Bethesda, U.S.A., showed that cryptopleurine damaged test tumours in mice, but its toxicity prevented further clinical development. Structurally related alkaloids with similar irritant properties also occur in *Tylophora crebriflora*, a vine with yellow latex related to the Wax Flower, *Ficus septica*, a shrubby fig, and *Boehmeria platyphylla*, a shrub of the nettle family. All belong to the wet tropical rainforest. Their alkaloids were shown recently to interfere with the synthesis of protein, which is of great biochemical interest. Tylocrebrine from *Tylophora* was found to be effective against lymphoid leukaemia under experimental conditions. Most of the chemical work on these plants was done by E. Gellert. Other plants from Queensland rainforests shown to be promising as anti-tumour agents by tests at the U.S. National Cancer Institute include species of Apocynaceae (frangipani family), Rutaceae (citrus family) and Hernandiaceae (related to the laurels).

Another spectacular alkaloidal plant is *Himantandra*, a large tree of the rainforests of north Queensland and New Guinea. Twenty-eight alkaloids have so far been isolated from its bark by E. Ritchie and co-workers — nearly a world record. This bark ('Argara') was chewed by New Guinea natives as a stimulant before tribal fights, and is reputed to cause dreams about the future and the man or animal intended to be killed. Two of its alkaloids, himandrine and himbacine, are considered to be of potential therapeutic importance.

One of the most interesting alkaloidal species is *Kreysigia multiflora*, a herb with pale pink flowers common in the wet sclerophyll forests of the subtropics. Several chemists have been involved in its investigation, including J. A. Lamberton, S. R. Johns, R. B. Bradbury and S. Mathieson in Australia, Battersby of the University of Liverpool, and Santavy of Czecho-Slovakia, a truly international collaboration. They showed that it contains a new class of alkaloids, as well as colchicine types and another related to morphine. Colchicine is well known as an agent which interferes with chromosome division and is used in plant breeding. Quite apart from any potential commercial use, this plant is of special interest to those who study biosynthesis, because it contains unusual alkaloids and gives added insight into the way that alkaloids such as colchicine and morphine are formed in the plant.

Another group of alkaloids which is of great economic importance to the livestock industry in Australia and abroad is found in common weed species such as Ragwort (*Senecio*), Rattlepods (*Crotalaria*) and members of the Heliotrope family such as *Heliotropium*, *Echium* and *Trichodesma*. These alkaloids are known by the formidable name of pyrrolizidines. Most of them are liver-poisons, and recent work by Culvenor, Dick, Bull and others in Melbourne has shown they are responsible for characteristic diseases in cattle, horses and sheep in various states, e.g. Kimberley horse disease or 'walkabout disease' of northern Australia, and a wasting disease associated with chronic copper poisoning of sheep in south-eastern Australia. It is thought that the alkaloids break down in the liver to form a substance which prevents cell division and causes cell enlargement, but only in the cell in which it is produced. If this interpretation is correct and the substance is stable, it may be of value as an anti-cancer agent.

But the harvest continues and the list of interesting alkaloids from Australian plants is almost endless. The alkaloids so far isolated represent only a tiny fraction of the unusual substances present in the plants, and which will eventually be studied if the species is available. One of the most realistic arguments for conservation is this continuing progress of science: improved chemical techniques enable substances to be isolated today which would have been missed by chemists a few years ago.

The same will be true of future research, which will undoubtedly discover many new and unexpected compounds, no matter how thoroughly the plant has been examined in the past. The great complexity of natural products and the fantastic variety of molecular structures present in them continually provide a stimulus to the chemist who is thus led to seek new synthetic reactions and to recognize new structural relationships.

Other Poisons

Besides alkaloids, there are many potent compounds in local plants. One of the most fascinating stories, in which the last chapter has yet to be written, concerns the cycads or Zamia Palms — mentioned in another chapter as living fossils. Scientific interest in these ancient plants is not new. They have been used as food and medicines for centuries, and native peoples who relied on the starch from the nut, stem and root were aware of its poisonous properties and ate it only after treatment (pounding, roasting, soaking, etc.). Although the toxic principle was first investigated a hundred years ago, it was not until 1941 that Cooper in Sydney isolated the poisonous glycoside, macrozamin, from the New South Wales species *Macrozamia spiralis*. Feeding tests in Queensland later proved that the leaves of *Macrozamia* spp. caused a progressive paralysis in cattle, popularly known as 'rickets' or 'wobbles'. The first feeding test on an Australian plant had, in fact, been performed on the ship's pigs by Captain Cook in August 1770, using the nuts of *Cycas media*: the ship's log laconically reports that the pigs were 'much disordered' and two of them died. Several adventurous members of the crew who had seen the Aborigines eating the nuts, but who were unaware of the special preparation required, became violently ill after sampling the nuts. Natives in various parts of the world who regularly ate cycads were sometimes reported to suffer ill-effects and fatal illnesses, presumably because preparation of the food did not remove toxins. A peculiar neurophysiological disease prevalent on the island of Guam focused chemical attention on *Cycas circinalis*, a staple food. It was observed that as the victim got older, there was loss of muscular tone of the facial muscles, then progressively of the limbs, so that the victim walked with a shuffle. Over a period of a few years, the muscular dystrophy developed so that he became 'a living vegetable' before death. In the early 1950s, N. V. Riggs and Japanese chemists established the chemical structure of macrozamin and cycasin, unusual plant products with an azoxy structure. Feeding tests with rats confirmed the toxicity of the cycads, the time of onset of death depending on the concentration of cycad in the diet. With low concentrations, the animals survived and apparently grew normally for some months, then began to lose weight and eventually died. Examination showed that they were suffering from cancerous growths in the liver and kidney. The same results were obtained experimentally by feeding cycasin. But feeding tests have not so far reproduced the neurophysiological disease in animals, although postmortem changes in the spinal cord of cattle affected with 'rickets' resemble those of human victims. The problem is still unsolved, and is the subject of regular international conferences, which have recommended that research be intensified over a wide range of localities, including Australia, where the plants are common.

Another unsolved chemical problem is provided by species of *Laportea*, the so-called Giant Nettles or 'Gympie Gympie'. These are trees or shrubs which regenerate in disturbed places in tropical and subtropical rainforest, and cause intense pain to anyone who comes in contact with the stinging hairs of the leaves. The pain recurs over a period of weeks whenever the affected part is washed, and swelling of the lymph glands under the armpit etc. is common. Even dead leaves on the floor of the forest are capable of stinging. Over the past twenty years, the fluid in the hollow stinging hairs has been investigated by several pharmacologists, and the mode of action on nerve endings has been established. The active principle was shown by McFarlane and Robertson to be a stable molecule of moderate size, but its chemical identity remains elusive, and no antidote has been established. In the meantime, visitors to rainforest areas, until they learn to avoid the plant, rely on old-fashioned bush remedies such as shaving the part and applying the juice of the cunjevoi plant, dettol, etc. Antihistaminic preparations do, however, help.

Perhaps the most notorious plant during the early settlement of north Queensland was *Rhodomyrtus macrocarpa*. It was called 'Wannakai' by the Aborigines, and was popularly known as Finger Cherry, because of the shape of the red fruits. It belongs to the same family as gum trees (Myrtaceae) and is a small tree fringing the lowland rainforests, generally in forests on poorer soils. It soon established a reputation for causing permanent blindness of some of the children who ate the fruits. Children of Europeans and of Aborigines on missions suffered, but knowledgeable Aborigines claimed that the fruits could be eaten at a certain stage of ripeness. The late Fred Martin of El Arish knew this, and ate a full plate of selected ripe Finger Cherries without ill effects, before a visiting team of scientists a few years ago. Several dozen cases of blindness, associated with eating Finger Cherries, were reported in the early part of the century. Blindness occurred suddenly, and could happen overnight: in the words of one victim, its onset was 'like a streak of lightning'. Medical examination of the victims revealed atrophy of the optic nerves. Blindness in goats and calves which ate Finger Cherries was also recorded. The coincidence of cases of blindness with areas in which the plant grew seemed significant, despite scepticism by some medical authorities, and conflicting reports from locals about the stage of ripeness at which the fruits were harmful. One 'theory' was that the over-mature fruits were attacked by a fungus which produced the toxin, another — based on an elementary chemical investigation at the beginning of the century — was that the immature fruits contained a saponin which was responsible. Public opinion was stirred by the succession of victims, and about 1915 the Queensland government accepted the plant as noxious. The Department of Education distributed posters to schools, railway stations, etc., in north Queensland, with a full-sized coloured plate of the leaves, flowers and fruits. The text illustrated the danger of the plant by a sinister anecdote; and concluded:

> Wherever you know of a Finger Cherry tree growing, tell your parents and ask them to have it destroyed. Never eat or handle or have anything to do with Finger Cherries, lest you become like one of the children of whom we have just read.

Small wonder that nervous fathers proceeded to hack down every Finger Cherry tree in sight in the Cairns district! This rather primitive reaction, in the absence of any attempt at scientific investigation of the plant's properties, reminds one of the natives of Calabar in Nigeria. They used to destroy the poisonous Calabar Bean (*Physostigma venenosum*) wherever they found it. Later the plant was shown to contain the drug physostigmine, used in ophthalmology, and became a valuable article of export.

In 1954, samples of Finger Cherries, both ripe and immature, were forwarded to the University of Cambridge for chemical examination. Trippett and Lythgoe showed that the *immature* fruits contained a toxic substance which they called rhodomyrtoxin, and which is a derivative of dibenzofuran. Although laboratory tests showed it was toxic to mice, the selective action of the compound on the optic nerve was not studied: at the time, these studies on experimental animals presented technical difficulties. Fortunately the plant still survives and regenerates abundantly in suitable habitats in north Queensland, and patiently awaits further investigation.

Chemical Curiosities

It is hard to believe that lobsters and pine trees have much in common, but current chemical research in Australia and Japan has revealed a dramatic relationship. Insects and crustaceans depend on hormones to trigger off the various processes associated with moulting. In 1966, Nakanishi in Japan reported the isolation of compounds with moulting hormone activity from the conifer *Podocarpus nakaii*. The same year, Galbraith and Horn in Melbourne identified crustecdysone, the major moulting hormone, in She Pine (*P. elatus*), a timber tree of subtropical rainforests in Queensland and northern New South Wales. Since then, compounds with moulting hormone activity have been recognized in other plants, including ferns. A log of She Pine may contain as much crustecdysone as tons of insects or lobsters! This ready availability of crustecdysone, and the difficulty of its synthesis, make local plants an important link in modern research on selective insect control. *Podocarpus* and certain ferns are known to be resistant to insect attack, and it is tempting to think that these plants elaborate hormones as an insect control measure. The hormones have no known action on vertebrates, including man. The fact that these substances act as hormones vital to the functioning of insect metabolism makes it unlikely that insects could develop resistance to them. So here is a most unlikely and unexpected avenue, literally between the pine trees, towards biological control of insect pests!

Another example of potent compounds concealed in odd places is the finding by P. R. Jefferies and co-workers that certain species of the Western Australian sand heaths (*Ricinocarpus*, *Beyeria* and *Phebalium*) contain substances with a gibberellin effect. Gibberellin, originally isolated from rice plants, causes seedling elongation and 'giantism' in plants. It has since been shown that the type of substances from the Western Australian heath plants occupies an important place in the synthesis of gibberellin within the living cell. As a result, and because there is no other useful source of these intermediates, the Western Australian plants have provided material for over thirty different research groups throughout the world.

The Australian wattles (*Acacia* spp.), common features of our natural landscapes, also play their part in the chemical sleuthing which so few members of the public hear about. The heartwood of Tasmanian Black Wattle (*A. melanoxylon*), which is a valuable furniture timber, contains a leucoanthocyanidin which was originally found on leaves of the grape vine in 1920. Its structure was worked out in 1954 by W. Bottomley and F. E. King. Related compounds have since been identified in other *Acacia* heartwoods by J. W. Clark-Lewis. This work stimulated related chemical research in many laboratories throughout the world, and hundreds of scientific papers have resulted directly or indirectly from it. The work on the leucoanthocyanidins is significant because it materially helped in the solution of a long-standing chemical problem and because it laid a firm foundation for an understanding of their biological role. Thus our native wattles can lay claim to great prestige in this field of organic chemistry, though in a more obscure way than our sportsmen and other heroes enjoy prestige.

An indirect effect of the Australian phytochemical survey was to stimulate the thinking behind A. J. Birch's acetate (or polyketide) theory. The ramifications of Birch's theory go well beyond the Australian scene, and embrace the first complete explanation of the biosynthesis of anthocyanins and flavonoids (pigments), antibiotics, and a huge range of other natural substances. The theory has been described as a fruitful, far-reaching and unifying concept in organic chemistry and plant biochemistry. It is good to think that it germinated in the fertile intellectual soil provided by the Australian phytochemical activity.

The glimpse of the beauty, practical uses,

scientific interest, and cultural implications of Australian native plants in this and the preceding chapter must surely cause us to challenge the ruling philosophy that native vegetation is simply an obstacle to 'development'. Exploitation of the rich genetic material evolved on this ancient continent, the last of lands, has already influenced social attitudes and scientific progress throughout the world. Chemical research on the Australian flora is just one of the many streams of real evidence that we can no longer continue ignorantly to loot our natural resources, lest we, in destroying forever some potent living tissue, throw away a pearl richer than our common wealth.

Glossary of Chemical Terms

ALKALOIDS: Basic nitrogenous substances found in plants. Almost always very bitter, often poisonous or with marked physiological action. Some are used clinically, e.g. morphine, quinine, reserpine, atropine.

AZOXY: Containing two linked nitrogen atoms with an oxygen atom attached to one of them. Related to the well-known azo dyestuffs.

COUMARIN: A relatively simple substance which is, for example, responsible for the odour of newly mown hay. The term 'coumarins' refers to more complex substances containing the same basic molecular structure. Some are insecticidal, some are fish poisons and one, 'dicoumarol', has marked anti-haemorrhagic properties.

DIBENZOFURAN: A relatively simple substance found in coal tar.

DITERPENE: see TERPENOID.

ENZYMES: Complex organic substances which function as catalysts in reactions in living cells. 'Life is one enzyme reaction after another.'

ESSENTIAL OIL: The relatively volatile oils of plants as opposed to the fixed oils such as olive and coconut oils. 'Essential' here connotes 'essence' and refers to odoriferous qualities, i.e. essential oils are responsible for the odours of flowers, leaves, etc.

FLAVONOIDS: A group of closely related substances responsible for nearly all of the off-white to yellow colours in flowers and other plant parts. In primitive societies some are still used as dyestuffs. The term is now usually extended to cover the very closely allied anthocyanins, the pigments of the palest pink to the deepest blue-black flowers, fruits, etc.

GLYCOSIDE: A general term denoting a substance whose molecule is made up of one or more sugar residues plus another unit which may be of almost any type, e.g. anthocyanins, saponins are glycosides, so are the powerful cardiac drugs from foxglove, etc.

LEUCOANTHOCYANIDINS: A group of colourless substances occurring in almost all parts of all plants, characterized by their ready conversion into anthocyanidins (i.e. the sugar-free pigment portion of an anthocyanin) on heating with acid.

LIGNANS: A widespread group of relatively simple substances closely related to the polymeric lignin which, together with cellulose, forms the bulk of wood.

SAPONINS: Substances which when shaken with water produce a stable foam. They are triterpene glycosides.

SESQUITERPENE: See TERPENOID.

STEROID: SEE TERPENOID.

TERPENOID: Originally the term terpene was applied to a large group of substances whose molecular skeletons are made up of two five-carbon units, the so-called 'isoprene' units. Most essential oils, e.g. eucalyptus oils, consist of terpenes, and other common terpenes are camphor, citronellal and turpentine. Sesquiterpenes are made up of three isoprene units, diterpenes of four and triterpenes of six such units. Triterpenes are very widespread in plants but also occur in all animals. The best known is probably lanosterol in wool wax. In general they have no marked physiological action.

In recent years it has been discovered that living cells first synthesize triterpenes and then convert them into other smaller molecules, e.g. steroids, including cholesterol, bile acids, male and female sex hormones, cortisone, aldosterone, and cardiac glycosides. Thus all these groups are now generally referred to collectively as 'terpenoids'.

The Vertebrates

J. H. Calaby

Australia is the driest continent; climatically seventy per cent is desert or semi-arid, and even the relatively well-watered eastern, northern, south-eastern, and south-western portions are not very wet when compared with some other parts of the world. The low rainfall, high temperatures and high evaporation, coupled with lack of topographical relief and consequent paucity of habitat diversity, is reflected in the vertebrate fauna of all Classes, which in terms of numbers of species is smaller than in any other area of comparable size, if the polar regions and the large deserts of the old world are excluded. What Australia lacks in quantity however, it certainly makes up in scientific and popular interest; many of the Australian vertebrates, such as the platypus and echidna, the great variety of marsupials, the Queensland Lungfish, the lyrebird, Mallee Fowl, parrots, bower birds, and others, are famous the world over.

This chapter is concerned with the land and freshwater vertebrates. The marine vertebrates are not dealt with as at least the great majority of species do not differ greatly from marine vertebrates in other parts of the world and in general most species are not endangered at present. Australia has played its part in the drastic reduction in numbers of two of the great whales, the Southern Right Whale (*Eubalaena glacialis australis*) and the Humpback (*Megaptera novaeangliae*), which formerly visited our shores in large numbers during the breeding season; and in the early years of the nineteenth century the only Australian breeding colony of the Southern Elephant Seal (*Mirounga leonina*) in Bass Strait was exterminated, and the two species of fur seals (*Arctocephalus*) were reduced to extremely small numbers. Legal protection has ensured the revival of the fur seals beyond the danger point but the Elephant Seal has never returned except as an occasional straggler.

The New Guinea-Australian area has been isolated by deep sea from other land masses since the Cretaceous period. All other continents have been connected at various times during the Tertiary and Pleistocene which has allowed faunal interchanges. As a consequence the Australian vertebrate fauna shows an essentially island pattern in its composition: there is a deficiency of basic types and some of these have radiated widely to fill available niches. There are a few very old endemic elements — forms that have originated in this region and have not been found elsewhere: the Lungfish (*Neoceratodus forsteri*), the monotremes, the marsupials, and perhaps the emu (*Dromaius novaehollandiae*) and cassowary (*Casuarius casuarius*). No other vertebrates are comparable to these in degree of endemism. The great majority of the ancestors of the Australian vertebrates have island-hopped across the Indo-Malayan island chain from Asia over a long period of time and their descendants have accumulated here.

The process is still going on. The amphibians and mammals are much more impoverished in basic kinds (Orders) than the reptiles and birds; the latter two groups have a much higher capacity for dispersal across water gaps. Land connections between Australia and New Guinea occurred from time to time during the Tertiary and Pleistocene, which led to faunal migrations between the two areas and consequent enrichment of their respective faunas.

The two most momentous events in the recent history of the vertebrates have been the colonization of Australia, firstly by Aboriginal man accompanied by the dingo, and secondly by European man. Although it is often stated that the Aborigines lived in equilibrium with the fauna and had little effect on it, Tindale has pointed out that their destructive uncontrolled hunting fires, in particular, probably had a drastic effect, changing the character of the vegetation over large areas and playing a major role in the extinction of the Pleistocene giant marsupial fauna. Merrilees has elaborated and documented the same theme.

European occupation has led to profound alteration of habitat due to clearing for agriculture, grazing and forestry; deliberate introduction of numerous herbivorous and predatory mammals, birds, fishes, and the Giant Toad (*Bufo marinus*); uncontrolled release of industrial wastes, pesticides, etc. The accumulated effects have led to increases in numbers of a few species, but large reductions in numbers of a great many more. Few animals appear to have become extinct however, and in view of the recent rediscoveries of supposedly extinct species, we can be certain of the extinction of only the species or subspecies of emus which formerly inhabited King and Kangaroo Islands. Discoveries in the last few years have reduced the list of probably extinct species of mammals to three marsupials and two rodents.

Freshwater Fishes

According to Whitley the freshwater fish fauna consists of about 180 species. A systematic revision using adequate material would no doubt reduce this number; on the other hand, other species surely await discovery. This depauperate fauna is no doubt a reflection of the general shortage of streams and other bodies of water, and the large expanses of arid country. Most species are concentrated in the well-watered coastal tracts and the Murray-Darling river system. All but two species are derived from marine families.

The most outstanding fish is the relict Lungfish originally confined to the Mary and Burnett Rivers in Queensland. Legal protection and its introduction to other streams in southern Queensland have ensured its survival. The order Dipnoi to which it belongs first appeared in the lower Devonian and was fairly abundant and widespread in the world in the late Palaeozoic and Mesozoic. Today there are three species in Africa, one in South America, and the Australian one, the only surviving species in its family. The Queensland Lungfish is a large species and may grow to a length of six feet. The African and South American forms can survive the drying-up of pools by aestivating in burrows, but the Australian one cannot do this, although it can survive in foul stagnant pools very low in oxygen by gulping air into its lungs. The only other Australian fish with claims to being old enough in origin to have arrived via an ancient land connection is the Barramundi (*Scleropages leichhardti*). It lives in fresh water in the Northern Territory, Queensland, and southern New Guinea, and a second species of the genus is found in parts of South-east Asia. The Barramundi is a large predatory fish growing to a length of about three feet. It is one of a number of fishes in which 'mouth-breeding' has independently evolved; the eggs are laid by the female into the male's mouth and are carried there until they hatch.

The majority of Australian freshwater fishes are small, and many have restricted geographical ranges. A few species have colonized the desert waterholes and one, the Desert Goby (*Chlamydogobius eremius*) is found in association with springs in the Lake Eyre basin, the part of Australia receiving the least amount of rain. The most widespread of the desert species is the Spangled Perch (*Therapon unicolor*) which is noted for its rapid dispersal over the countryside when the ground is covered by water following heavy rains. Among the more interesting fishes are two small pale and blind species living in the subterranean caverns of Northwest Cape, Western Australia. One is a gudgeon of the family Eleotridae, *Milyeringa veritas*, and the other is an eel of the family Synbranchidae, *Anommatophasma candidum*. The habitat is shared with two highly specialized species of blind shrimps.

Little is known of the biology of most species and in fact we probably know less about the freshwater fishes than any other vertebrates. Among the few species that have been studied to some extent are the large edible ones in the Murray-Darling system, Freshwater Catfish (*Tandanus tandanus*), Golden Perch (*Plectroplites ambiguus*), Murray Cod (*Maccullochella macquariensis*), Silver Perch (*Bidyanus bidyanus*), and the small Western Carp Gudgeon (*Carassiops klunzingeri*). It has been found that all of these species are well adapted to the conditions in the Murray-Darling system. Floods are important and the fish breed when there is a rise in water level accompanied by a rise in temperature. Water conservation and flood control by means of dams and weirs are detrimental to the survival of these fishes but favour the introduced species.

Amphibia

An excellent essay on the ecology and evolution of the Australian frogs has been written by Main. Of the three living orders of amphibians, the caecilians, salamanders, and frogs, only four families of the frogs have reached Australia, and two of these are represented by one or few species restricted to the extreme north. Many of the frogs are very colourful, the most outstanding being perhaps the small Corroboree Frog (*Pseudophryne corroboree*) which has a bold black and yellow striped pattern and inhabits the mountains of southern New South Wales and the Australian Capital Territory.

The known fauna consists of approximately 120 species in twenty-two genera but it is certain that further study will bring to light many more species. Of particular interest is the radiation of the largest family, the Leptodactylidae, otherwise found only in Central and South America. The other large family is the Hylidae, containing the tree frogs of which there are numerous species in the genus *Hyla*. They climb around on vegetation aided by the pads or discs on the ends of their toes.

The great majority of species are concentrated around the wetter coastal fringe but a number have successfully conquered the dry interior by a combination of physiological and behavioural adaptations. In eastern Australia there are a number of genera of leptodactylids, each with one or two species, found only in the very wet coastal and mountainous areas. These are believed to be old elements in the fauna, each with one or another of special habitat requirements such as high rainfall, moss or sphagnum bogs, clear streams, and so on. The desert species avoid desiccation by aestivating in burrows, and exploit the rain that falls by feeding and breeding only when water is present. The burrows of *Notaden nichollsi*, which lives among spinifex (*Triodia*)-covered sand dunes, may be five or six feet deep. Desert-adapted species are able to withstand greater dehydration than those from wetter areas, and can rehydrate quickly and thus take advantage of rain almost immediately. The well-known 'Water-holding Frog' (*Cyclorana platycephalus*) lives in desert clay pans and because of the hardness of the soil its burrows are quite short. It enters aestivation with its bladder and coelom filled with water, and a longer time elapses than with other species before dehydration becomes critical. This and other desert species enclose themselves in cocoons during aestivation which further reduces the rate of water loss. Non-burrowing desert species, for example *Hyla rubella*, *Glauertia russelli*, and *Pseudophryne douglasi* of north-western Australia, avoid the desert conditions to a large extent by living around soakages and pools in creeks and other more favourable situations.

All desert species have an aquatic larval life although the length of larval life may be relatively short. Strangely enough a few species in the high rainfall areas, such as *Metacrinia nichollsi*, *Crinia rosea*, and *C. lutea* of south-western Australia, have dispensed with the aquatic stage. These species have large eggs and, at least in the latter two, the larvae develop to metamorphosis in the broken-down egg membranes. The habitat contains few ponds and many fast streams, presumably an unsuitable aquatic habitat for small frog larvae. The most extreme adaptation in this group is shown by *C. darlingtoni*, a species virtually restricted to the Antarctic Beech (*Nothofagus moorei*) forest on the Queensland-New South Wales border. The female produces up to ten large eggs and the larvae develop to metamorphosis in paired brood pouches on the sides of the male. The streams in this area are fast torrents, again an unsuitable habitat for small frog larvae.

In their food habits all but one of the Australian frogs are generalized opportunist predators which snap at anything of suitable size which moves past them within range. The exception is a short-limbed, turtle-shaped frog, *Myobatrachus gouldii*, which lives in sandy areas of south-western Australia. It is a subterranean burrowing species and lives on termites which it takes from their foraging galleries encountered during its burrowing activities. No free eggs or larvae have been found but the large size of eggs in females leads to the belief that it also has no aquatic larval stage.

Reptiles

The most useful general works on the reptiles are Storr's essay on zoogeography and Cogger's introductory popular study. In contrast to the amphibians and mammals, the reptiles are a modern and reasonably varied segment of the fauna of the Oriental region and the old world tropics. There are no archaic relicts in any way comparable to the Lungfish and the monotremes, although the last of the extinct giant horned land tortoises (*Meiolania*) persisted here until the Pleistocene. The approximately 400 species of Australian reptiles are classified as five marine turtles in two families, one family of freshwater tortoises, two species of crocodiles, and five families each of lizards and snakes. Study of the reptiles is in many ways still in the exploratory phase; new species are described every year and no doubt many others have yet to be discovered.

The family Chelidae containing the river and swamp tortoises of Australia and New Guinea is found otherwise only in Central and South America. They are not found in Tasmania. There are eleven known species in Australia and they are usually common in the well-watered parts and are found in permanent pools in dry areas. Alteration of the countryside for agriculture apparently does not affect them and they quickly colonize farm dams. The rarest of them, the Swamp Tortoise, *Pseudemydura umbrina*, of south-western Australia, has had a remarkable history. The type specimen with no other locality than 'Australia' reached the Vienna Museum in 1839 but was not described until 1901. No further specimens came to light until 1953 when one was collected by an amateur naturalist within twenty-five miles of Perth. Research in recent years has shown that its total geographical range is apparently very limited and the total population amounts to only a few hundred. Its habitat requirements are rather specialized and it lives in shallow swamps that dry out in summer when the tortoise aestivates in suitable shelters and under litter. The two crocodiles are restricted to the far north. The small endemic species (*Crocodylus johnstoni*) is a fish-eater restricted to fresh water and is not dangerous to man. Both species have suffered severely in the past from uncontrolled and illegal hunting.

There are several genera and over forty species of dragon lizards in the family Agamidae, many of which are brightly coloured with patterns of red and yellow, etc. The most specialized is the thorn-covered harmless desert form, the Mountain Devil (*Moloch horridus*), which lives on small ants. One of its more interesting characteristics is its ability to take advantage of free water, normally a scarce resource in its habitat. The water rapidly moves all over its skin and is drawn up by capillary action in minute channels in the skin. It is swallowed when it reaches the mouth. Most species of the large genus *Amphibolurus* live in dry regions. They are active fast-running lizards. As they are diurnal they have to cope with very high temperatures, and behavioural postures and activity patterns have been evolved as a result of which the body temperature is regulated.

There are about fifty species of geckos in Australia of which a high proportion are desert species. Geckos are nocturnal predators of insects. They are most attractive soft-bodied lizards and many have colourful dorsal patterns. They are the most vocal of lizards and produce a variety of chirping and barking sounds. The only endemic family of lizards is the Pygopodidae (snake-lizards) the members of which are long and slender and mimic snakes in their appearance. The limbs have disappeared except for vestigial hind-limbs. There are about twelve species of which two occur in New Guinea and one is restricted to the island. Over 130 species of skinks (Scincidae) are known; it is the largest family of reptiles in Australia. There is a great diversity in size and body form. The large Blue-tongue Lizards (*Tiliqua*) and the Stump-tail (*Trachydosaurus rugosus*) are well known representatives. Goannas (Varanidae) are found from Africa to Australia but the majority of species are found here. The seventeen or so Australian species range in size from the very large Perentie (*Varanus giganteus*) of rocky arid areas which may grow to more than seven feet in length to the small Mulga Goanna (*V. gilleni*), a desert species about eighteen inches in length.

The Australian snake fauna consists of about 130 known species of which twenty are sea sna es not restricted to our area. A distinctive feature of the land snake fauna is the large representation of venomous species of the family Elapidae and the small number of species of Colubridae, the reverse of the situation in other parts of the world. The colubrids are obviously recent arrivals as no genera and few of the twelve species are restricted to Australia and the family is found only in northern and north-eastern coastal areas. Most species are non-venomous and the few venomous ones are back-fanged and thought not to be dangerous to man. The most common species is the handsome Green Tree-snake (*Ahaetulla punctulatus*) of the northern and eastern coast which grows to a length of about six feet. All of the approximately sixty species of elapids are venomous but most are too small to be dangerous to man. However, the family contains several large dangerous species including the Taipan (*Oxyuranus scutellatus*), Death Adder (*Acanthophis antarcticus*), Tiger Snake (*Notechis scutatus*), and a few others. None of these snakes are aggressive and all prefer to escape rather than attack. Many of the small species are very handsomely marked with coloured bands or brightly-coloured head patches, or bellies. This family has had a long history in Australia and has numerous distinctive members, notably the viper-like Death Adder.

We have twenty or more species of blind snakes in the genus *Typhlops* (Typhlopidae) which are relatively small rather worm-like subterranean burrowing creatures that live on worms, insects, and other small animals. They are harmless to man. The ten Australian species of pythons (Boidae) range in size from the Amethystine Python (*Liasis amethystinus*) of north Queensland which may grow to a length of twenty-five feet and is one of the world's largest snakes, to the Pygmy Python (*L. perthensis*) of south-western Australia, which is about two feet in length. The pythons are non-venomous and are not injurious to man if not molested.

Birds

Over the years a great many people have taken an interest in birds and consequently we know far more about them than other vertebrates. About 700 species have been recorded in Australia, although a considerable number are visitors only or vagrants, some known only from one or a few records. It was believed for many years that all endemic species were known but surprisingly two new species were discovered in the past few years. Hall's Babbler (*Pomatostomus halli*) of southern central Queensland was described in 1964 and the Grey Grass-wren (*Amytornis barbatus*) of north-western New South Wales in 1968. In addition careful studies of ecology and behaviour of ravens showed that there were two distinct species in south-eastern Australia rather than one.

Zoogeographically the land and freshwater birds resemble the reptiles in that they are a fairly well-balanced fauna and have been derived from the Oriental region and the old world tropics. The earlier arrivals have given rise to numerous endemic families, subfamilies, and genera. The immigration process is still going on and the latest well-established species to arrive unaided in the past thirty years is the Cattle Egret (*Bubulcus ibis*) which is now a breeding species in northern and eastern Australia. The Sarus Crane (*Grus antigone*) of South-east Asia was found recently in some numbers in the Atherton-Normanton region of Queensland and has apparently bred there. A recent arrival from the south, presumably New Zealand, is the Southern Black-backed Gull (*Larus dominicanus*) which appears to be establishing itself as a breeding species.

There are some notable absentees which are widely distributed in the rest of the world, such as woodpeckers, vultures, and flamingoes, although recently-discovered fossils show that flamingoes were common in Australia from mid-Tertiary to late Pleistocene. The last species to disappear (*Phoenicopterus ruber*) was the same as the common modern species of the Northern Hemisphere.

Many of the more outstanding species and their behaviour are well known to the ornithologist and public alike. Among these are the emu (*Dromaius novaehollandiae*), Laughing Kookaburra (*Dacelo gigas*), the lyrebird (*Menura novaehollandiae*) with its outstanding display and vocal mimicry, the several species of bower-birds and their elaborate display-structures, the Mallee Fowl (*Leipoa ocellata*) and other megapodes with their bizarre nesting behaviour, and the great variety of brilliantly-coloured parrots and cockatoos.

Among the dominant families is that of the honeyeaters (Meliphagidae) which has originated in the Australo-Papuan area and spread to the eastern Indonesian and Pacific islands, including New Zealand. One or more of the approximately seventy Australian species are found in virtually every habitat from rainforest to desert scrubs. They are especially abundant in eucalypt communities. Honeyeaters are probably chiefly insectivorous but their long slender beaks and brush-tipped tongues are adaptations for gathering the considerable quantity of nectar they consume. At least one, the Painted Honeyeater (*Grantiella picta*) has specialized food habits; its chief diet is mistletoe berries and it is a nomadic species, presumably following the fruiting of its food plants.

The Cracticidae, containing the magpies, currawongs, and butcher-birds, is another family with obscure relationships. The magpies (*Gymnorhina* spp.) are among the vertebrates that have benefited from land clearing. They are primarily birds of savannah woodland and need trees for nesting and open areas for foraging. Opening of the forest for agriculture and grazing has created more optimum habitat for them.

The Australian warblers (Malurinae) comprise a large endemic sub-family of about fifty species which have adapted successfully to a wide variety of habitat types. The well-known members are the many species of blue wrens 'wig lining burrows of the Trapdoor Spider, *nidiops villosus*, in linear *Acacia-Casuarina* litter ghtly disturbed by rabbits twenty miles north of Broad Arrow, north of Kalgoorlie, Western ustralia. PHOTO COURTESY B. Y. MAIN

A Dipluran of Family Campodeidae from Black Mountain, Australian Capital Territory.

Hedleyella falconeri, the Giant Panda Snail from Lamington National Park.

Hackeria veitchi, a Peloridiid from Lamington National Park, Queensland.

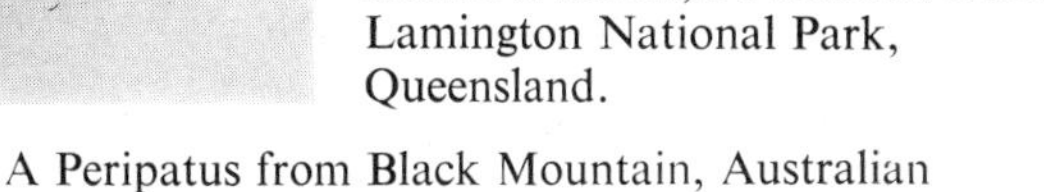

Macropanesthia rhinoceros female and newly-born young. PHOTO COURTESY C. LOURANDOS

A Peripatus from Black Mountain, Australian Capital Territory

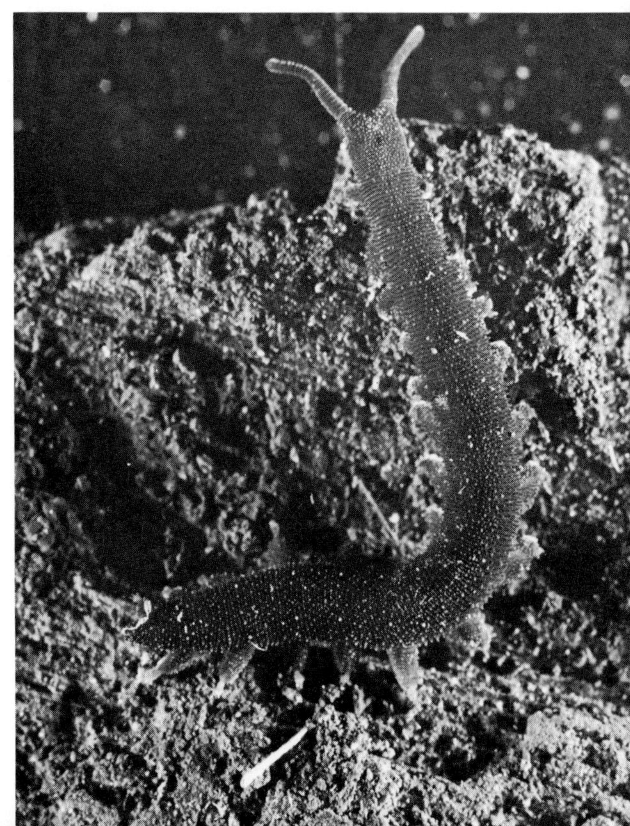

A portion of Crescent Reef, north of Cooktown, Queensland. Photographed about 1890 by W. Saville-Kent who described it as 'the most luxuriant expanse of living coral' he had ever photographed. REPHOTOGRAPHED COURTESY AUST. MUSEUM, SYDNEY

Colourful Damsel-Fish and a Moorish Idol swim over luxuriant co in the Swain Reefs, at the southern end of the Great Barrier Reef of Queensland. PHOTO COURTESY KEITH GILLETT

Male *Zelotypia stacyi* Scott, a Bent Wing Swift Moth, from Mt Keir N.S.W. The specimen has a wing span of 18.3 cm. PHOTO COURTESY C. LOURANDOS

(*Malurus*) and thornbills (*Acanthiza*). The group also includes the Rock Wren (*Origma solitaria*) restricted to the Hawkesbury sandstone in New South Wales, which builds its hanging nest in windblown caves and man-made substitutes such as sheds and culverts. The genus *Amytornis* (grass-wrens) contains eight species of desert and semi-desert country, and there are two species of *Stipiturus* (emu-wrens), one (*S. malachurus*) occupying the wet coastal area of south-eastern and south-western Australia, with a well-marked subspecies in the semi-arid mallee of Victoria and the nearby part of South Australia, and the other (*S. ruficeps*) living in the desert of north-western and central Western Australia.

Other than large endemic units, of which the above are examples, there are a number of remarkable and interesting endemic genera in families that are widespread in the world. For example there are several among the ducks, especially the Magpie Goose (*Anseranas semipalmata*), and Freckled Duck (*Stictonetta naevosa*) neither of which has any close relatives in the family. Other examples are the Flock Pigeon (*Lopholaimus antarcticus*), the Black-breasted Buzzard (*Hamirostra melanosterna*), and Square-tailed Kite (*Lophoictinia isura*) among the hawks, and the Australian Dotterel (*Peltohyas australis*) among the waders.

There is a large and successful bird fauna in the Australian semi-arid and desert regions. Many species have overcome the vagaries of the climate by dispensing with the normal pattern of seasonal breeding, and breed only after good rainfall irrespective of season. In some drought years many birds will not breed at all. This breeding pattern ensures that the young will be born when food is plentiful and they have maximum chances of survival.

On the whole the birds have stood up to European settlement remarkably well. Other than the island emus we cannot be sure that any other forms have become extinct. The Night Parrot (*Pezoporus occidentalis*) and the Paradise Parrot (*Psephotus pulcherrimus*) have not been seen for many years and a few species, including other parrots, have become rare. On the other hand, two species have been seen again after it was believed that they had become extinct. A colony of the Noisy Scrub-bird (*Atrichornis clamosus*) of south-western Australia was found in 1961 although there had been no definite sighting of the species since 1889. Also in 1961 a small colony of Goyder's Grass-wren (*Amytornis goyderi*) was discovered near Lake Eyre close to the locality where a handful of specimens were collected in 1874. No evidence of the existence of the species was obtained during the intervening years.

Mammals

The mammal fauna resembles the Amphibia in that it is an unbalanced one, typical of an island rather than a continent. The approximately 225 species are classified into only four orders — the monotremes, marsupials, rodents, and bats. At least the great majority of species are known and described. Some of them, such as the platypus, koala, and kangaroo are known to people the world over who know little else of Australia.

Because of their anatomical and reproductive peculiarities the platypus and the echidnas are the most distinct of all mammals. They have many reptilian features in their anatomy and are the only mammals that lay eggs. Their evolutionary history is unknown and they have no close relationships to any other mammals, living or fossil. They are relicts of ancient origin and it may well be that they have never lived outside the Australian region. In spite of their primitive features, the monotremes are among the most specialized of living creatures. The platypus (*Ornithorhynchus anatinus*) is found in eastern Australia from north Queensland to Tasmania and is quite common over much of its range. It is amphibious and digs burrows in the banks of the streams and lakes which it inhabits. When swimming the eyes and ears are closed and it relies on the very sensitive muzzle for locating prey. It swims close to the bottom and may stir up the mud or move stones; any insect larvae, small crayfish, or other small aquatic animals that touch the muzzle are snapped up. The eggs are laid and hatched in a nest of leaves in the burrow. The echidna (*Tachyglossus aculeatus*) is found all over Australia, including Tasmania, and also in southern New Guinea. Its prey, consisting chiefly of ants and termites, is presumably located by smell and is exposed by digging with the powerful forefeet. The insects are collected by the long sticky tongue and crushed against the palate before being swallowed. Its single egg is hatched in an abdominal pouch and the young is carried there for some time after hatching. In forested mountainous parts of New Guinea a much larger echidna (*Zaglossus bruijni*) is found. Large echidnas of the genus *Zaglossus* were common and widespread in Australia during the Pleistocene.

The ancestors of the marsupials were early arrivals in Australia and they presumably found a continent empty of mammals except monotremes. The outcome was the evolution of a whole range of marsupials that are parallels of the placental mammals of other parts of the world — a classic example of adaptive radiation. Thus there are marsupial equivalents of such placental mammals as the shrews (marsupial mice), mongoose (native cats), wolf (Tasmanian Tiger), anteaters (Numbat), African golden moles (Marsupial Mole), large burrowing rodents, such as marmots (wombats), and antelopes (kangaroos and wallabies). Australia has no monopoly of marsupials as there are about seventy species in Central and South America and one in North America. The Australian ones, however, are of fundamentally different kinds and are much more varied in form, anatomy, and habits. They range in size from the tiny insectivorous *Planigale* species, the smallest of all marsupials, weighing about a quarter of an ounce, to the Red Kangaroo, a large male of which may weigh over 180 pounds.

About forty species of insectivorous and carnivorous marsupials in the superfamily Dasyuroidea are found in Australia. The largest and among the rarest is the Tasmanian Tiger (*Thylacinus cynocephalus*), now confined to Tasmania although it lived in mainland Australia and New Guinea during the last few thousand years. It was savagely persecuted by landholders when it was reasonably common and now grave fears are held for its survival. The Numbat (*Myrmecobius fasciatus*), with its reddish coat and bold white and dark striping across the back, is probably the most beautiful of the marsupials. It is still fairly common in parts of the south-western Australian woodlands where its termite food and hollow log shelters are abundant. It is unusual among small mammals in that it is diurnal in habit. The blind burrowing Marsupial Mole (*Notoryctes typhlops*) lives in deep sand dunes in central and north-western Australia. Its relationships among the marsupials and its life history are unknown. It is subterranean and only encountered occasionally by accident but is probably not rare.

There are about twelve species of bandicoots some of which live on insects while others are omnivorous. Some species have adapted readily to settlement and others have become very rare. The Long-nosed species (*Perameles nasuta*) is common in eastern coastal districts including suburban areas of Sydney. The Rabbit-eared Bandicoot (*Macrotis lagotis*) has disappeared from a large part of its range in the southern farming and grazing areas but is still found in many places in the sparsely inhabited arid areas. The Pig-footed Bandicoot (*Chaeropus ecaudatus*) is one of the rarest of marsupials and has not been seen for many years.

The two kinds of wombats occupy very different habitats. The common species (*Vombatus ursinus*) is found in forested higher rainfall country in south-eastern mainland Australia and Tasmania, while the two species of Hairy-nosed Wombats (*Lasiorhinus*) occur in drier areas especially country characterized by limestone. The wombats are large herbivores and dig large burrows. The well-known koala (*Phascolarctos cinereus*) is the nearest living relative of the wombats.

The twenty-four species of possums (Phalangeridae) include a range of adaptive types. The most specialized is the tiny Honey Mouse (*Tarsipes spencerae*) of south-western Australia. It is a nectar-feeder with a long slender snout and a brush-tipped tongue, a parallel of the honeyeaters among the birds. These adaptations have enabled it to exploit the magnificent flora of its home region. Another specialized group are the possums commonly called gliders of which there are five species in three genera. Gliding membranes have independently evolved on three occasions in these possums. The Brush-tailed Possum (*Trichosurus vulpecula*) is probably the most familiar and adaptable of all Australian marsupials. It lives in most towns and suburbs and shelters in sheds, roofs of houses, and garden trees.

The kangaroo family includes roughly forty-five species and one or a number are found in all habitats. They range in size from the tiny Musky Rat-kangaroo (*Hypsiprymnodon moschatus*), a little more than a pound in weight, to the large Red Kangaroo (*Megaleia rufa*). In recent years a great deal of research has been carried out on the larger kangaroos and some of the wallabies. Among the more remarkable discoveries is that many species exhibit a reproductive phenomenon called embryonic diapause, or delayed implantation. The female mates soon after giving birth and the resulting fertilized egg or blastocyst increases in size for only a few days in the uterus and then ceases development. When the young leaves the pouch, or if it is lost, the stored blastocyst resumes development and in due course a new young is born. Another interesting finding is that the stomach anatomy and digestion physiology resemble those of ruminants in many features, which enables some species at least to make the most efficient use of poor quality low-protein food during hard times.

About fifty species of native rats and mice are found in Australia. Although they all belong to one family, the Muridae, they have radiated widely and various members have convergent resemblance to rodents of the family Muridae and other families in other parts of the world. The native rats and mice of the genus *Pseudomys* resemble the true rats and mice of the old world, the Broad-toothed Rat (*Mastacomys fuscus*) is like a vole, the hopping mice of the genus *Notomys* resemble the jerboas of the old world and the kangaroo-rats of North America, the tree rats of the genera *Mesembriomys* and *Conilurus* which live in tree hollows and feed on the ground have the habits of some kinds of squirrels, and so on. We do not know a great deal about our rodents and study has been hampered by the confused state of their systematics. There are many desert species. Two of these, *Notomys alexis* and *Pseudomys hermannsburgensis*, can live happily on dry seeds without drinking water, and have a greater ability to conserve water by producing concentrated urine and dry faeces than any other desert rodents on any continent.

The Australian bat fauna consists of about fifty species of which ten are fruit and nectar feeders of the suborder Megachiroptera, and the rest, which are normally insectivorous, are in the suborder Microchiroptera. On the whole our bats are not very different from those of South-east Asia, and there are few endemic genera. The best known of the bats are probably the flying foxes because of their reputation as pests of cultivated fruit. One of them, the Grey-headed species (*Pteropus poliocephalus*) is one of the largest of bats and may have a wingspan over four and a half feet. The Ghost Bat (*Macroderma gigas*) of northern and central Australia, is the largest of the Microchiroptera. It is a rapacious predator and its carnivorous diet consists of small birds, small mammals including other bats, lizards, large insects, etc.

There is no doubt that the marsupials and rodents have declined more than other vertebrates since European settlement began. A few species, such as the Red Kangaroo, have benefited from habitat changes but a large number have declined in numbers and geographical range. Although many explanations have been offered the main reason for the decline has undoubtedly been habitat changes due to clearing and especially grazing by domestic stock, aggravated by the rabbit. Possibly natural long-term environmental changes are also involved. A number of species of marsupials and rodents have not been seen for many years and some of them are thought to be extinct. In view of recent experiences with supposedly extinct mammals and birds, some or all of them may yet reappear. Leadbeater's Possum (*Gymnobelideus leadbeateri*) was known from only five specimens collected between 1867 and 1909, and was believed to be extinct when it was found again in 1961. It is now known to inhabit several hundred square miles of Victorian forest. The Pigmy Possum (*Burramys parvus*) was known only from Pleistocene fossil bones when a living example was found in Victoria in 1966. A third example is the New Holland Mouse (*Pseudomys novaehollandiae*) which until recently was known from only four specimens collected between 1840 and the 1880s. In December 1967 and February 1968 living examples were collected at two different localities in New South Wales, at one of which, near Port Stephens, it was surprisingly abundant.

Conclusions

The foregoing is a summary of our present knowledge of Australian vertebrates, and abundantly illustrates the importance of the fauna which we propose should be conserved. In spite of the profound changes that have taken place since Europeans came to Australia we have lost very little of the vertebrate fauna. It is our duty to ensure that the position does not deteriorate further and to rehabilitate the seriously depleted species. The provision of more reserves is most urgent. Probably a more urgent task is a fauna survey of the whole continent to determine what we have and where it is. We do not know where to find some animals and there is little or no information on the habitat requirements of most of them. Very few reserves or national parks have been chosen primarily for animal conservation: the chief reasons have been scenery or catchment preservation or reservation of state forests for economic exploitation. It cannot be expected that such reserves will necessarily be adequate for animals and there are numerous species that are not present in any reserve.

The job is not completed with the provision of reserves. We need to know the important requirements of the individual species — food, shelter, and adequate living space — and manage the reserves accordingly so that stable self-perpetuating populations are maintained. The habitat is never stable and may become unsuitable with time. Some examples may illustrate this point. The journals of explorers provide evidence that the Red Kangaroo was relatively uncommon in western New South Wales at the time of its discovery. The elimination of saltbush and shrubs by sheep and thinning of the tree cover has produced a relatively treeless short-grass plant community that has favoured the increase of the kangaroo. R. M. Warneke has found that the country in which Leadbeater's Possum now occurs was devastated in the disastrous bushfires of 1939. The optimum habitat of the possum is presumably the young regenerating Mountain Ash (*Eucalyptus regnans*) forest which still has a dense undergrowth of acacias and other small trees. As the forest matures the undergrowth disappears and it seems likely that the possum will again become rare. Our studies indicate that the habitat of the New Holland Mouse at Port Stephens is an unstable one. It is a rather open, dry sclerophyll forest on fixed dunes with a dense shrub understory chiefly of acacias and other legumes, an ideal habitat for a seed-eating mouse. The shrubby habitat is apparently a seral stage following a bushfire some years ago.

These observations indicate that if we wish to have some animals in reasonable numbers it will be necessary to preserve early successional stages in the vegetation by such management procedures as fire, the bulldozer, or grazing stock. Conversely, some species may become too abundant and threaten to change the habitat in undesirable directions. In such cases the surplus would have to be removed.

It may be that the best way to preserve some species in reasonable numbers is on land already utilized for economic purposes. In the higher parts of the north-eastern corner of New South Wales the dominant uses of land are beef-cattle grazing and forestry. This area supports a remarkably varied and abundant mammal fauna, including eleven species of kangaroos and wallabies. The eucalypt woodland is only partly cleared for grazing, and grazing intensity is in general not severe enough to prevent eucalypt regeneration. The effect has been to create a considerably greater amount of forest edge in which kangaroos and wallabies find shelter, and open feeding areas on which the grass is kept fairly short by cattle. The numbers of kangaroos and wallabies present are much higher than in untouched forest. Should this form of grazing management cease the number of native herbivores would inevitably decrease. The best thing to do for the wildlife in this situation would be to leave the area alone.

References

Bradshaw, S.D. and Main, A.R., 'Behavioural Attitudes and Regulation of Temperature in *Amphibolurus* Lizards', *J. Zool.*, 154: 193-221. London, 1968.

Calaby, J. H., 'Mammals of the upper Richmond and Clarence Rivers, New South Wales', *Div. of Wildl. Res. Techn. Paper No. 10*, CSIRO, 1966.

Cogger, H., *Australian Reptiles in Colour*, Reed, 1967.

Darlington, P. J., *Zoogeography: The Geographical Distribution of Animals*, John Wiley, 1957.

Frith, H. J. and Calaby, J. H., *Kangaroos*, Cheshire, 1969.

Keith, K. and Calaby, J. H., 'The New Holland Mouse *Pseudomys novaehollandiae* (Waterhouse) in the Port Stephens district, New South Wales', *CSIRO Wild Res.*, 13: 45-58, *1968*.

Lake, J. S., Principal fishes of the Murray-Darling river system in *Australian Inland Waters and their Fauna* (Ed. A. H. Weatherley), Aust. Nat. University Press, 1967.

Main, A. R., Ecology, systematics and evolution of Australian frogs in *Advances in Ecological Research* (Ed. J. B. Cragg), London: Academic Press, 1968.

Mees, G. F., 'The Subterranean Freshwater Fauna of Yardie Creek Station, North West Cape, Western Australia', *J. Roy. Soc. W. Aust.*, 45: 24-32, 1962.

Merrilees, D., 'Man the Destroyer: late Quaternary Changes in the Australian Marsupial Fauna', *J. Roy. Soc. W. Aust.*, 51: 1-24; 1968.

Rowley, I., 'A Fourth Species of Australian Corvid', *Emu*, 66; 191-210, 1967.

Storr, G. M., 'Some Aspects of the Geography of Australian Reptiles', *Senck. Biol.*, 45: 577-89, 1964.

Straughan, I. R. and Main, A. R., 'Speciation and Polymorphism in the genus *Crinia* Tschudi (Anura, Leptodactylidae) in Queensland', *Proc. Roy. Soc. Q.*, 78: 11-28, 1966.

Tindale, N. B., Ecology of primitive aboriginal man in Australia in 'Biogeography and Ecology in Australia', *Monogr. Biol.* 8, The Hague: W. Junk, 1959.

Whitley, G. P., *Native Freshwater Fishes of Australia*, Jacaranda, 1960.

The Invertebrates

Elizabeth N. Marks

Introduction

It has been estimated that over ninety-seven per cent of the known species of animals in the world are invertebrates, and over seventy-five per cent are insects. These figures include unicellular animals (Protozoa) and marine animals. No total count has been made for Australia but estimates of our known land and freshwater species include 1,440 vertebrates (A. Keast), 750 molluscs (D. F. McMichael) and over 55,000 insects (I. M. Mackerras).

Why then is it that our invertebrates, which make up the greatest part of our fauna, are so seldom considered in discussions and decisions on conservation? The enormous number of species, and often of individuals, coupled with the small size or obscure habits of many species gives an overall impression that invertebrates are so plentiful that few are likely to be in danger of extinction. Furthermore, the wording of legislation and of many popular writings has conditioned the average Australian to equate the terms 'fauna', 'wildlife' and 'animals' with vertebrates. A breakthrough in the official attitude is heralded in a 'Draft for a Wildlife Conservation Act' for New South Wales in which 'animal' means birds, mammals, and members of any other class of animals listed on a schedule of the Act, that are indigenous to Australia.

The reasons for the conservation of any animal or plant species may be scientific, aesthetic, and/or economic. A great variety of scientific reasons, often of potential economic importance, provide our strongest arguments for conservation of particular invertebrate species.

As our invertebrates, both fossil and living, become better studied, much more evidence of the history of our fauna will be revealed, both of ancient history concerning its origins, and of recent history concerning the evolution and distribution of existing species. A significant contribution to the latter can be expected from genetical studies, as is clearly indicated by the very few already undertaken.

L. Brundin has recently emphasized that we are short of time for the study of trans-antarctic phylogenetic relationships. He says

> We have to realize that the principal answer as to the history of austral life most probably will be delivered by invertebrates and that much more of basic, strongly specialized field work is badly needed. But the utterly important virgin biotypes of the southern lands disappear very rapidly as a consequence of human agency.

Another aspect of evolutionary importance concerns the internal parasites of our native vertebrates. Australia, because of its long isolation, offers a unique and important opportunity for study of the evolution of host-parasite relationships. Study of the interactions caused by infecting native Australian hosts with the parasites of closely related exotic animals or infecting the exotic animals with the parasites of their native relatives (e.g. infecting an introduced rat with the nematode of a native rat) can throw light on the rate at which a parasite can evolve a permanent relationship with its host. It may also help resolve whether host reaction is in fact an indication that association with the parasite is of recent origin, and whether in the final evolutionary stage of the association there is no host reaction at all.

Scientific interest of a different kind concerns the role a species plays in the community of which it is part. Almost all invertebrates are involved in 'food-chains' directly or indirectly providing food for other animals. Many play essential roles in the aeration of soil, in the decay of dead vegetable and animal matter, or in the pollination of plants. Some prey on or parasitize species which would otherwise increase in numbers sufficiently to cause severe damage to their environment. Thus there is a balanced system in each biological community. Just as man depends on an assortment of renewable resources which are directly useful to him (like crops which require soil fertility which requires microflora and invertebrates, leaf-litter chewers and decomposers etc.), so also do all other species depend on their own assortments of renewable resources. Thus those species upon which we depend indirectly are much more abundant than those which we exploit or enjoy directly.

Purely aesthetic reasons for conservation are more difficult to define. In the more spectacular of our butterflies, moths and beetles, there is beauty of colour and pattern which is not obvious in many other invertebrates of small size or cryptic habits. Nevertheless, under the keen eye of the naturalist, the study of their form, their habits, and their life histories provides a charm, a relaxation, even a philosophy. Australia may not produce a Darwin or a Fabre, but our invertebrates present a scarcely tapped resource for intellectual enjoyment to fill the leisure hours of this computer age.

Economic reasons for conservation involve immediate usefulness to man. Of obvious benefit are the invertebrate parasites and predators of pests that infest man, his livestock, or his crops; and the marine animals which are harvested for his food or which by their beauty provide a tourist attraction. The more obscure but essential role of invertebrates in man's environment has already been indicated. Destruction of many useful or harmless animals often accompanies chemical control of pests, but our knowledge is insufficient to prove that the role of one native species could not be taken by another if the first disappeared. There are, however, analogies in the disruption of the natural balance that has occurred in other countries; and it is usually only after the virtual disappearance of a species that this knowledge becomes available.

Problems in conservation of the various groups of land and freshwater invertebrates have much in common, but are entirely different from those associated with the marine fauna which are considered elsewhere. The necessarily few examples that can be discussed in this chapter have been selected not for their functional importance, but to illustrate that among Australian invertebrates are many fascinating animals worthy of preservation and that some are already in danger of extinction.

Living Fossils and Missing Links

Among the arthropods there are some groups which are best known as fossils but which still have one or more apparently scarcely altered living representatives. There are also several small but exceedingly interesting groups of animals which are indicators of the common ancestry of major groups.

Triops

The Shield Shrimps (Order Notostraca) are very primitive crustaceans with only nine living species in two genera. Their worldwide distribution is explained by their passive method of dispersal and their geological age.

They breed mainly in temporary surface waters, and have drought-resistant eggs which are blown about in the dust after the pools have dried out. The eggs are sticky when first laid so it is likely they may also be transported by birds. The shrimps' present distribution is thus not dependent on ancient land connections.

Triassic fossils 200 million years old closely resemble living *Triops*. Two modern tools of classification, spectrographic analysis of the blood haemoglobin and chromosome counts, show three of the four present-day species of *Triops* to be very closely related. The fourth species, which differs in chromosome numbers, but has not been subjected to blood analysis, is *T. australiensis*, the green Shield Shrimp of dry inland Australia.

T. australiensis is about two inches long, with a flattened, almost circular carapace about one inch across and slender abdominal segments projecting behind. Within a few days of rain in central Australia, every muddy pool is crowded with hundreds of these animals which are preyed on avidly by water birds and aquatic beetles, and which develop from the resting eggs to sexual maturity within two weeks. They swim on their backs, but finally flounder dorsal side up onto the mud or sand at the pool's edge and scoop a hole deep enough for the body to lie in. Presumably the females lay their bright red eggs there before they die. Their bodies half embedded in the dried mud appear like fossils in the making. In these depressions the dried mud often contains eggs from which young can be hatched and reared in aquaria.

Several interesting features of *T. australiensis* need investigation by naturalists living near their habitats. The proportion of males taken in samples has varied from ten per cent to forty per cent, which might be due to a difference in mortality rates between the sexes. To check this, samples would have to be taken regularly throughout the history of the pool from the time hatchings occurred. The number of limbless abdominal segments varies from seven to twelve, and it seems possible this may vary with seasonal or environmental (e.g. salinity) conditions. Although Shield Shrimps, because they differ so little from their ancient ancestors, may be said to exemplify evolutionary stagnation, *T. australiensis*, with its ability to live and disperse widely in the most arid parts of Australia, seems well equipped to survive in this modern age.

The same may not be true so far as Australia is concerned of its relative, *Lepidurus viridis*, a species known from all continents. In Australia it is restricted to winter rainfall areas with a typical mediterranean climate and is found only in ponds which carry an open shrubby vegetation and are dry during summer. A. R. Main has observed that of numerous breeding sites round Perth known to him ten years ago only one now remains, for they occurred in land that is easily cleared and drained for intensive agriculture. The remaining site is located in a reserve set aside by the Western Australian government for preservation of the Short-necked Tortoise (*Pseudemydura umbrina*) and within its fifty acres of apparently suitable ponds and ephemeral swamps, *L. viridis* is restricted to one pond about an acre in area. Other associated crustaceans are not similarly restricted and this suggests that the ecology of *L. viridis* is of peculiar interest.

Anaspides

Anaspides tasmaniae, the Mountain Shrimp of Tasmania, caused great excitement seventy years ago when it was realized that it belonged to the Order Syncarida, crustaceans hitherto known only from Carboniferous and Permian fossils in Europe and North America. It seems to have survived almost unchanged for 250 million years.

Since then other living syncarids have been discovered in Europe, Africa and Asia, and in Victoria, as have as well additional Tasmanian species. Part of the fascination about survivors of ancient groups is that we can learn from them about the way that the forms we know as fossils must have lived, and can compare their habits with those of more recently developed groups.

The largest *Anaspides* are nearly two inches long, very dark olive brown animals with long antennae and an elongate flattened body, rather like a shrimp except that the anterior segments of the body remain distinct. They walk or half-swim about on the pool bottom foraging for algae and detritus on weeds and stones and digging in the mud for small worms and other organisms, and although they are clumsy hunters they sometimes capture tadpoles as well. They sunbathe in moderate sunlight but seek shelter under weeds if it is strong and heats the water. When alarmed they can jump vigorously, in and out of water, and when conditions are unfavourable they move against the flow and may crawl out of the water.

Anaspides are now known to be widespread in the highlands of central, western, and southern Tasmania where they occur from 4,000 feet down to 1,000 feet in pools with flowing water. A specimen was killed without struggle when placed with a much smaller Caddis larva, suggesting that perhaps the species had survived here because predators were absent. Small trout and *Anaspides* have often been seen in the same pool, but the effect of introduced fish needs careful watching; otherwise, its survival seems assured for much of its home is already in national parks.

Another syncarid, *Paranaspides lacustris*, the Great Lake Shrimp, is known only from Tasmania's Great Lake. It is a little smaller than *Anaspides*, less flattened, and lighter brown in colour, and it swims and lives in the shelter of the weed on the lake floor at depths of twelve feet or more. Man has already severely tested its powers of survival, for in the 1920s the lake was dammed and its water level was raised about thirty-three feet, killing nearly all the weed in which *Paranaspides* had lived in abundance. Moreover, brown and rainbow trout were also introduced to the lake which had previously supported few large fish. For a while *Paranaspides* was thought to be extinct, but over the years, as the weed has become re-established round the new shores, it has again become reasonably common. Reports suggest that trout do not prey on it to a serious extent. *Paranaspides*, due to these vicissitudes, has been less studied than *Anaspides* and there is argument as to whether it may represent survival of a still more ancient stage. Proposed further large rises in the lake level may again threaten it with extinction.

Peripatus

The name *Peripatus* was given in 1825 to an animal discovered in the West Indies; now, about seventy species are known and they are grouped in the Class Onycophora of the Phylum Arthropoda. Although many, including the Australian species, belong to other genera, they are all referred to by the common name Peripatus.

They were at first thought to be slugs with feet and this well describes their appearance — little (half to two inches long) animals with a thin velvety skin, a soft muscular body wall, two protruding 'feelers' at the anterior end but no distinct head, and with fourteen or more pairs of small unsegmented clawed feet like those of a caterpillar. Some Australian specimens are black or brown, some striped with blue and orange, some patterned with red or indigo diamonds.

Peripatus forms a fascinating link between the annelids or true worms on the one hand and the arthropods on the other, having characters of both; all seem to be descended from a common ancestor. It is generally classed as the most primitive of living arthropods, and its ancient lineage is indicated by a mid-Cambrian marine fossil, 550 million years old, of a very similar animal. Its distinctness from other arthropods has helped to keep it in obscurity, for it is seldom mentioned in popular natural history books.

Most terrestrial arthropods breathe by means of tracheae with openings on the body surface that they can close if necessary. Peripatus cannot close their tracheal openings and so are unable to regulate the amount of air intake or water loss through the tracheae and are obliged to live in a very humid atmosphere to avoid desiccation. They are found in sites that are permanently damp, in or under rotting logs, under stones and in leaf-litter or moss. They move about at night in a rather deliberate leech-like manner and capture small arthropods by throwing over them a sticky secretion from glands beside the mouth.

The Onycophora are divided into two distinct groups, one with an equatorial distribution, and the other with representatives in Chile, South Africa, Australia, Tasmania, New Zealand, New Guinea, New Britain and Ceram. How could these slow, feeble little animals, obliged to live in humid hidden places, become distributed in this way unless the land masses had once been linked together?

They must be among our continent's oldest living inhabitants but we have learned comparatively little more about them since Australian zoologists and naturalists wrote about them sixty to eighty years ago.

Peripatus have been recorded from Queensland, New South Wales, Victoria, Tasmania and Western Australia. Three genera are distinguished (there is another genus in New Guinea which should be looked for on Cape York Peninsula) but the number of species is uncertain. A viviparous species occurs in south-east Queensland and there are oviparous Peripatus in the Blue Mountains of New South Wales and in Victoria. They are known from the wet tropical lowlands of the Cardwell district in north Queensland and from the slopes of Mount Kosciusko at an altitude of 5,700 feet; there is even said to be a species recorded from central Australia. The anatomy, physiology, and mating habits of Australian species have scarcely been touched on, yet these may be expected to provide essential information for a revision of their taxonomy, and until the latter is undertaken we cannot evaluate their distribution. Naturalists could add much to our knowledge by careful observation of them in the field and in captivity.

Many habitats of Peripatus are undoubtedly preserved in our national parks and many habitats are undoubtedly destroyed. Thus one swampy tea-tree area on the outskirts of Brisbane where they were collected thirty years ago is now an industrial site. But we simply do not know enough to say whether we are in danger of losing any species by habitat destruction.

Diplura

Diplura, which live in the same type of habitats as Peripatus, are hexapods (i.e. six-legged animals) belonging to an Order of primitive animals close to the insects. They are considered not to be true insects but probably to represent an early offshoot from the line from which the insects later evolved. Unlike most true insects, they have their mouth-parts enclosed within the head.

Diplura are often very small but Australian species of *Heterojapyx* are among some of the largest known, measuring one to two inches in length. They are long, slender, flattened animals (in appearance a little like a cross between a centipede and an earwig) with long antennae, no eyes, six short legs, and a long abdomen ending in a pair of strong forceps. The forceps are used for catching prey, and a European species guards its eggs and young. Little is known of the biology of Australian Diplura although H. Womersley has provided a handbook by which they may be identified.

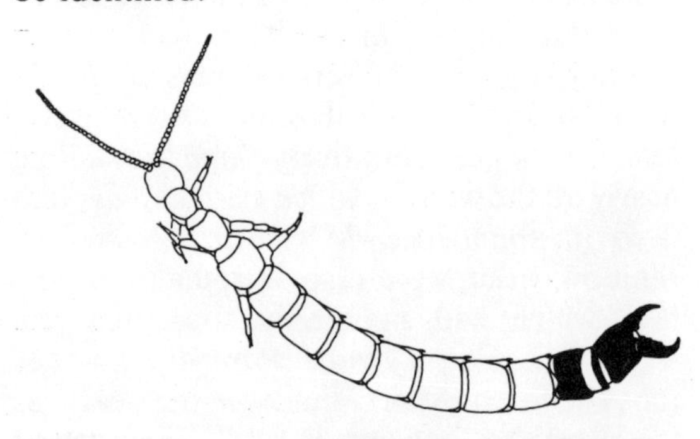

FIGURE 1: Heterojapyx tambourinensis *from near Killarney, Queensland.*

Machilidae

Machilids, known as Bristle-tails or Rockjumpers, are considered to be the most primitive surviving true insects. They are often placed with the better-known silver-fish (Lepismatidae) in the Order Thysanura.

Allomachilis froggatti was the first machilid to be described from Australia, in 1904. It is a silver-fish-like insect, with body about three quarters of an inch in length, large eyes, long antennae, and three long tail appendages, and is clothed with scales of a brownish colour with beautiful variable mottlings. It lives in cracks in cliffs along the sea-shore, particularly sandstone, on the southern Australian coast, and little is known of its biology. This primitive little animal should receive consideration in preservation of shore habitats, for it is of great evolutionary interest.

Peloridiidae

Peloridiids are a family of small and archaic Bugs (Hemiptera) of great interest both to biogeographers and to students of insect evolution. In insects the wings arise from the second and third of the three thoracic segments and are thought to have evolved from flap-like lateral projections of the thorax. Many fossil insects from the Palaeozoic and Mesozoic have flap-like projections on the first thoracic segment as well, and these occur in peloridiids and a few other relatively primitive present-day insects.

Of the twenty known species, nineteen are flightless and one either flightless or fully winged. They are tiny, flattened, straw-coloured slow-moving animals, about one eighth of an inch long, which feed on damp moss growing in conditions of permanently high atmospheric humidity and cool temperatures.

The family occurs in the south of South America, New Zealand, Lord Howe Island, Tasmania and south-eastern Australia as far north as the McPherson Range on the Queensland-New South Wales border. These bugs are often found associated with Antarctic Beeches (*Nothofagus*), a strong indication that both bugs and trees are adapted to similar conditions. *Nothofagus* has a generally similar distribution but there is none on Lord Howe Island, nor in some other peloridiid localities, and despite much searching, no peloridiids have been found associated with *Nothofagus* in New Caledonia or New Guinea. This is another group of animals which by their structure and habits seem to need past land connections to account for their present distribution. Conservation of Australia's peloridiids seems assured by national parks already existing.

Mastotermes

The Giant Termite of northern Australia, *Mastotermes darwiniensis*, which causes great damage to buildings, underground cables, and other structures and can even eat through lead piping, is an animal of great scientific and economic interest. It is not very closely allied to other living termites, and its nearest known relatives are six fossil species of *Mastotermes* thirty million years old from the Oligocene and lower Miocene of Europe. No plea for conserving *Mastotermes* is likely to be well received, but it is in no danger of extinction.

Some Especially Interesting or Vulnerable Species

Native Earthworms

Most native Australian earthworms seem to be unsuited to existence in cultivated soil where they also have competition from introduced garden worms of the family Lumbricidae. Earthworms cannot resist desiccation and they tend to 'stay put'. Whether any species are actually in danger is not known — but they are undoubtedly among the invertebrates whose survival would be aided by preservation of even small areas typical of varied plant and soil associations.

Probably our most famous native species is the giant earthworm of South Gippsland, *Megascolides australis*. A gurgly, sucking sound can be heard as it moves through its burrow. C. Barrett in 1931 pointed out that a worm four feet long, if suspended, will extend to seven feet, so that it is difficult to compare recorded measurements. He considered the average was about three quarters of an inch in diameter and a little over four feet long, with one authenticated specimen of eleven feet. Barrett thought the greatest enemy of this animal was the plough, but that it was so abundant that even intensive cultivation was unlikely to make it scarce. Farming practices have since changed greatly and the Victorian Fisheries and Wildlife Department in 1967 commenced a survey to establish the present status and distribution of *M. australis*.

A second giant earthworm, *Digaster longmani*, occurs in areas between Tamborine and Kyogle along the Queensland-New South Wales border; a suspended specimen measured five feet five inches long and about one inch thick. These animals are sometimes seen in rainforest when they emerge from the ground after heavy rain. Little is yet known about their natural history but they are well provided for by existing national parks.

Kosciuscola

On Mount Kosciusko above 5,000 feet, in the late summer and autumn, the predominant insects are little flightless grasshoppers, *Kosciuscola tristis*, which have a remarkable ability to change colour in response to temperature in a way unknown in any other grasshoppers.

These are rather sturdy animals about three quarters of an inch long, with strong hind legs and only rudiments of wings. On a warm sunny day they bask in the sunshine on or near plants of Snow Daisy (*Celmisia*) and tussock grass (*Poa*), sometimes feeding on the latter, and when disturbed they will jump several feet. In the late afternoon they become sluggish and burrow into the bases of the tussocks.

When they emerge from the tussocks about sunrise, the males are a dull, near black in colour, but two to three hours later, on a clear sunny day, they have become a bright greenish-blue; in the later afternoon they begin to turn dark again. The females show a similar change but from near black to brown or green.

K. H. L. Key and M. F. Day studied this phenomenon and showed that at temperatures below 15°C. the males were dark, and above 25°C. they were blue. The colour change was brought about by migration in opposite directions within the epidermal cells of two types of granules. Small, highly refractive granules were near the surface in the pale phase and larger, dark brown granules in the dark phase. They concluded that this ability of a black animal to become pale was an important advantage in an alpine environment, enabling it to make best use of the high solar radiation. While blackness facilitates a rapid rise of body temperature in the morning, the ability to become progressively paler as its temperature rises is thought to protect it against overheating; it thus has greater freedom to go about its business in an environment where survival of the species depends on a rapid rate of development and reproduction.

K. tristis ranges from the Kosciusko massif south to Mount Buffalo, and as its habitats are already in national parks, preservation of this interesting animal seems assured.

The Bent Wing Swift Moth

One of Australia's largest and most beautiful moths is the hepialid, *Zelotypia stacyi*, the Bent Wing Swift Moth, whose nearest relative is a South African species. The female may have a wing span up to nearly ten inches, with body length about three and a half inches; the male is smaller, with a wing span up to about seven and a half inches. The long wings are orange-brown, the forewings patterned with darker and paler patches and a broad outer margin of wavy lines. This species occurs in coastal forests from the Queensland border to Cambawarra Mountain south of

Sydney, though it is best known from the area between Taree and Gosford. The larva is a wood-borer and tunnels in the stems of saplings and small trees of *Eucalyptus saligna* and *E. tereticornis*, taking two to three years to complete its development, and growing up to six inches long. About February the adult moths emerge during the afternoon and fly at night. Newcastle miners sixty to eighty years ago made pocket money by rearing this species from timbers cut for pit-props, for it has always been much sought after by collectors. We should make sure that adequate habitats of *Z. stacyi* are included in national parks; it seems doubtful whether this is so at present. Recently the Australian Entomological Society recommended that it be listed as a protected animal in the proposed new Wildlife Conservation Act of New South Wales.

Native Land Snails

There are several groups of terrestrial gastropods that are confined to Australia.

About thirty-seven species of the genus *Bothriembryon* of the family Bulimulidae occur in south-west Western Australia, a few in South Australia and one in central Australia; many of them have distinctive shells. A. R. Main, who has studied them, says it is an old relict group which was probably declining before European settlement began. Many species have a very restricted distribution, and some consist only of two or three populations each occupying a few hundred square yards of suitable habitat. All species aestivate (become dormant) during the dry season. Species with long spired shells frequent the wetter habitats and aestivate under rocks and logs. The more globose species aestivate by burrowing to a depth of several inches in the soil beneath shrubs, mallee, or, on the Nullarbor Plain (where all the species have white shells), under saltbushes. In order to survive a dry period *Bothriembryon* secretes a tough mucous plate, the epiphragm, which seals the shell aperture and is apparently permeable to air but not to water vapour. This plate is thick in species from arid areas. Once sealed in, if undisturbed, the animal can live for months or years in a state of suspended animation. As soon as wet conditions recur, the epiphragm is discarded. On the Nullarbor, hundreds of these white discs have been observed under bushes after rain. The effectiveness of the epiphragm in regulating water loss is apparently dependent on the presence of the surrounding soil. If the sheltering shrubs and litter are removed or burnt, or the soil structure altered by trampling of stock, the aestivating animals fail to persist. Thus many species of *Bothriembryon* are particularly vulnerable to habitat alteration by fire or by hoofed animals.

Australia has several genera of the family Caryodidae, an endemic Australian group with relationships to the South American and South African faunas. The genus *Anoglypta* contains a single species *Anoglypta launcestonensis*, the Granulated Tasmanian Snail, which is confined to the dense tree fern country of the wet mountain gullies in north-eastern Tasmania. This has a rather flattened conical shell about one inch high and one and a half inches across; its upper surface is mainly yellowish green and granulated, the lower shining black with a bright yellow band.

The genus *Hedleyella* contains six species occurring on mountains along the east coast. *Hedleyella falconeri*, the Giant Panda, has a beautifully glossy brown rounded shell, up to four inches across and high. It ranges from Barrington Tops to south-east Queensland. On a damp night in rainforest it is fascinating to watch these animals moving about, for by day they are tucked away in crevices and more often the empty shells are observed. It would be interesting to know which vertebrates are their main predators. The Giant Panda feeds on fungi and rotting vegetation, and once its rainforest habitat is cleared it does not persist for long in an area.

These and others of our forest snails are

dependent for survival on preservation of suitable areas of their habitat.

Macropanesthia

The Cockroaches (Blattodea), which were the dominant group of insects at the end of the Upper Carboniferous Period (270 million years ago), are the most ancient surviving Order of insects. Today's cockroaches appear little different from their ancient ancestors. Australia has many interesting species, the largest of which is the wingless *Macropanesthia rhinoceros*. (See photo.) It is unfortunate that the term 'cockroach' conjures up the vision of a repulsive domestic pest, for *Macropanesthia* is a handsome and engaging creature. Nearly two and a half inches long, and half as wide, it looks from above like a newly-varnished, glossy brown, horizontally-grooved oval shield, for its head is hidden below the prothorax.

These animals live on forested sandy ridges in north Queensland where they burrow in the sandy soil, aided no doubt by their very stout legs which bear an array of heavy spines. At night they move about on the surface and in favoured habitats the soil may be quite churned over by their activities.

Macropanesthia is an advanced type of cockroach for instead of depositing its egg case in some secluded site, as our domestic species do, it carries it within its body until the eggs hatch, thus protecting them from predators and parasites. F. J. Gay has kept this species in captivity and finds the animals take three to four years to reach maturity, but little is known of their natural history in their native habitat.

It seems likely that as yet no habitats of *Macropanesthia* are included in national parks, and rapid changes in the agricultural and pastoral industries of north Queensland suggest there may be some urgency to assure its preservation. Its winglessness and its long life cycle make it more vulnerable to disaster than most insects.

Keyacris

Keyacris scurra is a very slender wingless grasshopper found on the southern tablelands and part of the south-western slopes of New South Wales and extending into northern Victoria. It is scarcely an inch long, with short, stout antennae, rather prominent ovoid eyes, attenuated hind legs, and a variable colour pattern in shades of grey, brown or buff (and, in females only, green) — in appearance not unlike a twig of grass. Although confined to habitats where the native perennial Kangaroo Grass (*Themeda australis*) predominates, it feeds not on this but on the Common Everlasting (*Helichrysum apiculatum*). Presumably the thick clumps of *Themeda* provide essential shelter either from predators or from adverse climatic conditions.

Adults mate in spring and each female lays about twenty eggs which hatch in December or January; there is only one generation a year. These little animals do not move about much and, though they may jump a foot or two when provoked, each individual probably spends its whole life within a few yards of where it emerged from the egg. It is likely that 130 years ago they were distributed fairly continuously over their present range, except on mountains, but since then intensive grazing by sheep has eliminated *Themeda* over vast areas, so that now *K. scurra* is found only in scattered 'ecological islands' with no chance of moving from one to another. Many of these 'islands' are in small country cemeteries where one to six acres have been fenced for many years to exclude stock, and native vegetation has survived; in these sites *K. scurra* colonies may consist of only a few dozen individuals in each generation.

Males of *K. scurra* have large and distinctively shaped chromosomes and M. J. D. White has made the species the subject of important genetical studies contributing to knowledge of the processes of evolution. He found two races with different numbers of chromosomes, one on the southern tableland

and one (presumably adapted to slightly drier conditions) on the south-western slopes. The two races interbreed successfully, but the hybrids are slightly less vigorous than the pure races. As a result, the zone of interbreeding in nature is as little as half a mile.

White concluded that thousands of generations of selection had perfected a genetic system adapted to the fluctuation of the environment that occurred before the coming of the pastoral industry, but this seemed inadequate to cope with the catastrophic changes resulting from grazing by sheep. He estimated that whereas *K. scurra* probably once occupied forty per cent of its total territory, it now occupies one per cent and as its remaining habitats gradually disappear either temporarily (e.g. by burning or mowing) or permanently, it may become extinct within the next century.

K. scurra belongs to a primitive subfamily of grasshoppers, occurring only in Australia, the Morabinae. Among its 200 species are many inhabitants of sclerophyll forest and savannah woodland, with very limited geographical ranges, and dependent on certain native plants for food and/or shelter. These plants may be almost entirely destroyed by sheep-grazing or by crop-growing, and there are undoubtedly other species whose survival is as precarious as that of *K. scurra*.

Trapdoor Spiders

In the Arthropoda, the Class Arachnida includes scorpions, spiders, ticks, mites, and several smaller and less familiar groups of animals. Because a few are venomous, and some are blood-sucking parasites, arachnids tend to be generally regarded with repugnance and often slaughtered without question. In fact they form an important section of the animal community, performing many useful functions, and only comparatively few are harmful to man or to his livestock, his crops, or his stored products. The worst of the arachnid pests in Australia are those he has introduced into the country himself.

An excellent example of the scientific interest of Australian arachnids is provided by the Trapdoor Spiders — which also, because of their special adaptations, are among the most vulnerable of our invertebrates to habitat destruction. (See photo.) They are members of the Suborder Mygalomorphae, the most primitive Australian representatives of the Order Araneida, the spiders.

In southern Australia, west of the Flinders Range, the dominant group of trapdoor building spiders is the tribe Aganippini, which is restricted to Australia, and has been extensively studied by B. Y. Main. Their life-history is tied to an autumn-winter rainy period. Females never leave their burrows, males leave them only at maturity, when they go in search of mates, after which they die. The animals moult in early autumn, and mature males wander with the first winter rains, usually in May or June. Mating takes place within the female's burrow. Before she begins to lay in October to November, she seals her trapdoor with silk. The young emerge from the cocoon in mid-summer but remain sealed in the burrow with the parent through the dry summer until the seasonal rain makes the ground soft and conditions cool and humid. They then emerge and each digs a burrow of its own, and begins to feed. Normally it will live out its whole life here, enlarging the burrow as it grows. Spiders of all ages can repair the door and rim of their burrows, but only the young ones have the ability to start a new burrow if the first is destroyed. They take several years to reach maturity, and females may live for some years more. The adult female aganippine is a thickset brown or black spider, about one to one and a half inches long, sometimes longer, and its burrow is about one inch in diameter. There are few records of their biting man but if they do, their bite may cause a severe reaction. Trapdoor Spiders are preyed on by scorpions, centipedes and some birds, e.g. magpies.

Main's biological studies have revealed a

fascinating story of adaptive radiation in this group of spiders.

Unmodified forms burrow among the damp dense litter of broad leaves in eucalypt-banksia forest, and their fragile burrow doors are made from litter. They have rather round soft hairy abdomens, and small widely-spaced forwardly directed eyes, and they catch their food, mainly beetles, without leaving the burrow entrance.

Species which burrow in clay-pans subject to seasonal sheet flooding, where there is little or no litter, make thick plug-like or dome-shaped soil doors which prevent collapse, flooding, and erosion of their burrows. Their abdomens have a slightly hardened cuticle, their eyes are moderately large, close together and directed partly to the side; they feed on any suitable prey, but never completely emerge from the burrow to capture it.

Aganippine species in semi-arid environments make a burrow in the dense linear type of litter beneath acacias and casuarinas and, radiating out from it, attach singly by silk to its rim, twig-lines up to ten inches long. These are used as feeling-lines for detecting prey, mainly ants, and the spider will run out along the twig-line to capture its prey, leaving its light door of litter and silk standing wide open. This greater foraging area compensates for the scarcer food, and the spider is physically adapted to it by having large close-set eyes which can look in all directions, and longer legs. From desiccation, it is protected physically by a thickened, often spiny abdominal wall, or by larger size, and behaviourly by deeper burrows sealed in summer by silk and soil.

This complex of behavioural-morphological adaptations has been independently developed in several genera and species, and is also found within races of one species of south-western Australia, *Aganippe raphiduca*. How did several species derived from a common stock and showing similar adaptations originate in the same general geographical area without major topographic barriers? Perhaps repeated westward migrations of an ancestral stock during moist pluvial periods were followed by selection for twig-lining forms during arid interglacial periods of the Pliocene and Pleistocene. Much can be learned today about the evolutionary processes within the group by study of polymorphic species such as *A. raphiduca*. In this respect the sclerophyll area approximating to the wheat-belt country of Western Australia is the most important, for it has within it a great many minor varieties of habitat close together, providing for almost every grade of adaptive level. Preservation of habitats in this area is urgent, for already in some places, undisturbed natural populations of Trapdoor Spiders survive only in ungrazed and unfarmed road verges.

Habitat destruction can befall Trapdoor Spiders without alteration of the main plant-cover. The twig-lining aganippines are absolutely dependent on a stable litter structure for construction and maintenance of their burrows and they live in the dense criss-cross litter mats under acacias and casuarinas. Grazing stock, particularly sheep, with their hooves and their nuzzling after seeds, break up these mats which deteriorate and become subject to erosion by wind and occasionally by water. Life of the spider is four to five years or more, during which alteration of the soil-litter structure of the habitat can mean loss of a generation. On bare ground habitats where the soil is bound by lichens, trampling of hooves affects spiders directly by damage to burrows and indirectly by erosive changes in the soil surface.

In Queensland, Main has recently observed an area of brigalow and vine scrub between Eidsvold and Cracow which had been stocked only one and a half to two years. Where cattle ran, Trapdoor Spider burrows survived close to logs, tussocks, and butts of trees and shrubs. In open ground hoof-damage had almost eliminated them. She estimates that two years of stocking may damage a habitat to the point where brood young are almost un-

Yellow-billed Spoonbill, *Platalea flavipes*. PHOTO COURTESY P. SLATER

On the Black Range, Mambray Creek National Park, southern Flinders Ranges, S.A. PHOTO COURTESY C.W. BONYTHON

Eastern Water Dragon, *Physignathus lesueurii*

Ochrosia elliptica, an important alkaloidal plant confined to rocky patches on the tropical coast of north Queensland. PHOTO COURTESY W. T. JONES

ommon Longicorn Beetle, *Tryphocaria mitchelli*

Splendid Blue Wren, *Malurus splendens*.
PHOTO COURTESY P. SLATER

Acacia baileyana (Cootamundra Wattle)

Orange Chat, *Epthianura aurifrons*. PHOTO COURTESY P. SLATER

Queensland Lungfish, *Neoceratodus forsteri*

Banksia coccinea

Broad-leafed Paperbarks, Wallis Lake, N.S.W. This area is about to be mined for rutile. PHOTO COURTESY A. M. FOX

Southern Short-nosed Bandicoot, *Isoodon obesulus*

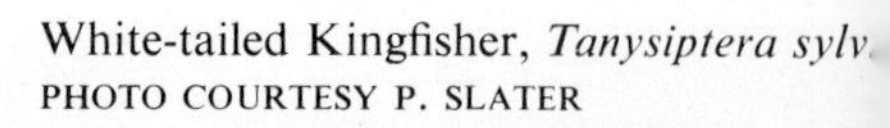

White-tailed Kingfisher, *Tanysiptera sylv.*
PHOTO COURTESY P. SLATER

Yuendumu area, Northern Territory

Orange-eyed Tree Frog, *Hyla chloris*

Platypus, *Ornithorhynchus anatinus*

Bushfire damage at Barren Grounds Nature Reserve, N.S.W.
PHOTO COURTESY A. M. FOX

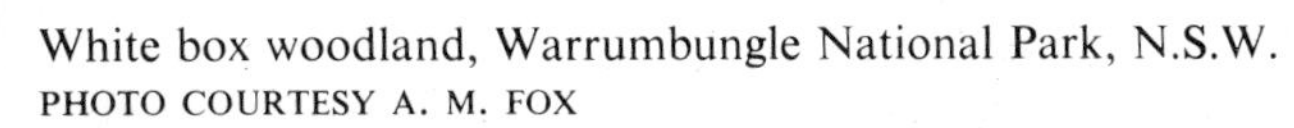

White box woodland, Warrumbungle National Park, N.S.W.
PHOTO COURTESY A. M. FOX

Rainbow bird, *Merops ornatus.*
PHOTO COURTESY P. SLATER

Common Wombat, *Vombatus hirsutus*

Balanophora fungosa, an unusual flowering plant which parasitizes the roots of tropical rainforest trees in north Queensland.
PHOTO COURTESY W. T. JONES

The lower Lachlan River and Gooawarra Nature Reserve, N.S.W. PHOTO COURTESY A. M. FOX

able to colonize. This particular vine scrub supports a unique assemblage of Trapdoor Spiders. One of the principal species in it, *Cataxia maculata*, belongs to a genus found only in Queensland in which each species is characteristic of a particular type of forest.

The animals that are associated with Trapdoor Spiders and often form their prey, e.g. ants, termites, beetles, terrestrial moth-larvae, are equally dependent on undisturbed soil-litter structure.

We can conclude that for preservation of Trapdoor Spiders and many other invertebrates found in the same soil-litter habitats, fauna reserves cannot, without detriment, be subject to any grazing whatsoever by hoofed animals. This often is not understood, or is disregarded by those responsible for administering national parks. On the other hand, if protection is complete and permanent, the area needed for preservation of a species assemblage need not be very great.

Conclusion

We have looked at a very small sample of Australia's invertebrates, and at whether survival of these is desirable and is or could be provided for in national parks or by other means. There are many species of comparable interest known, and undoubtedly many still to be discovered. With a better understanding of the scientific, aesthetic and economic importance of our invertebrates, and of what is happening to them at the present time, what positive steps might we take towards their conservation? There are three basic requirements, without which we are unlikely to achieve success, but if the second takes time to obtain, we can still proceed with the other two.

(1) We must have clear statements of facts concerning any animals about which action is likely to be needed. These can only be provided by invertebrate zoologists (including amateurs) many of whom must first be stirred out of their defeatist attitude that no one will be interested.

(2) We need a central clearing house to which zoologists can submit these facts, and where they can be collated and made known. For instance, information could be brought together concerning animals from the same habitats as *Macropanesthia*. It will probably need evidence from several animal groups before most arguments for invertebrate conservation can be strongly urged, but students of one group are often unaware of work on other groups. The Australian Conservation Foundation, when fully established, might provide this clearing house, but in the meantime the need is urgent and might be met by a leading Museum or a Commonwealth scientific institution. The clearing house need not necessarily press arguments itself, so long as it made the collated facts available to bodies concerned in conservation, both government and private.

(3) We need an increased public interest in and goodwill towards invertebrates, to provide strong backing to the efforts of zoologists. Writers, teachers, and naturalists can contribute most here, for the average zoologist has a very limited audience.

Apart from these three requirements, there are several points on which there needs to be wider understanding amongst those concerned generally with conservation. Grazing stock must be completely excluded from reserves in order to preserve natural communities of invertebrates dwelling in the soil and litter, or dependent on the natural herbage. Quite small reserves, adequately protected, may be sufficient to maintain populations of rare invertebrate species. Some species have a very restricted distribution, such as one mountain top. Some species are dependent for survival on a single plant species.

Clearly there is a tremendous need for study of our invertebrates in the field, so that we can understand what is required for survival of each species. Where it is obvious we cannot ensure its survival, we can at least find out as much as possible about it. Given a greater public and governmental understanding of the interest and importance of our invertebrates, and of the problems in conserving them, there seems no reason why we should not ensure survival of the great majority of these fascinating members of the Australian fauna.

Marine National Parks and Reserves

Donald F. McMichael

The concept of national parks and nature reserves now widely accepted throughout the world has developed almost solely in relation to the terrestrial environment, with the conservation of land areas of special scenic beauty and essentially natural conditions which are set aside primarily for recreation or the conservation of fauna and flora. Although some of these areas include freshwater habitats such as lakes and rivers as important features, and others include coastal land or off-shore islands, the conservation of marine areas, whether intertidal or subtidal, has been largely neglected until recently. This is because of the much greater urgency of conservation on land, where floras and faunas are rapidly disappearing, whereas man's impact on the oceans has been relatively insignificant until the present century. The oceans of the world have not in general been subjected to ownership by individuals, nor has public use of them been restricted, with the exception of waters closed to navigation or fishing.

In recent years, however, there has been increasing evidence of significant alterations to natural conditions in marine environments as a result of human activity. This is especially true in the intertidal zone — the seashore in the broad sense — and in the strip of land immediately adjacent to the shore, where there has been a striking increase in conflicting demands for land and water use, particularly for recreation, housing, mining, port and harbour facilities, commercial fishing, waste and sewage disposal. Such conservation measures as have been taken in the sea have largely been designed to protect commercially valuable species (including marine mammals, reptiles, fishes, molluscs and crustaceans) which have shown signs of depletion as a result of over-fishing. These measures have included the fixing of minimum legal sizes, the closing of waters (especially breeding or nursery areas), the application of closed seasons, and restrictions on fishing gear, and they have usually been aimed at maintaining fisheries on a sustained yield basis.

However, a number of events during the last two decades have stimulated a worldwide interest in the conservation of marine environments for both recreational and nature conservation purposes. These events can be summarized as follows:

(1) The development of the new recreational activity generally known as skindiving — a term which includes both surface swimming with the aid of a snorkel breathing-tube and underwater swimming with the aid of an aqualung or 'self-contained underwater breathing apparatus' (scuba) — has resulted in much greater awareness of the beauty of underwater environments. It has also made the taking of fish with spear-guns a relatively simple matter, and this in turn has had a dramatic effect on populations of some species of fishes.

(2) Several other groups of organisms which have provided the basis for recreational activities (shells, corals, crustacea and other edible marine organisms) have shown signs of depletion, partly as a result of the destruction of habitat by shell collectors and other reef fossickers who leave boulders overturned. The activity of coral collectors is also especially

damaging in coral reef areas, and further damage has been caused to fragile coral growths by large numbers of visitors. This has caused concern to biologists, conservationists, and those associated with the tourist industry.

(3) There has been increasing interest in the exploitation of marine resources, both biological and mineral, and increasing use of the sea for the disposal of wastes.

These events have led to an increasing concern for the establishment of national parks and nature reserves, embracing both foreshore and subtidal lands, and giving protection to the marine organisms living on and swimming in the waters above those lands. Before proceeding to a consideration of marine parks and reserves which have been established in Australia and elsewhere, some general remarks on problems of conservation in the marine environment are necessary.

Some Basic Data on Conservation Problems in the Sea

A study of the literature relating to the effects of man on marine organisms reveals a number of facts which are relevant to the need for conservation in the sea. From these, some principles emerge which should be borne in mind when marine parks and reserves are being established.

(1) It is clear that man can force some marine animals to the point of extinction, especially the larger, slower-breeding species such as the whales, the Dugong and the Manatee. Some species may indeed survive only if given complete protection from hunting, or sanctuary in marine fauna reserves. On the other hand, most marine species, by virtue of their wide distribution and the large number of eggs they produce, are unlikely to be brought close to extinction by overfishing, though there may be depletion of local populations. In general, marine animals have a larval stage which is widely dispersed by ocean currents, and so a population which has been depleted in one area can usually be re-established by the immigration of larvae derived from distant populations. Marine parks and reserves would therefore provide useful refuges for breeding populations from which natural replenishment of depleted stocks for fisheries could take place.

While there is some evidence that shell collectors and others seeking intertidal organisms can cause depletion of local faunas, primarily through the disturbance of habitat by leaving boulders overturned, there seems little to show that collecting of this kind has led to the reduction of any species towards extinction. It does, however, seem likely that sedentary or highly localized populations (such as Baler shells of the genus *Melo* or Giant Clams of the genus *Tridacna*) subjected to intensive collecting could be reduced to levels from which they might take many years to recover. In a few areas close to large cities, where especially heavy collecting of intertidal invertebrates for food or bait has occurred, there has been marked reduction in population size (for example at Gunnamatta Bay near Sydney, which in 1967 was closed to all forms of collecting).

(2) Massive natural destruction of intertidal organisms as a result of storms occurs in both tropical and temperate seas from time to time. It must be assumed that such catastrophes are among the normal hazards faced by marine communities. The destruction is sometimes accompanied by environmental changes which prevent re-establishment of the community, but recovery is usually rapid.

A recent natural phenomenon of great importance is the outbreak of a plague of the Crown of Thorns seastar (*Acanthaster planci*) in Great Barrier Reef waters. This seastar feeds on living corals, and is now so abundant that large areas of some reefs have been reduced to rubble. The cause of this population explosion is uncertain, and to date no method has been found to control it. The collection of shells of *Charonia tritonis*, the Trumpet Shell, has been suggested as a possible causative factor, since *C. tritonis* feeds on *Acanthaster* (as well as other Echinoderms). However, Trumpet Shells have not been collected commonly in Queensland waters south of Cooktown for quite a long time, and I can find no evidence that they were ever common. It seems unlikely therefore that collection of Trumpet Shells was the primary cause of the sudden increase in numbers of *Acanthaster* which has occurred in the last few years and which appears to be continuing. Nevertheless the collecting of *C. tritonis* has now been prohibited in Queensland waters as a precautionary measure.

(3) There are a number of marine foreshore environments which, though generally unattractive and at times offensive to man, are of great importance for various reasons. Among these may be mentioned the mangrove swamps and mudflats, which may be unpleasant to walk in, offensive to smell, the habitat of biting mosquitoes and sandflies, and areas where debris accumulates; yet these have been found to be among the most fertile areas of the world, the breeding grounds and nurseries of important commercial fishery species; and in addition they serve as silt traps and stabilizers of estuary foreshores.

(4) The marine environment is becoming contaminated with waste products of human society, especially near large urban and industrial centres. Some of these pollutants are spread widely by ocean currents and may affect marine organisms directly or indirectly. In general their effects are local and apparently transitory (e.g. sewage and most industrial waste products); but a few contaminants such as pesticide residues and radio-active wastes may be accumulated by living organisms, and could have long-term effects as yet unrealized. There is already much evidence that DDT and its breakdown products are now widespread in marine organisms throughout the world, and that the accumulation of these substances in some species, e.g. sea birds, may have serious effects on their breeding rate.

One of the most serious pollutants of comparatively recent concern is oil, of which great quantities are released into the sea each year, some coming from tankers sunk in World War II, some deliberately discharged during tanker cleaning operations, and some from accidental damage to tankers and oilwells. International Conventions for the Prevention of Pollution of the Sea by Oil, in 1954 and 1962, laid down some requirements to guard against pollution of coastal areas, and new techniques in cleaning tankers will help to reduce this threat; but the tonnage of oil being carried at sea is increasing, and offshore oilwells are becoming more widespread, so that the danger of accidental spillage is growing. Once released, oil slicks can drift for long distances, and various techniques have been used to destroy or disperse them before they reach the shore. In temperate waters oil, if left alone, will eventually disperse. Studies made after the *Torrey Canyon* disaster suggest that oil generally has little effect on marine organisms other than sea birds. As yet there has been no occasion to my knowledge when a large quantity of oil has settled on a living coral reef.

(5) The development of new techniques for offshore mineral extraction means that there will be increasing interest in mining the deposits lying on the continental shelf. The effects of silt arising from the mining operations are likely to be local, depending on the current systems, but some particular environments, such as coral reefs, are likely to be especially vulnerable to damage.

(6) There is some evidence that recreational activities, including the intrusion of underwater swimmers and the presence of fishing boats, affect the behaviour of some species of fishes, and according to F. H. Talbot such activities may be undesirable in areas required for the study of natural populations.

The Need for Conservation Areas in the Marine Environment and some Principles for their Establishment and Management

To preserve marine environments in a relatively natural state it is desirable to set aside areas of the sea floor as marine reserves in which the fauna and flora can survive unmolested. Such reserves could serve many purposes, but they generally would fall into the categories of national parks or nature reserves, and the two should be carefully distinguished. Nature reserves would include areas reserved specifically for fishery management purposes and those set aside for scientific reference or for the conservation of species generally. Examples of these types of reserve include the proposed Marra Marra Creek Nature Reserve in the upper reaches of the Hawkesbury estuary near Sydney, which is intended to preserve a large area of mangroves and the fauna associated with them; the proposed marine reserve off the far south coast of New South Wales adjacent to the Nadgee Nature Reserve; and areas closed to commercial fishing such as American River, Kangaroo Island, South Australia.

A marine park should primarily be an area of scenic beauty, principally underwater, but preferably also in its coastal landscape. Diversity of marine life is essential and a wide variety of underwater land forms is desirable, except in coral reef areas where there is usually a fairly simple landscape, but where coral growth provides the interest. Of the utmost importance are factors affecting sea conditions, especially shelter from exposure to waves of more than a gentle nature, and the absence of strong ocean currents. Clarity of water is also essential, and careful surveys should be made throughout the year before selecting sites, with special attention to any potential source of pollution or sediment which might subsequently affect water clarity.

A primary problem for marine parks and reserves is likely to be the avoidance of pollution. For this reason conservation areas should be situated well away from industrial and urban complexes (though marine parks obviously need to be relatively accessible to users), and away from areas affected by rivers and ocean currents which might carry pollution into them. Adequate oceanic surveys should be made before any disposal of wastes near conservation areas is permitted. Because many marine organisms are particularly susceptible to pesticides even in very low dilutions, the use of any kind of pesticide near these areas should be prohibited.

A continuous watch for evidence of pollution should be kept by management staff, and immediate action taken if any indication of pollution is found. One of the most likely sources of pollution is drifting oil, and the experiences of recent years, especially with the *Torrey Canyon*, suggest that the methods to be adopted for oil dispersal should be carefully worked out in advance. The use of detergents is especially undesirable close to the areas to be conserved, as detergents are highly toxic to marine organisms; but it would be permissible if the oil can be treated at a sufficiently great distance. Other methods of treatment which have been used include sinking the oil with chalk, but this has been criticized as leading to slow release of the oil over a long period of time. It seems that more research is necessary before adequate techniques can be developed to deal with this threat.

The design of laboratories, accommodation and other visitor facilities, the siting of boat anchorages, and particularly the method of sewage disposal and location of outfalls should be carefully considered in relation to possible pollution.

Legislation establishing marine parks and reserves should provide for the permanent reservation of the sea floor against all forms of mining, including oilwell drilling.

Commercial fishing for pelagic species generally need not conflict with the conservation of essentially bottom-dwelling organisms, and therefore could be permitted in marine conservation areas, provided that the bottom is not disturbed by the fishing technique. Other forms of commercial fishing should, however, be prohibited. Recreational fishing and collecting of marine organisms such as shells should be prohibited in marine nature reserves, although in order to attract visitors these may be permitted in some areas of marine national parks, provided that proper controls, including bag limits, are applied, and rare or biologically interesting species are rigidly protected. From a conservation point of view, there can be no logical distinction between fishing with spearguns, fishing with hook and line, and shell collecting. In each case organisms are being removed from the population and the effect depends on both the rate of removal and the abundance of the species being taken. Speargun fishing is generally more efficient than line fishing, and has been found to lead more rapidly to depletion of local populations of sedentary fishes. Shell collecting is generally selective, the rarer species being sought out and removed, while common species are left alone.

Any interference with the natural environment through careless anchoring of boats, turning of boulders, or walking on fragile coral should be discouraged, though obviously too many restrictions on activity in national parks will lessen their appeal, and some compromise may be necessary. Interference of any kind in nature reserves to be used for the study of natural communities should be kept to an absolute minimum.

The Development of the Marine Parks Movement

Several countries have shown interest in conserving both seashore and underwater environments in recent years. The United States has made most progress in this field, and now has well-established parks in several places, including the Virgin Islands and the Florida Keys, while others are in the blueprint stage. The U.S. National Parks Service has been evolving new techniques of management for these areas, and is thus pioneering once again in the national parks field. However, it seems that Australia may have been one of the first countries to establish a *de facto* marine park, when in 1939 the coral reef and adjacent waters at Green Island off Cairns, Queensland, were protected under fisheries legislation against the taking of all marine organisms, other than fishes caught by rod and line or hand line. In 1963, similar protection was given to the coral reef adjacent to Heron Island and to nearby Wistari Reef, in the Capricorn Group of islands and reefs at the southern extremity of the Great Barrier Reef. Like many of the Barrier Reef islands, Green and Heron are dedicated as National Parks under the Queensland Forestry Act, but this status extends only to highwater mark. The protection of the adjacent beaches and intertidal and subtidal areas by the Department of Harbours and Marine transformed them in effect into marine parks, although no real attempt at management has been made, nor has any permanent warden or ranger been appointed. In each case the islands have hotels and other ‘concessions’ operating on them, which provide the essential facilities for visitors such as accommodation, guided tours in glass-bottomed boats for non-swimmers, facilities for scuba diving, and at Green Island an aquarium and an underwater observatory. In Queensland these facilities are provided on land removed from the park, as a matter of policy.

Elsewhere in Australia there has been some interest expressed in the marine park concept in most states, but at the time of writing no parks have actually been established. In New South Wales, a marine nature reserve has been proposed adjacent to the coast of the Nadgee Nature Reserve. Nature reserves are established under the Fauna Protection Act primarily for scientific and conservation reasons, and their marine equivalents are envisaged as serving similar purposes. Nadgee is unsuitable for marine park purposes because of its exposed coastline and lack of spectacular underwater scenery. A marine park taking in the coral reef at Lord Howe Island has also been proposed. In Victoria, a number of foreshore areas are reserved for the protection of sea bird and seal populations, but none of these would qualify as a marine park. Local skindivers have recently expressed interest in a marine park within Port Phillip Bay, but this proposal has not been taken far. South Australia has a marine reserve established under fisheries legislation at Port Noarlunga, where all marine life associated with a rock reef about half a mile long is protected. This was established at the request of local skindivers, with a view to using it as an index of recovery of an area in which the fish and invertebrate populations had been severely reduced by hunting and collecting. Tasmania, Western Australia and the Northern Territory have no marine reserves yet.

A number of countries have been active in establishing marine parks and reserves in recent years, following Recommendation No. 15 of the First World Conference on National Parks, held in Seattle, Washington, in 1962. Among them are Japan, Israel, New Zealand, some South American countries and, most recently, Kenya. In view of Australia's greatest natural asset, the Great Barrier Reef, with its potential for science, tourism, fisheries and minerals, and the extent and variety of the rest of her coastline, the establishment of adequate marine parks and reserves in this country should receive high priority.

Some Aspects of Marine Park Management

The facilities desirable in a marine park would vary according to the nature of the area. In places where swimming is safe, the main provision should be for skindivers, who could use the park independently or in company with other swimmers. Self-guiding trails can be effectively laid out, with labels indicating either particular examples of sessile organisms or generally the motile species which frequent the area. Construction of underwater labels which will resist corrosion and the growth of fouling organisms poses problems, but successful techniques have been devised in some of the United States parks. (It does not follow, however, that these methods would necessarily suit another area where different fouling organisms might be present.) Stability of underwater structures (signposts, moorings, etc.) under storm conditions is another problem. Safety features should be paramount, and the provision of adequate resting places (e.g. moored rafts), resuscitation equipment, including decompression chambers for scuba divers, shark observation and general patrol vessels to watch over swimmers, and adequate signposting or patrolling to keep other vessels, especially power boats, away from swimming areas are desirable. In practice it has been found that a successful technique for guided tours is to have swimmers towed at the surface behind a powered boat driven slowly along a laid-out nature trail. An accompanying guide can then point out the features of the area to the visitors. Underwater communications systems have been developed which operate over short distances and are useful for interpretation and explanation of the features seen.

For non-swimmers the standard glass-bottomed boat or its modern equivalent will be necessary in any marine park. The cost of maintenance of such vessels can be very high, as indeed is that of any marine park equipment. The parts of the vessel designed for underwater viewing need to be carefully maintained if they are to be effective, control of fouling organisms and prevention of leakage being vital. The second generation of vessels for use in marine parks will be submersibles of various kinds. Some already developed have been operated satisfactorily, including Piccard's forty-man vessel which was used in Lake Geneva, but there is still a long way to go before such vessels can be considered both economic and completely safe. Obviously the guides, rangers, and other staff of marine parks will require new skills, quite different from those of terrestrial park staff, though in philosophy and attitude they will undoubtedly be similar. There will be many constructional problems, but provided that the organisms and underwater scenery are present, and that clear water of less than 100 feet in depth is available, there should be no problems in engineering which cannot be overcome, although the techniques to be used will have to be worked out anew for each park.

Perhaps the most difficult aspect of marine park management will be that of deciding what limits should be placed on fishing. Most parks permit line fishing but prohibit spearfishing and shell collecting, though, as stated above, there seems to be no rational ground for distinguishing between these activities. It seems likely that the regulations have been formed on the basis of tradition rather than scientific fact, and may be simply a transfer of practice from terrestrial parks, where angling is usually permitted but other forms of hunting are not. In general it seems that any taking of organisms from marine parks should be discouraged, and if permitted should be under strict supervision and regulation based on a full knowledge of the effects on the organisms concerned.

References

Arthur, D. R., 'Different Kinds of Death', *New Scientist*, 37: 625-7, 1968.

Barnes, J. H., 'The Crown of Thorns Starfish as a Destroyer of Coral, *Aust. Nat. Hist.*, 15: 257-261, 1966.

Bertram, G. C. L. and C. K. R., 'The Dugong', *Nature*, 209: 938-9, 1966.

Beynon, L. R., 'Oil Pollution', *New Scientist*, 38: 96, 1968.

Bone, Q. and Holme, N., 'Oil Pollution — Another Point of View', *New Scientist*, 37: 365-6, 1968.

Brockis, G. and Beynon, R., 'Keeping Coasts Clean', *New Scientist*, 37: 196-7, 1968.

Butler, P. A., 'Effects of Pesticides on Commercial Fisheries', *Proc. Gulf & Caribb. Fish. Inst. 13th Annual Session*, Publ. by Inst. Mar. Sci., Fla., 1961.

The Continental Shelf — Australia's Newest Mineral Frontier, Planet Metals Ltd, Planet Gold Ltd, Sydney, 1967.

Cooper, M. J., 'Destruction of Marine Flora and Fauna in Fiji caused by the Hurricane of February 1965', *Pacific Sci.*, 20: 137-141, 1966.

Føyn, E., 'Disposal of Waste in the Marine Environment and the Pollution of the Sea', *Oceanogr. Mar. Biol. Ann. Rev.*, 3: 95-114, 1965.

George, M., 'Oil Pollution of Marine Organisms', *Nature*, 192: 1209, 1961.

Harrison, G. G. T., 'Conservation of the Marine Life of Mangrove Swamps, Estuaries and Coastal Swamps', in *Caring for Queensland*. Publ. by Australian Conservation Foundation, Brisbane, 1967.

Hedley, C., 'The Natural Destruction of a Coral Reef', *Rep. Great Barrier Reef Committee*, 1: 35-40, 1925.

Hibbard, W. R., 'Mineral Resources: Challenge or Threat?', *Science*, 160: 143-9, 1968.

Hodgkin, E. P., 'Catastrophic Destruction of Littoral Fauna and Flora near Fremantle, January 1959', *West. Aust. Nat.*, 7:6-11, 1959.

Mauchline, J., and Templeton, W. L., 'Artificial and Natural Radioisotopes in the Marine Environment', *Oceanogr. Mar. Biol. Ann. Rev.*, 2: 229-279, 1964.

McVay, S., 'The Last of the Great Whales', *Sci. Amer.*, 215, No. 2: 13-21, 1966.

Robinson, J., Richardson, A., Crabtree, A. N., Coulson, J. C., and Potts, G. R., 'Organochlorine Residues in Marine Organisms', *Nature*, 214: 1307-1311, 1967.

Sladen, W. J. L., Menzie, C. M., and Reichel, W. L., 'D.D.T. Residues in Adelie Penguins and a Crabeater Seal from Antarctica', *Nature*, 210: 670-3, 1966.

Smith, J. E. (Ed.), '*Torrey Canyon*' *Pollution and Marine Life*. Cambridge University Press, 1968.

Talbot, F. H., 'A Description of the Coral Structure of Tutia Reef (Tanganyika Territory, East Africa), and its Fish Fauna', *Proc. Zool. Soc. Lond.*, 145: 431-470, 1965.

Tatton, J. O'G., & Ruzicka, J. H. A., 'Organochlorine Pesticides in Antarctica', *Nature*, 215: 346-8, 1967.

Wurster, C. F., & Wingate, D. B., 'D.D.T. Residues and Declining Reproduction in the Bermuda Petrel', *Science*, 159: 979-981, 1968.

Part III

Three Parks Three Rangers

Derek Whitelock

While you read this book, and while naturalists gather for leisurely conferences to deplore public apathy about conservation, the national park ranger is patrolling his park. He is the human element in all this talk about nature conservation which ranges the gamut from sugary sentimentality about koalas to clinical scientific jargon. The onus is upon him, more than any other, to apply conservation principles in practice. As well, as part of his job, he has regularly to get soaked to the skin, begrimed by fighting bushfires, to lead the search for lost hikers, and to confront the man with the gun — and often with the crate of beer — who sneaks into the park after brush turkey, as his father did, and would like to see anyone stop him. Much of conservation practice and, certainly, the entire system of national parks, hinge upon the ranger.

Yet, surprisingly, the ecological relationship of the ranger to his environment is rarely mentioned in treatises on conservation. This seems to me about as relevant as discussing military tactics without mentioning the infantry.

Who are the rangers and how did they come to be? By any standards, they are poorly-paid for what they do, and are expected as a matter of course to do. They have to take the knocks from the ignorant and the hostile. They are the unsung battlers on the frontier of conservation.

How does the ranger feel about his job?

During 1965 and 1966 I came to know the rangers working in the New England, the Gibraltar Range and the Dorrigo National Parks in northern New South Wales. I visited them often and became acquainted with their attitudes, their problems and the stretches of rugged terrain which were, to each ranger, his particular piece of Australia, his pride, his burden and his responsibility. Further, I got to know several more rangers from other parks in New South Wales and from other states at seminars on conservation arranged at the University of New England in Armidale. One such seminar was held especially to discuss the practical problems of national parks and most of the people attending were rangers. From these experiences emerged what seemed to be a fairly comprehensive picture of the difficulties as well as the pleasures of the ranger's life, and of the heavy demands made upon him by conservationists in particular and by society in general.

I suspect that the details of the work, the problems and the irritations faced by the three rangers described below are generally typical of those encountered by most Australian rangers and, further, that Tom Elliott of the New England National Park, Roly Paine of the Gibraltar Range and Neville Fenton of the Dorrigo are fairly typical of that decidedly special breed of men who become rangers. The conditions described below antedate, or course, the New South Wales National Parks and Wildlife Service Bill which became law in 1967 and which is examined elsewhere. Its implications for rangers in New South Wales are studied at the end of this chapter.

New England National Park

At the feet of Tom Elliott as he stands on Point Lookout (5,240 feet high), a precipice drops to steep slopes shelving down to Platypus Creek, one of the headwaters of the Bellinger River. From the Point, if clouds permit, you look across an enormous amphitheatre of deeply-gouged valleys and gorges, all thickly-forested, to the distant blue of the Pacific and the white ribbon of the surf beaches. You see the weals of the forestry tracks striping the sides of the lower coastal ranges beyond the park and many signs of the whittling away of the forest by the timber men. But the vast, variegated green spread of the rainforest canopy spreads virtually unbroken over the 56,000 acres of the New England National Park.

'How did all this survive?' you ask. 'How did the park come to be set up?' Tom is used to these questions. He is in his sixties, a tough, wiry and highly articulate bushman with over thirty years' experience of prospecting and timber-cutting in the New England district. He has a deep knowledge of the area and its history and knows the park as intimately as the dashboard of his battered Landrover.

'Well, the loggers did work it over in the early days,' he confesses. 'They took a lot of cedar out. And the miners had a go at it too. In fact they mined antimony down there from 1936 to 1956. You can still see the workings. The Park was set up in 1930. Local people like P. A. Wright, now Chancellor at the University of New England, and politicians like Earle Page and D. H. Drummond worked on the government until they got it. But they only got 34,000 acres when they asked for 100,000. We've been able to add about 26,000 acres more since in bits and pieces.

'The Trust's had to fight every step of the way to look after this park properly. They've always been short of money — they only had $400 a year to pay for everything, including a part-time ranger. To get an access road to the Point, they had to let some cedar be cut. They were forced to let the miners in. Most people didn't care a hang about national parks until quite recently. Even now the Trust's under pressure to permit aerial baiting for dingoes in the park. That'd mean "1080" — imagine what that would do to the wildlife! And timber interests are always trying to get their axes into the park. There's long been talk about pushing a new road to the coast right through the middle of the park. But the Trust won't have a bar of any of this.'

At the slightest encouragement, Tom will rattle off the names of the main peaks in the mountain panorama from Point Lookout. He will point out the distinctive crowns of the Antarctic Beech and the different types of vegetation of the montane, submontane and lowland zone that clothe the slopes down to Platypus Creek.

If you are wise, you will accept Tom's invitation for a look round the park. First he will move off at a great pace through the Snow Gums to show you the strip of territory at the top of the range, Wright's Lookout, the new, ultra-modern hikers' chalet that has recently been built and is in great demand, and stands of Antarctic Beech. Grey kangaroos and wallaroos will thump away through the scrub as you follow him along the excellent tracks that occasionally snake down the side of the precipice among massive boulders and through dense, dripping vegetation.

You will then be invited to climb into the park's Landrover and your bones will be shaken by a plunging descent down the old miners' track which now provides the main access for hikers and naturalists into the depths of the park. Tom will talk for as long as you want him to about the orchids, the trees, the koalas, lyrebirds, gliders, the rock formations, creeks and gullies of his preserve. He is a little hazy about some of the finer scientific points but has that intimacy with the bush that is only acquired by years of work in the open.

Over a cup of tea back at his house near Point Lookout, Tom yarns about his earlier days as a prospector and timber cutter.

'I'm a convert to conservation,' he says. 'When I was young I was paid to cut down trees, not to protect them. I've helped burn stands of Coachwood, Tallowwood, Cedar even, when we were clearing the Dorrigo. That was a great mistake. Some of those old cow cockies lived on the smell of an oil rag. They'd have been glad enough of the money for that timber if they'd used it properly.'

He is full of anecdotes about the Aboriginal tribes who once roamed these mountains and can tell tales of massacre and poisoning that are not for delicate ears. If he really takes to you, he might show you some magnificent bora grounds that still survive, totally unprotected, near the park.

Tom Elliott is of the old breed of ranger, self-taught, a bushman. 'A ranger's got to be a bushman,' he declares. 'Any amount of study won't teach him how to handle himself in the bush.' He concedes that bushmen are a fast-disappearing type but still argues that any young man who wants to be a ranger would be well advised to gain hard, practical experience of the bush first.

'Being a ranger is not a glove job,' says Tom. 'A good ranger has to know about nature but he's got to be a good plumber, carpenter, stonemason, mechanic and axeman as well. He's got to know how to handle vandals, and he has to keep smiling even when people get on his nerves with silly questions. I reckon in future he ought to have a university degree as well.'

He agrees that any ranger suffers a number of deprivations, and instances the case of his colleague, Bill Groom, who has been working with Tom on the park for several months now. This ranger has a young family and the problems he faces of transporting his children to and from school are severe.

'But it's a good job,' Tom Elliott concludes. 'Bill and I get on very well with the Trust. The public are beginning to appreciate what national parks are for now, and it's a pleasure to talk to most of the visitors. I'm out in the open most of the time and there's plenty of variety. It's a worthwhile job, that's the main thing.'

Gibraltar Range National Park

The new Gwydir Highway from Glen Innes to Grafton bisects the Gibraltar Range National Park, roughly sixty square miles of tangled gorges, plateaux and mountains clothed with sclerophyll forest and patches of rainforest. As you approach the centre of the park from the west along the highway you see grim traces of the bushfire of 13 and 14 December 1964 that destroyed half the vegetation before the park was gazetted on 30 May 1965. You see, mile after mile along the road, hosts of skeletons of great trees clutching at the sky with blackened fingers, the result of the most ruinous type of conflagration, a running 'crown fire'. How did it start? 'Burning off' in the brush to clear cattle leases or to encourage new grass? A fire left by picnickers? No one knows, and many have their suspicions, but what everyone in the area does know is that the fire was the worst in living memory. It destroyed thousands of trees and smaller plants, and killed mammals, birds, insects and reptiles whose numbers cannot be assessed. It is just another example of how vulnerable Australia's national parks are to uncontrolled fires, and another reminder of how little we know about how fire should be used in their management.

The park will soon be augmented by neighbouring forestry land so that it will be even bigger than the New England National Park, and one of the most extensive in the state. The country varies from exposed mountain ridges and tors to steep slopes plunging into rainforest on the eastward facing escarpments overlooking Grafton and the Clarence Valley. There are tremendous views of some of the wildest and most unspoiled country in New South Wales from the Summit (3,740 feet) in the heart of the park. Its very inaccessibility and ruggedness have been its natural safeguard. 'Developers' were not interested in the rocky wastes and poor soils of such a region. Scenery, fortunately, is not good fodder for sheep.

From the conservationist's point of view, then, the park is both a gigantic biological laboratory and a reserve for wildlife and recreation. Here are innumerable creeks, heathlands, swamps, eucalypt forests and vine forests. There are rarities such as the Rufous Scrub Bird, Feather-tailed Glider, Wampoo Pigeon, native cat and scrub turkey. Brilliant features of the park are the areas ablaze with Christmas bells and waratahs in season. A small colony of koala bears lives in the park. Giant land snails are plentiful in the rainforest and glow-worms flicker in the caves in the rock walls. Like most other New South Wales parks, Gibraltar Range is administered by a Trust of local people, most of them amateur enthusiasts. The Trust is preparing a master plan for the park, has built a ranger's cottage near the highway and is beginning to push trails through the forest.

The ranger, Roly Paine, has been in his time a steam engineer, fitter, plumber and dairy farmer. Like most rangers, he, too, has had a lifelong interest in natural history, was an honorary ranger at Brisbane Water for six years, and left a much better-paid job to come to Gibraltar Range. He has many interests and has, for example, for years searched for Aboriginal archaeological remains throughout Australia.

Again like most rangers, Roly Paine will drop everything to talk at length about his park to any sympathetic listener. He points out that Gibraltar Range, although at first glance apparently virgin wilderness, 'was raped before we got it'. The 1964 conflagration was just one of a series of catastrophic fires in the evolution of this living landscape. Some suitable patches of timber had been logged, much of the country had been grazed over by cattle and there had been desultory mining activity.

Roly's busiest times are when most other people are relaxing, at the weekends or on public holidays. His average day's work begins at 5.30 a.m.: for nearly all the daylight hours he is out on patrol. He checks on construction work in the park, talks to visitors, looks out for birds previously unrecorded in the area, keeps tracks clear with a brush hook and axe, descends like an avenging angel on shooters after turkeys, checks the temperatures and rainfall and records the notable events of the day in his log book. The smooth, broad highway which swoops across the Gibraltar Range National Park for eighteen miles is Roly Paine's main case of worry. While it enables well-intentioned visitors to reach the park, it is also a splendid access route for poachers and despoilers and has adversely affected the vegetation on either side of the road. Its traffic destroys animals and birds in large numbers. Careless picnickers or smokers on the highway could easily, and probably will, cause further bushfires.

Roly Paine watches over his park with that fierce, almost proprietary pride common to most rangers. When his day's work is done, he devotes much of his evening to study for he believes that all rangers should have a fund of soundly-based knowledge for the benefit of visitors to their parks. 'I've got a ton to learn,' he said. 'If I lived to be a thousand I still wouldn't know enough to be a perfect ranger.'

Dorrigo National Park

Travellers along the main road to the coast from Dorrigo pass the entrance to the Dorrigo State Park and flank it for the first mile or so of their seven miles descent down Dorrigo Mountain to the Bellinger River. It is a small park of 3,872 acres, compact, wedge-shaped and remarkably attractive. The greater part of it is on the steep upper reaches of the Dorrigo escarpment and is covered with luxuriant rainforest. Further down the slopes, more open sclerophyll forest prevails.

The area was dedicated as a fauna and flora sanctuary in 1927 and was later rededicated as a national park, entirely because of local initiative. True, the area set aside was largely useless to farmers and was too steep for the timber men to get at the giant

angrove forest (*Rhizophora stylosa*), north Queensland.
IOTO COURTESY W. T. JONES

Chillagoe Caves, north Queensland, are composed of limestone; the vegetation is a deciduous vine thicket which is a type of tropical monsoon forest. PHOTO COURTESY QLD FORESTRY DEPT

typical waterfall and creek in subtropical rainforest, south ueensland. PHOTO COURTESY S. AND K. BREEDEN

Aboriginal cave paintings on sandstone, Carnarvon National Park, south Queensland. Vandalism is not limited to accessible Aboriginal relics; 'rockhounds', oblivious to the idea of conservation, often break open rock masses with dynamite and destroy mineral deposits valuable because of their beauty, crystalline form, or rarity. PHOTO COURTESY QLD FORESTRY DEPT

ropical seasonal-swamp forest with Fan Palms (*Licuala muelleri*), ear El Arish, north Queensland. Note the Strangling Fig on the ght. PHOTO COURTESY L. J. WEBB

Snow-covered highlands of the Kosciusko National Park, N.S.W. PHOTO COURTESY NATIONAL PARKS & WILDLIFE, N.S.W.

Cottage Rock, on the shore of Ku-ring-gai Chase National Park, N.S.W. PHOTO COURT NATIONAL PARKS & WILDLIFE, N.S.W.

(LOWER RIGHT) The Nadjee Nature Reserve, looking from the north end of Wally Newton's Beach, southern N.S.W. PHOTO COURTESY NATIONAL PARKS & WILDLIFE, N.S.W.

(BELOW) Nest of the Mallee Fowl (*Leipoa ocellata*) in mallee scrub, Round Hill Nature Reserve, N.S.W. PHOTO COURTESY NATIONAL PARKS & WILDLIFE, N.S.W.

trees profitably at that time. But it was an imaginative act by the Dorrigo people, and perhaps betrayed the stirrings of conscience for the rape of the land to the west by the early settlers. Local people worked hard to clear trails through the forest and even planted dahlias by the sides of the main road near the park. For years the little park was cared for in this way, with a small Trust of local people to administer it. Now there are plans for expanding the park to double its present size. The first ranger, Jim Steenson, was appointed in 1965. A fiery conservationist who had been an honorary ranger at the Royal National Park near Sydney for years before, he abandoned his job as a construction foreman and endured a severe drop in income to take the post. Jim saw himself as a crusader for a cause and there were some unpleasant clashes with sections of local opinion when he fenced off the glade at the top of the park from motorists, enforced the law on shooters and refused to allow '1080' baiting for rabbits in his preserve. For several weeks before the building of an excellent ranger's house and office at the Dorrigo, Jim and his family lived in a caravan in the glade and here they were subjected on some nights to abuse and rowdyism from motorcyclists from the coast who objected to his methods. But before he left for a ranger's job at Ku-ring-gai Chase after about a year, Jim Steenson had constructed good facilities, refurbished the kiosk, cleared the trails and established a naturalists' club in town.

Neville Fenton, the present ranger at Dorrigo had previously worked as a prospector and a timber contractor in the eastern ranges, which 'gave me a great interest and love for the bush'. For eight years he was manager of the trout hatchery near Ebor and the New England National Park, a much-sought-after consultant and companion for the trout anglers who haunt the New England creeks, and he worked devotedly to establish rainbow trout in these alien waters. Neville finds that his job at the hatchery taught him a lot which is useful to him as a ranger — public relations, for example, planning and supervision, book-keeping.

A fit, modest, amiable young man whom everybody seems to like, Neville is obviously in love with his work. He appears easy-going, but one or two turkey hunters caught prowling in the park were rapidly disarmed and ejected. Neville is at home with the local dairy farmers, most of whom are but one generation removed from the first settlers. They bring him in an occasional echidna or native cat to release in the park, and yarn over cups of tea in his hospitable kitchen. Satin Bower Birds peck for crumbs outside the door, and orphaned Ring-tailed Possums clamber about the furniture.

Neville usually divides his day between public relations, which includes meeting and accompanying visitors and giving talks about the park illustrated with slides; park maintenance; park planning, in consultation with members of the Trust; survey and construction of nature trails; book-keeping and correspondence; and law enforcement—rare but as necessary as it is sometimes personally unpleasant. He is a keen nature photographer, and the Trust derives quite a sizeable income from the sale of his slides of the park.

In many ways, this ranger is lucky. His park is small, interesting, and accessible. It is only two miles from town. He has a very good house, office and other facilities. He is a local man, part of the local scene, and popular. Above all, he enjoys good relations with his Trust.

I know of other rangers who are by no means as fortunate, men living in poor conditions, isolated, over-worked and poorly-appreciated. Rangers in New South Wales are beginning to meet together more often now at training schools arranged by the new State Wildlife Service, and these meetings are generating a demand for reform and re-thinking in the rangers' world.

Like all the other rangers I have talked to, Neville Fenton has firm opinions on how job conditions could be improved for all of his colleagues.

'Many rangers are very poorly paid,' he says. 'They are made to suffer for the lack of finance for parks generally. I think it would be best if *all* rangers were employed by the National Parks and Wildlife Service so that they would be all working under the same principles and conditions.'

Conclusions

These rangers have much in common. They are keen naturalists, but they are essentially amateur naturalists who have learnt from observation rather than study. They are expected to have many talents — to build tracks, fell trees, do carpentry work, repair cars, fight fires. They have to be tough to do all this, and be able to cow the occasional villain with a gun or the carload of rowdies who want to revel in the park all night. They have learned to be thick-skinned and take abuse with philosophy.

Further, each is troubled by the problems that beset the emergent national parks system in New South Wales. Above all, they worry about the implicit contradiction between preservation and recreation. The Gwydir Highway is, as has been shown, more of a liability than an asset to conservation interests in Gibraltar Range. The main road by the Dorrigo, which is constantly being widened and repaired, has already eroded several acres from the park. How will the great amphitheatre of wilderness below Point Lookout fare if, in fact, a road is driven through it? These rangers are more than mere caretakers and handymen. They regard themselves as conservationists first and foremost. They are concerned about threats to the parks still posed by timber interests and pastoral pressure groups which consider fauna reserves as 'vermin refuges'. Most of all, they are concerned about the manifold problems set by the growing popularity of national parks. Like their colleagues in other parks throughout New South Wales, the rangers of these three parks are the direct intermediaries be tween their Trusts and, latterly, the Department of Lands and the Wildlife Service. As such, being in effect the public relations men of conservation, they are keenly conscious of the inadequacies of their own training. Such misgivings are common to most rangers. About sixty rangers from many parks throughout eastern Australia and the Northern Territory attended a special seminar on 'The Practical Problems of National Parks' held at the University of New England in February 1966. The following are the recommendations of a study group formed by the rangers themselves on the question of recruitment and training of staff for national parks:

Members strongly supported the idea that there is need for the provision of a true career course in National Parks administration as an incentive to people to enter this field. It was felt, too, that this should apply not only at the top administrative level, but also at the ranger level so that those entering this field of public service could have the security of some career line ahead of them.

Recruitment should be considered at two levels: sub-professional and professional.

Sub-professional group

This group should be recruited straight from school at the standard of the New South Wales School Certificate; this would mean recruits approximately sixteen years old. Over four years these recruits would be given training analogous to apprenticeship, that is, a combination of practical and theoretical training.

Training could be exclusively for a National Parks' Service or it could embrace training in forestry, fisheries and the like. If it were the latter, trainees would be eligible as employees in other services, and there would be common sub-professional groups. On completion of training, a certificate would be given to each youth as a recognition of the standard he has reached. These sub-professionals would hold positions up to ranger in the Park Service. It should be made possible for outstanding students in this group to enter the professional group in some way.

Professional group

Within this group are those with tertiary educational qualifications. There was considerable debate as to whether or not existing disciplines such as forestry, geology, zoology and botany were the best training for National Park personnel. It was generally agreed, however, that whatever the basic discipline, some special training was desirable for management. This would mean post-graduate training and perhaps a course for this could be established at the University of New England. This would be for the skilled staff who would be taking charge of National Parks and the top bracket of personnel who would be responsible for National Park administration generally.

Professional Park personnel would become members of a Park Service. The service would be conducted from a central office which would have, in addition to people trained in Park administration, specialists in particular fields to whom problems could be referred from the field. The professional administrators in the field could be put in charge of a major Park or be posted to a country town from which they could control a number of Parks. For instance, there could be a professional Park administrator stationed in Armidale who would control, say, the New England National Park, the Gibraltar Range Park and the Dorrigo National Park, the actual on-the-spot management of these particular parks being conducted by a ranger.

It would considerably help the creation of both a sub-professional and a professional service if greater emphasis were laid on conservation in schools.

In summary, the following recommendations were made:

* that National Park trainees should be recruited from school at the School Certificate level, to be given four years apprenticeship training with a certificate at completion.
* that it is a matter of urgency for conservation courses to be introduced into Universities at undergraduate and post-graduate levels. These courses should place emphasis on National Park administration and forestry.
* that emphasis should be laid on teaching conservation at school.

As well as considering training for future staff, seminar members expressed concern over the need for a course for those already employed as rangers; here, cadetships were not appropriate. Moreover, many Park staff were removed from centres wherein they could follow technical college courses, or a university course, in any form. Some form of correspondence courses would thus have to be set up for their training. It was then suggested that a suitable correspondence course for rangers might be set up in conjunction with the Department of External Studies at the University of New England. Suggested was a two weeks crash programme of an introductory nature at the University, after which the rangers could take their texts away for study during the year. Another two weeks' programme at the end of the year could consolidate the theory learnt by practical field work under supervision of university staff and other lecturers.

These are detailed and practical recommendations made by men who have first hand experience of the work.

The New South Wales National Parks and Wildlife Service Bill of 1967, on paper at least, went a fair way towards rationalizing the position of the ranger. Its re-classification of parks and reserves, plans for zoning and formation of the Wildlife Service gave much-needed clarity and organization to a system which had previously suffered from confusion and much benevolent but often bungling amateurism.

In practical terms, the new Act has already provided the New South Wales rangers with smart uniforms and badges. More importantly, it is giving them a greater sense of purpose. They already see themselves as part of a definite scheme of things rather than the mere servants of the local Trust. One of two seminars and training schools for rangers have already been arranged by the Service. Rangers are generally pleased about the new *esprit de corps* that is beginning to emerge.

At this point, let me say a few words about the New South Wales park Trusts which, with their rangers, have until recently carried most of the work and worries of the national parks in this state. There have been criticisms of some of them, and a number have already been abolished by the new Act, but this should not be allowed to obscure the excellent work for conservation that they have done for years. The Trusts for the three parks mentioned in this chapter, for example, have devoted an immense amount of time and effort to administering and safeguarding the interests of their parks against various pressures. Had it not been for the activity of such people, the New England National Park, for instance, would probably never have been established back in the days when both official and public opinion was apathetic, to put it kindly, about nature conservation. Indeed, several Trusts in the northern half of New South Wales in particular are still functioning, not only because they have richly proven their value, but because the National Parks and Wildlife Service simply does not have the staff to work the system without them. I hope, as many people do, that this will not be an obituary for the New South Wales park Trusts. Informed amateurism can mitigate the bureaucratic excesses of centralized official control — New South Wales has many grisly examples of the latter. Conservationists in northern New South Wales are anxious that in future the Service should continue to rely upon and respect local advice and help by people who have already demonstrated their worth. On this, it is to be hoped that the Service will eventually make provision for the education, not only of rangers, but of the Trust members who are their natural allies and guides. From the present transitional turmoil in New South Wales parks there could and should emerge a virtually unique system, a hybrid of professionalism animated and given sinew by amateurism and local participation in a worthy cause.

The Act has certainly improved the general position as described earlier in this chapter, yet we still have little to be complacent about. It is frequently remarked that Australia loiters along in the wake of the United States. There, rangers are professional people, graduates, well paid for an exacting job with its own particular disciplines. Such professionalism needs to be grafted on to the enthusiasm of the Australian ranger, and quickly. We have no time to afford for our national parks to be anything other than efficient. It would seem that the ranger is a most vital factor in the ecological systems we wish to protect in our national parks. And in the last analysis a national parks system is only as good as its rangers.

National Parks and Other Reserves of Queensland

J. K. Jarrott

Geographic Features and Environment

Queensland covers 667,000 square miles; it is triangular in shape, with a latitudinal spread from 10½° S. at Cape York to 28° S. at Point Danger. Two-thirds of this area lies within the Great Artesian Basin, which covers much of the land west of the Great Dividing Range.

This range ,which hems in the eastern plain, is of a modest height. At Mount Bartle Frere it just exceeds one mile above sea-level and at its most inland point near Lakes Galilee and Buchanan (longitude 146°) it is gently sloping and is only 1,000 feet above sea-level. There are lengthy cuestas at points where the Great Divide is near the coast such as from Cooktown to Atherton and from Bunya to the New South Wales border. The dominant cuesta appearance comprises a gentle westward slope with an abrupt eastern scarp.

The 3,236 miles of coastline provide a wide variety of habitats. It includes high sand dunes on Stradbroke, Moreton and Fraser Islands, on the coast north of Noosa and along considerable sections of Cape York Peninsula, particularly at Cape Bedford. The coastal soils from Sarina to Mossman sustain the greater proportion of the sugar production of Queensland; the many miles of red cliffs at Weipa have recently acquired world importance as a major source of bauxite.

Paralleling the eastern coast is the longest belt of coral reef in the world — the Great Barrier Reef — running from Torres Strait south-east to terminate at the Bunker Group opposite Gladstone (a distance of 1,200 miles). Between the low islands of the reef and the coast are several groups of mountainous islands such as the Whitsunday group (20° south latitude), Gloucester Island, Magnetic Island, Palm and Hinchinbrook Islands (18½° S.) and the Flinders Group (14° S.). These islands rise abruptly from drowned coastlines and achieve their greatest height at Mount Bowen (3,650 feet) on Hinchinbrook.

Western Queensland, on the other hand, includes part of the Simpson Desert, which has been rated as the fourth most arid region of the world. The rainfall in the vicinity of Poeppel Corner seldom reaches five inches per annum. By contrast, the rainfall of the Babinda-Tully area on the east coast exceeds 160 inches annually. Several cyclones cross the Queensland coast annually, and may travel as far south as Brisbane.

The wide variety of climate supports a considerable diversity of vegetation types. The coastal ranges are largely covered by eucalypt forests, and these regions contain most of Queensland's rainforest. The drier tropical regions also contain largely savannah woodlands. In addition to these types there are some 200 million acres of Flinders and Mitchell grassland, dominating the area to the west of the Great Divide. In the same area are twenty million acres of brigalow forest, and several million acres each of cypress pine and mulga. The coastal sand dune areas support several million acres of wallum heath.

Evolution of the Reserve Systems

Conservation of wildlife in Queensland had its beginnings in 1877 when fauna legislation protected certain game and insectivorous birds. In 1898 further legislation provided in part for preservation of animals (including birds) deemed to be of economic value.

In 1906 a State Forests and National Parks Act was proclaimed and with some amendments provided the legislative authority over state forest, timber reserves and national parks until 1 August 1960 when the Forestry Act of 1959 was proclaimed. This was amended in 1968.

Partial protection of koalas and possums granted in 1906 was extended by legislation in 1910. The Animal and Birds Acts 1921 to 1924 listed certain fauna, fixed periods of protection, prohibited the sale of some and prescribed open seasons for other fauna and declared lands to be sanctuaries. This Act was replaced by the Fauna Protection Act of 1937 and later by the Fauna Conservation Act of 1952. In the 1952 Act, fauna is classified as:

(a) permanently protected
(b) protected (except for certain open seasons)
(c) pest

All fauna until legally taken or kept are the property of the Crown. The Act does not extend to marine animals, mice, rats (other than water rats) and feral cats. Administration of this Act comes under the care of the Minister for Primary Industries. There is a Chief Fauna Officer and several fauna officers are biologists. Police officers, senior officers and inspectors of the Primary Industry Department, forest officers, land commissioners and assistant commissioners and land rangers are also fauna officers. Honorary Protectors are scattered throughout Queensland.

The Native Plants Protection Act of 1930 lists certain plants as protected for unlimited periods in Queensland. The list comprises twenty-two ferns, six palms, thirty-three orchids, fourteen miscellaneous plants and two specified areas — Bishop Island in Moreton Bay and Friday Island in Torres Strait.

Marine reservations are few and far between. The taking of coral in Queensland waters or on the foreshores is prohibited except under licence while the green turtle is fully protected south of 15° latitude. Dugongs are fully protected.

Sanctuaries are numerous and include all state forests, all national parks, all islands that form part of Queensland as well as some leaseholds and freeholds.

In the nineteenth century, early reserves such as scenic reserves and reserves for public purposes (waterfalls) were established under the Lands Acts. The scenic reserves were largely under the control of Shire Councils. The reserves for public purposes mainly stayed under the control of the Lands Department and differ from camping and water reserves which are primarily intended for travelling stock. Eight waterfall reserves of two square miles each in the Herbert River basin were examples of the reserves for public purposes and have since been proclaimed as national parks as a nucleus of a large national park envisaged along the southern and northern slopes of the Herbert River Gorge.

A national park is defined as land set aside and declared or deemed to be set apart and declared under the Forestry Act (1959 to 1968) as a national park. The Forestry Act comes under the control of the Minister for Conservation. The Conservator of Forests is responsible for policy and management of national parks. The Secretary of the Forestry Department is the officer in charge of the administration of national park matters.

The Queensland Parliament votes funds each year from revenue and also provides some loan funds. Clerical, drafting, photography and survey services are provided by Forestry staff while examination of areas under consideration as possible national parks is often conducted by expert foresters. Sections 40 and 41 of the Forestry Act provide that:

40. The cardinal principle to be observed in the management of National Parks shall be the permanent preservation, to the greatest possible extent, of their natural conditions and the Conservator of Forests shall exercise his powers under this Part of this Act in such manner as

appears to him most appropriate to achieve this objective.

41. Consistent with this Act, the Conservator of Forests may within any National Park from time to time construct, carry out, improve, maintain, operate, protect, control, and otherwise manage any works, or do any act or make such provision as he considers necessary or desirable for the preservation, proper management, or public enjoyment of the National Park.

The 1968 Act provides for the following classifications within the national park system: primitive, scientific, historical, recreational, and combinations of these. Recreation areas are limited to 400 acres in the largest parks and much less in the smaller ones.

Until 1960, an Act of Parliament was necessary to reduce or abolish a national park except for excision of small areas for tourist facilities. The Forestry Act (1959 to 1968) provides for revocation in whole or in part of a national park in the following manner—the Governor in Council shall cause to be laid on the table of the Queensland Legislative Assembly, a proposal for such revocation. A resolution (of which fourteen days or more notice has been given) passed by the Legislative Assembly that such proposal be carried out, is followed by an Order In Council completing the revocation.

Classification of national parks with features of interest is given in the Table below.

The main reason for the large number of national parks in Queensland is the method of individual gazettal. Grouping of islands and regazettal would reduce considerably the numbers and increase the average size of the parks.

A resolution carried unanimously at the First World Conference on National Parks at Seattle in 1962 stipulated that there should be an unrestricted right of access by the public to visit national parks subject to occasional seasonal restrictions. Queensland complies with this worldwide concept and indeed levies no entrance fee as occurs in some countries.

The latest Queensland government statement on national parks is contained in the publication, *The National Parks of Queensland*, of June 1964, in which the Honourable

	Number of Reserves in Sizes (acres)				Total
	1,000-10,000	10,001-50,000	50,001-100,000	Over 100,000	
Island groups	3	1	1		5
Single islands	4		1		5
Portions of islands	2				2
Coastal (to shore line)		1			1
Headlands	1				1
Coastal (no shore line)	2				2
Mountains, ranges (Great Divide or easterly mainly with rainforest and waterfalls)	4	3	2	2	11
Mountains (mainly isolated)	8	2			10
Tableland (mainly lakes and waterfalls)	9				9
Inland (sandstone ranges, gorges with some brigalow)		2	2		4
Desert				1	1
Limestone caves	1				1
	34	9	6	3	52

H. Richter, Minister for Conservation, stated:

The National Parks of Queensland are dedicated to the people. They have been established for our enjoyment, our education and our inspiration. I am sure that they will achieve this purpose in increasing measure year by year. Visitors to the National Parks are guests of the people of Queensland.

The National Parks of Queensland are sanctuaries of Queensland itself. Their aim is the preservation of nature intact. Once destruction has occurred, man can never rebuild what nature has produced throughout the untold centuries. It is essential to protect and preserve unspoiled parts of the original Queensland whilst we still have the opportunity, so that these areas will be safeguarded for our generation and for future generations for all foreseeable time.

Areas dedicated for this purpose must be managed so that they are accessible and available for scientific, educational, aesthetic and recreational purposes, but in so doing their future values for these very purposes must not be destroyed. The administrators of the National Parks must accept the inescapable responsibility of preserving them in their unspoiled naturalness. This is no easy task and for its full achievement requires the co-operation and help of all visitors to these Parks.

Australians have a sense of national responsibility. Let us individually accept this responsibility as applied to the National Parks by each doing our share to preserve them.

The Act incorporates previous Cabinet policy whereby no timber or forest products shall be harvested from Queensland national parks. Official policy does not permit accommodation within the mainland national parks nor are areas excised from these reserves for such purpose. Tourist accommodation leases on the island national parks have been cancelled in most instances and small areas excised to cover the existing and future buildings. Camping is permitted within national parks under permit issued by the Forestry Department. The administration of national parks is the responsibility of the Minister for Conservation, of the Conservator of Forests and of the Secretary, Department of Forestry. Staff comprises three rangers, a research biologist, a zoologist, a graduate forester, and approximately fourteen overseers and thirty-six workmen in the field. Honorary rangers provide valuable assistance in their spare time. All foresters are national park officers. There are no trustees for individual parks nor is there any Statutory National Park Board or Advisory Council.

Distribution of the Parks

The national parks of Queensland may be conveniently separated into four geographical regions: island, coastal, subcoastal and inland.

Island National Parks

Australia is fortunate that Queensland has reserved many island national parks including the largest ocean national park in the world—Hinchinbrook (97,200 acres) near Cardwell. The mountain ridges drop 3,150 feet to the sea and are densely covered with rocks and heath type vegetation. Along the main ridge to the north is Mount Bowen (3,650 feet). On the western side, miles of mangrove flat extend from the base of the mountains to Hinchinbrook Passage. Sand dunes and mangroves are an unusual combination along windswept Ramsay Bay.

Among many islands in the region of the Great Barrier Reef visited by tourists in north Queensland, the following have been reserved as national parks — Orpheus, Whitsunday, Hook, Gloucester, Long, South Molle, Lindeman, Shaw, Brampton and North Keppel. The greater part of Magnetic Island and Dunk Island are national parks. There are further national parks islands large and small and the principal of these is Flinders Island in Princess Charlotte Sound, north of Cooktown.

Coastal Reserves

The lack of coastal national parks is a disappointing feature of the Queensland system. Sixty miles south of Brisbane is an excellent but tiny scenic area on Burleigh Head. Its fifty-eight acres contain some dense rainforest as well as open forest. The southern slope of the headland has low windswept trees streamlined by the constant south-easterly wind. Koalas live in this reserve.

One hundred and thirty miles to the north, is Noosa Heads (930 acres) where a small colony of koalas has recently been released. Noosa is noted for its wide variety of trees (both rainforest and hardwood) and of wildflowers, and for its picturesque coastal track with she-oaks and pandanus (breadfruit).

The Noosa Parks Development Association has recorded an impressive list of birds at Noosa. Many trees on the tracks have been named on tags by the Forestry Department.

From the mouth of the Noosa River northward to Double Island Point, the coastal sand dunes reach several hundred feet in height. The exposed coloured Teewah sands are an outstanding scenic and geological feature, and the heath and wallum-type vegetation to the west are of botanical interest. This area has not yet been included in the national parks of Queensland.

Between Yeppoon and Emu Park (east of Rockhampton) there are a few headlands reserved for scenic puproses. These are Rosslyn, Bluff Point, Mulabin and Double Head. Twenty miles to the north of Mackay, Cape Hillsborough National Park is two and a half square miles in area, and is studded with caves and covered with rainforest.

Conway Range, east of Proserpine, is Queensland's largest coastal national park (48,000 acres) and forms a magnificent western backdrop to Whitsunday Passage. To the state government's everlasting shame, several hundred acres were excised from the park and are being sold to pay for the cost of the road, yet every other tourist road in Queensland has been financed from Main Roads or Special funds.

From here to the tip of Cape York, and southwards along the Gulf of Carpentaria the coastline is without a national park.

Subcoastal (between the mountains and the coast)

On Thornton Peak (north of Daintree) in north Queensland, the upper slopes as well as the peak (4,508 feet) have been reserved for botanical and historical reasons. Extension of the area (5,760 acres) to the north and north-east is advisable. This would include Mount Alexander, Mount Hemmant, Mount Pieter Botte and could terminate at Cape Tribulation for historical reasons.

A little to the west is Queensland's second largest national park — Windsor Tableland and Upper Mossman Gorge (133,000 acres). Here is a high plateau and ranges covered mostly by rainforest and with swiftly flowing streams, such as the Mossman and Daintree Rivers. The tableland is the last extensive elevated area north of Atherton Tableland and averages 3,500 feet with some peaks including Mount Spurgeon rising to 4,300 feet.

Farther south, the Chillagoe Caves National Park protects some limestone caves at Mungana and Chillagoe. So far, these are the only extensive caves reserved in Queensland. The more accessible ones are Royal Arch, Donna, Markham and Ryan Imperial.

Incidental to the reservation of the caves is the preservation of the overlying vine scrub or monsoon forest of the limestone hills with scrub turkeys and bower birds, and Aboriginal art in caves and overhangs nearby.

Bellenden Ker and Bartle Frere National Park occupies 80,140 acres and contains Queensland's highest range and peaks reaching 5,275 feet. A. Meston (June 1889) described the vegetation of Bartle Frere as different from that of Bellenden Ker yet there is only a deep valley between.

Baron von Mueller had prophesied that the Bellenden Ker Range would contain *Rhododendron* and this has proved to be true.

Palmerston National Park overlooks the North Johnstone River and protects rich tropical rainforest along the Palmerston Highway. Cassowaries, rifle-birds, scrub turkeys and pigeons are among the birds of the park. An Aboriginal bora ring is situated on the eastern boundary.

The Herbert River Gorge to the west of Ingham is noted for its spectacular waterfalls. Small national parks have been set aside as the nucleus of a larger national park. These are of two square miles each around Herbert, Sword, Garrawalt, Wallaman, Herkes, Broadwater and Yamanie Falls. Wallaman is Queensland's highest sheer fall, 937 feet. Platypus and grebe share the pools above Wallaman.

Mount Spec to the north of Townsville and Mount Elliott to the south provide contrasting national parks. The rainforest and the catchment area of Townsville's water supply at Crystal Creek form part of Mount Spec's reserve of 17,700 acres. On the other hand, Mount Elliott's 62,770 acres have a blend of open forest on the ridges and peaks with some rainforest in the gorges. The rainfall is less than at Mount Spec and the drier type of vegetation gives shelter to birds and mammals different from those at Mount Spec. Birds include finches, catbirds, whipbirds, pigeons, cockatoos, scrub turkeys, parrots and the southern kookaburra. Mount Burrumbush Park is just across the Bruce Highway from the eastern slope of Mount Elliott. The swamps around the mount give shelter and breeding ground to many brolga. These birds are often seen in the early morning from the Sunlander train.

Fifty miles west of Mackay on the Clarke Range is Eungella National Park (122,600 acres). Mount Dalrymple, 4,190 feet, and other peaks are covered with palms and vine jungles on the eastern slopes while there are extensive eucalypt forests on the western side of the range. Platypus can often be seen near the picnic area at Broken River.

Mount Walsh to the west of Maryborough, is noted for its elevated heath vegetation and for rainforest in the gorges. It is accessible from nearby Biggenden and contains 7,380 acres.

Small reserves on Montville such as Kondalilla are visited by thousands of holiday makers from Brisbane's near north coast seaside resorts. Just to the north of Brisbane are the Glasshouse Mountains, for many years the favourites of climbers, scouts, bushwalkers, photographers and botanists.

A little nearer to Brisbane at Mount Glorious is Maiala National Park, which has a self-guiding nature trail. This is a very popular area for Brisbane people.

Mount Tamborine to the south of Brisbane was once extensively covered with rainforest and has several small parks and scenic areas. Birdlife includes the Albert Lyrebird.

At Springbrook, the national parks are mainly confined to the deep gorges of Warrie, Gwongorella and Natural Bridge. As Springbrook receives approximately 100 inches of rain annually, the waterfalls — Billbrough's, Purlingbrook, Twin, Blackfellows, Reids — are spectacular for several months of the year. From the lookouts on the ridges can be seen many miles of coastline both to the north and south.

Queensland's favourite and best known national park is Lamington (49,000 acres). Accommodation is provided at Binna Burra (eastern boundary) and O'Reilly's (central boundary) but the park can be visited from several roadheads including Running Creek, Christmas Creek and Numinbah Valley. Over 100 miles of graded track are available to visitors. It is noted for its waterfalls, Antarctic Beeches, orchids, wildflowers and an immense variety of birdlife.

Mount Barney National Park is about twenty miles to the west and is accessible from the Mount Lindesay Highway. The peaks of Barney (4,449 feet) have been climbed by thousands of people. Nearby, Mounts Lindesay, Maroon and May have also been reserved and these too are favourites of campers and climbers. Mount Maroon particularly is noted for its wildflowers. A small reserve has been set aside at Wilson's Peak on the junction of the Great Dividing Range and McPherson Range and extensions have been sought at

Mount Neilsen. Just to the north of here is Cunningham's Gap National Park astride the Cunningham Highway between Brisbane and Warwick. Here and at Wilson's Peak and Lamington can be heard and occasionally seen the shy but vocal Albert Lyrebird. The Gap is noted for its tree ferns, orchids and the rock lily (*Doryanthes palmeri*) on Mounts Cordeaux and Mitchell.

Inland National Parks

One of our oldest national parks in Queensland is at the Bunya Mountains north-west of Toowoomba, where Bunya Pine (*Araucaria bidwilli*) trees reach nearly 180 feet in height. Since the original reservation in 1909 the national park, with additions, occupies 24,230 acres. There are Bottle Trees on the drier western slopes, and many birds have been recorded.

Robinson Gorge north-west of Taroom and Isla Gorge north-east of Taroom in central Queensland are fairly recent national parks. Robinson Gorge is more spectacular and a plentiful flow of water occurs in Robinson Creek. Leichhardt named and explored the creek in 1844. Access has, until recently, been very difficult.

Carnarvon National Park farther to the west and north of Roma is more widely known. It is approached from Rolleston to the north or from Injune to the south. It is noted for its Aboriginal paintings. Carnarvon Gorge is about twenty miles long and the top level of the plateau is about 3,000 feet high. The area reserved is 66,480 acres which together with Isla Gorge (11,500 acres), Robinson Gorge (22,000) and Salvator Rosa (64,900 acres) provide a fine start for inland national parks.

Salvator Rosa was first visited by Sir Thomas Mitchell in 1846. Access to this park is normally by four-wheel-drive vehicle from the Springsure-Tambo road.

Probably the most spectacular wildflower area in Queensland is located in the granite belt near Wyberba in Girraween National Park. The great granite domes and nearby forests within the reserve provide shelter for wombats and the southern lyrebird as well as many other birds.

Away in the north are the only lake national parks in Queensland. These are on Atherton Tableland and comprise The Crater, Barrine and Eacham. Unfortunately the two latter have been affected by the introduction of speed-boats and waterskiing which certainly do not go hand in hand with national parks. Queensland has very few lakes but at the present time investigation is being carried out with a view to creating a new national park near Lake Buchanan and Lake Galilee on each side of the lowest part of the Great Dividing Range and north-east of Aramac.

Tully Falls, Barron Falls, Millstream Falls, Elizabeth Grant Falls and Cannabullen Falls, Jourama (Waterview) Falls are also in national parks in north Queensland.

Simpson Desert National Park of 1,250,000 acres was gazetted in Queensland in May 1967 following representations by the National Parks Association of Queensland to the Queensland government and to the authorities in South Australia and the Northern Territory. This large area of parallel sand hills with ephemeral plants and low rainfall (under five inches annually) should prove of great scientific and scenic interest.

Other Reserves

State forests (6,202,000 acres) and timber reserves (2,043,000 acres) play their part in giving some protection to habitat and to our mammals, birds, reptiles and invertebrates. It must be remembered that tree harvesting must seriously disturb nesting and breeding cycles and in some cases may even destroy age-old territories of Australian fauna.

A reserve for scientific fauna conservation has been set aside north of Noosa and contains 10,800 acres of wallum and lake. In addition, authorization is given under the Fauna Conservation Act of 1952 for the establishment and protection of fauna sanctuaries.

Many of these are on private or lease-hold land and are not policed. Sanctuaries do include all of the islands off the Queensland coast, all state forests, timber reserves and national parks and certain government lands such as Swans Lagoon near Burdekin River (fifty miles upstream from Ayr) and Lake Moondarra (Mount Isa's water supply).

Problems in Queensland

The centralized Queensland system of control by the Forestry Department has in general worked well. The system of access within the parks limited to graded tracks is greatly appreciated by young and old visitors from near and far. Roads are provided to the boundaries of the reserves with small picnic areas on some of the boundaries; and on the mainland government policy has kept accommodation outside the boundaries.

Nevertheless, the overall picture cannot be regarded as satisfactory.

At the time of writing, the area gazetted as national parks and scenic areas in Queensland has increased to 2,323,617 acres but this has taken sixty years to achieve. In this period, large areas ideal for preservation as national parks have gone for ever. The bulldozers are on the march in Queensland and time is running out if 3,000,000 acres (one suggested target) are to be set aside for national parks. Even when this target is reached, and it will need to be reached before 1974, only three-quarters of one per cent of the total area of Queensland will have been set aside in perpetuity as national parks.

Impatience and concern at the apparent lack of funds for national park purposes have been shown by the National Parks Association of Queensland. The Queensland Minister for Conservation in a recent reply has quoted expenditure on wages and improvements in 1957-8 as $91,624 and that this has risen in 1966-7 to $152,190. The Minister added:

> the salaries of all permanent officers, either full time or part time, on National Park work in Queensland is charged against the Salary Vote of the Department and not against the special appropriation for National Parks. Furthermore all the other work carried out by the Department in its Drafting and other Sections is not costed directly to the National Park allocation. A point which should also be recognized is the fact that to date no charges whatsoever are made for facilities provided on National Parks in Queensland.

This author can compare total government expenditure in 1957-8 and 1966-7 and also can look at the Queensland Tourist Bureau allocations in the same nine years. With a twofold increase in total government expenditure and a many times increased vote for tourist purposes, a reasonable conclusion is that the Queensland government should almost double the national parks by 1969-70 to bring this state's needs into line with a decade of government spending in other directions. The number of visitors to national parks in the last nine years has more than doubled.

The quality of the staff is excellent but numerically it is barely adequate now and lack of money for training and recruitment of dedicated personnel could soon cause a crisis of interpretation and control. Visitors from other states and other countries will expect to see and speak to overseers, rangers, park naturalists, about the national parks they visit. They will want popular brochures about these reserves. So far there are only eight official Queensland publications, with some in preparation.

Although Australia was commended at the First World Conference on National Parks in 1962, for Queensland's reservation of more than 500,000 acres of rainforest, Dr L. J. Webb at Armidale in 1965 listed twelve types of rainforest not reserved in Queensland. A detailed submission of these unreserved types as apply on northern coastal lowlands is now being examined by the Conservator of Forests. In response to his invitation to government departments such as C.S.I.R.O., Lands, Mines, Geological Survey and to conservation bodies, the Conservator now has received numerous submissions of valuable information about areas considered suitable for national park purposes.

The National Parks Association of Queensland to date has submitted proposals for national parks in Queensland to the extent of 2,400,000 acres and has been gratified to see gazettal in Queensland of 1,900,000 acres of these proposals with 400,000 acres still under consideration. Approximately 100,000 acres have been preferred for pastoral or forestry purposes.

Among the areas not covered in existing national parks in Queensland are western grasslands, kangaroo habitat, brigalow, coastal wallum and breaks in vegetation types in Cape York Peninsula. Among areas under consideration by the government are the following:

Rainforest to the south of Cape York
Tozer Range to the west of Iron Range
McIlwraith Range north-east of Coen
Annan River Gorge and Mount Finnegan south of Cooktown
The Great Basalt Wall
Flinders and Porcupine Gorges north-east of Hughenden
Gregory River Springs north of Mount Isa
Herbert River Gorge (west of Ingham)
The northern end of Fraser Island
Wallum areas between Bundaberg and Noosa
Brigalow areas

The Queensland government and its Forestry Department are faced with several problems in national parks but no more so than similar authorities in other countries. Some are of the government's own making and some are presented by opportunists who cast avaricious eyes on some of the national parks.

New South Wales

A. A. Strom

The Environments

New South Wales has an area of approximately 200 million acres — about three times the size of the British Isles — with significant variations in climate and a diversity of environmental conditions.

The Great Dividing Range running generally parallel to the coastline separates the narrow coastal plain from a considerable area of western slopes and plains. A broad drainage pattern, based on the Murray-Darling River System, dominates the entire western area of the state.

The Great Dividing Range has a peneplain topography giving rise to three separate tablelands: the Northern (New England) Tableland, with some peaks 4,000 to 5,000 feet in altitude, the Central Tableland 2,000 to 3,000 feet, and the Southern Tableland (and Monaro), which contains the highest country in Australia, including Mount Kosciusko of 7,316 feet.

The Southern Tableland, particularly the Monaro region, experiences annual falls of snow and severe winters, while all areas on the tablelands are subjected to low winter temperatures and severe frosts.

Westward of the tablelands the elevation drops slowly over the western slopes, following the general drainage pattern of the west-flowing streams from the Range. There are several interesting remnants of ranges left on the western slopes and plains, some of which are directly linked with the main Divide by low lines of hills, two being particularly important, the Nandewar and Warrumbungle Ranges.

The western plains are generally continuous from the slopes to the South Australian border, the Darling River entering from the north-east and dissecting the plains well to the west by a north-south line. The lower reaches of the Lachlan, Murrumbidgee and Darling Rivers and their confluences with the Murray, present a special set of conditions with billabongs, lakes and interconnecting river systems of particular value for waterfowl conservation. It is in these areas, which were originally subject to regular flooding, that control of water supplies by dams and weirs in the upper reaches is having a most significant effect upon environmental conditions and the conservation of fish and waterfowl.

The climatic conditions in New South Wales vary considerably in different regions. These are broadly:

(a) High rainfall regions (up to seventy inches or more per annum) on the north coast
(b) Wet areas at other points along the coast and on the tablelands
(c) Tablelands subject to frigidity, particularly in the south where alpine conditions are well developed
(d) A region of slopes of moderate rainfall, increasing in aridity westward towards plains
(e) A region of riverine conditions at the confluence of the inland rivers in the south-west
(f) Plains with a semi-arid climate

All regions may vary significantly from normal, giving periods of extreme drought or high rainfall.

The coastal strip and the western slopes

have suffered the most significant alterations to vegetation cover by the activities of man. Large areas of subtropical rainforest were eliminated from the far north coast ('big scrub' area). Patches of rainforest now survive mainly in state forests and the more inaccessible parts of the eastern escarpment. There is a transition along the coastal and tableland regions, from rainforest to wet sclerophyll and thence into dry sclerophyll and coastal heathlands.

A major area of alpine complex occurs in the Kosciusko area northward into the Brindabella Ranges, west of Canberra. Remnant alpine environments are to be found at various other sites where the elevation is great enough, interestingly at Mount Kaputar (Narrabri), also on the Northern Tableland, but particularly on the Barrington/Gloucester Tops at the southern extremity of the Northern Tableland.

Most of the remainder of the tablelands and westward over the slopes, is an area of altered woodland and savannah woodland, which finally gives place to the scrubs of the more arid plains. The scrubs in the southern areas are largely mallee interspersed with savannah woodland, and mulga with box and Leopardwood in the north. There are widely distributed areas of saltbush-bluebush steppe, tussock grasslands (Mitchell and Wallaby grasses) in the north, and riverine marshlands in the Riverina (south-west).

Evolution of the Parks and Reserves Systems

New South Wales has the distinction of possessing Australia's oldest national park, The Royal National Park, just south of Sydney. The Royal is also one of the oldest national parks in the world having been set aside in 1879.

Although the Royal National Park (originally called 'The' National Park) was set aside 'for the use of the public for ever as a national park', there are strong reasons to believe that its sponsors were not entirely guided by altruistic motives. They apparently knew very little of the true meaning of 'national park' and saw no need to establish a programme to conserve the resources of nature. The early history of 'The Royal' contains many efforts on the part of the mangement to exploit the resources of the park, including the logging of timber and the organization of shooting parties.

The second national park in the state was the Ku-ring-gai Chase north of Sydney, which was set aside in 1894. At the time of establishment, both the Royal and Ku-ring-gai would have represented isolated and barren patches of sandstone country surrounding the then small city of Sydney. While it is extremely fortunate for the population of Sydney that these areas were set aside, it is obvious that at the time of reservation, at least, no great sacrifice was being made in terms of arable or valuable land being 'locked-up away from the people'. Ku-ring-gai in contradistinction to Royal, was set aside (at the inspiration of non-professional interests) with the specific aim of providing a breathing space and playground facilities for the future large metropolis of Sydney. Three or four decades were to elapse before further reservations of significance were made.

Impetus for the establishment of a comprehensive system of national parks seems to have resulted largely from the inspired and voluntary efforts of one man, Myles J. Dunphy, whose interest in primitive lands and excellence in cartography led him to study the experience of workers in the same field in the United States. Dunphy became familiar with the concepts of national parks and primitive areas (now known as wilderness areas) which he conveyed to bushwalkers and nature lovers. In the late twenties and early thirties this led to efforts aimed at ensuring the reservation of lands for recreation — largely walking and wilderness experience. However, the propaganda did bring about a wave of interest in preserving places of scenic charm and naturalness, with a concurrent claim to the 'preservation of flora and fauna'. By and large, many of the schemes produced by Myles Dunphy are the national and state parks of today.

The thirties saw the reservation of the Mark Morton Primitive Reserve (now Morton National Park) in the lower Kangaroo Valley and along the Shoalhaven River, as a result of the drive of the late Mark Morton, M.L.A.; the reservation of the New England National Park on the eastern escarpment of the Northern (New England) Tableland and along the catchment of the Bellinger River, with the inspiration of P. A. Wright (Snr.); the reservation of the Bouddi Natural Park (now Bouddi State Park) on the seaboard near Gosford following the efforts of Marie B. Byles and the Federation of Bushwalking Clubs; and the reservation of Garrawarra Park on the southern end of Royal (now absorbed in the Royal) and the Heathcote Primitive Reserve (now State Park) adjacent to Royal, as a result of campaigns organized by bushwalking and allied interests.

At the same time, schemes were produced for a Greater Blue Mountains National Park (a noble and comprehensive inspiration largely conceived and presented by Dunphy in 1932), the future Kosciusko State Park, a Kariong National Park and several others. It must be of great satisfaction to Myles Dunphy, now in his seventies, to see so many of his schemes, not so readily accepted at official levels in the thirties, being hailed as achievements of the century.

The Kosciusko State Park (now National Park) was established under Act of Parliament in 1944. Following the Fauna Protection Act of 1948, the fifties saw a new development towards nature conservation.

The Warrumbungle National Park near Coonabarabran was reserved in the mid-fifties, followed by the Brisbane Water National Park near Gosford (Dunphy's Kariong proposal) and Gloucester Tops later in the same decade. Blue Mountains and Gibraltar Range (near Grafton) followed, largely as the result of the special effort and interest of the late Charles Elphinstone, then Surveyor-General.

In the Fauna Protection Act of 1948, provision was made for the dedication of lands as faunal reserves 'for the preservation, care, propagation and study of fauna'. From the very beginning, the Fauna Protection Panel (the administrative authority set up under the Fauna Act) moved towards the establishment of a faunal reserve system. The intention was to secure samples of various natural environments to preserve the indigenous fauna. The idea of establishing 'reserves of nature' subsequently led to the substitution of the title 'nature reserve' for 'faunal reserve', a connotation which was authenticated in the National Parks and Wildlife Act of 1967.

The task which the Fauna Protection Panel set itself met with considerable official opposition since the concept of a system of reserves designed largely for scientific reference purposes was not readily understood. But by the end of 1967, there were fifty-five such nature reserves covering a wide variety of habitats and about 150,000 acres. Each of the reserves has a special significance, as a sample of one or more ecosystems, as a bird-nesting site, or as some other aspect of importance to wildlife conservation.

A major problem which faces nature conservation is the diversity of the Australian biota represented in this state. Moreover, many of the indigenous fauna are migratory or opportunist in habit, a feature related to the transient condition of drought and floods. The inevitable conclusion is that no system of reserves vested solely in the nature conservation administration can hope to succeed in ensuring the survival of the optimum number of species, or to secure a full and comprehensive representation of the diverse natural communities of the state. For some time then, the erstwhile Fauna Protection Panel expended much effort to establish and manage a third system of wildlife refuges and game reserves based on multiple land use principles.

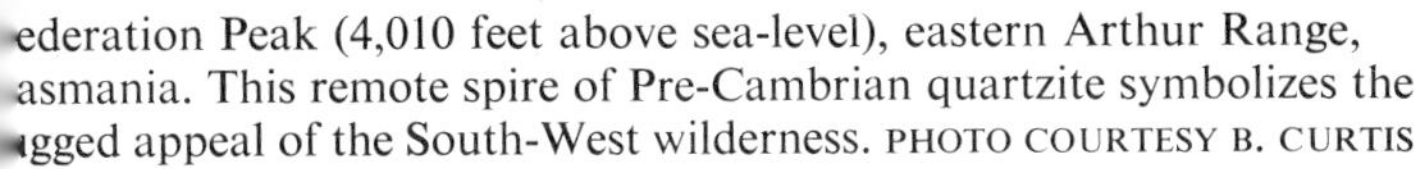

ederation Peak (4,010 feet above sea-level), eastern Arthur Range, asmania. This remote spire of Pre-Cambrian quartzite symbolizes the ugged appeal of the South-West wilderness. PHOTO COURTESY B. CURTIS

'ool temperate rainforest (moss forest), Tasmania, with the tree layer omposed of Antarctic Beech (*Nothofagus cunninghamii*).
HOTO COURTESY UNIVERSITY OF TASMANIA

ntally National House, Tasmania. The house of an early colonial landowner, it was estored by the Scenery Preservation Board and is open for inspection by the public.
HOTO COURTESY R. GOSS

Ayers Rock, Central Australia. This huge monolith stands 1,100 feet high and is 7 miles in circumference. PHOTO COURTESY AUST. TOURIST COMMISSION

Visitors from overseas at an Australian fauna park. PHOTO COURTESY AUST. TOURIST COMMISSION

The Olgas, Northern Territory; viewed from the west. Note the crocodile figur on top of the tallest monolith. Landsca features, whether as spectacular as this or more subtly of interest to science, deserve preservation as geological monuments for their own sake — as 'type' areas for particular rocks and ro sequences and as fossil localities. PHOTO COURTESY SOIL CONSERVATION SERVICE, N.S.W.

This system aimed to encourage private individuals and other land use authorities to agree to management plans over the whole or part of their properties which would preserve natural communities, develop simulated environments, and encourage the preservation and rehabilitation of particular species.

The multiple use concept was not intended to be restricted to lands held only by private or other authority and it seemed desirable to urge the nature conservation administration itself to practise multiple land use. Furthermore, there is an urgent need to establish game reserves, to encourage the breeding of native game species for recreational purposes including hunting.

An amendment to the Fauna Protection Act in 1964 enabled the Fauna Panel to proceed with this approach, and by the end of 1967 there were about 150 wildlife refuges (mostly on privately held lands) covering approximately two million acres, and some game reserves in various stages of progress towards proclamation. It is believed that the wildlife refuge and game reserve concepts deserve a great deal more attention and development.

Status of Parks and Reserves

Moves to have the administration define the nature and function of the national parks, to establish a professional service for national parks, to expand the national park system commensurate with the contemplated demands of future generations, and to secure adequate funds to manage a comprehensive national park system, have been included in the campaigns of nature conservationists over the last half-century. The early reports of the Wild Life Preservation Society of Australia (est. 1909) contain reference to representations made to the government of the day.

Dunphy and his colleagues campaigned throughout the twenties, thirties and forties, spurred on by the successes of the United States National Parks Service established in 1916.

During the fifties, established and encouraged by the work of the Fauna Protection Panel, several local wildlife conservation societies, together with some of the larger state-wide organizations, began to meet at regular intervals to discuss matters of mutual interest and concern. In 1955 it was agreed to present a proposal to the government for a National Parks Act. The organizations met the Minister for Lands, Mr Roger Nott, in March 1957. Subsequently, the National Parks Association of New South Wales was established and the spearheading of the campaign for the National Parks Act was turned over to that association.

The National Parks and Wildlife Act, 1967, restricts the use of the names 'national park' and 'state park' to those areas dedicated under the terms of the Act, or subsequent dedications. This clarifies a position which had become complicated by previous enactments for the Royal, Ku-ring-gai and Kosciusko Parks, as well as other areas gazetted under the Crown Lands Consolidation Act 'to be known' as national parks.

Although the legislation which was finally enacted took on a much more complex form than that originally proposed by the amateur nature conservationists, it did bring about what might be termed a 'legitimate' system of national and state parks. Those parks which were scheduled in the Act are shown in Table 1. The total area of all parks and nature reserves is just in excess of two million acres or about one per cent of the state. Five to six per cent of the state has been suggested as the optimum figure.

It is difficult to determine the intended nature and function of parks placed under the care, control and management of the Director of National Parks and Wildlife by the 1967 National Parks and Wildlife Act, since the Act does not provide a definition or a statement in context. However, a general direction is given as to the principles which

Table 1

NATIONAL PARKS AND STATE PARKS OF NEW SOUTH WALES

National Parks	Type	Area in Acres*
Kosciusko	From the Victorian border north along the Great Dividing Range and south-west of Canberra, A.C.T. Alpine	1,322,000
Blue Mountains	A significant part of the sandstone range country west of Sydney, north and south of the Great Western Railway	243,000
Kinchega	Plains country immediately south of Menindee. Includes some land alongside the Darling River and Lakes Menindee and Cawndilla	87,100
New England	On the edge of the New England Tableland, east of Armidale and largely the catchment of the Bellinger River	56,000
Morton	Along the Kangaroo River and tributaries and part of the Shoalhaven River, between Moss Vale and Nowra	45,000
Gibraltar Range	High granite country, some valley with rainforest between Grafton and Glen Innes on the Gwydir Highway	38,000
Royal	Sandstone country and coastline between Sydney and Illawarra	36,700
Ku-ring-gai Chase	Sandstone country and estuaries between Sydney and the Hawkesbury River	35,300
Mount Kaputar	Parts of the Nandewar Mountains near Narrabri including the Mount Kaputar plateau	35,200
Dharug	Sandstone country north of the Hawkesbury River near Wiseman's Ferry between Broken Bay and Windsor	29,000
Brisbane Water	Sandstone country immediately west of Gosford and Woy Woy and north of Broken Bay	16,500
Warrumbungle	Part of the Warrumbungle Mountains between Coonabarabran and Coonamble and including the cones of recent volcanic activity	15,400
State Parks		
Warning	Rainforest and the tall peak of the historic Mt Warning (Capt James Cook) near the head of the Tweed River, Murwillumbah	5,230
Heathcote	Along part of Heathcote Creek and Woronora River south of Sydney and west of the Royal National Park	3,900
Dorrigo	The rainforest-clad slopes on the eastern side of Dorrigo Mountain between Bellingen and Dorrigo	3,870
Gloucester Tops†	Alpine country and rainforest on high tops at the head of the Gloucester River, west of Gloucester	3,832
Bundanoon	Sandstone country and gullies along Bundanoon Creek between Bundanoon and the Morton National Park	3,330
Barangary	Belmore Falls and rainforest at the head of a gorge on Barangary Creek, a tributary of the Kangaroo River near Robertson	1,970
Bouddi	About twelve miles of coastline, adjacent valleys and moors between Kilcare and McMaster's beaches in Gosford district	1,310

* These figures as at 31 December 1967. There have been some additions since that time.

† Gloucester Tops State Park will be absorbed in the 34,000 acres Barrington Tops National Park, the dedication of which has been announced. Two other National Parks, Kanangra/Boyd in the Southern Blue Mountains, and Cocoparra on the range of that name near Griffith, are also reported for early dedication.

shall be observed in recommending additional areas for parks:

(a) National parks are to be spacious areas 'containing unique or outstanding scenery or natural features'
(b) State parks are 'large areas containing unique or outstanding scenery or natural features' but without the size of national parks.

Later under Section 29, the Director of National Parks and Wildlife is required to prepare a plan of management for each national park and state park reserved. These plans of management shall have the following objectives:

(a) Encouraging and regulating appropriate usə
(b) Preservation of natural conditions, protection of special features and conservation of wildlife
(c) Preservation of the park as a catchment area
(d) Protecting the park against fire and erosion
(e) Setting apart the whole or part of a park as a wilderness area.

While this statement provides guidelines for management, it does not placate fears that parks may be used intensively and for activities which are permanently damaging to conservation for scientific purposes. There is a total absence of any definition of 'wilderness' or for that matter, of any further reference to 'wilderness', except under Section 29(7) where we are told that a wilderness area 'shall be kept and maintained in a *wilderness* condition' and only essential survival huts will be permitted.

It is obvious, however, that intensive usage of at least parts of some parks is intended, since Section 30 enables the minister to grant leases of land (to any approved person, presumably) for the purpose of:

(a) The erection thereon of accommodation hotels or accommodation houses
(b) The provision thereon of facilities and amenities for tourists and visitors
(c) Occupying or using lands ('use' is not defined) within a national park or state park.

Section 32 enables the minister to grant a franchise to any person for the sale of goods and services, the provision of public transportation or the supply of other facilities and amenities.

Since the National Parks and Wildlife Service was only recently established, it is too early to draw conclusions from policies implied by recent management procedures, and as far as is known, no intended policy has been publicized.

The pattern of usage, however, has been already set in some parks where policies of the previous administration (i.e. the Trusts) have permitted roading, proliferation of picnicking and camping sites, leasing for accommodation, business operations and grazing. One presumes that it will be difficult to amend these policies and indeed, in some cases, amendment may not be desirable. Perhaps the following statement taken from *Wildlife Service*, Vol. 3, No. 8, a publication now produced under the aegis of the National Parks and Wildlife Service, is a balanced statement of the position:

> National Parks are for people and will provide these people contact with their natural environment. Thus naturalness is an essential quality and maintenance of this will be the major management problem. As a bonus, one can expect those forms of wildlife which can ignore Man's usage of the environment to survive as a natural population. Those which cannot adapt will become animals dependent upon an artificial and purposeful manipulation of their habitat.

Fortunately New South Wales has the basic legislation to enable administration to face up to 'a picture of wildlife conservation which demands flexibility, which demands recognition of the fact that it should be part and parcel of the whole land use spectrum from the restricted nature reserve to the city park' (*Wildlife Service*, Vol. 3 ,No. 8). The nature reserves which may be dedicated under Section 9 of the Fauna Protection Act, 1948, as amended, are primarily for the maintenance of natural environments for scientific use by man, with a bonus of strictly limited recreational use, while for the many more mobile animals and for the various other interests of wildlife generally, the wildlife refuges and game reserves of Section 23A of the same Act, have particular significance.

Section 9 of the Fauna Protection Act states that the purpose of nature reserves is 'the protection and care of fauna, the propagation of fauna and the promotion of the study of fauna'.

In later subsections of Section 9 and other sections of the Fauna Act, it is amply demonstrated that the intention is to provide protection for nature reserves so that they will serve as scientific reference areas and as natural areas for study and contemplation. There are fifty-five nature reserves in New South Wales, ranging in area from three acres (Moon Island near Swansea) to 29,247 acres (at Nadgee in the extreme south-eastern corner of the state).*

The nature and function of wildlife refuges and game reserves are set out under Section 23A(4) of the Fauna Act which states:

> The Director may prepare a scheme of operations the object of which shall be the maintenance or restoration of natural environments, and the encouragement of the care, propagation, preservation and conservation of protected fauna and the appreciation of protected fauna in their natural environments.

On a wildlife refuge, only unprotected species of fauna may be taken at any time under licensed conditions, but on a game reserve certain species of 'game fauna' may be taken under licence as approved by the Director of National Parks and Wildlife.

Legislation and Administration

Legislation covering the interests of nature conservation in New South Wales, while diverse, is centred in three major enactments administered by the new Director of National Parks and Wildlife:

(a) The Wild Flowers and Native Plants Protection Act, 1927-1967
(b) The Fauna Protection Act, 1948-1967
(c) The National Parks and Wildlife Act, 1967.

The Wild Flowers and Native Plants Protection Act provides for the proclamation of a list of protected native plants and for a system of licences to enable protected plants to be taken for scientific purposes and protected plants to be grown for sale.

The Fauna Protection Act provides for the preservation of natural habitats through nature reserves, wildlife refuges and game reserves; for the protection of most native birds and mammals with special cover for certain 'rare' species and for certain areas of land to be proclaimed 'sanctuaries'; for education towards a better appreciation of wildlife values and for the extension of knowledge through research and scientific enquiry; for management of wildlife, to control, regenerate and use the resource.

The National Parks and Wildlife Act provides for the establishment and management of national parks, state parks and historic sites; for a Director of National Parks and Wildlife and a National Parks and Wildlife Service to administer the provisions of the National Parks and Wildlife Act, the Fauna Protection Act and the Wild Flowers and Native Plants Protection Act. (Note: This Act abolished the Fauna Protection Panel.)

Other legislation which provides incidental assistance to nature conservation includes the Crown Lands Consolidation Act, whereby Crown lands may be dedicated or reserved for a number of 'public purposes' which are in the interests of nature conservation; the Forestry Act, in its general provisions and in the provision for the dedication of flora reserves; and various other enactments which afford protection to catchment areas or limit the destruction of natural cover on Crown and other lands.

* This was the situation as at 31 December 1967. The position now is sixty nature reserves with a total area of about 340,000 acres. The largest is Pilliga (160,000 acres) in the central west of the state.

Problems

There has been little effort so far to bring together all facets of conservation in this state. Consequently the public find it difficult to secure an integrated, comprehensive picture. The rigid categorization of conservation into soil, water, forests, fisheries and nature, each with a largely independent administration, is unfortunate. In addition, the term 'conservation' does not acknowledge non-renewable resources. The inevitable outcome is conflict and competition for land and an individual canvassing of public support. It is difficult to see a way around the impasse at this time, as each subdivision of conservation tries to entrench itself for better financial attention and a greater say in land use. In the neighbouring state of Victoria where land development has already outstripped that of New South Wales, a Land Utilization Advisory Council has been set up and this may well provide some answer to the perplexing problems of sustained-yield use.

Natural environments, natural phenomena and places of historical importance may be preserved under the existing legislation through national parks, state parks, historic sites and nature reserves. In selecting sites for parks and reserves, an attempt is made to secure diversification of nature. This is hampered by an absence of ecological surveys of the state and by the availability of land to satisfy the demands of diversification. Recent work by a Scientific Committee organized by the Minister for Lands is helping to rectify the situation. The selection of nature reserves has always been geared to the sampling of ecosystems, but parks have in the past been chosen to satisfy the needs of recreation, the utilization of significant scenery, or some other natural amenity, such as the snowfields in the Koskiusko National Park.

New South Wales is fortunate to have the opportunity to develop a dichotomy of reserves — the national parks to enable people to contact the natural environment, and the nature reserves for scientific reference and where applicable, very low density experience of nature. The new National Parks and Wildlife Service has yet to announce publicly its understanding of the purpose and functions of the parks and reserves. One might expect the plans of management to demonstrate the guide lines which the Service has in mind for the purpose and functions of parks, particularly in regard to the amount of each park to be devoted to 'wilderness', which will be, in pure terms, the significant contributing factor of parks to wildlife conservation. The Service would do well to define 'wilderness' and any other categories designated.

It is acknowledged that the Fauna Protection Act and the Wild Flowers and Native Plants Protection Act are in need of revision, and a new Wildlife Conservation Act is in draft. This should define wildlife to mean both plants and animals and to include other animals besides birds and mammals. New South Wales is also fortunate to have some authority to develop a broad pattern of wildlife management under a common head with management of natural environment. The proposed Wildlife Conservation Act should bolster, broaden and emphasize wildlife management.

The administration of all segments of nature conservation under a single nature conservation authority appears a suitable approach to balancing the reservation of natural environments and the management of wildlife stocks over the entire state. Undoubtedly there are many unresolved questions, not the least of which concern the involvement of fisheries and the place of general conservation education. The present nature conservation administration — the National Parks and Wildlife Service — is so new that it has more than enough to handle with the management of national parks, nature reserves and general plant and animal populations, without the added burdens of fisheries management and conservation education.

The immediate task now is to develop a

concept and an expression of local problems of nature conservation in its widest sense, then to forge a comprehensive and workable link with the management of the total resources, through soil, water, forest and fish conservation.

The community looks to the new National Parks and Wildlife Service to demonstrate understanding that nature conservation is much more than resource management. Conservation means the protection of a variety of units of nature; the total biomass, and individual land forms, geomorphological features and natural ecosystems. All of these units may then be used by man in a variety of ways: for enjoyment of nature, for the benefit of harvesting as a recreation or as a commercial enterprise, or for reference and scientific research.

National Parks and Nature Conservation Reserves in Victoria

J. Ros Garnet

Environment and Ecological Factors

Victoria occupies less than three per cent of the mainland of Australia, and is slightly smaller in area than Great Britain. Yet, as the result of the great diversity of the environment, Victoria supports an extensive range of biotic communities of great scenic and scientific interest.

The major physical divisions of Victoria are the Murray Basin plains, the central highlands which reach over 6,000 feet, and the east-west belt of lowlands (Western and Gippsland plains) flanked by the southern uplands.

The climate is varied and is partly related to the geographical position of the state. The inland area to the north-west experiences continental heat and drought, whereas the eastern and southern portions of the state have warm and cool oceanic influences respectively. Summer days are hot (with temperatures occasionally over 100°F.) and typically dry. Rainfall is highest during the winter months, although in much of the southern half of the state, spring is the wettest season. Rainfall is higher near the coast and on the highlands, where it reaches forty to sixty inches per year, decreasing to less than fifteen inches in the north-west interior. Hot, dry northerly winds during the summer drought regularly provide 'blow-up' conditions for disastrous conflagrations, in which the fire runs through the tree crowns and 'spots' ahead of the main fire-front. During the winter, frosts are common away from the coast, although regular snowfalls are confined to the highlands.

The most spectacular forest, in the central and southern highlands, is dominated by the Mountain Ash (*Eucalyptus regnans*). According to Patton, the greatest height officially recorded for this tree is 326 feet, and the greatest girth, 88 feet. Adjoining forests are dominated by Messmate, Peppermint, Mountain Grey Gum, Silvertop and other eucalypts, commonly with species of *Acacia*. Temperate rainforest dominated by Antarctic Beech (*Nothofagus cunninghamii*) occurs in favorable situations, and a typical fire sere in fern gullies is composed of various wattles, e.g. Blackwood (*Acacia melanoxylon*), with a well-developed understorey often with tree ferns. As the rainfall decreases, sclerophyll forests dominated by various eucalypts and characterized by a dense sclerophyllous understory occur. On the high plains of the alpine zone, there are alpine grasslands, sphagnum bog and sclerophyll scrub. In lowland areas on suitable soils, there are extensive grasslands and tree savannas. To the north-west, mallee associations (mallee, heath, scrub, etc.) are common. One of the most picturesque associations of the lowlands is fringing forest with River Red Gum (*Eucalyptus camaldulensis*) along the rivers and billabongs. The southern lowlands and uplands have a varied cover of vegetation, including sclerophyll forest, heath, swamp, sand dune, salt marsh, mangrove etc. The Lilly Pilly (*Eugenia smithii*, sens. lat.) is the characteristic tree species of the subtropical 'jungle' patches to the east. The tropical character of this habitat is emphasized by the composition of the bird fauna and the presence of the Grey-headed Flying Fox.

Victoria has been subdivided into five

faunal regions, related to vegetation type, rainfall and physiography. In all these regions, the native fauna has become restricted to smaller and smaller areas with the spread of settlement and increased destruction by bushfires.

Evolution and Status of National Parks

Tower Hill, the famous geological monument in the western district, was temporarily reserved in 1866 and in 1892 its 1,360 acres were permanently reserved for public recreation by the Tower Hill National Park Act. Yet by that time Tower Hill was little more than a monument to the geological past of the western district and to man's unrivalled capacity for destruction. It exemplified the disconcertingly slow development of public awareness of the need for conservation. When von Guerard painted his scenes on Tower Hill in 1859 it was a place of exceeding charm and immense scientific interest. Fifteen years later the picture of Tower Hill had been altered almost beyond recognition. Most of the forest had been destroyed, the wildlife had dwindled. What hadn't been shot had been burned. After 1892, being Crown land, it continued under the administration of the Lands Department's Board of Land and Works which delegated the management of the park to the local borough council. The sad tale of public and civic vandalism in this park would take too long to tell, but is equally applicable to many other scenic places in Victoria. Finally, in 1960, Tower Hill was proclaimed a state game reserve and a total of 1,500 acres were transferred to the care of the Fisheries and Wildlife Department. There is no evidence that it has lost any value thereby.

The early dedication of Tower Hill led to requests for national parks in other parts of the state where scenery was endangered, as was the continued existence of animals such as the koala, platypus, echidna, lyrebird, bower-bird, brolga, bustard, lowan, emu, and even the common kangaroo and wallaby.

Werribee Gorge, a notable geological feature about forty miles west of Melbourne, would have suffered the same destruction as Tower Hill had it been more accessible. The gorge itself had been temporarily reserved in 1881, but it was not until 1907 that the lower entrance was set aside as a public park. Its 573 acres, it is understood, are soon to become a national park.

About 412 acres of forest and fern gully on the south-western slopes of Mount Dandenong were temporarily reserved in 1887, and formed the nucleus of what was to become, forty years later, Fern Tree Gully National Park (now 927 acres).

In 1898, after fourteen years of spasmodic campaigning, 75,000 acres of Wilson's Promontory were temporarily reserved as 'a site for a national park'. This was reckoned a sufficient political gesture to quieten those persistent nature lovers in a decade when grandiose land settlement schemes were engaging the attention of the more astute politicians. But by then what the area possessed in the way of exploitable resources — so far as could be determined at the time — had been harvested. What remained was deemed to be useless for any other purpose than exhibiting attractive scenery, although some native animal and plant species were inadvertently preserved.

Settlement and clearing in the Strzelecki Ranges were fast destroying hundreds of square miles of some of the state's magnificent forests. But fifty acres of rainforest on the Mesozoic sediments of the Ranges were spared, and in 1904 were gazetted as Bulga Park (now ninety-one acres). Wilson's Promontory, farther south, seemed likely to have its reservation revoked because of its possible use to graziers. The threat was real enough to arouse naturalists to immediate action, and in 1908 practically the whole of the Promontory (102,379 acres) was gazetted as a national park. During the Second World War the park was taken over by the Army and used as a commando training centre. The public was, of course, debarred from entry into their park: what little was learned about happenings within the sanctuary did nothing to allay fears that the wildlife was having a sorry time. Whether the damage was as great as many were ready to believe will never be known. After the war, the park has become a favoured tourist area, and the centre of active biological research by the university.

In 1898, some 2,880 acres of the north-eastern subalpine Mount Buffalo plateau had been temporarily reserved, and in 1908 rather more than 20,000 acres of the plateau were added to form the Mount Buffalo National Park (27,280 acres). The following year, 4,730 acres of the foreshore of Wingan Inlet — a site of historical significance — were set aside, and 11,225 acres of the lovely environs of Mallacoota Inlet were reserved.

In 1909, about 9,600 acres of mallee country were excluded from development and declared a sanctuary for native fauna. In 1921, a further 16,000 acres were added to form the Wyperfeld National Park. This action so much upset nearby landholders that they arranged a deputation to seek the revocation of the reserve. They argued that it was only a breeding ground for vermin and noxious weeds, although one suspects that these may have entered the reserve from their own properties. The official reaction was heartening for the public at large. A further 7,680 acres were added to the reserve! But more than thirty years elapsed before the antipathy of the local settlers abated. Today, Wyperfeld is the state's largest national park and has grown to 139,760 acres. It is recognized by the new generation of settlers as a proud possession. Most of them are reconciled to the prospect of living with its kangaroos and emus, and they no longer fear it as an uncontrollable breeding ground for rabbits.

Early in the century, the habitat of the Mallee Fowl was being rolled and fired so recklessly that the civic conscience was stirred to demand that some of it be kept intact. The result — one and a half square miles of sanctuary! At least something had been achieved. During the Second World War there were matters more urgent than conservation, and it was felt that the population could not afford the luxury of too much waste land.

However, the decade 1920 to 1929 was possibly the most productive period in the history of nature conservation in Victoria. Besides the enlargement of reserves in the mallee country, fragments of other habitats were salvaged. In 1921, some 145 acres of the Tarra Valley which somehow had miraculously survived the wrecking of the surrounding countryside were temporarily reserved as a companion to Bulga Park. Tarra Valley National Park now comprises about 315 acres. In 1926, the Alfred National Park of 3,351 acres on Mount Drummer, east of Cann River was gazetted. It is a place where the Gippsland Waratah flourishes, and the present area of 5,406 acres includes about 300 acres of subtropical-type rainforest or 'jungle'. At the same time, 2,882 acres of the lovely Euchre Creek valley in the same County Croajingolong were permanently reserved as Lind National Park. The special virtues of these two areas might not have come to notice had not the then newly proclaimed Princes Highway transected them.

By the end of 1929, an extensive area of burnt-out forest and devastated bushland had graduated to the status of a permanent reserve known as Kinglake National Park. Some cynical observers suggested that the reserve was granted only because some incompetent official failed to recognize the great economic potential of a fire-blackened waste. Time ensured the growth of mighty forests to tantalize saw-millers and loggers. The area of Kinglake National Park is now 14,093 acres.

A few other sites of public interest were brought within the scope of Section 14 of the Land Act of 1928, under which all national parks and nature reserves had been proclaimed. Scenic places and formations deserving attention as national monuments were brought to official notice from time to time. Sometimes the requests were merely filed for future reference, or the sites unofficially withheld from alienation by simply blue-pencilling the area on the office master plan. Places like Mount Wellington and Lake Tarli Karng were treated thus.

Following the National Parks Act of 1956 and the creation of the National Parks Authority, over 56,000 acres have been added to the parks system. Only a small proportion of recommendations for reserves seems to have been accepted, and some acquisitions appear to be ill-advised. Thus it is unlikely that an experienced Authority, of its own volition, would have chosen the 7,749 acres which were thrust upon it as Fraser National Park.

Its scenic attractions largely depend on the artificial Lake Eildon and it is unimportant as a nature conservation reserve. It was run-down grazing property which could well have been maintained as a tourist resort without burdening the National Parks Authority with the cost and responsibility of managing it in accordance with its very specialized requirements.

Another acquisition was 1,534 acres (now increased to 2,036 acres) at Mount Richmond, near Portland in the far south-west of the state, which is well-selected and will conserve a fraction of the flora of the south-west which is fast disappearing with settlement.

Mount Eccles (84 acres), the extinct volcano with its beautiful little crater lake, Lake Surprise, came into the hands of the Authority because the local shire council found its maintenance as a public reserve too much of a burden. It may be more appropriately labelled a state geological monument, and its inclusion in the schedule of national parks is a precedent for the consideration of other small areas of special scenic, scientific or historical interest. Eight hundred and ninety acres of broken rubble to the north-west of Mount Eccles were recently added, to make the total area 974 acres.

Hattah Lakes, another charge of the Authority, is 44,000 acres in extent, and measures up well to the specification of a good national park and nature conservation reserve. It provides ample space for the free movement of fauna and the development of stable populations, as well as embracing some of the more important mallee associations. It is a pity that two features not yet represented in any Victorian national park were not included: the historical associations of an old and famous pastoral run, in this case Kulkyne Station, and a section of the Murray river and one of its 'bends'. The exclusion of most of the Chalka Creek anabranch system of freshwater lakes was especially disappointing, and renders the several delightful little lakes which were included vulnerable to permanent damage if economic development (such as vegetable growing aided by irrigation) occurs.

Glenaladale National Park, of 403 acres, is an area of river gorge with surrounding forests which was retrieved by the cooperation of Australian Paper Mills. Besides a special type of subtropical community in a picturesque setting, it possesses rich historical associations with early exploration in Gippsland and with Aboriginal legends.

A recent acquisition, in 1964, was a narrow coastal strip of Tertiary sand heathland and scrub between Princetown and Curdie's Inlet near Peterborough: the highlights of Port Campbell National Park (1,750 acres) are the picturesque offshore islets and eroded rocks whose very nature and situation are a sufficient guarantee that they could never be destroyed by man's neglect or by normal destructive agencies.

Lakes National Park (5,238 acres) was formerly known as Sperm Whale Head, so named because of the peninsula which extends eastward towards Lakes Entrance and separates Lake Victoria from Lake Reeve and the Ninety Mile Beach. It is the only known

Victorian habitat of *Thryptomene micrantha.*

Churchill National Park (477 acres) is a small enclave of timbered country in a larger public reserve known as the 'Police Paddock', and is situated on the southern slopes of the Lysterfield Hills three miles from Dandenong. The area was used to train the horses of mounted police of an earlier era, but the reserve is much too vulnerable to serve any valuable nature conservation purpose.

The most recent addition to the national parks system is Morwell, comprising 342 acres of fern gully about 100 miles south-east of Melbourne. It is one of the few remaining natural habitats of one of Victoria's epiphytic orchids — *Sarcochilus australis.* Its small size gives no assurance that the plant association will continue to survive now that public access has been facilitated.

Proclamation is pending for several national parks. Sydenham Organ Pipes, an example of columnar basalt in the gorge of Jackson's Creek about sixteen miles from Melbourne, is at present situated on freehold, but the area is expected to be about 150 to 200 acres.

Kiata Lowan Sanctuary, about one square mile of mallee scrub five miles south of Kiata was recently extended to 2,870 acres and dedicated as Little Desert National Park. It is expected to finally cover 80,000 acres.

It is expected that 6,000 to 7,000 acres of the southern part of Yanakie Isthmus, between the soldiers' settlement of Yanakie and the northern boundary of Wilson's Promontory National Park, will be added to the latter. It was part of the old Yanakie Pastoral Run, and is mainly sand dunes overlying Recent marine limestone deposits. It should form a good buffer for the preservation of the richer flora of the Promontory.

Administration and Legislation

On 25 October 1956, Victoria's National Parks Act was assented to, and it came into operation in May, 1957.

The groundwork for this Act had been laid towards the end of last century by certain eminent individuals and the organizations to which they belonged: University, National Museum, Royal Society, Field Naturalists' Club, Australian Natives' Association and even the Acclimatization Society.

In more recent times, a report by the Field Naturalists' Club of Victoria activated a series of public conferences on problems and policy of nature conservation in the state. That was in 1948. The government was urged to recognize by statute the state's national parks and to establish a competent public authority for their administration.

In 1952, a Parliamentary State Development Committee endorsed most of the recommendations of the Field Naturalists' report. It was officially recognized that the 530 square miles of national parks already existing in Victoria were a valuable asset, and that new parks were needed.

A combined standing committee representing societies interested in nature conservation was transformed into a new national parks association, which helped draft the Bill on Victoria's national parks. The Act of 1956 provided for the establishment and control of national parks, the preservation of indigenous plant and animal wildlife, and features of special scenic, scientific or historical interest, besides the maintenance of the existing environment of national parks and the education and enjoyment of visitors.

That these objectives might be properly pursued, the Act authorized the creation of a National Parks Authority of eleven persons. It comprised the Premier (or a Minister nominated by him) as Chairman, a Director who is a permanent public servant appointed to act as the Authority's chief executive officer, five departmental heads or their nominees (from Lands, Forests, Public Works, Soil Conservation, and Fisheries and Wildlife), and four persons appointed by the Governor-in-Council to represent organizations concerned with the protection of native fauna and flora, plus citizens with a special interest in national parks, as well as the Victorian Ski Association and the Government Tourist Bureau.

The duties of the Authority, as set out in Section 10 of the Act, are:

(a) unless inconsistent with any special purpose for which a national park has been proclaimed, to maintain every national park in its natural condition and to conserve therein ecological associations and species of native plants and animals, and to protect the special features of the park and, so far as practicable, to exterminate exotic plants and animals therein,
(b) to encourage and regulate the use of national parks by the public and to provide for the enjoyment thereof by the people in such a way as to leave parks unimpaired for the enjoyment of future generations,
(c) to protect national parks from injury by fire.

The employees of the National Parks Authority may be regarded as the nucleus of what could develop into a National Parks Service, which will be essential if nature conservation is to be served adequately and effectively in Victoria.

A serious weakness in the present system of national parks control in Victoria is the lack of certainty about who is really responsible for shaping policy — is it the committee of management? Or the Authority? Or Cabinet? From recent events, one can be excused for believing that political considerations outweigh all others.

So much for national parks and the Authority. But they are not the only agencies for nature conservation. Crown reserves of one kind and another, many of them of considerable significance for conservation, are administered by the Lands Department, Forests Commission, Fisheries and Wildlife Department, State Rivers and Water Supply Commission, Melbourne and Metropolitan Board of Works, Country Roads Board, State Electricity Commission, and provincial water supply and sewerage authorities.

All these reserves are for specific purposes which, in some cases, actually preclude or restrict public access. Thus the watershed reserves of the Board of Works are almost ideal nature reserves because the only catastrophic change they are likely to suffer will be from bushfires.

The State Rivers Commission reserves are less important because they generally embrace only the immediate environs of reservoirs and man-made inland lakes.

The Victorian Forests Commission plays an important part in the protection and preservation of scenery and wildlife, and administers reserves created by Order in Council. These have no statutory permanence and their status is maintained largely by force of public opinion. Forest parks (reserves exceeding 1,000 acres) are situated in the Grampians, Lerderderg Gorge, Sherbrooke, and You Yangs. Following the recent severe drought in Victoria, the Lerderderg River almost dried up, and approval was given for the harvesting of river gravel by private interests. The bulldozers have despoiled the approaches to Lerderderg Gorge, and the gravel royalties provide a tangible cash harvest. But under such circumstances park values mean little. Gravel quarrying in the You Yangs also destroyed a large area of Yellow Gum (*Eucalyptus leucoxylon*) forest which was a favoured nesting area for many birds. The Baw Baw Alpine Reserve of 13,000 acres is an important subalpine reserve administered by the Forests Commission. Several alpine reserves have been established, including a quite extensive area on the Bogong High Plains, controlled by the State Electricity Commission; a reserve containing Mt Hotham controlled by the Lands Department; and one established by the Forests Commission at Mt Buller.

Scenic parks (less than 1,000 acres) also administered by the Forests Commission number more than thirty, and like the forest parks are immune from normal forestry practices. Since the Commission has no obligation to provide accommodation for tourists most of the reserves remain in good condition because the impact of visitors is too transient to do much damage. Good forestry roads, along which the modern motorist is tempted to keep on driving, are largely responsible for this.

The only governmental agency other than the Forests Commission and the Melbourne and Metropolitan Board of Works which contributes in any significant way to nature conservation in Victoria is the Department of Fisheries and Wildlife. It has gained considerable public support for its programme of acquiring reserves over which it may have exclusive control. These are known as wildlife reserves, and are areas of public land (or land purchased for the purpose) set aside under the Lands Act specially for the conservation of wildlife. There are three categories. The state game reserve is open to duck shooting during the proclaimed season. The state game refuge is recognized as a haven for wildlife at all times, including declared open seasons, and no shooting is permitted. The state faunal reserve is established for the rehabilitation and/or maintenance of specified species of wildlife or of a particular faunal association.

Sale Common, about 760 acres in the City of Sale, is the only state game refuge. There are at least sixteen state game reserves which, with the exception of Tower Hill already mentioned, are mostly wetlands — lakes, marshes, and morasses, varying in size from 900 to over 13,000 acres. There are over twelve state faunal reserves, including range, creek and island habitats, for the protection of rock wallabies, fur seals, mutton birds, fairy penguins, sea birds, Mallee Fowl, the Helmeted Honeyeater, mammal fauna etc.

The department's programme involves control of various remaining swamps and marshes as drainage has been a major factor in the permanent destruction of habitat. Since the preservation of wildlife involves land form and its vegetational cover, the wildlife reserves are simultaneously fauna and flora reserves. Unfortunately these do not have the same guarantee of permanency as the national parks, which can be revoked only by Parliament. The Forest Commission's reserves are similarly vulnerable, and, while gazetted by Order in Council, may be revoked by ministerial decision without reference to anyone but the Commission.

Problems

The report in 1948 of the national parks and national monuments sub-committee of the Field Naturalists' Club highlighted the deficiencies of the previous administration of national parks in Victoria. Few of the parks which existed then had an assured income. Those that did generally obtained a substantial part of their revenue from such dubious sources as grazing fees or leases, logging royalties, bee range licences, or quarrying!

Wyperfeld, the Promontory, Mount Buffalo and Tower Hill were valued more for the benefits they yielded as grazing leases than as nature conservation reserves. Committees of management struggled on conscientiously at their own expense. Voluntary efforts or occasional municipal grants allowed one or two of the parks to provide a few facilities for picnic parties. But in the absence of inspection and maintenance, the combination of weather, vandals and bushfires usually destroyed the facilities.

However, if a national park happened to be favoured as a tourist resort, its committee of management could depend on obtaining a small allocation from a special fund set up by the government for assisting tourist development. Thus Wilson's Promontory, Mount Buffalo, Kinglake and Fern Tree Gully national parks were enabled to benefit, but places like Wyperfeld, Lakes, Tower Hill or Werribee Gorge could not get a penny. They were officially regarded simply as nature conservation reserves: as such they had no appeal to the ordinary run of money-spending tourist.

The present government of Victoria is dedicated to the belief that 'development' at maximum speed and intensity is only possible through the agency of private enterprise: no opportunity should be lost to harvest a known natural resource. Now national parks are seen to provide a natural resource which the public, in its role of tourist, wants to use. Tourists bring in easy money to the state. If tourists at Wilson's Promontory or Mount Buffalo want Gold Coast (of Queensland) treatment, why shouldn't they have it?

To facilitate this harvest, the National Parks Act was amended to provide for the virtual alienation of fifty acres in any national park for up to seventy-five years by any business concern which would be prepared to spend $200,000 on buildings to accommodate tourists. Other sites would be available for exploitation for a lesser term of thirty-three years without any obligation to spend money on buildings. The promptness with which advantage of this amendment was taken at Mount Buffalo and the Promontory by private investors indicated clearly enough the source of inspiration of the amendment. One surmises that the National Parks Authority merely acquiesced to a Cabinet decision. The present structure of the Authority leaves it peculiarly vulnerable to political control and, consequently, the future of national parks and nature conservation in Victoria will depend largely on what influence conservationists can exert on politicians.

Nor is the procedure for the establishment of new reserves to be accepted as satisfactory. Recommendations come from private citizens or their organizations who, instead of submitting them to the Lands Department or Forests Commission or the Fisheries and Wildlife Department, direct them to the National Parks Authority. The Authority may or may not examine the proposals before making its own recommendations to Cabinet. Because of the unbalanced composition of the Authority, community considerations can easily be neglected in favour of political expediency. There is a feeling among Victorian conservationists that this ever present threat to the integrity of national parks would be lessened were the Authority to be reconstructed. If it possessed a better balance between official and community representation it would be buffered against undue political interference.

At present, the two members appointed by the Governor-in-Council to speak for scientists and naturalists have little hope of successfully opposing a Cabinet decision which the rest of the Authority would feel obliged to support. An infusion of some new blood into the National Parks Authority would be worthwhile — such as a botanist, zoologist, geologist, and a representative of the Victorian National Parks Association.

As for safeguards against mining in national parks, Section 11 of the Act could, at first glance, engender a warm glow of approval. There is the assurance that no lease or licence shall be granted under the Mines Act 1958 or the Petroleum Act 1958 in respect of a national park except with the consent of the Authority. Unfortunately, a proviso allows appeal to the Governor-in-Council against an adverse decision of the Authority. A mining company, if influential enough, would almost certainly get its way 'in the public interest'. This may seem an unkind thing to say, but the very fact that the long lease amendments which were incorporated into Section 9 of the Act were introduced, and carried in spite of unusually persistent opposition from the public (the intended 'beneficiaries') shows that exploitation of a natural resource will find greater favour in the eyes of a politician than will the cultural value of scenery and wildlife.

The Future

The conservationists' ideal is to have a reserve containing a representative section of each of the major formations and an adequate portion of every important biotic community. To date, the National Parks Authority of Victoria has not announced any policy for achieving such an aim. The reason may be that no one quite knows what is lacking in the present system, nor what is the potential of now unreserved land for making good the present deficiencies. No public authority has the power nor, possibly, the inclination, to make a survey of the situation. For this reason, the National Parks Association undertook a nature conservation survey, financed by private subscription from its members.

Shortly, Victorian conservationists (and the Victorian government) should have the answer to at least some of the problems of land utilization which have been a perennial headache to departmental administrations and, often enough, a source of disappointment to the conservationist.

There are countless lessons to be learned from the successes and failures of the steps taken for nature conservation in Victoria. One is that it does not do to have one's eggs all in one basket. The tidy mind might think that it would be best to have all nature conservation reserves under a single controlling authority so that duplication of effort and resources could be avoided. However, the scope is so vast that the single authority would soon be forced to subdivide itself and the end result would surely be much the same as it is at present. Perhaps the greatest benefit derived from the creation of the National Parks Authority is that it has brought together the four great public agencies concerned with land utilization for the single and undivided purpose of furthering the interests of nature conservation. In the years before the Act was passed, each of them went its own sweet way without much thought as to what the other one was doing or even wanted to do. Now they co-operate and even if a little competition does occur, the conservationist — and, of course, the community at large — stands to gain.

Scenic Reserve and Fauna Sanctuary Systems of Tasmania

J. G. Mosley

The Tasmanian Environment

The island state of Tasmania, a detached part of the eastern uplands of Australia, roughly the size of the Irish Republic, is situated between 40° and 44° south of the Equator, stands in the track of the prevailing westerly air flow, and has a temperate oceanic climate which is wetter and cooler than the mainland's. These basic physical circumstances lead one to expect a considerable degree of distinctiveness in land forms, plant cover, and animal life.

One result of Tasmania's southerly position is that its mountains were more severely modified by the Pleistocene glaciation than other parts of the eastern highlands. On the Central Plateau thousands of small lakes remain on the site of a former ice cap, while the slopes of the higher western ranges are marked by cirques, rock basin lakes, and morainic ridges. Another response to position and climate is the natural vegetation which contains a comparatively great number of Southern Oceanic components.

Rainfall is the main influence on the character and distribution of vegetation and there are three forest zones: temperate rainforest in the wetter west; a transition zone comprising wet sclerophyll, and mixed forest (rainforest as an understory to tall eucalypts); and open sclerophyll forest in the drier rain shadow country of the east. Botanical interest focuses on the western and montane communities where there are many species having affinities with the plants of similar regions in New Zealand and Chile.

The western third of the state is exposed to persistent moist westerly winds and as a result large parts of it have an annual average rainfall of sixty to ninety inches and the greatest number of cloudy days of any part of Australia. The terrain consists of a series of north-south oriented sharp-crested ranges and poorly drained, flat-bottomed valleys. The major communities are temperate rainforest in which Evergreen Beech (*Nothofagus cunninghamii*) is dominant, ranging from sea-level to 4,000 feet, and sedgeland, an edaphic climax of the poor podsol peats of the valley bottoms, in which the Button Grass (*Mesomelaena sphaerocephala*) dominates.

The montane moorland occurs at altitudes of over 3,500 feet in the north and 2,000 feet in the south. The main elements are microshrubbery, fell field, coniferous shrubbery, and coniferous forest. Many plants of this region are endemic, including the conifers, cushion plants, and several heath species.

Tasmania's insularity has been too limited in time and space for a distinctive island fauna to develop. Many of the native birds and mammals of the mainland are present and one of the significant features of Tasmania for the preservation of Australian fauna is the abundance of certain species including large numbers of bandicoots, small macropods, and marsupial carnivores. The sclerophyll forests support the richest fauna of the main vegetation zones in both population and diversity of species.

When European colonization commenced in 1803, the vegetation had already been considerably modified by several thousand years of occupation by Tasmanian Aborigines. The general effect of their use of fires for hunting appears to have been to extend the non-forest

ind-distorted Snow Gums and subalpine herbfield, Mt Stillwell, above
osciusko Chalet, N.S.W. PHOTO COURTESY N.S.W. SOIL CONSERVATION SERVICE

'et sclerophyll forest with *Eucalyptus regnans*, Cumberland Valley, Victoria.
nis is the tallest eucalypt in the world, reaching over 300 feet in height.
IOTO COURTESY AUST. TOURIST COMMISSION

he Tower Hill State Game Reserve, Victoria. The causeway leads to the island
1 which the Natural History Centre is being erected. PHOTO COURTESY
SHERIES AND WILDLIFE DEPT, VICTORIA

The 'Quokka' or Short-tailed Pademelon (*Setonix brachyurus*) of south-western Australia is the smallest of the scrub wallabies. PHOTO COURTESY V. SERVENTY

'Donga' on the Nullarbor Plain, near Nareth with native willows, false sandalwoods and masses of wildflowers including Sturt Pea. PHOTO COURTESY V. SERVENTY

Wet sclerophyll forest of Karri (*Eucalyptus diversicolor*) near Pemberton, W.A. PHOTO COURTESY V. SERVENTY

Turtle Frog (*Myobatrachus gouldii*) of south-west Australia is a subterranean burrowing species of sandy areas, and lives on termites. PHOTO COURTESY V. SERVENTY

Kangaroo Paw (*Anigozanthos manglesii*), the state floral emblem of Western Australia, is a tourist attraction among native wildflowers in King's Park, Perth. PHOTO COURTESY V. SERVENTY

communities at the expense of the forest, and the more open forest at the expense of the heavier forest.

Fire caused by human agency continued to be influential after the European occupation, helping to maintain the mixed forest against conversion to the climatic climax condition of temperate rainforest. Because of the ruggedness and infertility of the greater part of the island much remains of the landscape of 1803, and 60 per cent of the state is still Crown land.

Evolution of the Reserve Systems

Knowledge of the main facts about the evolution of the reserve system is essential for an understanding of the current position. Reserves for the protection of natural scenery and wildlife were set aside under Crown land legislation from the 1860s onwards, but these had only slight security of tenure. After 1891 scientific, private tourist, and field naturalist bodies campaigned for more permanent reserves under the control of rangers. These demands were met by the Scenery Preservation Act of 1915. At this stage Tasmania's sixty-year-old tourist industry was regarded as a relatively important facet of the island's economy, and the passage of legislation for scenery preservation and the subsequent acquisition of reserves were closely connected with the government's tourist industry promotion policy. In 1914 the new Labour Government assumed full responsibility for administration of tourism. A logical step the next year was to arrange better protection for the industry's scenic and historic resources.

The newly created Scenery Preservation Board, which was made responsible for the recommendation of new reserves, was linked administratively with the Lands Department, and there were no major obstacles to the setting aside of a large reserve acreage from the extensive public domain, especially after the Act had been amended in 1921 and 1938 to make reserve alienation easier for such a purpose as mineral exploitation. By 1941. 516,000 acres had been set aside as scenic and historic reserves.

The Animals and Birds Protection Act of 1919 (considerably reinforced in 1928) complemented the Scenery Preservation Act, providing machinery for the creation of more secure fauna sanctuaries and measures for the conservation of the wild animals and birds in the state at large. Many of the former Crown Lands Act fauna reserves were redeclared under the new legislation.

Between 1941 and 1955 emphasis was placed on the acquisition and care of historic sites and because of revocations the total scenic and historic reserve area was increased by only 70,000 acres. Between 1955 and 1967 there was a strong reaction against the creation of further large reserves; only eighteen sites were reserved, all under 10,000 acres, and the total area of the scenic reserve system was increased by only 23,000 acres.

Proposals for large new reserves and reserve extensions have been rejected mainly on the grounds that the suggestions are premature and that first priority should go to the consolidation of the existing reserves, but the underlying reason for the change of attitude is not hard to find. Since the twenties the government has become increasingly preoccupied with a programme of expanding secondary industry, based on the exploitation of Tasmania's mineral, forest and hydroelectric power resources. Tourist promotion has become proportionately less important as an aspect of state policy. Large areas of Crown land which would otherwise be suitable for addition to the scenic reserve system have acquired potential for economic development. That priority is now given to these new values is demonstrated by the successful opposition of the Forestry and Hydro-Electric Commissions to a number of new reserve suggestions since 1945.

Nature and Function of the Reserves

Scenic and Historic Reserves

In proportion to its size and population

TABLE 1

MAIN FEATURE	NO. OF RESERVES IN EACH GROUP (ACRES)				
	0-99	100-999	1,000-9,999	10,000 & OVER	TOTAL
National parks (not differentiated)			2	7	9
Coastal reserves	10	4	2		16
River reserves	1	1	2		4
Scenic roads		2	1	1	4
Forests and fern gullies	7		2		9
Waterfalls		5			5
Cave reserves	1	4			5
Thermal springs and chalets	3				3
Lookouts	2				2
Historic sites and buildings	19	2			21
TOTAL	43	18	9	8	78

Tasmania has the largest of the Australian state national park systems, though no reserves over 10,000 acres have been created in the past twelve years. By June 1967, seventy-eight reserves had been set aside under the Scenery Preservation Act, totalling 609,000 acres, in addition to the hundreds of low security reserves established under Crown land legislation. Nine of the major units have the informal title of 'national park', but the term has no legal significance.

Sixty-one of the reserves are under 1,000 acres and comprise stretches of coastline, river banks, waterfalls, fern gullies, limestone caves, roadside bushland, and historic buildings. The larger reserves consist of nine units of between 1,000 and 10,000 acres, seven of between 10,000 and 60,000 acres and the Cradle Mountain - Lake St. Clair National Park of 338,000 acres. Details of the number and size of the main types of reserve are given in Table 1; the reserves are classified according to the descriptive categories used by the Scenery Preservation Board.

The organic scenery preservation legislation laid down no specific criteria for the selection of reserves and the park agency has never elaborated a policy or decided on a programme for this aspect of its work. Although the Scenery Preservation Board rejected some proposals which lacked national significance, evaluation was cursory, and many inferior sites were reserved.

Generally, areas were reserved either because they contained some feature of scenic or historic interest, or, in the case of the larger reserves, because they combined scenic beauty with interesting native flora and fauna. This approach resulted in an emphasis on the more inhospitable and more scenic west, and four-fifths of today's reserve acreage is in the western half of the state. This preference was doubly fortunate in that this region contains the Tasmanian environments which are of greatest interest to science. The characteristic sedgeland, temperate rainforest, high moor, and mixed forest communities, are all well represented. The drier forest communities of the east are sampled in two large scenic reserves and one major fauna sanctuary. The only Tasmanian ecosystem not well sampled is the coastal heath association which occurs around parts of the north-east and north-west coasts. This is also inadequately represented in the reserves of the other states.

Tasmanian governments have taken care to make extensive provisions for reserve alienation, and these have been used to alienate scenic reserve land for a variety of purposes including mining and quarrying, water impoundment, and timber exploitation. In 1950, a 3,680 acre area of Mount Field National Park containing some of the finest surviving stands of *Eucalyptus regnans*, the world's tallest hardwood, was revoked for Australian Newsprint Mills in spite of emphatic opposition by the Scenery Preservation Board and nature conservation bodies from many parts of Australia. In 1967 Parliament gave approval for the construction of the Middle Gordon hydro-electric power scheme which will create a ninety-seven square mile water storage flooding the Serpentine and Huon Plains, including the lower parts of the Lake Pedder National Park, to a depth of about fifty feet (the proclamation of the park is unchanged).

The value of the reserves for scientific reference is enhanced by the relatively undisturbed condition of the larger units. This is due to a number of factors including their position amongst vast areas of unalienated land, the absence of commercial values to date, and the limited demand for the use of the parks for recreation. However, some deterioration has resulted in the past from various non-conforming uses such as grazing and many of the reserves are not well supervised. Only three national parks have full-time rangers, and the Board has to rely upon sometimes unfriendly agencies for fire-fighting services. The reserves are far from safe against alienation. It is possible for a whole reserve to be alienated by Parliament without the approval of the Scenery Preservation Board and for part of a reserve to be alienated without the consent of either the Board or Parliament. It is also possible, with the approval of the Board, for reserve land to be exempted from any of the specified provisions of the Act.

As Australia's second oldest colonial settlement, Tasmania has many relics of interest for their historical associations and comparatively great age. The reserve system contains a wide range of historic places, including monuments to the marine explorers, the sites of the first settlements in the north and south, and relics of the penal era at Port Arthur, Saltwater River, Richmond, and Macquarie Harbour. The whole of the extensive penal settlement at Port Arthur is administered by the Scenery Preservation Board and some of the buildings have been restored. In 1965-6 some 38,000 people paid the guided tour inspection fee at this reserve. Tasmania's colonial domestic architecture is also of great interest, but the only examples reserved are a pioneer cottage at The Steppes, and elegant Entally House an example of the country house of an early well-to-do landowner. Because of a time lag in the adoption of new styles the state's heritage of Regency town and country houses is particularly rich. None of these is included in the reserve system and it is fortunate that the Tasmanian branch of the National Trust of Australia, founded in 1960, is attempting to correct this deficiency and has already acquired two late-Georgian houses in the north midlands.

Since the individual units in the reserve system range from extensive mountain areas to small historic sites, the system as a whole attracts many kinds of recreational use. The many scattered scenic and historic reserves and the seven national parks which have road access are popular with tourists from the mainland and Tasmanian weekend motorists. At Mount Field National Park an estimated 60,000 visits were made in 1965-6. Several of the national parks and larger reserves with road access have picnicking and camping facilities and simple huts which are generally located near the park entrance and harmonize well with their surrounds. In contrast there is only one high-class chalet in the national parks. All of the state's snow-fields are in national parks but these are not highly developed.

The two roadless national parks and the unroaded interior of the other major reserves contain some of the state's most spectacular mountain scenery and are used mainly by the hardier type of bushwalker. The fifty-three-mile overland walking track through the Cradle Mountain-Lake St. Clair National Park attracts walkers from all over Australia. In two national parks the Boards have provided unattended shelter huts which are available free of charge.

Other groups who also use the reserves include persons with a special interest in field natural history, speleology, and historic places. The only major interpretative facility is a trailside museum at Cradle Valley. Nevertheless, formal educational use of the reserves is growing. Four mountaineering schools organized by the Tasmanian Adult Education Board have been held at Mount Field National Park and an increasing number of high school and university parties are visiting the parks.

Fauna Sanctuaries

Four of the large national parks are also fauna sanctuaries under the Animals and Birds Protection Act (1928), but there are also an additional fifty-five sanctuaries with an area of 117,000 acres (June 1967) outside the scenic reserve system. Ten of these are between 1,000 and 10,000 acres and two are over 10,000 acres.

The areas reserved as sanctuaries were chosen for their usefulness for fauna conservation and not because of the intrinsic interest of all parts of the environment. As with the scenic reserves they have been acquired in a piece-meal fashion. The main function of the sanctuaries outside the scenic reserve system is the conservation of waterfowl. A number of them are lakes and lagoons which are refuges and breeding grounds for black swan (three reserves) and wild duck (eight reserves). But the reserves make only a small contribution to the preservation of Tasmania's duck habitat. Eighteen sanctuaries are breeding grounds for the mutton bird (*Puffinus tenuirostris* — Short-tailed Shearwater). The largest sanctuaries are the 56,000 acre Tooms Lake which was created as part of an attempt to preserve the Grey Kangaroo (*Macropus giganteus*), and the sub-antarctic Macquarie Island of 29,000 acres.

Fauna sanctuaries on Crown land may be alienated only after a resolution of both Houses of Parliament. The Animals and Birds Protection Board, known locally as the Fauna Board, has direct control over these reserves and conserves them for the sole purpose of fauna conservation but sanctuaries established on private lands with the owner's consent can be used for other purposes and be revoked without formality on change of ownership. Most of the privately owned sanctuaries have little biological significance. Land may be declared a sanctuary either with respect to all animals and birds, or to any particular species. The Board has scientist members, employs a scientifically qualified curator, and is conscious of the practical value of research. Its management of the wild animal population in Tasmania generally is on ecological lines. The Fauna Board also has responsibility for habitat reserves and a faunal district. The habitat reserves consist of conditions in land titles designed to preserve wildlife habitat. The five reserves of this kind, which have been established to date are all lagoons with associated swamps and marshes, of value as nesting and refuge areas for wildfowl. There is a single faunal district — The South-West Faunal District — of 1,600,000 acres. Special regulations have been made for this area prohibiting the unauthorized carrying of firearms and entry of dogs.

Administrative Organization

The main provisions of the Scenery Preservation Act reflect the problems and doubts which troubled the government of 1915 and have continued to influence the attitude of later governments. The fundamental concern was, and is, the scant financial resources of a small state. In 1915 the government was anxious to avoid committing the state to a major new field of expenditure, and therefore gave the park agency no direct statutory authority to provide facilities for park visitors. Although anxious to avoid making expensive administrative arrangements the government of 1915 mistrusted the wisdom of relying solely on voluntary trusts, and it therefore created a central body — the Scenery Preservation Board — consisting chiefly of senior officers of government departments, under the direction of the Minister of Lands and Works and with authority to delegate powers to subsidiary boards.

The existing arrangements make scenery preservation to a considerable extent an administrative appendage of the Lands Department. The limited size and status of the secretariat and field staff partly reflects the heavy dependence on unsalaried boards. At present there are four special boards appointed by the Governor on the advice of the parent Board. The members, who are appointed for three-year terms, are mainly representatives of government departments and park-user bodies. In the past the special boards undertook most aspects of reserve management, but gradually their function has become limited to the recommendation of development proposals to the parent body.

The strengths and weaknesses of this organization have been detailed in an earlier paper. Generally, it has become less satisfactory as the scope of the work has widened, and as the problems of managing the reserves have become more complex. In the early period of the Board's history when the main task was the acquisition of reserves from the extensive domain of freely available Crown lands, its composition and part-time nature did little harm, although, as mentioned, reserves were not carefully selected. Today, when there is considerable competition for Crown land, the presence on the Board of public servant representatives of such authorities as the Mines and Forestry Departments, and the Hydro-Electric Commission, reduces its independence. Furthermore, the departmental representatives have little time to devote to the ever-growing business of the Board, and basic matters such as policy determination and planning have been neglected. The interest and sympathy of the members and the Chairman is not guaranteed and friction during the past few years has led the Board to favour making the Chairman's position elective. There is little doubt that association with the Lands Department facilitated reserve acquisition, but in the post-Second World War period, as the emphasis of the Board's work shifted to the acquisition and restoration of historic properties, provision of visitor facilities, and control of roadside hoardings, the technical skill of the Lands Department became less relevant to scenery preservation. The government's policy has been to try to make the existing arrangements work, but there is ample evidence that the powers of the park agency are inadequate and that the strained relations have affected the work of scenery preservation. This has become so obvious that the granting of greater autonomy and wider powers to the national park agency seems to be but a matter of time.

For two years the government has been considering amendments to the Scenery Preservation Act which would create a position of Director and make the Scenery Preservation Board more independent of the Lands Department. The demand for these changes was given fresh impetus during the public debate over the plan to flood part of the Lake Pedder National Park. The fact that, as constituted, the Board could not adequately express the conservation viewpoint, and that it was considered by the government to be incapable of protecting a large area proposed as a national park in the South West, caused considerable public concern. A Select Committee of the Legislative Council which was appointed to report on various aspects of the Gordon River power development noted what it referred to as 'a changing community attitude to the principles of conservation and preservation of natural environment', and accepted the need for integrated control of parks. It recommended the repeal of the Scenery Preservation Act and the appointment of a new national parks authority headed by a Director and an Advisory Council comprised mainly of representatives of voluntary nature conservation bodies and special boards. It also suggested that the special boards should be retained in an advisory capacity to the Director. The government has promised to bring down new legislation for national parks and fauna conservation before September 1968 and it appears likely that the recommendations of the Select Committee will be implemented.

The arrangements for the control of the fauna sanctuaries are similar to those for scenic reserves but less cumbersome. A greater independence of outlook than the Scenery Preservation Board enjoys is ensured by the fact that membership of the Fauna Board, which is under the oversight of the Minister for Agriculture, is predominantly of user organizations rather than public servants and the Chairman is elected. The Board relies on seconded police officers as rangers but can also appoint and pay its own staff. The work of the Scenery Preservation Board and the Fauna Board is not co-ordinated and the two agencies have little contact, but it seems likely that this will be changed by the promised legislation.

Management Problems

If it is accepted that the main objective of park and reserve administration in Australia should be to manage selected natural areas in a manner which will meet distinctive scientific, recreational and educational needs whilst preserving them intact for the use of future generations, then the Tasmanian reserve systems are to date a qualified success. Although selected unsystematically, the scale of the system is such that they include a great variety of natural environments. The reserves are in a good state of preservation and are performing, or are capable of performing, diverse functions.

The reserves retain their value for scientific reference and recreation not because of the success of any special park management concepts, but because of the favourable demand-supply circumstances and because the governments policy on park spending and the unwillingness of private enterprise to undertake risky ventures has inhibited the development of more intensive uses. While the economy approach to national park administration has had some advantages so far, this, and the lack of clear definition of objectives, may have overwhelming drawbacks in the future. Most of the favourable factors are now rapidly disappearing, but the park administration has not yet been adjusted to handle the changing circumstances.

The Scenery Preservation Act contains no statement about the purpose of the reserves and the Board has not elaborated its policy on management. There is for instance no awareness of the value of preserving areas free of roads, and roads have been built whenever funds became available. The Board has been slow to recognize the advantages of planning, and the only plans in existence are three or five year works programmes drawn up by the special boards.

These problems inevitably lead one to the conclusion that the existing amateurish organization and loose management concepts and practices are inadequate for a task which is daily becoming more complex.

The likely problems of a more affluent and more crowded future are twofold. Firstly, there is the question of whether the reserves can be protected against encroachment by alienation for other forms of land use which at present are given high-priority by the government. Crown lands, including national parks, continue to become more valuable for economic exploitation as Tasmania's industrialization programme gathers momentum, and many of the state's former wastelands are now undergoing rapid change. The power resources of two major river systems have been harnessed, work is proceeding with a third, and a fourth project in the hitherto remote south-west has been approved. It seems likely that hydro-electric power developments and also forestry and mining will result in demands for further alienation of park lands and place strong obstacles in the way of reserve expansion. There is a real danger that the government will allow the commercial use of national park timber. Any proposal of this kind would be completely contrary to the world-wide national park concept, and should be strongly resisted.

Secondly, it is a problematical question whether the scientific and primitive recreational values can be defended against internal pressure from the increasing demands of intensive and mechanized recreation. The number of park visitors is growing faster than the growth of both the population and the out-of-state tourist traffic. Eventually, the point may be reached when commercial interests will feel confident in building resort-type hotels in the parks. The government has no conceptual reasons for not building new roads, so that the park road network may be gradually expanded as finances permit. If these civilizing tendencies are not controlled, the parks may become dominated by high density recreation and lose their value for the more distinctive uses.

Remedies

The decision to prepare new legislation for national parks and wildlife conservation and to create a new authority to administer the Act presents an excellent opportunity to provide remedies for these problems. The first necessity is for better definition of national park objectives and priorities. This can be provided in the Act and in a public declaration of management policy by the park agency, including definition of the recreational, scientific and educational goals of the parks, and an outline of the methods to be used to ensure their achievement.

The unsatisfactory nature of the existing administrative organization appears to have been recognized. The composition of the Scenery Preservation Board gives no guarantee that members will have either sympathy for the Board's work or specialized knowledge, and tends at times to work against the very interest of nature conservation. The results of this and the part-time nature of the Board are seen in the failure to attend to fundamental matters. The fragmentation of authority and responsibility has also impeded decision-making and planning, and the special nature of the task suggests that there is a good case for giving greater authority to the park agency. Management by an autonomous government department with a qualified staff headed by a Director would have the advantages of clear location of authority in a professional body, and time and technical skill for basic planning and management tasks.

In a small state such as Tasmania it would be relatively easy to achieve completely centralized control of the reserves, and if an effective central agency is provided the subsidiary boards will become largely redundant. There is an overlap of function between the Scenery Preservation Board and the Fauna Board and there would be many advantages in unified control or, at least, greater coordination of the two administrations, including common research, reserve supervision, publicity, and educational programmes. If a new national park and wildlife department is created it would be an advantage to have separate divisions for each major function.

The Select Committee on the Gordon Power Scheme noted that there is an interest in more rational methods of control and management of national parks. A desirable improvement is the legislation for different functional categories of park and reserves, and for management plans for each reserve unit. The park management plans could provide for zoning into 'development', 'limited development', and 'wilderness' areas. In some of the more primitive parks such as

Frenchman's Cap and the proposed park in south-west Tasmania the ideal conservation solution would be to zone the whole or the greater part as 'wilderness'. Planning in a classified system would be best carried out by the central park and wildlife agency and based on the results of surveys of needs and resources, rather than, as at present, on the whims and caprices of individual park boards. If the special boards are retained it would be desirable to match the composition of each board to the particular function of the park in its charge.

A vital part of the reform of the system would be a review of the adequacy of the existing reserves and the selection of additional sites to fill gaps. Investigation of sites should be by the park agency. Greater emphasis on research as a basis for reserve selection, as well as for planning and management, and park interpretative programmes is essential. Any list of desirable additions to the reserve system would probably include an area containing a sample of the poorly represented coastal heath formation. The elimination of a number of biologically valueless fauna sanctuaries is overdue, and there is a need for additional units to give better protection for duck habitat, and possibly for individual species such as the Cape Barren Goose and the Grey Kangaroo. The recently proposed Norfolk Range-Pieman River National Park of 100,000 acres would do much to preserve a sample of the sedgeland, dune coast and rainforest environments of north-western Tasmania.

There is also an outstanding opportunity to improve the range of recreational environments offered by creating a large roadless national park of nearly one million acres in the far south-west of Tasmania. In addition to its unique biological importance this is the largest primitive tract in temperate Australia and therefore has outstanding values for wilderness recreation. The government has decided to accept the recommendation of the Select Committee on the Gordon River that this national park should be established. The south-west can be preserved as one of the world's finest wilderness parks and if the park is created it will be one of the most important events in the history of nature conservation in Australia.

The problems of the reserves cannot be solved solely by action within. Ideally, park planning should be undertaken as part of a broader process of land use planning. The planned use of public forests and hydro-electric power schemes as multiple purpose areas with recreation as an integral feature would do much to prevent the future destruction of the reserves by their conversion to high density use. Where natural values are threatened by economic developments there is no authority responsible for putting the case for their preservation unless an existing reserve is involved. It seems that the national interest would be served by also giving the national park agency some responsibility for developments affecting natural values in any part of the state.

Postscript

Since this section was written the preparation of new national parks legislation and the creation of a large reserve in the south-west has changed the picture considerably.

The South-West National Park of 475,000 acres, which was gazetted in October 1968 and placed under the control of a special board, included the Lake Pedder National Park and the Arthur Ranges but left out some of the most valuable areas recommended by the Legislative Council's Select Committee on the Gordon Power Development, including Port Davey, and Precipitous Bluff. The creation of this reserve brought the total acreage of scenic and historic reserves and Crown land sanctuaries in Tasmania to 1,187,000 acres; 6.7 per cent of the state.

In November 1968 the National Parks and Conservation Bill was introduced. It provided for the replacement of the Scenery Preservation Board by a National Parks and Conservation Board of nine part-time members with corporate body status, greater autonomy, and increased and better defined powers; the appointment of a Director as the Board's chief executive officer; and improved arrangements for the employment of staff by the Board. Provision was also made for the special boards to be retained.

During the debate the conservation societies pressed for the more fundamental changes recommended by the Legislative Council's Select Committee including a National Parks and Wildlife Service headed by a Director. Although the government would not agree to an executive Director and Service it promised to give the Board control of the Animals and Birds Protection Act before July 1969.

The Bill also contained provisions for the classification of reserves, the preparation of management plans, and the declaration of 'hazardous areas' (areas considered dangerous to visitors which can be closed to entry).

The Bill sought to strengthen the security of tenure of reserves by making the consent of Parliament necessary for any revocation of reserve land. The ease with which reserves could be made available for incompatible forms of land use such as timber cutting and mining, was not greatly changed and there was still no explicit statement on the purpose of the reserves and the priorities to be sought in management.

The proposed legislation, whilst an improvement, did not go far enough. Control by part-time bodies was perpetuated and the limitations and guidelines affecting reserve land use were unchanged. The 'hazardous areas' provision was a great disappointment. If enacted this measure could result in a serious reduction in the opportunity for Australians to enjoy wilderness. In spite of these defects, the provisions which were made for the employment of qualified officers, the co-ordination of national parks and fauna conservation, and the introduction of management planning were all signs of a gradually dawning awareness of the need for a more vigorous and more carefully calculated approach to nature conservation.

The Bill had a speedy passage through the House of Assembly, but was held over until the New Year by the Legislative Council. Since the government called an election in May 1969, the Bill automatically lapsed, but it can be revived by a resolution of both Houses when the new Parliament meets after the election.

In his policy speech delivered in April, the Premier promised to create a new Ministry of Tourism headed by a Director-General of Tourist Services who would control all tourist activities including national parks, scenery preservation, fauna conservation and inland fisheries. The Liberal Party's promises included the establishment of a conservation authority advised by a board, and the creation of a National Parks and Wildlife Service.

National Parks and Reserves in South Australia

C. Warren Bonython

The Geographical Features and Environment

South Australia comprises thirteen per cent of mainland Australia, with an area of 380,000 square miles. It has predominantly a low rainfall, but in view of the political boundaries, drawn with complete disregard of the natural geographical regions, and in view also of the eleven to one rainfall range (forty-five inches to four inches) it is an unjustifiable simplification to accept a popular appellation — 'the driest state in the driest continent'.

While eighty-five per cent of the state has a rainfall of less than ten inches per annum, there are some substantial areas of fertile and comparatively well-watered country in the south. A tongue of higher rainfall country reaches inland along the axis of the Mount Lofty and Flinders Ranges, some parts of the former having a precipitation of over forty-five inches per annum. Northwards from the coast the rainfall steadily decreases to an irregularly-fluctuating four inch annual average round Lake Eyre. The rainfall of the southern, coastal part of the state is of the winter (Mediterranean) type, brought by the prevailing moist westerly winds and accentuated orographically over the coastal ranges. In the far north there is a predominantly summer rainfall resulting from occasional incursions of moist, tropical air. Thus South Australia may be divided into a series of rainfall zones.

Water coming from other than direct rainfall is also of importance. The River Murray brings water from the eastern states through the dry Murray Valley to the sea at Encounter Bay; the erratic Cooper's Creek and Diamantina bring Queensland water to the parched Lake Eyre Basin, and underground water from western Victoria flows towards the sea through the porous limestone of the south-east.

The seasons are characterized by hot, dry summers and cool winters. The day-to-day weather of the settled coastal areas tends to show pronounced variations dependent upon whether northerly winds bring warm, dry air from the extensive arid interior, or whether westerly and southerly winds bring cool, moist air from the vast expanses of the Great Australian Bight and Southern Ocean.

The majority of the state is of low relief, but within the Mount Lofty and Flinders Ranges there is a significant area at an elevation of 2,000 to 3,000 feet above sea-level (St Mary's Peak — the highest point — is at 3,900 feet), and there is another high area in the Musgrave Ranges in the north-west (Mount Woodroofe at about 5,000 feet). In contrast, the Lake Eyre Basin is depressed to fifty feet below sea-level.

South Australia may also be divided into some nine geographical regions, each with its characteristic topography, rainfall regime and vegetation as summarized in Table 1.

In view of this diversity the statement that national parks and reserves represent less than one per cent of the area of the state has little meaning. The different zones and regions should be considered separately.

The Evolution of the National Parks and Reserves System

The national parks and reserves system in South Australia evolved in several ways, and under several bodies which are now described.

Table 1

Region	Topographical Relief	Rainfall	Vegetation
Adelaide Plains, Mount Lofty Ranges and near north	varied	moderate to high	dry sclerophyll forest and savannah woodland
Yorke Peninsula and Kangaroo Island	low	moderate	mallee, savannah woodland and dry sclerophyll forest
Eyre Peninsula	low	moderate	sclerophyllous mallee
Murray Valley	low	low	mallee
South-east: upper	low	low to moderate	mallee, sclerophyllous mallee, mallee-heath and heath
South-east: lower	low	moderate to high	dry sclerophyll forest and savannah woodland
Flinders Ranges	high	low to moderate	savannah woodland (inc. sclerophyll shrub savannah)
Northern Interior	generally low	low	desert complex, salt-lakes, low layered woodland, shrub steppe and tussock grassland
Far west coast	low	low	as for northern interior

The National Parks Commission

A body entitled the Commissioners of the National Park was constituted by Act of Parliament in 1891 to hold and control one piece of land — the National Park, at Belair. For sixty-five years this was the only land held, but in 1955 the Act was amended to provide for the holding of the wild life reserves.

In 1956 three of these reserves were added, and three more in 1960, while in 1962 began the transfer of the many flora and fauna reserves which had previously been loosely controlled by the Flora and Fauna Advisory Committee. Further areas were subsequently reserved and added.

A new National Parks Act was passed in 1966, and the controlling body — now called the National Parks Commission — was reconstituted with fifteen members. The new Act contained some valuable innovations, such as greater security of tenure — any alienation of national parks land has now to be agreed to by both Houses of Parliament — and restriction of mining in national parks. Under it, most of the holdings are termed national parks, while those of minor importance (mostly very small) are called national parks reserves. Those that are essentially of a wilderness nature may be called wilderness national parks.

Areas continue to be added, and at present there are thirty-nine holdings, totalling 881 square miles. Most of these are listed in Table 2. The main additions currently being made are Simpson Desert National Park — 2,670 square miles (Northern interior), Yumbarra National Park — 410 square miles (Far west coast), and Elliot Price Wilderness National Park — 250 square miles (Northern interior). These will increase the total area to 4,200 square miles.

The Fauna and Flora Board of South Australia

The reserve on Kangaroo Island called Flinders Chase is controlled by the Fauna and Flora Board of South Australia, which was constituted under the Fauna and Flora Reserve Act in 1919, the real creation date of the reserve. (However, part had previously been reserved in 1906 as the Cape Borda Reserve.) The Board is competent to hold land nowhere else except in Kangaroo Island, and Flinders Chase is the only holding. Now of 212 square miles, it is considered the premier reserve of the state.

The South Australian Government Immigration, Publicity and Tourist Bureau

The Tourist Bureau currently holds twenty reserves, totalling 23,000 acres, and designated national pleasure resorts. These are used primarily for tourist purposes, and the conservation of flora, fauna, etc., appears to be only secondary.

Some of those areas of significance from the nature conservation point of view have already been transferred to the National Parks Commission, but the Bureau continues to hold the important Wilpena Pound, with its outstanding scenery, its unusual geological structure and its interesting arid vegetation.

TABLE 2

A SELECT LIST OF NATIONAL PARKS AND RESERVES IN SOUTH AUSTRALIA

No.	Name	Region	Rainfall Zone	Area in Acres	Type	Remarks
1	Flinders Chase	B	d	135,680	O	
2	Wilpena Pound	F	b	19,900	NPR	
3	Lincoln National Park	C	c	35,521	NP	more area to be added
4	Alligator Gorge National Park	F	c	9,466	NP	contiguous with (5)
5	Mambray Creek National Park	F	c	6,560	NP	more area to be added
6	Canunda National Park	E	e	22,120	NP	
7	Messent National Park	E	c	28,000	NP	
8	Billiatt National Park	E	b	90,874	NP	
9	Mt. Rescue National Park	E	c	70,149	NP	
10	Hambidge National Park	C	b	93,865	NP	
11	Hincks National Park	C	c	163,315	NP	largest in state
12	Mt. Remarkable National Park	F	c	673	NP	more area to be added
13	Cleland National Park	A	f	1,749	NP	contains native fauna reserve
14	Belair National Park	A	f	2,058	NP	
15	Para Wirra National Park	A	e	2,697	NP	
16	Morialta Falls Reserve	A	f	539	NPR	
17	Coorong National Park	E	c	7,800	NP	
18	Big Heath National Park	E	e	5,809	NP	
19	Jip Jip National Park	E	d	350	NP	
20	Fairview National Park	E	d	2,690	NP	
21	Peebinga National Park	E	b	7,775	NP	
22	Kelledie Bay National Park	C	d	4,321	NP	
23	Kyeema National Park	A	e	800	NP	
24	Horsnell Gully National Park	A	f	346	NP	
25	Ferries-McDonald National Park	D	b	2,085	NP	

26	Sandy Creek National Park	A	d	258	NP	notable for birds
27	Warren National Park	A	e	847	NP	
28	Spring Gully National Park	A	d	716	NP	conserves Red Stringy Bark
29	Hale National Park	A	e	471	NP	
30	Mt. Magnificent National Park	A	e	293	NP	
31	Mundoora National Park	A	b	1,352	NP	
32	Koonamore Reserve	G	a	960	O	
33	G. S. Sandison Reserve	A	d	$3\frac{1}{2}$	NT	conserves striated glacial pavements
34	Glenelg River Reserve	E	e	309	NT	on S.A.-Vic. border
35	D. B. Mack Reserve	D	a	655	NT	conserves mallee fowl
36	Kelly Hill Caves Reserve	B	d	1,672	NPR	limestone caves
37	Bool Lagoon Fauna Reserve	E	d	477	FR	contiguous with B.L. Game Res.
38	Greenly Is. Fauna Reserve	C	d	500	FR	offshore island
39	Perforated, Price and Four Hummocks Is. Fauna Reserve	C	d	605	FR	offshore islands
40	Eyre Is. Fauna Reserve (in Nuyt's Arch.)	H	b	2,500	FR	offshore island
41	Waldegrave Is. Fauna Reserve	C	c	800	FR	offshore island
42	North and South Neptune Is. Fauna Reserve	C	d	1,000	FR	offshore islands
43	Manning Reserve	A	e	111	O	also Fauna Res.

KEY

Regions

A Adelaide Plains, Mount Lofty Ranges and near north
B Yorke Peninsula and Kangaroo Island
C Eyre Peninsula
D Murray Valley
E South-east
F Flinders Ranges
G Northern interior
H Far west coast

Rainfall Zones

a 10 in. p.a. or less
b 11-15 in. p.a.
c 16-20 in. p.a.
d 21-25 in. p.a.
e 26-32 in. p.a.
f 33 in. p.a. or more

Type

NP National Park
NPR National Pleasure Resort
NT Reserve under National Trust of S.A.
FR Fauna Reserve
O Other Reserve

The National Trust of South Australia

This body was constituted under the National Trust of South Australia Act of 1955. It has already received a number of geological and nature reserves, mostly as private gifts or bequests, and some of these are of significance in the present survey.

The Field Naturalists' Society of South Australia

This society holds two relatively small reserves one of which — the Manning Reserve — deserves mention (see Table 2, No. 43).

The University of Adelaide

Through its Botany Department, the University of Adelaide controls the 960 acre Koonamore Reserve which has been for a long time the only one in the low rainfall country conserving the low layered woodland and shrub steppe vegetation communities.

Department of Fauna Conservation

The Minister of Agriculture, through the Department of Fauna Conservation, and, under the Fauna Conservation Act, 1964, controls a number of reserves outside the national park system — viz. prohibited areas, fauna reserves, fauna sanctuaries and game reserves. Those other than the fauna sanctuaries have adequate security of tenure, and total approximately 20,000 acres. Recently all the more important offshore islands have been declared fauna reserves.

Other Bodies

Other bodies include the Minister of Agriculture's Flora and Fauna Advisory Committee and the Royal Society of South Australia.

A Select List of National Parks and Reserves

Forty-three of the more important and significant national parks and reserves are listed in Table 2. This is modified from the list prepared by the Australian Academy of Science National Parks and Reserves Subcommittee for South Australia. The fossil reserves are now omitted, as these protect fossils only and not the other values of the land. As before, the extensive Aboriginal reserves are excluded.

The areas range in size from three and a half acres to 163,000 acres (or a much greater area when some pending parks are proclaimed), in climate from that of the arid interior to that of the moist coastal ranges, and in purpose from preserving striated glacial pavements to conserving complex biological systems embracing soil, vegetation and fauna. The total area represented by all significant national parks and reserves in South Australia (i.e. with some further to the select list of Table 2) is 770,000 acres, or 1,206 square miles.

TABLE 3

AREAS IN NATIONAL PARKS AND RESERVES ACCORDING TO RAINFALL ZONES

RAINFALL ZONE	TOTAL LAND AREA IN ZONE	RESERVED AREA	
		ACTUAL	RELATIVE TO TOTAL LAND
10 in. p.a. and less	323,000 sq. m.	4 sq. m.	less than 0·01%
11-15 in. p.a.	29,300 sq. m.	340 sq. m.	1·2%
16-20 in. p.a.	14,300 sq. m.	560 sq. m.	3·9%
21-25 in. p.a.	9,450 sq. m.	240 sq. m.	2·5%
26-32 in. p.a.	3,130 sq. m.	53 sq. m.	1·7%
33 in. p.a. and more	620 sq. m.	9 sq. m.	1·5%

Most of the areas listed are national parks, the others including seven fauna reserves, three national pleasure resorts and three National Trust reserves.

In Table 3, the reserved areas are considered in relation to rainfall zones. (For the purposes of Tables 3 and 4 there have been included some additional areas of land shortly to become national parks or reserves, but not the three major pending national parks previously referred to.) The distribution over the rainfall range is uneven; there is a maximum in the middle of the range with minima at either end. This is true both as regards the total reserved area and the percentage of land reserved in a zone. The explanation is that in the higher rainfall zones much early land development occurred, and little bushland in its original state remained there when the need for reservation was fully recognized. In the intermediate rainfall zones development was slower, and much has been reserved in the last thirty years. In the low rainfall zones it has not been felt necessary to reserve arid or 'waste' areas until quite recently, but some important developments are pending there.

In Table 4 reserved area is considered in relation to geographical regions of the state. A reasonable percentage of Yorke Peninsula and Kangaroo Island, Eyre Peninsula and the south-east is reserved, but it should be noted that in Yorke Peninsula itself the only land is a pending 12,000 acre reserve at the southern end. The poorness of representation in the Adelaide Plains, Mount Lofty Ranges and near north region is due to the advanced state reached by land development before the need for reservation was recognized. The tendency to believe that reservation is unnecessary in remote and arid areas is responsible for the low representation in the northern interior and far west coast, and similar thinking probably explains the situation in the Murray Valley. The Flinders Ranges are a special case which is discussed later.

Other Reserves

A fauna sanctuary under the Fauna Conservation Act, 1964, is land which can be utilized for other purposes while being

TABLE 4

AREAS IN NATIONAL PARKS AND RESERVES ACCORDING TO GEOGRAPHICAL REGIONS

REGION	TOTAL LAND AREA IN REGION	RESERVED AREA	
		ACTUAL	RELATIVE TO TOTAL LAND
Adelaide Plains, Mount Lofty Ranges and near north	9,700 sq. m.	20 sq. m.	0·2%
Yorke Peninsula and Kangaroo Island	4,300 sq. m.	232 sq. m.	5·4%
Eyre Peninsula	18,800 sq. m.	505 sq. m.	2·7%
Murray Valley	9,400 sq. m.	5 sq. m.	less than 0·1%
South-east	15,000 sq. m.	370 sq. m.	2·5%
Flinders Ranges	15,800 sq. m.	60 sq. m.	0·4%
Northern interior	282,000 sq. m.	2 sq. m.	less than 0·01%
Far west coast	25,000 sq. m.	12 sq. m.	less than 0·1%
All South Australia	380,000 sq. m.	1,206 sq. m.	0·32%

simultaneously used for conservation. The proclamation can be revoked simply at the request of the owner.

The fauna sanctuaries, while theoretically being not very secure, nevertheless play an important role in fauna conservation — particularly in that of birds. There are approximately eighty of them, most with an area of a few hundred or a few thousand acres, and one of as much as 553,000 acres.

Administrative Organization

Creation of National Parks and Reserves

National parks are government-owned land appropriately dedicated and vested in the National Parks Commission. The government annually budgets for a fund for the purchase of 'land for national park purposes', and the amount provided has been approximately $150,000 per annum for several years. It is administered by the Department of Lands. National parks may be created on unoccupied Crown lands or on land purchased by means of the fund.

Administration and Management

THE NATIONAL PARKS COMMISSION This is not a government instrumentality but it is virtually responsible to the Minister of Lands through whom the annual government grant is arranged.

There is a chairman and deputy chairman, and a Director of National Parks responsible to the Commission. There is a full-time staff of twenty-six and two part-time employees. Only three national parks — Belair, Para Wirra and Cleland — have resident staff, but a resident ranger is shortly to be installed at Canunda National Park in the south-east, and it is planned as soon as practicable to install others at Lincoln National Park (Eyre Peninsula) and Mambray Creek National Park (Flinders Ranges). Two field officers are continually visiting the unstaffed national parks.

The current annual budget of the Commission is $156,000, of which $121,000 is for maintenance and general running and $35,000 is for capital improvements (but not including land acquisition). Most is spent on those three national parks near Adelaide most patronized by the public (i.e. Belair, Cleland and Para Wirra National Parks), and only some $30,000 on the remainder. However, the proportion devoted to the remainder is likely to increase considerably.

THE FAUNA AND FLORA BOARD OF SOUTH AUSTRALIA Besides holding Flinders Chase the Board manages Kelly Hill Caves for the Tourist Bureau, and is responsible to the Minister of Agriculture. Management is by a resident ranger and an assistant. Its annual budget is currently $14,000.

THE DEPARTMENT OF FISHERIES AND FAUNA CONSERVATION This comes under the Minister of Agriculture, and is headed by a Director. There is a field staff of four solely devoted to wildlife duties and a further ten whose duties cover both fisheries and wildlife. In addition there is a central administrative staff of seven. The annual budget of the Department is $170,000 of which some $50,000 may be arbitrarily assigned to fauna conservation.

Its main work on the fauna conservation side is the policing of the fauna laws, and this is for the state at large as well as for the four categories of reserve controlled by the Department.

THE SOUTH AUSTRALIA GOVERNMENT IMMIGRATION, PUBLICITY AND TOURIST BUREAU The Tourist Bureau has no administering board, and is controlled by a Director responsible to the Minister of Immigration. The Deputy Director has charge of the national pleasure resorts, but funds and staff for nature conservation purposes are rather limited.

OTHER BODIES Other bodies holding reserves have limited funds for their maintenance, and rely principally on voluntary help in managing them.

Gibber plains, near Woomera, S.A., are part of the arid centre of the continent. PHOTO COURTESY AUST. NEWS & INFORMATION BUREAU

he emu is a feature of Australia's coat-of-arms. ut as his habitats are being removed faster than ver before due to extensive clearing of arginal scrubland for farms in southern ustralia, where is he to go? PHOTO COURTESY UST. TOURIST COMMISSION

Mungerannia Creek and sandhill, South ustralia. PHOTO COURTESY AUST. TOURIST OMMISSION

The educational aspects of conservation are excellently served by this display at Minnamurra Falls Reserve, N.S.W. — one the many interpretative devices common in overseas parks but which, for want of sufficient funds, Australian reserves' administrators can scarcely afford to construct at this stage. Without such public education there can be little hope of the ai of conservation being supported and understood by the general public. PHOTO COURTESY AUST. TOURIST COMMISSION

Freshwater lake habitat near Cooloola, coastal south Queensland. PHOTO COURTESY S. AND K. BREEDEN

(ABOVE) Royal Arch Cave in the Chillagoe Caves formation, north Queensland. Although many of Australia's spectacular caves are well known tourist attractions, as yet little has been done to bring the underground world into the sphere of conservation. Cave habitats are most easily despoiled; the major threat is from mining interests wishing to exploit the limestone in which most of our caves are found. PHOTO COURTESY QLD FORESTRY DEPT

(BELOW) Aboriginal carvings of emus at Flat Rock, Dharug National Park, N.S.V Emus are now extinct in this area. PHOTO COURTESY A. M. FOX

Problems and Remedies

Interpretation of the Purpose of National Parks

For the general public the purpose of national parks has followed the tradition of the Belair National Park, for over fifty years the one and only such park. This was a public recreation and pleasure ground, with numerous tennis courts and ovals, albeit set in natural surroundings. The old tradition dies hard.

The new National Parks Commission takes a different view, and in general appears to interpret two broad purposes:

(1) to provide a place for the enjoyment by the people of natural scenery and surroundings

(2) to conserve for posterity samples of the natural environment which are of scientific importance on account of their floral, faunal, geological, pedological, anthropological and allied values.

Its attitude is that it should no longer promote organized sport except in those parks where facilities for it already exist and where such activities have traditional acceptance. Emphasis is now on the appreciation-of-nature aspect of public recreation.

Sufficiency of Area and Ecosystems Conserved

Reserved area in South Australia is insufficient. If, as according to international thinking, an optimum of five per cent and a minimum of two per cent of a country should be conserved in national parks, reference to Tables 3 and 4 will reveal inadequacy in the state as a whole and in most of the rainfall zones and regions. If the major plant communities are considered in relation to the reserves some are found to be completely unrepresented, and others to have minimal representation. Further reservation must be made in order to fill these gaps.

The need for further reservation is well appreciated by the National Parks Commission and others. However, while more must be done to impress on those in government the need for greater funds for land purchase, it should be noted that money is not necessary for the acquisition of unoccupied Crown lands.

Fauna conservation is helped in general by conserving more of their habitats in further national parks, but in some cases (e.g. the Hairy-nosed Wombat, the Yellow-footed Rock Wallaby and the Plain Rat Kangaroo) conservation must start by studying the specific needs of these fauna. National parks will not provide adequately for fauna, including birds, that range all over the state. The remedy seems to be to continue the move started by a former Minister of Agriculture of persuading private landholders individually to set aside and enclose a small proportion of their holding to be kept in its natural state.

Funds for Land Acquisition and Park Management

While it is urgent to secure the land for more and larger national parks, the present funds available for maintenance and general running are inadequate for the existing parks; proper staffing and management are urgent problems.

There is current financial stringency in South Australia, but the real problem is to convince the government and the electors that national parks are vitally important to the community, and that they should raise their sights to the level accepted in many overseas countries in respect of the funds made available per head of population.

Opposition to National Parks by Surrounding Landholders

Landholders with properties adjoining national parks and reserves often tend to oppose them because, they claim, these areas harbour 'vermin', and are a bushfire danger. Others oppose the existence of large parks because, since the land is withheld from exploitation, the development of the local town and district is thereby restricted.

There can be merit in the claim that native fauna from bushland parks do emerge to make sorties on the farmers' crops. This can be countered by adequate fencing, or by providing open grazing strips for the fauna along the edge of parks. The National Parks Commission has a policy of subsidizing fencing between parks and adjoining land. The wide firebreaks simultaneously created may serve as grazing strips as well as countering the fire hazard.

The charge that parks 'strangle development' continues to be levelled by Eyre Peninsula farmers who have an action committee seeking the alienation of the Hambidge National Park; it continues to cause concern at ministerial level, and among conservationists generally.

Roads in National Parks

The new National Parks Act allows national park land to be dedicated as public roads. Although it is understood that all such proposals would first be discussed with the Minister of Lands, this provision remains a constant threat to national parks within which it is desirable that road-building be minimized, if not avoided altogether.

Another problem is the maintenance cost of those roads considered necessary in national parks. Wear under modern traffic can make these costs excessive, and in the absence of a toll charge the only recourse seems to be to come to terms with the highways authorities; this may result in a loss of sovereignty, and insistence on an increase in through traffic to justify the outside help.

Reserves and the Shooting of Fauna

Shooting must be regarded as a legitimate form of recreation for a section of the community, but the shooter is finding himself increasingly restricted as further land is closed to him with the creation of more national parks, fauna reserves and sanctuaries, and with further clearing or closing of private land. This could lead to an increase in surreptitious, illegal shooting on reserved land.

A remedy is to create more game reserves (as provided for in the Fauna Conservation Act, 1964), but good natural bushland, already scarce, should not be requisitioned for this purpose.

Conservation of the Flinders Ranges

If there is unique country in South Australia meriting conservation, it is surely the picturesque Flinders Ranges, already much visited by tourists, and yet less than one per cent is reserved. The creation there of further national parks would be likely to little more than double the area at present reserved. The main problem is that practically all the land has been alienated in the form of pastoral leases. The solution seems to be in instituting a planning control similar to that used in the national parks of Britain. While pastoral activities would still continue as before, the planning control would prevent or limit developmental changes that would impair the essentials of scenic landscape and natural amenity while providing the public with legal access to certain sites of beauty and interest.

The Future of the North-west Aboriginal Reserve

A few years ago it seemed likely that this great area of 27,000 square miles, still very much in its original, natural state, would eventually be vacated by its few remaining tribal Aborigine inhabitants, and so could become available for a huge Central Australia National Park.

More recently, however, a new government policy was announced — although it has not yet been implemented for the North-west Reserve. This is that Aboriginal reserve lands be deeded to the Aborigine and that he be encouraged to exploit their productive potential, for example, by the development of grazing. This would mean bringing cattle into unspoiled country never affected by grazing. Further, the unsophisticated Aborigine in developing this land would be shouldering a responsibility for practising effective conservation — a responsibility that the sophisticated European has largely failed to meet in his own field.

Nature Conservation in Western Australia

Vincent Serventy

The Environment

In Western Australia there are two major physical regions, the coastal plain and the great plateau. The latter averages 1,000 to 1,500 feet in altitude but rises in places to slightly over 4,000 feet, and roughly coincides with the Pre-Cambrian Shield, a geological complex of igneous, sedimentary and metamorphic rocks. The coastal plain is of varying width and runs along the south and west coasts to the area near Broome.

Whereas the Pre-Cambrian Shield covers two-thirds of the state and contains many important minerals which have been worked commercially, the sedimentary basins cover the other third of the state and are now assuming greater importance as commercial oil fields and artesian basins. Among the superficial deposits, laterite is the most striking feature and helps to shape many of the land forms. It is believed that this hard crust was developed over much of the state when the great plateau was a low-lying peneplain. At a few feet in depth the laterite generally merges into weathered country rock, then into unweathered rock at depths varying from a few feet to a hundred feet. The laterite has been exploited mainly as a source of iron and aluminium ore.

Salt lakes, although small in area, also add character to the land forms. They are an important habitat for certain species, e.g. the Banded Stilt, whose breeding is associated with the presence of brine shrimps in such lakes.

In the southern portion of the state are large areas of sand plain whose origin is in dispute. In the more arid areas are extensive developments of parallel red sand dunes. The sand dunes at the southern end of the Swan coastal plain in the south-west are being exploited for their mineral content, and with further exploration other sand dune zones may face similar exploitation.

The horizontal limestones of the Nullarbor Plain stand about 600 feet above sea-level, and are bounded to the north by the sand ridges of the Great Victoria Desert. To the south the Nullarbor falls abruptly to the sea with cliffs about 300 feet in height.

Three natural regions in Western Australia are conveniently recognized, and are correlated with rainfall distribution. The south-west region, which is the most densely populated, has a temperate climate with assured winter rainfall. Sandheaths are well developed along the coast on the northern and eastern ends of the region and extend east of the forests, continuing into the semi-arid and arid areas. The distribution of the forest types in the south-west is correlated with differences in rainfall and soils. Wet sclerophyll forest dominated by Karri receives a high winter rainfall with some summer falls and is the most spectacular of the forest lands. Early attempts to clear Karri forest for dairying were ill-advised and ruinous and are not likely to be repeated.

Dry sclerophyll Jarrah forest is found in the drier zone on poor lateritic soils, sharply bounded to the east by the thirty-inch rainfall line. Jarrah forest has always been safe from farming pressure. Tuart forest is limited to limestone areas near the west coast, and Wandoo forest flanks the Jarrah forest where clay soils develop. Wandoo forms a pleasant open sclerophyll woodland abounding in native animals, and, being rich in plant species toxic to livestock, was saved until recent times.

To the east of the Jarrah forest, Salmon Gum and Gimlet woodlands occur on the heavier soils. These woodlands were easily cleared and were settled early, so that this is one area where it is now impossible to obtain adequate reserves.

The sandheaths and thicket formations of the drier areas of the south-west are now under heavy pressure, through use of trace elements and the development of new methods of farming semi-arid lands. It is here that the first major battle must be fought within the next ten years to save the present reserves and to establish new ones.

The winter rainfall region shades off into a huge semi-arid and arid central region which covers two-thirds of the area of the state. It receives some rainfall in the summer, particularly from tropical cyclones and also some from winter cyclone systems. This region is conveniently coupled with the pastoral area between the Murchison and De Grey Rivers in the north-west. Many species of *Acacia* (e.g. the well-known mulgas), *Cassia* and *Eremophila* are common in the central semi-arid and arid region. In southern sections, rock outcrops often carry many species from the south-west zone. An interesting ecological boundary is the so-called mulga-eucalypt transition belt. This begins on the western coast at Shark Bay and runs south-east toward Mount Jackson, then eastwards past Goongarrie. South of this line the woodland is mainly eucalypts and the ground water is salty. North of the line the ground water is fresh and the vegetation is mulga, with eucalypts usually restricted to the watercourses. The fresh ground water led to the extensive exploitation of the northern areas for sheep-raising. For various reasons the sheep numbers have declined and now the south-west corner carries the largest population. Generally speaking, much of the central semi-arid and arid region is still unoccupied and adequate reserves could be set aside without difficulty at present.

Finally, there is the northern region, with summer rainfall and winter drought, and characterized by a number of deciduous trees in the woodland and by grass as the dominant ground cover (savanna types). Remnants of tropical monsoon forest, with many deciduous species, occur along the rivers where soil moisture is adequate. The attractive Baobab tree is a feature of the area. Mangroves are found in quantity from the mouth of the Fortescue River northwards, and occur as outliers on the Abrolhos and as far south as Bunbury. The northern region was first settled almost a hundred years ago and has remained largely cattle country. Some extensive irrigation projects are proposed.

Present National Parks

National park is used here in a broad sense to include public recreational parks, nature reserves, geological reserves, wilderness areas, anthropological reserves etc. all of which have adequate parliamentary protection.

South-west region

Abrolhos 3,000 acres
John Forrest National Park 3,648 acres
Cape le Grand 39,500 acres
Kalbarri 358,000 acres
Kalamunda 919 acres
Lake Magenta 233,000 acres
Neerabup 2,785 acres
Nornalup 32,229 acres
Porongurups 5,531 acres
Rottnest 4,726 acres
Stirling Range 285,874 acres
Walyunga 4,000 acres
Yanchep 6,840 acres
Yalgorup 7,683 acres
Serpentine 1,571 acres
Nambung 9,286 acres

If we take into account the present national parks and the dedicated state forests we have eight per cent of the south-west region permanently reserved. This is satisfactory in terms of area, particularly where forests are concerned. Should there be a change in forest management policy, the position could change drastically since the dedicated forest area is over three times the area of the national parks. The major weaknesses are the lack of national parks along the coastal fringe where pressures are greatest, and in the wheatbelt where farms have removed most of the original plant cover. Also there is new farming pressure eastwards into the drier areas.

North-west and Central Regions

Cape Range 33,171 acres
Barrow Island 50,000 acres
Bernier and Dorre 26,000 acres

These are obviously inadequate though there are a number of fauna and flora reserves whose status could be raised to national park level.

Northern Region

Geikie Gorge 7,750 acres

There is, however, a big flora reserve at the Prince Regent River.

National Parks Needed

The reservation of natural areas in Western Australia is complicated by the number of Acts giving power to authorities to interfere in various ways with reserves. Thus there are three classes of reserves, each with different degrees of security against alienation.

CLASS A: These are of various types but can only be alienated by an Act of Parliament, or by over-riding powers of the Commonwealth in regard to defence.

CLASS B: These reserves can be cancelled by proclamation in the Government Gazette. Reasons have to be given by the Minister for Lands to both Houses of Parliament.

CLASS C: These can be cancelled by proclamation alone.

A full coverage of the position is given in the publication *National Parks and Nature Reserves in Western Australia* by the Subcommittee of the Australian Academy of Science Committee on National Parks (W.A. Government Printer, 1965). This report included recommendations for various areas and reserves to be raised to national park status, and these, with minor amendments, are briefly described below for the different regions.

South-west Region

MARGARET RIVER-HAMELIN BAY: Mixed state forest and some Class A reserves. Area 34,000 acres.

Jarrah forest dominates but there are smaller areas of Karri. Famed for its caves, it would be worth considering as a multipurpose type of park which would include farms and towns along the lines of English national parks. There is also an urgent need for a classification of roads into general and tourist, so that the devastation which has occurred along the main access road will not extend to the narrower tourist and farm roads.

SERPENTINE: Water catchment. Area 86,400 acres.

Set aside as a sample of unworked Jarrah forest, this would be valuable for assessing effects of use in the commercial forests. Such effects may be quite subtle and we do not know what happens when mature trees only are removed from such a forest, or the effects of the present fire control policy.

LUDLOW STATE FOREST: Area 5,000 acres.

This area contains a beautiful stand of Tuart forest and because of its tourist value it has not been milled. The mining of mineral sands could be a threat to the area.

MANDURAH: Some Class A, some Class C reserve. Area 30,000 acres.

This is the last chance to save a portion of this important coastal strip between Perth and Bunbury. Unchecked and poorly planned development has reduced much of the coastline to an ugly ribbon of holiday homes and shacks. Large areas of green belt are urgently needed to prevent an unbroken line of buildings between Geraldton and Cape Leeuwin. These parks would also have maximum public use and would need careful planning and control. Yalgorup and Nambung have recently been set aside in this area.

PINGELLY-DRYANDRA RESERVES: Some Class A, some state forest and some Class C reserve. Area 80,900 acres.

Since forestry practice is tending to abandon natural regeneration in favour of artificial plantings, action is needed urgently. The East Pingelly Reserve is being organized along the lines of basic research and educational work with the general public. This pleasant Wandoo forest has a very high potential in terms of public use along educational lines. Nature trails and hides from which observations on such fascinating creatures as Mallee Fowls and Numbats are needed.

TOODYAY STATE FOREST: Area 84,268 acres.

Original Wandoo forest at present. Should natural regeneration be abandoned as forestry practice, this should then be declared a national park.

FITZGERALD RIVER: Some Class C reserve. Area 604,000 acres.

Mr C. A. Gardner estimated the total number of endemic plants in the reserve to be about twenty-five. There is magnificent coastal scenery.

MOUNT LESUEUR: Some Class C. Some Crown land. Area 230,844 acres.

This is a very rich area, in coastal and dunes country, which carries a fascinating variety of plant life.

CAPE ARID: Class C reserve. Area 642,000 acres.

An area rich in plant life with over fifteen endemic species.

BREMER RANGE: Crown land. Area 576,000 acres.

This area was selected by the committee because of the botanical associations with the salt lake systems so well developed in this state. In addition it is near the edge of the semi-arid areas of the state.

LAKE BARKER: Class C reserve. Area 516,240 acres.

This is also on the edge of the semi-arid areas of the state to the south-east of Southern Cross. It has endemic plants and is of potential historical interest.

TWO PEOPLE BAY: Class C reserve. Area 10,900 acres.

This area was set aside to protect the colony of Noisy Scrub-birds which occur in this area, the only known colony at present. Nothing indicates the sympathetic attitude of the government to conservation better than the decision to cancel the proposed townsite of Casuarina planned for this area. The next logical step is the raising of its status and the appointment of a full-time warden. At present it is being controlled by a warden stationed in the Albany district, but this is only one of his responsibilities.

BALD ISLAND: Class C reserve. Area 2,000 acres.

Biological surveys have revealed that this island is of outstanding scientific interest.

RECHERCHE ARCHIPELAGO: Class C reserve. No recorded area.

There are hundreds of islands in this chain, some heavily wooded, which provide unique ecological situations.

GARDEN ISLAND: Held freehold by the Commonwealth. Area 2,800 acres.

It is under increasing use as a tourist resort with no planned development. Rottnest Island nearby has a local board of control and from this experience it is obvious that such boards must be forced to work under the general control of a master plan if the unique qualities of such places are to be conserved. The present policy seems destined to destroy the very qualities which made Rottnest one of the world's finest island resorts. Soon it could be indistinguishable from thousands of others.

OTHER ISLANDS

All coastal islands, besides their own intrinsic biological associations, form important havens because of their isolation from introduced species on the mainland. A blanket raising of all islands to Class A status is desirable.

THREATENED SPECIES

Noisy Scrub-bird: The only known colony in the Two People Bay area has been protected in two ways: a reserve of nearly 11,000 acres has been set aside and a gazetted town site cancelled. With less than a hundred pairs, its position is precarious.

The Short-necked Tortoise: Partly by public subscription but mainly by government funds, land has been purchased to provide sanctuary for this reptile. In addition, an active research programme into its biology is being undertaken.

North-west Region

NORTHERN NULLARBOR: Crown land. Area 5,552,000 acres.

An area which includes Nullarbor Plain as well as sand ridges to the north. It is physiographically complex, with great floristic diversity.

MOUNT MANNING RANGE: Crown land. Area 449,000 acres.

An important mulga reserve. Grazing on mulga communities in leases to the west needs such nature reserves for assessment of effects.

LAKE DISAPPOINTMENT: Crown land. Area 800,000 acres.

This also includes the Canning Stock Route. Sandy desert country of biological and historic interest and scenic grandeur.

QUEEN VICTORIA SPRING: Aboriginal reserve. Area 618,750 acres.

BARLEE RANGE: Crown land leasehold. Area 265,000 acres.

HAMERSLEY RANGE: Some class C reserve. Some Crown land. Area 1,437,000 acres.

This area contains some of the most beautiful desert country in Australia, only equalled by Ayers Rock and adjacent country. It has high tourist potential.

DAMPIER ARCHIPELAGO: Crown land. A number of islands of unrecorded area.

TWILIGHT COVE: Crown land. Area 1,263,000 acres.

This is the boundary zone between the arid and south-west regions, and is part of the old coastal migration route of animals and plants between western and eastern Australia.

Northern Region

DAMPIER LAND: Crown land. Area 313,600 acres.

This is a reserve needed to preserve the pindan, an interesting association where a fairly dense cover of mainly acacia and tall grasses forms a typical savannah.

PRINCE REGENT RIVER: Class C. Area 1,600,000 acres.

The Academy of Science Report stresses that this could become 'one of the world's outstanding and scenic natural history reserves'.

DRYSDALE RIVER: Crown land. Area 1,086,000 acres.

NAPIER-OSCAR RANGES: Leasehold. Area 123,000 acres.

An area of outstanding natural beauty and wildlife interest.

Practically all the areas recommended are at present unused Crown land or are already reserved for fauna and flora, but at lower status than a Class A reserve.

MARINE RESERVES

This category has not been investigated in Western Australia, yet it is a field which should not be neglected. Rottnest Island is a research area and the prevention of spearfishing and use of pots for catching crayfish in certain national park sections would seem advisable. Similar reservations in the Abrolhos would be important also from the viewpoint of assessing the exploitation of the crayfish populations, by allowing unfished reefs to be available for study. This is one field where a survey needs to be made.

Tentatively one might indicate the following areas which should become marine national parks.

Recherche Archipelago: Certain specified islands after a survey has been made.

Rottnest: Some of the offshore reefs should be closed to all types of fishing and developed as a properly organized marine national park.

Swan Coastal Plain: Certain sections are important as teaching areas — Trigg's Island is one. After a survey these should be declared marine reserves.

Abrolhos Islands: Part of the Pelsart or Southern Group should be made into a marine national park to link with the sea bird colonies.

Not sufficient is known about other marine areas to indicate what other marine national parks should be declared.

Legislation and Control

Security of Reserves

There is no complete legislative security for any reserve which would be acceptable under the definition of national parks as understood internationally, where such parks can only be revoked by an Act of Parliament.

1. COMMONWEALTH POWERS

A classic use of Commonwealth powers was shown in the atomic explosion at the Monte Bellos. Although a Class A reserve, there was no prior consultation with the state government departments most concerned. The pre-explosion biological survey carried out by the British government was pitifully superficial and amateurish compared to the careful work done by the United States in the Pacific. The protests of naturalists were dismissed in contemptuous terms by the Prime Ministers concerned.

2. STATE POWERS

Mining Act: This over-rides all other Acts and therefore mining can be carried out on reserves; for example, Barrow Island is being developed as an oilfield; bauxite mining has been approved in the John Forrest National Park though not yet carried out.

Public Works Act: In essence this takes control of all streams out of the hands of the National Park Board should water needs arise.

Forests Act: This gives the Forests Department wide powers in reserve.

Fisheries Act: There is no method by which a reserves board could stop fish being introduced into its streams. European trout have already been released in most south-west streams and the American *Gambusia* has been set free on an extensive scale in an ill-advised mosquito control scheme.

Vermin Act: Vermin boards can destroy 'vermin' on any reserve.

Bushfires Act: This allows bushfire control officers to enter a reserve and burn to reduce a fire hazard. So far the greatest destruction under this Act has been the burning of road verges. The native flora is being rapidly replaced by introduced grasses and other plants.

Other: Departmental incompetence can also destroy reserves in remote areas. Slope Island in Shark Bay was a reserve for native fauna. It was one of the few islands in Australia which are breeding places for the two phases of the Wedge-tailed Shearwater. The island was handed over to a salt company and the whole habitat is likely to be destroyed. Apparently this was a case of administrative inefficiency.

Summary

It is obvious that no reserve has adequate legal protection. Even if a Director of National Parks were appointed he would find interference by outside organizations a continual problem under the present Act.

Control of Reserves

NATIONAL PARKS BOARD: Most Class A reserves listed as national parks are under the control of this government-appointed board. All members are civil servants and the board employs no scientific personnel and conducts no research. At present 832,285 acres of reserves are under its control. Its early years showed the lack of interest in conservation and also lack of scientific knowledge. Recently more biologists have been appointed to the board and one is now the vice-chairman. However, for all members such an appointment can be no more than a hobby with their real professional duties elsewhere. Should this board be retained as an advisory panel, it would need a much greater range of skills than at present. An educationalist is essential so that this aspect of a good national park will not be neglected. At present this is almost entirely ignored in all parks. In addition a landscape architect is urgently needed. One of the most magnificent views in the Stirling Ranges has been marred by the over-conspicuous placement of water closets and other facilities. Also this has flouted the basic principle of keeping large congregations of people in places where they can do the least damage.

WESTERN AUSTRALIA WILD LIFE AUTHORITY: This is a statutory, corporate body set up under the Fauna Conservation Act. It has as its chairman the Director of Fisheries and Fauna while the Chief Warden of Fauna is its deputy chairman and chief executive officer. Other *ex officio* members are the Chief Vermin Control Officer and the Conservator of Forests. Of the seven appointed members, one must be a botanist and two zoologists and the remaining four must be persons who are not members of the state public service and at least one must represent country interests. The seven persons currently appointed include the Curator of the State Herbarium, Mr Royce, the Director of the Western Australian Museum, Dr Ride, and Professor A. R. Main of the Department of Zoology at the University of Western Australia, and Dr D. L. Serventy of C.S.I.R.O. The three other members are Mr A. H. Robinson of Coolup, Mr N. A. Beeck of Katanning, and Mr H. G. Hall of Dangin, all farmers who are also experienced naturalists and who thus bring wide practical experience to the Authority. At the present time, the Department of Fisheries and Fauna, which finances and services the Authority, has provision for three graduate research officers each of whom has one or more technical assistants. One heads a wetlands and waterfowl research unit, another a reserves management unit, while the third was appointed to study the bionomics of the Grey Kangaroo.

OTHER BOARDS: There are some which control specific reserves, e.g. King's Park, Rottnest. Local boards such as this have had an unhappy record regarding nature conservation and a full statement of King's Park is included in the bibliography. Rottnest Board has already been mentioned. It would seem doubtful if such boards could have any future function except as an advisory panel.

Fauna and Flora Protection Laws

Flora

This Act is mainly designed for the protection of flowers, rather than conservation of flora. Destruction of flora along roadsides, Crown lands, reserves and state forests is banned. However, bushfire boards, main road gangs, P.M.G. workers and other public servants are rapidly removing most of the bushland still left along road edges. In addition in new road planning, practically no attempt is being made to allow for the preservation of nature strips.

Fauna

This excellent Act allows a blanket protection for all vertebrate fauna except frogs. Certain pest species are unprotected and there are open seasons for game animals. Sensible provision is made for students who wish to keep protected fauna for study.

Public Education

In National Parks

As already mentioned, public education is the grave weakness in most parks. King's Park has begun a more comprehensive educational programme, including nature trails and flower shows. At Pingelly Reserve, steps are being taken to educate the public.

Education Department

This department has been particularly effective. There is a Nature Advisory Service which provides all teachers with an effective service in teaching conservation ideas. One of the major aims of the science curriculum is to teach the meaning and the value of conservation. Western Australia was the first state to introduce a Nature Conservation Day so that the importance of the subject could be brought home to children. In addition an Arbor Day is celebrated each year. These celebrations are not mere 'window dressing'. In the majority of cases they represent an intelligent and determined attempt to teach conservation.

Societies

There are a number dedicated to the study and conservation of fauna and flora. Interestingly enough one of the largest and most powerful, the Tree Society, is government subsidized. Others prominent in the field are the Western Australian Naturalists' Club, the Gould League, the Royal Society and the National Trust. The Naturalists' Club and Gould League stage a large natural history exhibition each year. This takes conservation to the general public. In addition both clubs publish a large amount of material on natural history topics. Regional societies are weak. A co-ordinating Nature Conservation Council has recently been established.

The Future

The future outlook for nature conservation in Western Australia is very favourable. The public is in general interested, and an opportunity exists to set aside sections of the original environment at little or no expense. With little management, these should hold their own, although the long dry summer makes wildfires a problem. The occasional firings before white occupation are rapidly being changed into regular burnings. Undoubtedly uncontrolled fire is one of the major problems facing many reserves.

In the older settled areas we will have to be content with small fragments of the original habitat. Here very complex problems face conservationists. The history of King's Park, a thousand-acre reserve in the heart of Perth, has shown how difficult it is to conserve an island of bush in a suburban area. 'Developers' interested in cheap land launch attack after attack, under various guises, but always mislabelled as 'progress'. Conservation is equally difficult in an agricultural area. Research will assist in this problem and a start has been made on such basic work.

State governments of all political shades have shown themselves to be interested in the problems of nature conservation in Western Australia, and an authoritative blueprint for action has been prepared by the Academy of Science Sub-committee.

The only danger is inertia. The next ten years are vital, and naturalists' organizations and governments must take action in these major tasks:

(1) *The setting aside of the national parks recommended*

This would give a total area of 17,495,000 acres which still only represents about three per cent of the state. This is well below the suggested minimum of five per cent for an adequate national park coverage. Moreover, the larger reserves are in areas which in the foreseeable future will never be used for agricultural purposes. Small nature reserves, even of a few acres, are also of biological importance and should not be neglected.

(2) *The establishment by the government of a unified Nature Conservation Authority*

This should be done by amalgamating the functions and personnel of the numerous instrumentalities at present operating independently in this field. In doing so, the principle should be accepted that conservation of fauna, flora and natural areas (i.e. of habitat) is indivisible. The Nature Conservation Authority should appoint as its executive officer a competent person with adequate training, and provide finance for the appointment of other qualified staff.

The newly formed Nature Conservation Council in Western Australia is working towards the achievement of similar aims.

Reserves in the Northern Territory

Lionel Rose

The Environment

Australia has been described as 'the last wilderness'. This may have been true enough when the phrase was coined, but as this book shows, it is no longer true in the 1960s. Certainly, when compared with most other countries, Australia is fortunate in the vast areas of 'undeveloped' land it still possesses, but these are rapidly being whittled away. It would then seem fair to claim that the Northern Territory, the last of the Australian frontiers, is also the last main stronghold of wilderness in this enormous country and that therefore it has striking implications for Australian conservation.

The Territory includes the uninhabited Ashmore and Cartier Islands and has an area of 520,280 square miles. Approximately 1,000 miles from north to south and 580 miles from east to west, it represents over a sixth of the Australian continent. It has 1,040 miles of winding coastline indented with numerous bays and inlets and the estuaries of hundreds of creeks and rivers. Some of these, such as the Daly River, have formed extensive alluvial plains.

The Northern Territory is an area of gentle to moderate relief with some stretches of rugged or mountainous country, such as the Macdonnell Ranges. More than four-fifths of the Territory lies north of the Tropic of Capricorn and the greater part has a climate subject to the influence of the north-west monsoon. Rainfall declines from over sixty inches annually in the northern rivers region to about ten inches at Alice Springs and barely five inches at Finke. In the monsoonal area especially, there is no marked seasonal change such as in temperate regions. Instead the year has two main climatic seasons: the 'wet' and the 'dry'.

The relatively few soil types in the Territory have a fairly simple distribution pattern. For example, red and clayey sands predominate over half the area of central Australia; red earths extend from central Australia to the higher rainfall areas; lateritic podzolics and leached gravelly brown earths are common in the northern part of the Territory.

Throughout the Territory, the vegetation has to withstand regular droughts. In the north, where the annual rainfall exceeds fifteen inches, eucalypts predominate except in areas with heavy clay soil. Elsewhere they occur only in small specialized habitats. There are extensive areas of treeless grassland on heavy clay soil, especially in the south. In the south too, are huge areas of spinifex country, dotted with shrubs such as acacias (including mulga) and low trees. In the far south relatively small areas of saltbush shrubland occur.

The Northern Territory's mineral deposits have not yet been completely surveyed, tested and mapped, but the indications are that there are rich mineral resources in the area. Gold, manganese, uranium and copper are already being mined in various parts of four main areas — the Darwin hinterland, the Gulf of Carpentaria and around Tennant Creek and Alice Springs. Exploitation has thus far been limited mainly because of distance and shortage of water but modern technology and the growing demand for minerals are rapidly overcoming such restrictions.

Reserves in the Northern Territory

The 520,280 square miles of the Northern Territory are allocated as follows:

Freehold, lease, licence	299,625 sq. m.
Aboriginal reserves	94,115 sq. m.
Unoccupied	125,494 sq. m.
Reserved	1,046 sq. m.
	520,280 sq. m.

The reserved land includes 590 square miles dedicated to the Northern Territory Reserves Board and this area may be accepted as the amount of land set aside for national parks. It amounts to 0.11 per cent of the total.

In addition, two sanctuaries set aside under the Wildlife Conservation and Control Ordinance are virtually inviolate areas, that is 'spacious land areas essentially of a primitive or wilderness character'. These are Tanami Sanctuary (14,490 sq. m.) and the Coburg Sanctuary (740 sq. m.). Together with the Reserves Board areas, these amount to just over three per cent of the total area.

Areas set aside as National Parks

The Territory now has three areas large enough to be called national parks — the Ayers Rock-Mount Olga National Park, the Katherine Gorge, and the Palm Valley Flora and Fauna Reserve, all of which contain 'outstanding scenery and natural wonders'. Their boundaries were probably fixed because of the availability of vacant land, and a flora and fauna survey is required to assess the adequacy or otherwise of the areas.

The Ayers Rock-Mount Olga Park covers 487 square miles and lies 300 miles south-west of Alice Springs. The vast, many-coloured Rock is one of Australia's outstanding single tourist attractions: its spectacular appearance is well-known locally and overseas thanks to the efforts of Australian tourist and airline interests. It stands in predominantly desert country with about five inches annual rainfall and clothed with spinifex and some mulga, ironwood and desert oak. Ayers Rock itself is a monolith looming 1,143 feet above the plain. About one and a half miles wide and two and a half miles long, it is one of the biggest isolated rock masses in the world. The Olga group lies about twenty miles to the west of the Rock and contains nineteen large and a number of smaller monoliths. Mount Olga itself rises to 3,507 feet above sea-level.

Twenty-two miles to the west of the town of Katherine, the Katherine Gorge runs through 56,609 acres of reserve land. The gorge itself has been formed by the Katherine River cutting through an abrupt rock escarpment. Although a complete survey has still to be carried out, the gorge is evidently rich in subtropical bird and marsupial life.

The Palm Valley Flora and Fauna Reserve covers 177 square miles astride the Finke River, eighty miles west of Alice Springs. It contains a series of permanent waterholes with high, colourful sandstone cliffs and groves of the relict palm *Livistona mariae*.

Other areas

An attempt has been made (as yet unsuccessful) to secure an area of approximately 1,000 square miles adjacent to the Arnhem Land Aboriginal Reserve, although suggested boundaries may need revision. Other areas, representing different land systems as classified by the CSIRO Division of Land Research Survey should be examined and substantial portions set aside if they qualify for inclusion in the definition of 'national parks', or are considered to be useful reference areas.

Overlapping of functions between National Parks and Gardens Ordinance and Wildlife Conservation and Control Ordinance

A committee consisting of the Assistant Administrator, the Chief Inspector of Wildlife, and the Chairman of the Reserves Board was set up to examine this problem. Submissions were prepared by the latter two members, but nothing has been resolved or decided. This issue must be decided sooner or later and here it is sufficient to say that a single authority is more desirable than are multiple ones. The Animal Industry Branch of the N.T. Administration is now the Primary Industry Branch and includes a Wildlife Section. It should be asked whether an organization such as Animal Industry, which is concerned with production of domestic species, is suitably equipped to consider preservation and conservation. It is the age-old problem of the short-term versus the long-term approach: history shows that too often the short-term view has won.

Legislation for Reserves Board

Prior to 1955, when the National Parks and Gardens Ordinance was passed by the Northern Territory Legislative Council, no specific authority existed for the acquisition and preservation of places of scenic, historic and other value. The legislation provided for the creation of a Board of not less than five, nor more than seven persons, to be appointed for a term of three years. Board members are now appointed by the Administrator's Council, which normally reappoints persons and fills vacancies, on the recommendation of the Board. However, if an appointed member proves of little or no value, it is not easy to displace him.

Owing to the vastness of the Territory, efforts are made to select Board members on a geographic basis so that the special requirements of all districts will be brought to the Board's notice by members who live in them.

The legislation has conferred on the Board the responsibility for the care, control and management of land reserved as:

a place for the recreation or amusement of the public
a national park
a monument
a botanical garden
a zoological garden
a reserve or sanctuary for the protection of flora and fauna
any other similar purpose.

It further allows the Board to develop its reserves by any of the many means available to it, including the construction and management of kiosks, hostels, hotels or places of entertainment or by granting licences to do so. It may also demand and receive rents and fees.

The staff is under the administrative control of the Executive Officer, Mr W. T. Hare, assisted by a secretary, both of whom are located at head office in Alice Springs. There is an Assistant Secretary in Darwin and full-time curators at Howard Springs, Alice Springs Telegraph Station, Ayers Rock, Simpson's Gap and Katherine Gorge, most of whom are supported by one or more assistants to make a total staff of eighteen, including a Field Supervisor whose duties are to supervise all field staff and activities and to understudy the Executive Officer.

Consistent with funds and public need, full-time curators are based at principal reserves to ensure that they are properly maintained, improved and secured against vandalism, and this involves the provision of a first-class residence. Water supply is always the first need and is invariably costly. It is required for the preservation of lawns, trees and shrubs, and is reticulated to hostels, etc., and to the Board's own camping areas which are equipped with toilet, washing and other facilities.

Other improvements are dictated by the nature of the reserve in question, but invariably it is the policy of the Board to erect an entrance archway of natural stone pillars, surmounted by a wrought iron title, with one of the pillars carrying a bronze plaque briefly describing the reserve. To assist visitors in understanding the significance of a place, there are bronze plaques describing features of particular interest.

Within the principal reserves, the Board has erected barbecues for the use of the public and to deter the indiscriminate lighting of fires. When adequate water is available, natural pools are developed for swimming, with special provision being made for children.

Procedure in Acquiring Reserves

A Board member brings to the notice of the Board an area that he feels should be acquired. This is then inspected by all members who decide whether a bid should be made for it. A proposal is then placed before the Administrator, fully supported with details of area, objective, and possible expenditure. If approved by the Administrator, a recommendation is sent to the Minister. If favourable, surveys are carried out and the land is acquired either by voluntary surrender or by resumption, but it has not, so far, been necessary to resort to this latter course.

These procedures sound simple enough, but may involve years of delay, which is unfortunate for administration and planning. Delay has meant, too, that some very beautiful and valuable places have, in the absence of a policing authority, been discovered by the tourist companies and the public, resulting in destruction and vandalism.

TABLE 1

NAME	AREA IN ACRES	TYPE	WHEN COMMITTED
John Flynn's Grave	·83	NR	1957
John Flynn's Memorial Monument	1	NR	1957
Howard Springs Recreation Reserve	700	RR	1957
Simpson's Gap National Park	640	NP	1957
Heavitree Gap Police Station	1	NR	1958
Ayers Rock — Mt Olga National Park	311,680	NP	1958
Berry Springs Recreation Reserve	320	RR	1959
Devil's Marbles Reserve	4,519	SR	1961
Alice Springs Telegraph Station National Park	1,096	NP	1963
Corroboree Rock Scenic Reserve	18	SR	1963
Green Valley Scenic Reserve	1,239	SR	1963
Attack Creek Memorial	·54	NR	1963
Central Mount Stuart Memorial	·51	NR	1963
Katherine Gorge National Park	56,069	NP	1963
Henbury Meteorites National Park	40	NR	1964
Gregory's Tree National Park	5	NR	1963
Edith Falls National Park	402	SR	1964
Glen Helen Gorge National Park	954	SR	1965
Katherine Low Level	40	RR	1965
Trephina Gorge Scenic Reserve	4,378	SR	1966
Emily and Jessie Gap Scenic Reserve	1,718	SR	1966
Kintore Caves Scenic Reserve	1,046	SR	1966
Palm Valley Flora and Fauna Reserve	113,280	NP	1967
Ellery Creek	2,400	SR	1968
Katherine 16 Mile Caves	640	SR	1967
Ormiston Gorge	11,520	SR	1966
Stuarts Tree	9	NR	1966
Serpentine Gorge	1,920	SR	1968
Mataranka Springs	9,600	RR	1967
Daly River	75	SR, RR	1967

Key:
NP National Park NR National Reserve RR Recreation Reserve SR Scenic Reserve

Reserves Already Committed to the Board

A list of these is summarized in Table 1.

Description of Some Reserves

The Board has learnt that good reserve planning can only be done where the Board is in possession of reliable basic data. It therefore secures a contoured map of the area and submits this, with its basic requirements, to a town-planning authority, from which it receives an architect's recommendation on development. Armed with this, Board members who have a detailed knowledge of the area modify the plan to suit local needs. In doing so, they take into account the engineering or works costs, things which are often not taken into consideration by professional and abstract planners. The descriptions which follow are intended to give some idea of what some of the Northern Territory reserves are like and how the Board has, so far, endeavoured to improve them for the public and secure them for posterity.

HOWARD SPRINGS. Situated about thirty miles from Darwin, four miles off the Stuart Highway, this reserve is reached by a sealed road. The area of 700 acres has, as its main feature, a permanent spring which feeds an expansive and deep pool of clear water held back by a concrete weir which was put in by the Army during the last war, when the place was used for the recreation of Service personnel. Below the weir, the stream trickles through a small belt of rainforest which greatly adds to the appeal of the reserve. The Board's improvements are a curator's lodge, water supply by pumping for storage and reticulation, toilets and showers, a children's bathing pool, a kiosk and a caravan park.

BERRY SPRINGS. This seems to be a 'second string' to Howard Springs as a place of recreation for the people of Darwin, who now number almost 20,000. The Berry River comes gushing down through the reserve in bubbling cascades, spilling into broad clear pools which are ideal for swimming. The Board is acquiring more land additional to the initial 320 acres, which will give access to more pools, extending to where the fresh water becomes brackish and then to the salt water of the bay. This extra land will also provide high ground facilities for the construction of camping, recreation and other facilities.

KATHERINE GORGE. This magnificent park is some seventeen miles up river from Katherine, and, until recently it was inaccessible because of the poor track. However, this has been largely remedied and now many hundreds of people go there, particularly at week-ends and long week-end holidays, taking with them their bathing gear, fishing tackle and outboard-motor dinghies. The area of 56,069 acres includes several miles of gorge where the river cuts its way through a narrow passage flanked by sheer cliffs. The gorge cannot be navigated all the way because of rapids, but this hazard is being successfully overcome by enterprising people.

At the lower limit of the gorge proper, the river opens out into an expansive sheet of deep water which is almost a lake and this is the main attraction for swimmers and boaters.

An important feature of this reserve is that it is sufficiently large in area for the Board to regard most of it as a conservation area for the great variety of fauna and flora living within its boundaries. Also, for those interested in Aboriginal art, the gorge contains many good examples of Aboriginal paintings.

ALICE SPRINGS TELEGRAPH STATION. This reserve, which is in effect the original 'Alice Springs', is situated about two miles north of the existing town and is 1,096 acres in area. Its survival is now assured by its dedication to the Board, which is developing it both as an historical feature of current and future interest, and as one of the very few places of recreation available to the people of Alice Springs.

The waterhole was found by surveyor Mills in 1871 and named by him after the wife of Charles Todd, who was responsible for constructing the Overland Telegraph from Port Augusta to Palmerston (now Darwin). The railway reached Alice Springs from Adelaide in 1929, and, as the town became established at the terminus, the Post Office was moved from 'Alice Springs' to its present site in 1932, and the old 'Bungalow' as it was called was used as an Aboriginal settlement until the Board took possession of it in 1963.

Improvements put in by the Board include a costly and secure boundary fence, constructed to preserve the flora from depredations by stock; the provision of a sealed access road; a curator's lodge, water supply, toilets, barbecues, entrance archway and commemorative bronze plaques. In addition spacious lawns have been developed and some 800 shrubs and trees have been planted, all of which have not only survived the prolonged drought but have grown to impressive heights. A good start was made in restoring the original buildings, and though some difficulties were encountered, these have been overcome and substantial progress has been made in this important work.

The Board's plan is to restore the place to the period 1890 to 1900 and, in doing this, it is assisted by original photographs and drawings of the buildings from the very start and by the provision of original equipment to install in the telegraph room and office. With patience and perseverence, the Board's efforts should reach satisfactory completion in the next few years.

SIMPSON'S GAP. This beautiful little rift in the great range, only fifteen miles from Alice Springs, is reached by sealed road most of the way. It is only one square mile in area but this is sufficient for its preservation and for the enjoyment of the public generally; and very few indeed of the many visitors fail to call here. The Board's improvements include a secure boundary fence, the usual entrance archway, through which the Gap itself can be effectively photographed and a level parking space. Simpson's Gap Reserve is maintained and policed by a curator whose responsibilities also include Standley Chasm.

STANDLEY CHASM, of 2,735 acres was found, on survey, to be part of the Jay Creek Aboriginal Reserve of 74,240 acres and, by ministerial edict, it cannot be excised from the Aboriginal Reserve. The Board had anticipated events and had spent a considerable sum in winning water, providing amenities and in levelling an area for a vehicle stand. Visitors usually arrange to have their midday meal here because this chasm is so narrow and high that good photographs may only be taken about midday, when the sun penetrates into its colourful interior.

AYERS ROCK-MT OLGA. 'The Rock' was first seen by Ernest Giles in 1872 and named in the following year by William Gosse in honour of Sir Henry Ayers, then Governor of South Australia. For the next eighty or more years it remained in splendid isolation except from the Aborigines, for whom it had a special significance. Indeed, when the writer first came to the Centre, over twenty years ago, the only approach was by camels, over seventy or more miles of sand hills, from Curtin Springs. Then, in the late forties, a tourist organization recognized its potential and an obliging Works Officer cut a graded track to it, by a long tortuous route which circumnavigated most of the steeper sand ridges. Others quickly followed, so that long before the area became vested in the Reserves Board, permanent tourist camps, in a variety of forms, became established close to the Rock.

Ayers Rock lies about 300 miles to the south-west of Alice Springs and is reached by a road which is normally quite trafficable for conventional vehicles, provided that their drivers are accustomed to some of the hazards of bush driving. Many visitors, by private vehicle or bus, approach it from the South Australia side, making a detour there en route to Alice Springs and other places of general attraction in the Centre.

The provision of a stable water supply has

been one of the Board's major problems here. The Rock's three camping areas are each equipped with the usual amenities and homes are provided for the curator and his assistant. Other appointments include sign-posting, the usual entrance archway, bronze plaques commemorating lives lost on the climb, a hand-rail at the more dangerous parts of the climb etc. Five tourist organizations have been granted leases of from five to ten acres on which they have built permanent tourist accommodation with a total capacity of 150 beds, all of which are booked out during the tourist season. The airstrip, right at the base of the Rock, receives many flights daily during the tourist season. Visitors to Ayers Rock-Mt Olga in 1968 numbered 22,000 and this number increases each year by about twenty per cent.

Additional Reserves Currently Being Sought

Negotiations are being conducted for the acquisition of the places listed in Table 2.

The Board is still striving to secure major areas representative of the far north and of the Centre, so that they may be preserved in their natural state, together with their often unique flora and fauna.

Conclusion

The present state of the Territory's parks, reserves etc., prove that a real and determined effort has been made, in the ten years of the Board's existence, to make up for past neglect. We are now approaching a standard near to that of the various states in regard to the development and maintenance of at least some of the Territory's areas of scientific, historical or recreational value.

TABLE 2

NAME	APPROX. AREA IN ACRES	TYPE
Berry Springs (additional area)	308	RR
Chambers Pillar	840	NR
Redbank Gorge	3,200	SR
Ooraminna Rock Carvings	15	Aboriginal rock carvings
Umbrawarra	2,560	SR
Douglas Hot Springs	7,680	RR
King's Canyon	14,720	SR
Illamurta Springs	320	SR and NR
Northern Area National Park	758,400	NP
Simpson's Gap Station	75,520	NP
Anna's Reservoir	to be determined	NR
Fort Dundas	to be determined	NR
Waterfall Creek	760	SR and RR

KEY:
NP National Park NR National Reserve SR Scenic Reserve RR Recreation Reserve

AUSTRALIAN NATIONAL PARKS AND EQUIVALENT RESERVES

30 June, 1968

State	Population 1966 ('000 persons)	Number of Parks and Reserves	Area ('000acs)	Area of Nat. Parks & Reserves ('000acs)	% of State Area	Acres per Capita
New South Wales	4,231	89	198,037	2,144	1.1	0.5
Victoria	3,218	48	56,245	497	0.9	0.2
Queensland	1,661	258	426,880	2,364	0.6	1.4
South Australia	1,091	110	243,245	2,889	1.2	2.6
W. Australia	836	380	624,589	3,042	0.5	3.6
Tasmania	371	113	16,885	712	4.2	1.9
Northern Territory	37	34	332,979	11,638	3.5	315.0
Australian Capital Territory	96	1	601	12	1.9	0.1
Australia	11,541	1,033	1,899,462	23,295	1.2	2.0

Information supplied by Dr J. G. Mosley, Australian Conservation Foundation, Inc., Canberra.

Notes on Contributors

C. W. BONYTHON, B.SC., F.R.A.C.I., F.R.G.S., F.R.MET.S., is a member of the Executive Committee of the Australian Conservation Foundation, and in South Australia is President of the Nature Conservation Society and Chairman of the Policy Advisory Committee, National Parks Commission. He is particularly concerned with the expansion of national parks.

J. H. CALABY, Principal Research Scientist of the Division of Wildlife Research, CSIRO, is concerned with the biology and taxonomy of native mammals, especially members of the kangaroo family. He is also engaged in fauna surveys. He has published a considerable number of papers on Australian mammals, birds, frogs and insects in scientific journals. He is Chairman of the Marsupials Group, Survival Service Commission of the International Union for the Conservation of Nature and Natural Resources; a member of the Conservation Committee, Australian Mammal Society, and editor of its *Bulletin*.

M. F. DAY, B.SC., PH.D., graduated from the University of Sydney and from Harvard University in biology. He is a member of the Executive of CSIRO, Canberra, and prior to that was a member of the CSIRO Division of Entomology. He has had a long-standing interest in conservation and was Chairman of the Australian Academy of Science's Committee on National Parks and Reserves, and has served on the Kosciusko State Park Trust.

R. G. DOWNES, M.AGR.SC., F.A.I.A.S., F.S.C.S. AM., is Chairman of the Soil Conservation Authority of Victoria, the Land Utilization Advisory Council and the recently established Pesticides Review Committee; he is a member of the National Parks Authority and the Wildlife Reserves Investigation Committee of Victoria. He is also Vice-President of the Australian Conservation Foundation, a member of the I.U.C.N. Ecology Commission and Chairman of the Committee on Ecological Aspects of Soil and Water Conservation. Since 1960 he has, on several occasions, been called on by the Food and Agriculture Organization of the United Nations to act as a technical consultant on land use, hydrology and soil conservation to the Israeli government and the government of Iran. He has written many articles on aspects of conservation in a wide range of publications.

J. ROS GARNET for many years has worked as a biochemist and bacteriologist in the Commonwealth Serum Laboratories. He has been Hon. Secretary and then President of the Field Naturalists Club of Victoria and a member of its Council for over twenty years, and was one of the founders of the Victorian National Parks Association and its Hon. Secretary since its inception. He is a Past-President of the Native Plants Preservation Society of Victoria, a member of the Royal Society of Victoria, of the Society for Growing Australian Plants and of the Committee of Management of Wyperfeld National Park. His sustained activity on behalf of conservation was acknowledged by the Australian Natural History Medallion which he received in 1966. He has contributed to many scientific journals, to natural history journals and magazines, has lectured frequently on nature conservation and national parks, including radio broadcasts and television appearances.

J. K. JARROTT has been Hon. Secretary of the National Parks Association of Queensland since 1947. He is the editor of the N.P.A. *News* and has prepared N.P.A. submissions to the Queensland government of areas suitable for national parks. He was an Australian representative at the First World Conference on National Parks at Seattle in June 1962, and has contributed articles on Australian national parks to various publications.

J. LE GAY BRERETON, B.SC. (SYD.), D.PHIL. (OXON), Associate Professor of Zoology at the University of New England, is an ecologist whose research is in social behaviour and animal population regulation. He is a Councillor of the Australian Conservation Foundation, a member of the Advisory Council of the National Parks and Wildlife Service of New South Wales, and a Trustee of the New England National Park.

ELIZABETH N. MARKS, M.SC. (QLD.), PH.D. (CAMBRIDGE), is Senior Research Officer, National Mosquito Control Committee, working in the Entomology Department at the University of Queensland. Her research on mosquitoes is supported by a grant from the Queensland Department of Health. She is currently the Queensland Naturalists' Club's Hon. Editor; Vice-President and Chairman of the Executive of the Australian Entomological Society; and a member of the Executive of the Australian Conservation Foundation.

JUDITH WRIGHT MCKINNEY, best known as a writer and poet, is co-founder and President of the Wildlife Preservation Society of Queensland, which has numerous branches throughout Queensland. She is also a member of the Australian Conservation Foundation's Council and of its Queensland Regional Committee. She has participated in various conservation seminars, previously edited the magazine *Wildlife in Australia* which is published by the Wildlife Preservation Society of Queensland, and has published articles on conservation in journals.

D. F. MCMICHAEL, B.SC. (HONS.) (SYD.), M.A., P.H.D. (HARVARD), is the first Director of National Parks and Wildlife in New South Wales. He was on the staff of the Australian Museum, Sydney, from 1948 till 1967, and became Curator in the Department of Molluscs, and finally Deputy Director of the Museum. From 1967 to 1968 he was Director of the Australian Conservation Foundation. He has published numerous papers and two books on molluscs, and has had extensive field experience throughout Australia and New Guinea, and especially on the Great Barrier Reef during recent years. He attended the Symposium on Marine Parks held in association with the eleventh Pacific Science Congress in Tokyo in September 1966.

J. G. MOSLEY, M.A. (NOTTINGHAM), PH.D. (A.N.U.), is Assistant Director of the Australian Conservation Foundation and is currently working on a survey of Australia's national parks and reserves. He has studied national park problems in several countries, and his experience includes work as an education officer, as a supervisor of the Canadian Rocky Mountain chain of youth hostels, and as a member of the New Zealand National Resources survey team. He is a member of the official New South Wales Scientific Committee for National Parks and Native Reserves, and the Resource Management Committee for the Kosciusko National Park.

W. F. MUSGRAVE, M.SC.AGR. (SYDNEY), PH.D. (NEW ENGLAND), is now Lecturer and Senior Lecturer in Agricultural Economics in the Faculty of Agricultural Economics at the University of New England. In 1959, he was with the Reserve Bank and in 1966 was Visiting Lecturer, Department of Resource Development, Michigan State University.

J. D. OVINGTON, PH.D., D.SC., F.F.S., F.I. BIOL., a graduate of Sheffield University, is head of the Department of Forestry of the Australian National University, Canberra. He was on the staff of the British Nature Conservancy for sixteen years and has been closely associated with the International Union for the Conservation of Natural Resources. He has travelled extensively in Europe, Africa, Asia and North America visiting national parks and nature reserves.

R. D. PIESSE, LL.B., B.A., DIP. ED. (HONS.), a graduate of the University of Melbourne was in October 1968 appointed Director of the Australian Conservation Foundation. He joined the Australian National Travel Association in 1955; his duties over the period 1956-59 included the editing of *Walkabout* magazine. He has travelled widely in all parts of Australia and overseas, visiting national parks and other reserves. In 1964-65 he co-ordinated the field work and report on 'Australia's Travel and Tourist Industry' by two U.S. firms of consultants. He contributes to various journals and was the author of the special article on travel and tourism in the Commonwealth Year Book, 1966.

B. N. RICHARDS, B.SC. FOR., PH.D. (QLD.), Senior Lecturer in Botany at the University of New England, is concerned with soil-plant-microbe interrelationships, and teaches a course in microbiology which emphasizes the role of micro-organisms in ecosystem structure and function. Before coming to New England, he was for a number of years a research officer with the Queensland Forest Service, where his interests lay primarily in the fields of silviculture and tree nutrition.

W. C. ROBISON, M.A. (CALIF.), PH.D. (BOSTON), is Chief of the Geography Division, U.S. Army Natick Laboratories, and Chairman of the Conservation Commission of Framingham, Massachusetts. He visited Australia a number of times between 1942 and 1968, including a three-year period as Lecturer in Geography at the University of New England. He has contributed articles to the *National Parks Journal*, *Geographical Review* and other journals.

COLONEL LIONEL ROSE, O.B.E., B.V.SC., the first Director of Animal Industry in the Northern Territory was, during his twelve years in that appointment, responsible for wildlife preservation and the control of noxious species. He was appointed a member of the Northern Territory Reserves Board in June 1958 and Chairman of the Board in June 1963. He was responsible for subsequent publications of the Board, and produced the Board's booklets on the Alice Springs Telegraph Station National Park, 'The Significance of Ayers Rock for Aborigines', and the forthcoming booklet on the Ayers Rock-Mt Olga National Park.

V. SERVENTY, B.SC., B.ED., is at present editor of *Wildlife in Australia* and President of the Wildlife Preservation Society of Australia. He is a member of the New South Wales Nature Conservation Council and of the National Parks and Wildlife Advisory Council of New South Wales, and is on the Councils of the Gould Leagues of Western Australia and New South Wales. He was previously Senior Lecturer in Science and Mathematics at Claremont Teachers' College, Western Australia, then in charge of the Western Australia Nature Advisory Service. His numerous publications include the books *A Continent in Danger*, and *Wildlife Conservation in Australia*. He has also conducted television programmes on conservation and natural history.

J. A. SINDEN, B.SC. (HONS.), PH.D. (WALES), and Master of Forestry (Michigan), is now Lecturer in Agricultural Economics at the University of New England, specializing in natural resource economics. From 1965 to 1967 he was at the Forest Research Institute, Forestry and Timber Bureau, Canberra.

A. A. STROM, A.S.T.C.(SC.) WITH HONS., is Advisor in Conservation, New South Wales Department of Education. At first a schoolteacher he was later the pioneer Education Officer at the Australian Museum, lecturer at Balmain Teachers' College and Sydney Technical College. He was a foundation member of the New South Wales Fauna Protection Panel in 1949, and became its Chairman and Chief Guardian of Fauna in 1958. In March 1968, subsequent to certain amendments to the Fauna Protection Act, Mr Strom returned to the Department of Education to develop a positive place for conservation in education.

J. G. TRACEY, Q.D.A. (LAWES), Rainforest Ecology Unit, Division of Plant Industry, CSIRO, Brisbane, has a wide botanical experience in eastern Australian rainforests, which was developed during the phytochemical survey and subsequent ecological studies. He specializes in the field identification of species including seedlings in tall complex forests. He is an active member of the Council of the Wildlife Preservation Society of Queensland.

L. J. WEBB, M.SC., PH.D. (QLD.), of the Rainforest Ecology Unit, Division of Plant Industry, CSIRO, Brisbane, has worked for the last fifteen years on the ecological relations of Australian rainforests. Before this, he was responsible for chemical screening and botanical collecting in the Australian phytochemical survey which he helped to develop. He is especially interested in the classification of vegetation by the use of structure and life-forms, and has collaborated with various specialists in the identification of habitat-types as a basis for their conservation. He has contributed to a number of conservation seminars and journals, and wrote 'The Rape of the Forests' in *The Great Extermination* and *Impressions of Nature Protection in Europe*. He is a Councillor of the Australian Conservation Foundation and a Vice-President of the Wildlife Preservation Society of Queensland.

D. WHITELOCK, M.A. (OXON.), is Assistant Director of the Department of Adult Education at the University of Adelaide. From 1963 to 1968 he worked in the Department of University Extension at the University of New England and as a keen amateur naturalist arranged the adult residential seminars on conservation at the university which provided the initial stimulus for this book. He co-edited (with Clement Semmler) *Literary Australia* (1966), is editing *Adult Education in Australia* for Pergamon Press, is general editor of the Australian Institute of International Affairs *Problems of Countries* series, reviews regularly in a number of newspapers and journals and has written several articles for anglers' magazines.

J. B. WILLIAMS, B.SC. (SYDNEY), Lecturer in Botany at the University of New England, has been for many years a member of the New England National Parks Trust. His research activities embrace the morphological adaptations of plants to changes in environmental factors, and the ecology of subtropical rainforests, montane beech forests and the littoral rainforests found on coastal sand deposits.

W. T. WILLIAMS, A.R.C.S., PH.D., D.SC., D.I.C., F.L.S., B.I.BIOL., of the Division of Tropical Pastures, CSIRO, Brisbane, is concerned with the application of computer methods to biological problems, especially those of ecological survey, and is known to his colleagues as 'The Computer Botanist'. He was Professor of Botany at Southampton, England, from 1951 to 1965 and has been a member of the Agricultural Research Council of the U.K., Secretary of the Society for Experimental Botany, editor of the *Journal of Experimental Botany* from 1960-65, member of the Annals of Botany Company and Secretary of the Sherlock Holmes Society of London. He joined CSIRO in 1966 and worked first in Computing Research, Canberra. He is a Past-President of Section M of ANZAAS and a member of the Fauna and Flora Committee of the Australian Academy of Science.

Further Reading

Allen, S. W., *Conserving Natural Resources*, McGraw-Hill, 1955.

Arvill, R., *Man and Environment*, Penguin, 1967.

Australian Conservation Foundation Viewpoint Series: Conservation of Kangaroos; The Cape Barren Goose; Waterfowl Conservation. Special publications: *The Conservation of Norfolk Island; National Parks and Equivalent Reserves in Australia.* Other publications: *Conservation and Australia.* A.C.F., 191 Royal Parade, Parkville, Victoria.

Australian Plants, Vols. I, II and III and current quarterly, published by the Society for Growing Australian Plants, 860 Henry Lawson Drive, Picnic Point, N.S.W.

Anderson, E., *Plants, Man and Life*, Univ. of California Press, 1967.

Bird, E. C., *Coastal Landforms*, A.N.U., 1964.

Blombery, A. M., *A Guide to Native Australian Plants*, Angus & Robertson, 1967.

Bonython, C. W. and Daily, B., *Report of the South Australian Sub-committee, National Parks Committee*, Australian Academy of Science, Canberra, 1963.

Bonython, C. W., and Daily, B., *National Parks and Reserves in South Australia*, Proc.Roy. Geogr. Soc. A/asia., S.A.Bs., 65:5-15, 1964.

Bourlière, F., *Problems of Space and Human Crowding in the World of Today and Tomorrow*, The Ford Foundation, Conference on Natural Resources, 1964.

Breeden, S. and K., *The Life of the Kangaroo*, Angus & Robertson, 1966.

Bride, T. F. (ed.), *Letters from Victorian Pioneers*, published for the Trustees of the Public Library of Victoria by the Govt. Printer, Melbourne, 1898.

Brooks, A. E., *Tree Wonders of Australia*, Heinemann, 1964.

Burch, W. R., Jr., 'Two Concepts for Guiding Recreation Management Decisions', *Journal of Forestry*, 62:707-712, 1964.

Carson, R., *Silent Spring*, Penguin, 1965.

Cayley, N., *What Bird is That?*, Angus & Robertson, 1966.

Chauvin, R., *The World of an Insect* (World University Library), Wiedenfeld & Nicolson, 1967.

Chisholm, A. H., *Bird Wonders of Australia*, Angus & Robertson, 1965.

Chisholm, A. H., *Land of Wonder*, Angus & Robertson, 1964.

Conservation in Education, Proceedings of the Univ. of New England Seminar, January 1966, (Dept. of University Extension, Armidale).

Coolidge, H. J., *International Significance of National Parks in Conservation Education*, International Union for Conservation of Nature and Natural Resources, Morges. 7:11-14, 1963.

Corner, E. J. H., *The Life of Plants*, Wiedenfeld & Nicolson, 1964.

Costin, A. B., *Interdependence of Man and Environment*, International Biological Programme Symposium on Biology in the Modern World, Australian Academy of Science, Canberra, 1967.

Costin, A. B., *Problems and Practice of Nature Conservation in Sub-alpine and Alpine Ecosystems of Australia*, Proc. Eleventh Pacific Science Congress, Special Symposium No. 4, Tokyo, 1966.

Cotton, B. C. (ed.), *South Australian National Parks and Wild Life Reserves*, Govt. Printer, Adelaide, 1964.

Dakin, W. J., *The Australian Seashores*, Angus & Robertson, 1960.

Dakin, W. J., *The Great Barrier Reef*, Ure Smith, 1963.

Darling, L., *Penguins*, Angus & Robertson, 1961.
Darling, L., *Seals and Walruses*, Angus & Robertson, 1961.
Dasmann, R. F., *Environmental Conservation*, Wiley, 1966.
Eastman, W. R. and Hunt, A. C., *Parrots of Australia*, Angus & Robertson, 1966.
Elton, C. S., *The Ecology of Invasions by Animals and Plants*, Methuen, 1958.
Erickson, R., *Orchids of Western Australia* (2nd ed.), Lamb Paterson, 1968.
Erickson, R., *Plants of Prey*, Lamb Paterson, 1968.
Erickson, R., *Trigger Plants*, Lamb Paterson, 1968.
Farb, P., *Ecology*, Time-Life International, 1965.
Fenner, F. and Ratcliffe, F. N., *Myxomatosis*, Cambridge Univ. Press, 1965.
Fleay, D., *Nightwatchmen of Bush and Plain*, Jacaranda, 1968.
Forest Trees of Australia, Forestry and Timber Bureau, Canberra, 1962.
Fox, Allan M., 'Nature Conservation in New South Wales', *Australian Parks*, February 1968.
Francis, W. D., *Australian Rainforest Trees*, Forestry and Timber Bureau, Canberra, 1951.
Fraser, R., 'Coastline and Landscape', *Australian Parks*, August 1966.
Frauca, H., *Birds from the Seas, Swamps and Scrubs of Australia*, Heinemann, 1968.
Frauca, H., *Harry Frauca's Book of Insects*, Jacaranda, 1968.
Frauca, H., *Harry Frauca's Book of Reptiles*. Jacaranda, 1967.
Frith, H. J., *Waterfowl in Australia*, Angus & Robertson, 1968.
Galbraith, J., *Wildflowers of Victoria* (3rd ed.), Longmans, 1968.
Gardner, C. A., *Wildflowers of Western Australia*, W.A. Newspapers, 1959.
Gazzard, D. (ed.), *Australian Outrage*, Ure Smith, 1966.
Gibbons, F. R. and Downes, R. G., *A Study of the Land in South-western Victoria*, Soil Conservation Authority, Victoria, 1964.
Gilbert, J. M., *Forest Succession in the Florentine Valley, Tasmania*, Pap. and Proc. Roy. Soc. Tasm., 93:129-151, 1959.
Gillet, K. and McNeill, F., *The Great Barrier Reef and Adjacent Islands*, Coral Press, 1962.
Good, R., *Geography of Flowering Plants* (2nd ed.), Longmans, 1953.
Gray, C. E., *Victorian Native Orchids*, Longmans, 1966.
Guiler, E. R., 'Animals' in Davies, J. L. (ed.), *Atlas of Tasmania*, Hobart, 1965.
Harris, T. Y., *Naturecraft in Australia*, Angus & Robertson, 1968.
Harris, T. Y., *Wildflowers of Australia*, Angus & Robertson, 1966.
Harrison, R. E., *Know Your Trees and Shrubs*, Reed, 1965.
Hawkins, S., *Australian Animals and Birds*, Angus & Robertson, 1962.
Hill, R., *Bushland and Seashore*, Lansdowne, 1962.
Huxley, Julian, *The Conservation of Wild Life and Natural Habitats in Central and East Africa*, Unesco, Paris, 1961.
Jacaranda Pocket Guides:
- I. F. B. Common, *Australian Moths*.
- I. F. B. Common, *Butterflies of Australia*.
- S. Domm, *Guide to the Corals of the Great Barrier Reef* (in press).
- Edgar Riek, *Insects of Australia*.
- Gilbert P. Whitley, *Marine Fishes of Australia*, 2 vols.
- Basil Marlow, *Marsupials of Australia*.
- Gilbert P. Whitley, *Native Freshwater Fishes of Australia*.
- Peter Goadby, *Sharks and Other Predatory Fish*.
- D. R. McPhee, *Snakes and Lizards of Australia*.
- Allan Keast, *Some Bush Birds of Australia*.
- D. F. McMichael, *Some Common Shells of the Australian Seashore*.
- H. Oakman, *Some Trees of Australia*.
- Barbara Main, *Spiders of Australia*.

Jacaranda Wildflower Guides:
- Chippendale, T. M., *Wildflowers of Central Australia*.
- Scarth-Johnson, V., *Wildflowers of New South Wales*.
- Burns, T. E., and King, H. J., *Wildflowers of Tasmania*.
- Rosser, C., *Wildflowers of Victoria*.

Scarth-Johnson, V., *Wildflowers of the Warm East Coast.*

Jackson, W. D., 'Vegetation' in Davies, J. L. (ed.), *Atlas of Tasmania*, Hobart, 1965.

Jennings, J. N. and Mabbutt, J. A., *Landform Studies from Australia and New Guinea*, A.N.U., 1967.

Jones, O. A. and Endean, R., 'The Great Barrier Reefs' in *Science Journal*, November 1967.

Keast, A. et al, *Biogeography and Ecology in Australia*, Den Haag, 1959.

Keast, A., *Window to Bushland*, Angus & Robertson, 1965.

Kinghorn, J. R., *Snakes of Australia*, Angus & Robertson, 1964.

Landsberg, H. H., Fischman, L. L., and Fisher, J., *Resources in America's Future*, Johns Hopkins Press, 1963.

Laseron, C., *The Face of Australia*, Angus & Robertson, 1964.

Leach, J. A., *An Australian Bird Book* (9th ed.), Whitcombe & Tombs, 1947.

Leach, J. A., *Australian Nature Studies*, Macmillan, 1952.

Leigh, J. H. and Mulham, W. E., *Pastoral Plants of the Riverine Plain*, Jacaranda, 1965.

Luke, R. H., *Bushfire Control in Australia*, Hodder & Stoughton, 1961.

Lyne, G., *Marsupials and Monotremes of Australia*, Angus & Robertson, 1968.

Main, B. Y., *Between Wodjil and Tor*, Jacaranda, and Landfall, 1967.

Marsh, M., *Mammals*, Longmans, 1965.

Marshall, A. J., *The Great Extermination*, Heinemann, 1967 (and Panther paperback).

Marshall, T., *Fishes of the Great Barrier Reef*, Angus & Robertson, 1964.

Marshall, T., *Tropical Fishes of the Great Barrier Reef*, Angus & Robertson, 1966.

Mass, N., *Australian Wildflower Magic*, Writer's Press, 1968.

Mass, N., *Flowers of the Australian Alps*, Writer's Press. 1968.

McArthur, K., *Queensland Wildflowers*, Jacaranda, 1959.

McKeown, K. C., *Australian Spiders* (2nd ed.) (Sirius Books), Angus & Robertson, 1963.

McMichael, D. F. (ed.), *A Treasury of Australian Wildlife*, Ure Smith, 1968.

Morgan, D. (ed.), *Biological Science: the web of life*, Australian Academy of Science, Canberra, 1967.

Mosley, J. G., *Classification of National Parks and Reserves*, Proceedings of the Univ. of New England Seminar on Practical Problems of National Parks, 1966.

Mosley, J. G., *National Parks*, Nelson Doubleday, 1968.

Mosley, J. G., *National Parks and Equivalent Reserves in Australia: Guide to Legislation, Administration and Areas*, Australian Conservation Foundation Special Publication No. 2, 1968.

Mosley, J. G., *Tasmania's National Parks — Policy and Administrative Problems*, Proceedings of Univ. of New England Seminar on Practical Problems of National Parks, 1966, (Dept. of University Extension, Armidale).

Murray, K. G., *Alpine Flowers*, Grenville, 1962.

Murray, K. G. (ed.), *The Alpine Flowers of the Kosciusko State Park*, Murray, 1962.

National Parks, Proceedings of the National Parks School, Univ. of New England, 1964, (Department of University Extension).

National Parks Committee, *Report of the National Parks Committee England and Wales*, London, 1947.

National Parks and Nature Reserves in Western Australia, Australian Academy of Science and National Parks Board of Western Australia, Govt. Printer, Perth, 1965.

National Parks and Reserves in Australia, Australian Academy of Science, Canberra, 1968.

Nicholls, W. H., *Orchids of Australia*, Georgian House, 1951-58.

Odum, E. P., *Ecology*, New York, 1963.

Officer, Brig. H., *Honeyeaters of Australia*, Bird Observers Club, Windsor, Victoria, 1968.

Outdoor Recreation for America, U.S. Outdoor Recreation Resources Review Commission Report, Washington, 1962.

Patton, R. T., *Know Your Own Trees*, M.U.P., 1961.

Pizzey, G., *Birds and Animals in Australia*, Cassell & Co., 1966.

Pollock, H., *Menura, the Lyrebird*, Jacaranda, 1968.

Practical Problems of National Parks, Proceedings of the Univ. of New England Seminar' Fcbruary 1966, (Dept. of University Extension, Armidale).

Ratcliffe, F., *Flying Fox and Drifting Sand*, Angus & Robertson, 1963.

Restoring the Quality of Our Environment, Report of the Environmental Pollution Panel, President's Science Advisory Committee, The White House, U.S.A., November, 1965.

Richards, P. W., *The Tropical Rainforest*, Cambridge Univ. Press, 1952.

Ridpath, P., *Possum Moods*, Ure Smith, 1966.

Ripley, T. H., 'Recreation Impact on Southern Appalachian Campgrounds and Picnic Sites', U.S.D.A. Southeastern Forest Experiment Station Paper, 153, 1962.

Roughley, T. C., *Wonders of the Great Barrier Reef*, Angus & Robertson, 1961.

Rule, A., *Forests of Australia*, Angus & Robertson, 1968.

Saville-Kent, W., *The Great Barrier Reef of Australia, its Products and Potentialities*, Allen, 1893.

Serventy, V., *Australia's Great Barrier Reef*, Georgian House, 1966.

Serventy, V., *Continent in Danger*, Deutsch, 1966.

Serventy, V., *Landforms of Australia*, Angus & Robertson, 1968.

Serventy, V., *Nature Walkabout*, Reed, 1968.

Serventy, V., *The Australian Nature Trail*, Georgain House, 1965.

Serventy, V., *Wildlife of Australia*, Nelson, 1968.

Sharland, M., *Stones of a Century*, Oldham, Beddone & Meredith, 1952.

Sharland, M. S. R., *A Territory of Birds*, Rigby, 1964.

Slater, P. and Breeden, S., *Birds of Australia*, Angus & Robertson, 1968.

Slater, P., *Wild Life of Western Australia*, W.A. Newspapers, 1966.

Sparnon, N., *The Beauty of Australia's Wildflowers*, Ure Smith, 1968.

Specht, R. L. and Cleland, J. B., *Flora Conservation in South Australia, Part* 1, Trans. Roy.Soc.S.Aust., 85:177-196, 1961.

Speechley, D. A., 'Cars in the Recreational Environment', paper at the National Conference of Australian Parks, Adelaide, 1967.

Stanley, H. J., *State Legislation for National Parks*, in Proceedings of the National Parks School, Univ. of New England, 1964.

Stead, D., *Sharks and Rays of Australian Seas*, Angus & Robertson, 1965.

The Australian Environment (4th ed.), CSIRO, Melbourne, 1969.

'The Great Barrier Reef', special issue of *Australian Natural History*, Vol. 15, No. 8, December 1966.

The Insects of Australia, CSIRO, M.U.P. (in press).

Thomas, W. L. (ed.), *Man's Role in Changing the Face of the Earth*, Univ. of Chicago Press, 1956.

'Tourism Today and Tomorrow', *Current Affairs Bulletin*, Vol. 14, No. 12, Univ. of Sydney, November 1967.

Troughton, E., *Furred Animals of Australia*, Angus & Robertson, 1965.

Udall, S. L., *The Quiet Crisis*, Holt, Rinehart & Winston, 1963.

Victoria's Resources, a quarterly magazine published by the Natural Resources Conservation League of Victoria, Springvale Road, Springvale South, Victoria.

Wakefield, N., *Naturalist's Diary*, Longmans, 1968.

Waterfowl in New South Wales, CSIRO and N.S.W. Fauna Panel. (Booklet.)

Water Resources, Use and Management, Australian Academy of Science, M.U.P., 1965.

Weatherley, A. H., *Australian Inland Waters and Their Fauna*, A.N.U., 1968.

Wildlife Conservation, Proceedings of the University of Adelaide Seminar, August 1966, (Dept. of Adult Education, Adelaide).

Wildlife Conservation in Eastern Australia, Proceedings of the Univ. of New England Seminar, January 1965, (Dept. of University Extension, Armidale).

Wildlife in Australia, a quarterly magazine published by the Wildlife Preservation Society of Queensland, Box 2030, G.P.O., Brisbane.

Williams, W. D., *Australian Freshwater Life: the invertebrates of Australian inland waters*. Sun Books, 1968.

Willis, J. H. (with Cochrane, Fuhrer and Rotherham), *Flowers and Plants of Victoria*, Reed, 1968.

Willis, J. H., *A Handbook to Plants in Victoria*, M.U.P., 1962.

Woldendorp and Slater, P., *The Hidden Face of Australia*, Nelson, 1968.

Worrell, E., *Australian Wildlife*, Angus & Robertson, 1966.

Worrell, E., *Dangerous Snakes of Australia and New Guinea*, Angus & Robertson, 1965.

Worrell, E., *Reptiles of Australia*, Angus & Robertson, 1964.

Worrell, E., *The Great Barrier Reef*, Angus & Robertson, 1966.

Worrell, E., *Trees of the Australian Bush*, Angus & Robertson, 1968.

Yonge, C. M., 'The Biology of Coral Reefs' in *Advances in Marine Biology*, Vol. 1, 1963.

Yonge, C. M., *A Year on the Great Barrier Reef*, Putnam, 1931.